SCOTS AND CATALANS

UNION AND DISUNION

J. H. ELLIOTT

YALE UNIVERSITY PRESS
NEW HAVEN AND LONDON

For information about this and other Yale University Press publications, please contact:
U.S. Office: sales.press@yale.edu   yalebooks.com
Europe Office: sales@yaleup.co.uk   yalebooks.co.uk

Set in Minion Pro by IDSUK (DataConnection) Ltd
Printed in Great Britain by TJ International, Padstow, Cornwall

Library of Congress Control Number: 2018934510

ISBN 978-0-300-234954 (hbk)

A catalogue record for this book is available from the British Library.

10 9 8 7 6 5 4 3 2 1

CONTENTS

ACKNOWLEDGEMENTS

The distant origins of this book are to be found in the 1950s, when I was fortunate enough to be given the opportunity to undertake some two years of research in Spain. Much of my time was spent in Catalonia, hunting down documents in its central and regional archives for a doctoral dissertation on the origins of the Catalan rebellion of 1640 against the royal government in Madrid, eventually published in 1963 under the title *The Revolt of the Catalans*. During that time I immersed myself in Catalan life and made many friends with whom I remained in contact, but I moved on to other topics and assumed that my close engagement with Catalan history was at an end. The publication of this book shows that I was mistaken.

It so happened that, at the time when the movement for Scottish independence was gathering momentum, I was casting around for a historical subject that would lead me into new fields. At the same moment separatists in Catalonia were also embarking on a bid for independence. I found myself wondering if there were any parallels between the two movements that might be worth exploring. Among those I consulted was the eminent historian of early modern Scotland, the late Jenny Wormald, who encouraged me to go ahead. I only regret that she is no longer with us to deliver a characteristically forthright verdict on the way the project turned out.

As far as I was concerned, the history of Scotland was unknown territory, and I have learnt a great deal, not only from the historical literature, much of which is of the highest quality, but also from Scottish friends and acquaintances who have done their best to keep me on the right lines and point me in the right direction. Among them are Colin Kidd, who read and made valuable comments on an earlier draft of the book; John Robertson, whose writings have taught me much about the origins and consequences of the Anglo-Scottish Union of 1707; Dauvit Broun and Murray Pittock, both of whom I met at a recent symposium in Edinburgh on Scottish identity; and Robert Frost, who shares my interest in composite monarchies and who has enriched the subject through his deep knowledge of the Polish-Lithuanian version of the genre. I am also grateful to him for welcoming my wife and me on a visit to Aberdeen in August 2015 and taking us on excursions that enabled us to get a sense of the region and acquaint us with some of its most important and picturesque sites. On that same Scottish tour we were welcomed in Glasgow by Hamish Scott and Julia Smith, who again generously devoted their time to driving us to historic houses and sites, including that of the old Scottish coronation ceremony at Scone.

Over and above his kindness to us in Glasgow I am deeply indebted to Hamish Scott for all that he has done to improve my book, even when in the midst of moving house from Glasgow to Oxford. While disclaiming any specialist knowledge of the history of his home country, he has read the entire text, offered many helpful and informed suggestions at every stage of the proceedings, and saved me from many errors. In making his comments he has never allowed me to forget the importance of placing the history of Scotland within the broad context of British and European history. No author could hope to find a more acute unofficial editor.

Catalonia, unlike Scotland, was hardly *terra incognita* for me. My knowledge of the history of Catalonia, however, as of Spain more generally, tended to peter out at the turn of the nineteenth century. Angel Smith of the University of Leeds, an expert on nineteenth-century Catalan nationalism, kindly read my nineteenth-century chapters and set me right on a number of points. James Amelang of the Autonomous University of Madrid has generously allowed me to take advantage of his unrivalled bibliographical knowledge, while Jon Arrieta Alberdi of the Faculty of Law of the University of the Basque Country has shared with me over the years the fruits of his pioneering researches into Spanish and Basque juridical and institutional history and his explorations into different types of historical union.

I have also done my best to keep abreast of current developments. In doing so, I have gained much from discussions with Spanish friends, including my former Oxford pupil, Cayetana Álvarez de Toledo, who provided various opportunities for me to try out my ideas in Spain, both in private and in public, and arranged what proved to be instructive personal encounters in the monastery of Poblet and Barcelona's City Hall. I have also received helpful information and advice over the years from William Chislett of the Instituto Elcano in Madrid; and, during the last few months, from the Madrid correspondent of the *New York Times*, Raphael Minder.

Where I needed advice on constitutional questions I was fortunate to be able to draw on the expertise of Professor Josep M.ª Castellà Andreu of the University of Barcelona's Faculty of Law.

Above all I had the benefit of expert readings of early drafts of the entire book by Josep M.ª Fradera of the University Pompeo Fabra, and Xavier Gil Pujol of the University of Barcelona, who between them cover the history of the last five centuries of Spain and their native Catalonia. Their suggestions and comments not only saved me from many mistakes, but also transformed my text. If I could not follow all their suggestions this is because I did not feel able to expand it any further without unbalancing a book in which there was always a danger of tilting too far away from Scotland. My indebtedness to Xavier Gil has increased still further over recent months as he has commented on successive drafts of revised sections, and brought to bear on them his eagle eye for detail.

The technicalities of preparing the book for the press would have defeated me if Laura Jiménez-Aguado, a member of the administrative staff of the University of Oxford's History Faculty, had not offered to come to my rescue. She skilfully juggled her way between different and sometimes incompatible computer programmes, picked up even the smallest errors and discrepancies in the text, and compiled and checked the bibliography. Her dedication and enthusiasm have carried me through difficult moments, and I owe her a deep debt of gratitude.

Robert Baldock, the former director of the London branch of Yale University Press and the editor of several of my earlier Yale publications, may have felt some initial scepticism when I first came to him with my proposal for a comparative study of Scotland and Catalonia. But if he had any doubts he quickly swallowed them, accepted the challenge and once again agreed to be my editor. As always he has been a staunch champion and candid friend, coming up with imaginative suggestions about content and layout, and struggling with me to find an appropriate title for a book that has required navigation through a number of minefields.

I am also grateful to the current staff of Yale University Press and in particular to the head of editorial management, Rachael Lonsdale, who has cheerfully come up with answers to my sometimes awkward questions and has skilfully piloted the book through successive stages as it moved towards publication. The copy-editor, Richard Mason, has pointed out several discrepancies and saved me from errors, and I am indebted to Martin Brown for preparing the family trees and maps.

Oriel College, Oxford
January 2018

NOTE ON STYLISTIC USAGE

It has been impossible to maintain complete uniformity in the use of Spanish (Castilian) and Catalan words and names in the text of this book. I have tended to keep the names of institutions in their original Catalan (e.g. Generalitat). While some placenames are the same in both languages (e.g. Tarragona), others differ (e.g. Lérida in Castilian, Lleida in Catalan). I have usually opted for the Catalan version. The names of individual Catalans present an intractable problem. For most of the nineteenth century it was common for them to use the Castilian version on public occasions, even when they normally spoke Catalan to each other. Nowadays the Catalan form is the one commonly used in Catalonia itself (e.g. General Joan Prim, and not Juan Prim). I have followed this practice from around 1800 onwards, although with occasional exceptions. For instance, the seventeenth-century rebel leader is always known as Pau Claris and not Pablo Claris, and it would be absurd to use the Castilian version of his name. Names of authors are particularly difficult, since, far into the Romantic movement, their books are likely to be published under Castilian names, and this is how they appear in bibliographies and library catalogues. Thus, the late seventeenth-century merchant and projector, Narciso Feliu de la Peña, tends nowadays to be known by the Catalan version of his name as Narcís Feliu de la Penya, but his treatises were published in Castilian, with his name in Castilian. I have respected this practice up to around 1800, which I have taken as a rough dividing line, although long hesitating between Antonio de Capmany and Antoni de Capmany, the well-known historian and politician whose career straddled the two centuries. My final choice, the Catalan form, is purely arbitrary. I have used the English version of names of Spanish monarchs (Philip II and not Felipe II), with the exception of Charles II of Spain, who appears in the text as Carlos II to distinguish him from his contemporary, Charles II of England and Scotland.

It should be noted that dates in the chapter headings are intended to serve as chronological indications of the general period covered by each chapter, and should be regarded as no more than approximate.

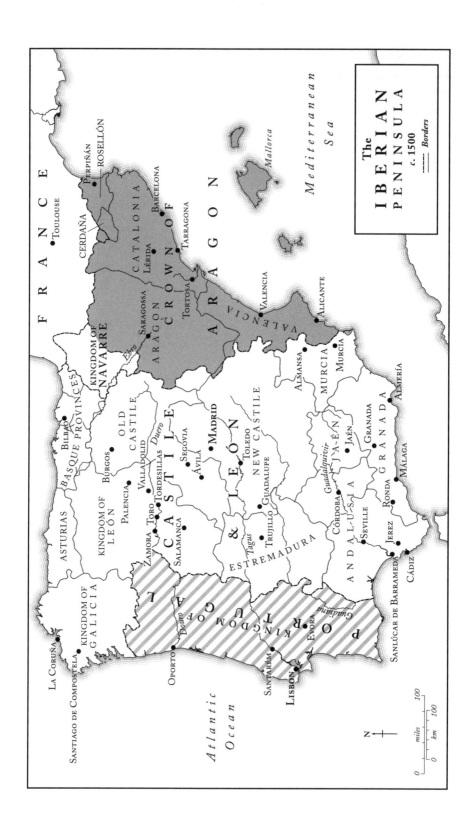

The
**IBERIAN
PENINSULA**

c. 1500

------- *Borders*

*Mediterranean
Sea*

F R A N C E

TOULOUSE

KINGDOM OF NAVARRE

PERPIÑÁN • ROSELLÓN

CERDAÑA

BARCELONA

CATALONIA

LÉRIDA

TARRAGONA

SARAGOSSA

ARAGON

CROWN OF

TORTOSA

A R A G O N

Ebro

VALENCIA

VALENCIA

ALICANTE

Mallorca

BASQUE PROVINCES

BILBAO

OLD CASTILE

BURGOS

VALLADOLID

Duero

SEGOVIA

MADRID

ÁVILA

ALMANSA

MURCIA

MURCIA

C A S T I L E

TOLEDO

NEW CASTILE

ALMERÍA

GRANADA

GRANADA

KINGDOM OF LEÓN

PALENCIA

ZAMORA

TORO

TORDESILLAS

& L E Ó N

SALAMANCA

GUADALUPE

TRUJILLO

Tagus

ESTREMADURA

Guadalquivir

J A É N

JAÉN

CÓRDOBA

A N D A L U S I A

MÁLAGA

RONDA

SANTIAGO DE COMPOSTELA

ASTURIAS

KINGDOM OF GALICIA

LA CORUÑA

Douro

OPORTO

I

K I N G D O M

O F

P O R T U G A L

SANTARÉM

LISBON

ÉVORA

Guadiana

SEVILLE

JEREZ

SANLÚCAR DE BARRAMEDA

CÁDIZ

*Atlantic
Ocean*

N

miles 100

km 100

0

0

N

F R A N C E

SALSES

PERPIGNAN

ROUSSILLON

ANDORRA *CERDAGNE* PORTBOU
LLÍVIA
LA SEU D'URGELL *CERDANYA* PUIGCERDÀ CADAQUÉS

FIGUERES *L'Empordà*
RIPOLL OLOT
G I R O N A
A SOLSONA
R *Pla de Vic* VIC
A L L E I D A GIRONA
G *El Gironès*
O CENTELLES PALAMOS
N MANRESA
CERVERA *B A R C E L O N A*
IGUALADA TERRASSA SABADELL
LLEIDA MONTSERRAT *El Vallès* MATARÓ
POBLET BADALONA
T **BARCELONA**
A VALLS
R *El Penedès*
R REUS SITGES
A CAMBRILS TARRAGONA
G
O
N
A
V
A TORTOSA
L
E
N
C
I
A

M e d i t e r r a n e a n
S e a

Mallorca

Modern
C A T A L O N I A

---- *Borders*

Territory lost to France, 1659

0 *miles* 50

0 *km* 50

SCOTLAND

✗ Major battle
----- Border

0   miles   50
0   km   50

Orkney

KIRKWALL

Shetland

LERWICK

CAITHNESS   WICK

Outer Hebrides

STORNOWAY

SUTHERLAND

ULLAPOOL

R O S S   *Moray Firth*   FRASERBURGH

ELGIN

ELGIN

PORTREE   INVERNESS ✗ *Culloden*   B A N F F

Skye   I N V E R N E S S   *Spey*   A B E R D E E N

Loch Ness

Inner Hebrides   *G R A M P I A N S*   ABERDEEN

BALMORAL

H I G H L A N D S   KINCARDINE

GLENFINNAN   ATHOLL   FORFAR

MONTROSE

Tiree   ANGUS

Mull   DUNKELD   ARBROATH

OBAN   *Tay*   SCONE   DUNDEE

PERTH   ST ANDREWS

A R G Y L L   MENTEITH   F I F E

STIRLING ✗   DUNFERMLINE   *Firth of Forth*

Bannockburn   LEITH ✗ *Dunbar*

Islay   DUMBARTON   EDINBURGH

GLASGOW

Firth of Clyde   C L Y D E   L O T H I A N

Bute   RENFREW   BERWICK-UPON-TWEED

Kintyre   *Arran*   *Clyde*   *Tweed*

AYR   B O R D E R S   N O R T H U M B E R L A N D

Mull of Kintyre   K Y L E   HAWICK

C A R R I C K

DERRY   DUMFRIES

U L S T E R   GALLOWAY   CARLISLE

STRANRAER

Loch Neagh   BELFAST   E N G L A N D

I R E L A N D

N

INTRODUCTION
Nations and Nation-States

This book is the story of two self-proclaimed nations which, at least at the time of writing, do not have states of their own. In recent years both Scotland and Catalonia have seen the growth of powerful movements whose goal is independence from the larger political entities, Great Britain and Spain, into which they have long been incorporated. Scotland asked for, and in 2014 secured, a referendum that the advocates of independence hoped would enable them to achieve their goal by way of a popular mandate. In the event, the electorate failed to deliver the desired result, leaving the disappointed minority with the hope that another referendum in the not too distant future would produce a different outcome. For their part the proponents of Catalan independence, who commanded a majority in the Catalan parliament, approved on 6 September 2017 the holding of an independence referendum. In accordance with this vote the regional government, in defiance of the Spanish state and the 1978 Spanish Constitution, arranged for the holding of its own, illegal, referendum on 1 October 2017, and unilaterally proclaimed an independent Catalan Republic nine days later.

In seeking to turn their nations into sovereign states the leaders of these independence movements have been following a well-travelled path. Europe between the end of the eighteenth century and the middle of the nineteenth experienced an upsurge of nationalist sentiment in the course of which minority peoples and ethnicities aspired or attempted to break loose from the larger political formations to which they belonged, and establish themselves as independent nation-states. In doing so, they drew inspiration from the two great intellectual and ideological movements of the period: liberalism with its insistence on the rights of citizens to some form of political representation, and Romanticism, with its emphasis on the organic nature of societies and the historical, ethnic and sentimental ties that gave them their cohesion.

These same influences were simultaneously at work in the dominant political formations of the time – nation-states, lesser polities and great monarchical empires – as they sought to transform their subjects and peoples into comprehensive national communities, endowed with a sense of common origins, common purpose and common identity. Their height-ened nationalism both provoked, and was countered by, the equally height-ened nationalism of their minority peoples, who, as the 1848 revolutions demonstrated, were by now on the march. In the Austro-Hungarian Empire in particular, with its multiplicity of submerged or partially submerged nationalities, a constant balancing act was required to hold the competing nationalisms in check, and the empire collapsed when the imperial armies went down to defeat in the final stages of the First World War.

At the end of the conflict the Versailles peace settlement and its accom-panying treaties grappled with some of the underlying problems that had led to the outbreak of the war by acknowledging the strength of the demands coming from stateless regions and communities for nation-states of their own. Yet although the recognition of the right to national self-determina-tion may have resolved some of the problems it sought to address, it created many others. The attempt to endow nations, or would-be nations, with appropriate territorial boundaries, itself became another source of conflict.

The process also raised the question of the extent to which a theoreti-cally noble ideal should be realized in practice. Once nationalism was given free rein, where would it stop? Not only did it bring rival communities or ethnic groups into collision, but it also threatened the integrity of the historical centralized nation-states or empires which had established them-selves over the centuries through a mixture of dynastic accident and polit-ical design and were now being pressed to acknowledge the right to self-determination of subjects and citizens whom they had long regarded as their own. As the Anglo-Irish Treaty of 1921 made all too clear, nationalism and separatism were two sides of one coin.

To some extent the problem of Europe's submerged or suppressed nationalities was both obscured and shelved by the outbreak of the Second World War in 1939 and the Cold War that followed. The old state structures were now visibly under strain. Weakened by six years of conflict, Europe's imperial states were progressively forced to relinquish their overseas empires in the face of uprisings and armed resistance by subject peoples who had learnt their European lessons all too well, and were imbued with a growing sense of their own national identity and their right to independence. The loss of overseas empire was accompanied by the diminution of some of the historic powers of the states of western Europe as a desire to escape from the apparently ceaseless round of fratricidal conflict and the challenge of the Cold War pushed them into accepting the need for new forms of military, political and economic partnership. This inevitably involved some sacrifice of sovereignty.

In a changing world temporarily dominated by the two superpowers into whose orbits they were pulled, old-style nation-states therefore lost, along with their freedom of action, something of their former relevance. It was ironic that, at a time when new nations were multiplying across the globe, national independence itself was beginning to look increasingly like a relic of the past, with interdependence rather than independence becoming the order of the day. This fact of international economic and political life was not fundamentally changed by the emergence of new states and the revival of old ones as a consequence of the collapse of the Soviet Empire in 1989 and the ending of the great ideological divide of the post-war years. The accelerating pace of globalization suggested that there could be no going back. As a result, the unified nation-state that had once seemed to be the logical culmination of a millennium of European history found itself in the last years of the twentieth century being pressed from above by supranational organizations and the transnational requirements that came from living in an increasingly interconnected world.

Yet just as nation-states were being subjected to a variety of pressures from above, they also found themselves being subjected to increased pressures from below. The pressure arose in part from a general sense in many parts of the western world that highly bureaucratized central governments had become too remote to understand the true needs and problems of the governed. The natural response, whether of individuals, communities or regions, was to demand a greater say in the management of their own affairs. The demand was especially insistent when it came from those regions, stateless nationalities and ethnic groups which, for historic reasons, felt maltreated and misunderstood, and their interests disregarded.

In a world in which the enjoyment of rights had become an article of faith, such a response was not surprising. Less expected, and largely unanticipated, was the resurgence of two of the deep historical forces that impelled it, and that were thought to have been laid to rest by the apparently triumphant march of cosmopolitanism and secularization. These forces were old-style nationalism and religion, especially in its fundamentalist form. Sometimes the two banded together, at others they did not, but by the start of the twenty-first century both were visibly on the rise.

Whether resurgent nationalism took the form of demands for a greater degree of autonomy or for outright independence, it looked to the past to stake its claims to the future. In this it was doing little more than follow the pattern of the nationalist movements of an earlier age. Over the nineteenth and a large part of the twentieth centuries nations and nation-states tended to be depicted in essentialist terms as fixed and permanent entities, the natural and predetermined products of a territorially grounded sense of collective identity inspired by kinship and ethnicity, along with shared faith, customs, language and historical experience. During the last two or three decades of the twentieth century this essentialist understanding of the nature and origins of nationalism came to be challenged by historians who argued that nations are in reality 'imagined communities' based on inherited traditions and the stories, or 'myths', they have come to believe about themselves.[1]

Whether or not these communities were the products of collective imagination or were grounded in remote social realities, their current high visibility has added one more element of uncertainty in a world that has come increasingly to look as if it is in the throes of a major transformation. The old order is disappearing, the outlines of a new order have yet to become clear. One of the tasks of today's historians is to provide some long-term perspective on the process of transformation, and on the developments and events that have shaped, and are continuing to shape, the world in which they find themselves.

This book is an attempt to explore the origins and fluctuating trajectories of national sentiment in Scotland and Catalonia, and of the separatist movements to which it is currently giving rise. 'Nation' and 'state' are both problematic words, whose meaning, as this book hopes to show, has changed over the centuries, acquiring in the process new understandings and connotations as circumstances alter and new ideas take hold. As the words are currently understood, however, both Scotland and Catalonia tend to be classified as nations without states. In a recent Spanish study of the constitutional background to the referendum movements in the two countries, the author writes: 'Scotland and Catalonia are two nations without a State which, especially since the beginning of the twentieth century, have demanded, with greater or lesser intensity and with greater or lesser support from the population, the recognition of their singularity, greater degrees of self-government, and, recently, independence.'[2]

Yet it is an indication of the uncertainty that now surrounds the definition of 'nation' and 'state' that in the second (2001) edition of David

McCrone's valuable sociological survey, *Understanding Scotland: The Sociology of a Stateless Nation*, first published in 1992, the word 'stateless' had disappeared from the subtitle, leaving the more anodyne *Sociology of a Nation* in its place. Explaining the change, the author writes: 'Recovering its parliament, albeit a devolved one, after almost 300 years of union means that Scotland is no longer stateless.'[3] But does it? Is Scotland's possession of a devolved parliament sufficient to transform the Scottish nation into a state, and can a state be truly a state without being 'independent', as the word is currently understood? Words take on different meanings at different times, and concepts that once seemed fixed can overnight become fluid. Nations 'imagine' themselves in different ways at different historical moments, adding or subtracting from the self-image they have created, and prioritizing some particular aspect or aspects at the expense of others.

Scotland and Catalonia both have long historical ancestries. Both were integrated, with varying degrees of success, into emerging polities, Britain and Spain, whose histories form part of the larger story that also has to be taken into account; and both have lived over the centuries in the shadow of a more powerful neighbour, to which their histories need to be constantly related. It is hoped that a comparison of the two, in attempting to identify and explain the similarities and the differences between their respective experiences, will shed some light on the development of European state structures over more than five centuries, and on the forms taken by nationalist movements and the secessionist demands that some of them inspired. Whatever the outcome of the decisions currently being taken, theirs is a story that will run for many years to come.

CHAPTER 1

Dynastic Union
1469–1625

The Background to Union

On 14 October 1469 Ferdinand, King of Sicily and heir to the throne of Aragon, after several days spent riding in disguise through hostile territory, arrived after dark in the Castilian city of Valladolid, where he would meet for the first time his intended bride Isabella, Princess of Asturias and the contested heiress to the Crown of Castile. The terms of a marriage treaty had previously been agreed, and the couple were married four days later. Isabella became Queen of Castile on her brother's death in 1474 and Ferdinand succeeded to his father's Aragonese inheritance in 1479. From this moment they became joint sovereigns of Castile and Aragon, and rulers of the country that came increasingly to be known as 'Spain'.

In 1503, thirty-four years after the Spanish royal marriage, Margaret Tudor, the daughter of Henry VII of England, was married to James IV of Scotland in a ceremony held in the chapel of Holyrood Abbey and celebrated with all the courtly spectacle expected of a monarch who prided himself on possessing all the accomplishments of a Renaissance prince.[1] When Queen Elizabeth I died childless exactly a century later, the great-grandson of this couple, James VI of Scotland, succeeded to the English throne. Travelling south by stages, in a royal progress very different from the furtive journey of Ferdinand of Aragon, he finally reached his new capital, London, and was crowned as James I of England on 25 July 1603. As ruler of the combined kingdoms of Scotland and England, which were henceforth to be governed by a single monarch, he chose to style himself king of 'Great Britain'.

These two new political entities, Spain and Great Britain, were the consequence of the dynastic marriages by means of which European monarchs traditionally concluded peace treaties, forged alliances, acquired new territories and sought to enhance their power and reputation. While matrimonial alliances were endlessly discussed, and their possible advantages and disadvantages calculated down to the minutest detail, their outcome, both short-term and long-term, was always a lottery. Shifting dynastic and state interests could turn today's friends into tomorrow's enemies; but, above all, even the best-planned matrimonial policy could all too easily founder on the unpredictable chances of life and death. Henry VII, in marrying his daughter Margaret to James IV in 1503 in order to bring about peace between England and Scotland, had every reason to expect that, with two sons who had survived into adulthood, the future of the new Tudor dynasty on the English throne was secure. But shortly afterwards his elder son, Prince Arthur, died, and with the failure of any of the children of his second son, the future Henry VIII, to have children of their own, the succession went by default to Margaret's descendant. It was the monarch of the lesser power, not the greater, who would unite the two kingdoms in his own person.

In Spain, by contrast, it was the greater power – Castile – and not the lesser that eventually prevailed in the dynastic sweepstakes. The union of the Crowns of Castile and Aragon brought about by the marriage of Ferdinand and Isabella, however, was no less subject to the vagaries of fate than the Anglo-Scottish matrimonial alliance. Its survival was placed in jeopardy when Isabella died in 1504 with no male heir to succeed her as a consequence of the death of their only son John in 1497. Following the queen's death the Crown of Aragon remained in Ferdinand's possession, but that of Castile passed to the eldest daughter of their marriage, and eventually to their foreign-born grandson, Charles of Ghent, the future Habsburg Emperor Charles V. It was the failure of Ferdinand's second marriage to produce a surviving child that ensured that his Aragonese territories would take their place alongside Castile as part of Charles's vast inheritance.

If the union of different and often disparate territories beneath a single ruler was frequently the result of dynastic accident, it could also be the product of dynastic design. This was particularly true of the Iberian Peninsula in the fifteenth century. Apart from the still unconquered Moorish kingdom of Granada, the peninsula was at that time divided into rival and competing political and territorial units – the Crowns of Castile and Aragon, the kingdom of Portugal, and that of Navarre, straddling the Pyrenees. The Crowns of Castile and Aragon were both the outcome of territorial accretions. At the heart of the Crown of Castile were the medieval kingdoms of Castile and León, permanently united from 1230.[2]

The Crown of Aragon, for its part, was made up of a complex of territories, joined together in the course of the long southward advance of the *Reconquista* – the great movement to recover the Iberian lands from Moorish domination.[3] The region of the eastern Pyrenees that was later to be known as Catalonia began its life as a Christian frontier region confronting the Muslims. The Franks under Charlemagne recaptured Barcelona in 801, and the county of Barcelona, as it developed under its ninth- and tenth-century counts, became the core territory of 'Old Catalonia', the marchland known by the Franks as the Spanish March, which would in due course stretch from the Pyrenees to the river Ebro. The mountain passes served as a passageway for generations of warriors and settlers as they streamed south from France into lands that were being reconquered from the Moors. But there would be another Catalonia too – a coastal Catalonia looking out towards the Mediterranean. The contrasting geography of these two Catalonias, later extended to include a western Catalonia of fertile plains and a central and more southerly Catalonia of plateaux and valleys, created a tension between the peoples of the mountains and the sea that would do much to shape Catalonia's development and the character of its inhabitants.[4]

Did the county of Barcelona's future lie with the Mediterranean, or with the Occitanian France of Provence and Languedoc, or perhaps with the Aragonese interior of the Ebro valley? In 1137 Count Ramon Berenguer IV seized the Aragonese option when he married Petronilla, the daughter of the King of Aragon. The marriage created a dynastic union between the kingdom of Aragon and what came to be called the principality of Catalonia – a name first given it in the twelfth century and possibly derived from the *castlàns*, the lords of the castles that dotted the landscape of the old Carolingian marchland and whose presence symbolized the emergence under the counts of Barcelona of a feudal order of castellans, knights and an enserfed peasantry.[5]

The Mediterranean, however, was another magnet of attraction, and all the more so after the failure of a short-lived incursion into southern France in the early thirteenth century. In 1229 the Count-King Jaume I, 'the Conqueror', seized Majorca from the Moors and then went on to conquer the remaining Balearic Islands. After recapturing the city of Valencia in 1238 he subsequently added the kingdom of Valencia to his dominions. This vast territorial expansion, to which a string of conquests in the Mediterranean, including Sicily, would later be added, marked the beginnings of what was to be a composite state system, the Crown of Aragon, often described by nineteenth- and twentieth-century historians as the Catalan-Aragonese federation. Although this agglomeration of territories was ruled by the kings of Aragon, the principal driving force behind later medieval Aragonese expansionism was Catalonia and its mercantile port-city of Barcelona, the hub of a maritime and commercial empire that for a time reached as far as Greece, following the conquest of the duchy of Athens by the Catalan Company of adventurers and traders in the early fourteenth century. Barcelona was famed, too, for the rules and ordinances devised in collaboration with its Consulate of the Sea (Consolat del Mar) – rules that came to be adopted as an international legal code for the regulation of maritime affairs across the Mediterranean.

Martin the Humane, the last monarch of the old line of the counts of Barcelona, died in 1410 without an heir. Two years later, nine commissioners agreed the 'Compromise of Caspe', which adjudged the Aragonese throne to a blood-relative of the Aragonese royal house, Ferdinand of Antequera, a member of the junior branch of the Trastámaras, the ruling Castilian dynasty. The establishment of the same dynasty in Castile and Aragon encouraged constant interference by the two branches of the family in each other's affairs, but the ensuing conflicts went hand in hand with marriage negotiations that each party hoped would one day allow it to inherit the two Crowns. Meanwhile, alongside this jockeying for position of the ruling houses of Castile and Aragon, the Portuguese monarchs were also involved in the matrimonial game. The ruling dynasties of Portugal and Castile had intermarried on no fewer than seven occasions in the 200 years before 1450,[6] and an eventual union between the two was just as possible an outcome as that between Castile and Aragon. In deciding in favour of Ferdinand rather than her other suitor, King Alfonso V of Portugal, Isabella made what proved to be a fateful choice, although eventually, in 1580, Portugal, too, would be united to the Crown of Castile, if only for sixty years, as the combined result of dynastic design and accident.

Lurking in the shadows behind the dynastic ambitions that gave rise to these different matrimonial negotiations were memories of a Roman Hispania, and subsequently of its successor state, a Spain united by its sixth-century Visigothic monarch Leovigild, and converted from Arianism to Roman Catholicism by his son King Recaredo in 587. In 711 came the great breaking point in the history of a Christian Iberian Peninsula when the Visigothic kingdom succumbed to the Muslim invasion launched across the straits of Gibraltar by Arabs and their Berber mercenaries. Throughout the succeeding centuries of conflict and coexistence with the Moors, however, the memory of a unified and Christian Hispania lived on, until it was given fresh vigour by fifteenth-century humanists like the Catalan Cardinal Margarit, chancellor to Ferdinand the Catholic's father, John II of Aragon.[7] It was not therefore surprising that Ferdinand and Isabella, in uniting in their persons the Crowns of Castile and Aragon, should have been known to their contemporaries as the joint rulers of *Spain*, although the Council of Castile decided in 1479 against making 'King and Queen of Spain' their official title for reasons that remain unexplained. One consideration may have been that, without Portugal, they could not claim to be ruling over all 'Spain'.[8]

If, at least in the eyes of the outside world, they were indeed the rulers of Spain, they were sometimes described as rulers of 'las Españas' – the Spains. For theirs was a plural political entity, a composite monarchy similar to those found elsewhere in the Europe of their day. Composite monarchies were conglomerates of territories owing allegiance to a single ruler. When these territories were acquired by marriage or inheritance rather than by conquest, the resulting union was commonly deemed to be a union *aeque principaliter*, in which the newly acquired territory enjoyed at least nominal parity of status with the political unit to which it now found itself joined. It thus preserved its own distinctive identity, along with the laws, customs and institutions it possessed at the time of its incorporation into the dominions of a monarch who came from a dynasty other than its own.[9]

Another such composite monarchy was that inherited by James VI of Scotland from Elizabeth I in 1603, although, until James succeeded to the English throne, this was a composite monarchy made up of conquered rather than inherited lands. Twelfth-century England itself formed part of a composite state, straddling the British Isles and France, that was later to be known as the Angevin Empire, but the French connection did not prevent Henry II (r.1154–89) from asserting, or more correctly reasserting, the claims of his predecessors to English overlordship over all of Britain. But for a long time the claims lacked real substance, although Norman military incursions into Wales and Ireland, and to a lesser extent Scotland, ad been accompanied by colonization and settlement that brought a degree of anglicization in its train. It was in 1282–3 that Edward I (r.1272–1307) transformed the English conquest of Wales into something approaching a real conquest. During the later years of his reign the English Crown effectively asserted its authority, too, over extensive areas of Ireland, and in 1291 Edward would claim that 'the realms of England and Scotland have, by God's favour, been united by reason of the superior lordship that the king [of England] had in Scotland' – a claim that he backed up with military force when he was victorious over the Scots at the battle of Dunbar in 1296.[10]

Conquest made Wales a part of the dominions of the King of England, in the shape of a principality, like Catalonia, though the Catalan reality, in terms of power and influence, was at this time very different from the Welsh. Although Owen Glendower made a bold attempt at the start of the fifteenth century to recover Welsh freedom, the subordinate status of the principality would not be undone. Yet, by a twist of fate, it was a Welshman, Henry Tudor, who laid claim to the English Crown by right of conquest when he defeated Richard III on the battlefield at Bosworth in 1485 and ascended the throne of England as Henry VII. In 1536, by Act of Parliament, the principality was to 'stand and continue for ever from henceforth incorporated, united and annexed' with England, with its government controlled from Westminster, its administration remodelled along English lines, and the Welsh to possess the same laws, liberties and rights as the English, including the right to representation in the English parliament.[11]

Where sixteenth-century Wales, under the government of a Welsh dynasty, acquiesced in these changes without rising in revolt, and accepted, if it did not embrace, the Protestant Reformation, it would take several centuries of struggle for the English to bring Ireland under some form of control. But Irish resistance did not deter Henry VIII from proclaiming himself King of Ireland as well as of England. By an Act of Parliament in 1541 the two realms were in principle to be equal, with the Irish Crown as an imperial Crown, but 'united and knit to the imperial crown of the realm of England'. In reality the Act made little difference to what had long been a complicated and ambiguous relationship, although it meant that Ireland remained outside the Anglo-Welsh state, and retained its own parliament, even though this would meet only four times between 1543 and 1613.[12]

Anglo-Scottish relations, however, were to take a very different course. Scotland's most conspicuous features, like those of Catalonia, were the mountains and the sea,[13] and its history and character were shaped, as with Catalonia, by the dialogue between them. The Highlands, encompassing the northwest of Scotland, were a rugged and sparsely populated region divided by its mountain ranges from the more fertile Central Lowlands and Southern Uplands. In many respects the region long remained a world on its own, a world of rough justice, bloodfeuds and faction fights between rival clans. In this it bore some resemblance to the lawless, bandit-ridden Pyrenean region of northern Catalonia, so different from the urban and mercantile Catalonia away to the south.

Where Catalonia possessed a single, Mediterranean, coast, Scotland faced different seas, and looked outwards in several directions – across the North Sea to Scandinavia and northern Europe, across the waters of the northern Atlantic to the North American continent that would one day be revealed, and across the Irish Channel to Ireland, only thirteen miles from the south-western tip of the Scottish mainland at the Mull of Kintyre. From the early Middle Ages onwards peoples arriving by land or sea from the surrounding lands and islands made their mark on Scotland. Around the year 500 Gaelic-speaking Scots emigrants from north-eastern Ireland crossed the Irish Channel to colonize the islands and the Argyll shore. Soon afterwards the Angles moved northwards from the areas they had occupied in southern and eastern Britain to begin colonizing the south-eastern Scottish Lowlands. Behind them came Scandinavians who raided and settled the Western Isles and moved into the Scottish Highlands between the eighth and eleventh centuries.

These various migratory movements were followed by competition among the emerging kingdoms of England, Norway and Scotland for territorial domination. Before the early thirteenth century, 'Scotland' was not the Scotland of today's borders, but only the territory north of the Firth of Forth. This was seen as a largely impassable dividing line (at least before a bridge was built at Stirling) between a separate northern 'island' of the British Isles, the Pictish kingdom of 'Alba', and Lothian, Galloway and 'Cumbria' (the old kingdom of Strathclyde) to the south of it, even though most of this southern territory fell under the rule of the King of Scots in 1069–70.[14]

It was by no means a foregone conclusion that the kings of Scots would eventually emerge the victors over rival kings and lords, and would succeed in transforming Scotland into a sovereign and unified state. Indeed it seemed more likely that the Scots' powerful Anglo-Norman neighbours to the south would prevail in north Britain as they were to do in Wales. The Scottish kings, however, were more successful than their Welsh counterparts in holding the English at bay. One explanation of their success was the continuity of the dominant royal line of the descendants of Malcolm III (r.1058–93) and his queen, St Margaret, the granddaughter of the English king Edmund Ironside. The line remained unbroken until the death two centuries later of the 'maid of Norway' and its continuity established a centre of stability in a changing world.

While successive Scottish rulers of this line paid homage to English monarchs for lands they held in England, they showed themselves increasingly reluctant to accept that their own kingdom was in any way subject to the rulers of the neighbouring realm. 'Independence' in today's meaning of the word did not exist in the political vocabulary of the age, but between the beginning of the tenth century and the end of the thirteenth, Scottish monarchs and their advisers were gradually articulating the idea of Scotland as a sovereign kingdom with its own defined geographical limits and possessing supreme jurisdiction in all secular affairs. Territorial sovereignty was defined geographically by the Pictish, and later Gaelic, concept of Alba as covering the landmass to the north of the Firth of Forth. Originally meaning 'Britain', Alba became the Gaelic term for the kingdom of the Scots somewhere around the year 900. Built up round the notion of this territorial entity, the 'kingdom of the Scots' – an expression that made its first appearance around 1160 – also came to be depicted as an ancient historical entity in a process that reached its culmination in the thirteenth century. At the inauguration ceremony of the seven-year-old Alexander III at Scone in 1249 the idea of the King of Scots as the sovereign ruler of a unified territory was clearly articulated. As ruler of an independent Scotland he was not prepared to accept any form of subjection to the King of England.[15]

Historical legitimacy was necessary to counter English claims to lordship over all Britain, but for much of the time the English claim to overlordship over Scotland was couched in relatively vague terms. It was only after the extinction of the Scottish dynasty in 1290 that Edward I began to press his claims seriously. In spite of the existence of such claims there was unbroken peace between the two kingdoms from the end of 1217 to early 1296, and an increasingly close relationship as the century advanced.[16] In 1251 Alexander III married Margaret, the daughter of Henry III of England, and in 1290 Edward I was laying plans for the marriage of the couple's granddaughter, also Margaret, the 'maid of Norway', to his son, Edward Prince of Wales, only to see them frustrated when she died that year on the voyage from Norway to take up the Scottish throne.

It was not only at the royal level that a close Anglo-Scottish relationship was developing. During the twelfth century the gift-giving of lands by successive Scottish rulers had attracted Norman magnates from England and elsewhere to their kingdom of Alba, or 'Scotia', as the north of Britain was also beginning to be called from the late tenth century onwards. This increasingly territorial aristocracy, many of them landowners in England, intermarried with the Gaelic-speaking Scottish nobility, who themselves became landowners south of the border.[17] With growing contacts between the two realms, aspects of English culture and language made their presence felt at the royal court and through the Scottish Lowlands.

During the reigns of Alexander II (1214–49) and Alexander III (1249–86) the Scottish Crown, borrowing and adapting for its own purposes English practices and institutions like the sheriffdom, did much to consolidate its authority and extend its territorial dominion. Benefiting from the peaceful relationship with England, the two Alexanders, building on the achievements of David I (r.1124–53), were able to move out from their core region of Scotia and Lothian into the Gaelic- and Norse-speaking regions of Scotland, and subdue or eliminate one after another the rival power centres. By the 1250s they had secured dominance over mainland Argyll; in 1264 the King of Man submitted to Alexander III and in 1266 the King of Norway recognized Alexander's recent conquests and agreed a treaty settlement that allowed him to purchase the Isle of Man and the Western Isles. Although Orkney and Shetland remained part of the kingdom of Norway until the mid-fifteenth century, by the late thirteenth the dynasty ruled over the entire Scottish main-land. Scotland was now unified under a dominant royal house; the threat of its fragmentation into alternative power blocs, whether Gaelic or Hiberno-Scandinavian, had been removed; and the kingdom of Scotland had largely secured the boundaries that it possesses today.[18]

Scotland and England now faced each other as two distinct kingdoms, sharing between them the space that constituted the whole island of Britain. Yet although territorial expansion had given the dominant Scottish royal line authority over all north Britain, the kings of the Scots can only loosely be called kings of Scotland in the full sense of the word. Medieval Scotland, like medieval England, was a state whose construction was the work of many generations, and it took longer than its southern neighbour to consolidate itself as a sovereign territorial polity. Not only was there a long delay before the incorporation into the emerging Scottish state of the Outer Hebrides, Orkney and Shetland, but much of western Scotland was geographically and historically closer to Ireland, and more deeply involved with Ireland and Ulster in particular, than with the seat of royal power in Edinburgh. For long, therefore, substantial areas were more subject in name than in practice to the kings of Scots; local potentates and Highland chieftains held court like petty kings; and a loosely constructed kingdom of Scotland can itself be seen as a composite monarchy in miniature up to the late Middle Ages and beyond.[19]

The Scottish kings did, however, enjoy several advantages, including the support of the clergy, who were anxious to remain free of ecclesiastical control by the archdiocese of York. But the monarchs lacked a strong bureaucracy, and above all they lacked an army to enforce their will. In effect they were therefore dependent on the compliance of the great landed nobles in the Lowlands and clan chiefs in the Highlands, and this was more likely to be secured by grants of land, privileges and administrative respon-sibilities than by hollow-sounding threats of coercion.

Consequently, state-building was a slow and complex process involving continuous and protracted negotiation with a powerful landed elite. The outcome was the emergence of a political and administrative system that harnessed the aristocracy to the tasks of government, even as royal officials moved deeper into the localities. While nobility and chieftains enjoyed extensive territorial rights, and exercised almost unlimited judicial powers over tenants and clansmen, they also came to be embraced within the institutional structures of royal government. The constant interaction of the Crown and aristocracy that was needed to make the system work meant that the two parties developed in unison rather than moving down their own separate paths. Their power-sharing enduringly shaped the pattern of the emerging Scottish state.[20]

By the time of the succession crisis that followed Margaret's death in 1290, the kingdom of Scotland was an effective sovereign state, and recognized as such by other European monarchs, including, even if somewhat reluctantly, the kings of England. But any prospect of the development of a permanently amicable Anglo-Scottish relationship based on parity of esteem between two sovereign states was shattered by the response of Edward I to the succession crisis. With his invasion of Scotland in 1296 and the transfer of its regalia to Westminster, the 'Hammer of the Scots' had apparently made himself monarch of all Britain, and was celebrated as such in contemporary chronicles. That year, however, was to prove the high watermark of his, and English, power.[21] William Wallace launched his uprising in the following year, and in 1306, in the wake of Wallace's capture and execution, Robert Bruce was crowned King of Scots at Scone. By 1314 Scotland was largely under Bruce's control. That same year he won the independence of his country by defeating Edward II's army at Bannockburn, although it was only in the Treaty of Edinburgh of 1328 that the English renounced their claims to lordship and accepted the existence of Scotland as an independent kingdom.[22]

During its Wars of Independence, Scotland reaffirmed and consolidated its identity as a territorially defined kingdom and as a national community, a *communitas regni Scotie*, that embraced both the king and his free subjects.[23] In 1320 the Declaration of Arbroath, which was designed to secure definitive papal recognition of Scotland's independence from English vassalage, emphasized both the concept of national sovereignty and Scotland's sense of itself as a country in which the relationship between ruler and ruled was, as in the Crown of Aragon, contractual in character. Robert Bruce was hailed in the Declaration as 'the person who hath restored the people's safety in defence of their liberties. But, after all, if the prince shall leave these principles he hath so nobly established, and consent that

our kingdom be subjected to the king and people of England, we will immediately endeavour to expel him as our enemy.'[24]

Although there were moments in the following years when it seemed
that English military power would prevail, from the middle of the fourteenth century the prospects of union of the two kingdoms, through
conquest or otherwise, receded, not least because of England's fresh involvement in war with France.[25] The convergence between the two realms that
had characterized their thirteenth-century relationship had now been
replaced by mutual hostility. The fourteenth and fifteenth centuries were a
period of endless cross-border warfare. They also saw the cementing of the
'auld alliance' between the Scots and England's traditional enemy, France,
first negotiated in 1295. By the beginning of the sixteenth century, Scotland,
under the government of its Stewart monarch James IV (r.1488–1513), had
taken its place among the reinvigorated monarchical states of Europe; and
although James himself was killed and his army crushingly defeated by an
English army at Flodden Field in 1513, a Scotland enjoying the support of
France was strong enough to hold Henry VIII at bay.

The coming of the Protestant Reformation would in due course transform both Scotland and England, bringing with it the prospect of some form
of reconciliation, but Henry's awkward combination of militancy and bluster
with the periodical offer of an olive branch only served to alienate the Scots
still further and drive them into the arms of the French. James V's marriage
in 1538 to Mary of Guise, the daughter of Claude of Lorraine, produced a
daughter, Mary, who was only seven days old when James died four years
later. Henry VIII, reaffirming in 1542 the claims made by Edward I at the
end of the thirteenth century, declared his sovereignty over Scotland,[26] but
his resort to invasion in order to bring about a marriage between Mary
Queen of Scots and his son and heir, Prince Edward, failed miserably.

Henry's 'rough wooing' of the Scots, which would be followed by an even
rougher wooing conducted by the Protector Somerset between 1547 and
1550, simply strengthened the hand of the pro-French faction in Scotland.
An English marriage was rejected, and instead Mary was promised to the
son of the French king Henry II. In 1548 the French dispatched a large force
to Scotland and carried her off to France for safe-keeping, while a regency
government under Mary of Guise turned Scotland into a French satellite. In
place of the Anglo-Scottish state envisaged by Henry VIII, the French king
could exultantly declare: 'Now Scotland and France are one State.'[27]

When Henry II of France was killed in a tournament in 1559, the seven-
teen-year-old Mary Stewart, as the wife of the new French king, Francis II,
became Queen of France. She was also in the direct line of succession to the

English throne if Elizabeth I, who had ascended it in the previous year, should die childless; and indeed Mary claimed that, as a Catholic, the throne was legitimately hers. Quite apart from any claims put forward by Mary, Elizabeth found herself at the very start of her reign confronted with an acute Scottish problem. French influence was dominant in Edinburgh, but Scottish Protestants, inflamed by the preaching of John Knox, were up in arms against the deeply unpopular regency government of Mary of Guise, who turned to her compatriots for help. Reluctant to support rebels against their legitimate queen, but fearful of a French-dominated Roman Catholic state on her northern border, Elizabeth let herself be coaxed by her principal secretary of state, William Cecil, into intervening in Scotland. In January 1560 she dispatched a fleet to the Firth of Forth and followed this up by sending an army across the border to besiege the French at Leith. With France at this point facing the prospect of civil and religious war at home, its commissioners agreed that all French troops should be withdrawn.

Cecil benefited from the fact that the Scots' hatred of the French now exceeded even their hatred of the English, but throughout the crisis he played his cards with skill.[28] He may well have had in mind an eventual union of the two kingdoms, but he was careful to avoid the bullying and bluster that had traditionally characterized England's approach to its awkward northern neighbour. His statesmanship did much to ensure that Scotland followed England in adopting the Protestant Reformation. A Protestant state north of the border, even if it assumed a Calvinist form, was far more welcome, and manageable, than a subordinate kingdom, like Ireland, whose people clung so obstinately to their Roman Catholic faith.

Although the return of the devoutly Catholic Queen of Scots to her homeland following the death of her French husband in 1560 would prove a source of endless trouble to Elizabeth and Cecil in the years ahead, at least Mary in Scotland was preferable to Mary as queen both of the Scots and the French. Her turbulent reign was in any event short-lived. Her marriage in 1565 to another descendant of Henry VII, her cousin Henry Stewart, Lord Darnley, was a personal and national disaster. His insolent and erratic behaviour in his new role of king consort soon alienated both his wife and his fellow nobles, and finally provoked his spectacular murder following a gunpowder explosion at Kirk o' Field in Edinburgh in February 1567. Mary's marriage that May to the Earl of Bothwell, widely suspected of orchestrating Darnley's death, precipitated the loss of her throne. Confronted by rebellion she was forced by the Scottish Lords to abdicate in July 1567 and her infant son James, her child by Darnley, was crowned King of Scotland in her stead. Her flight to England in the following year removed the immediate danger posed by her continuing presence in her own country, and Scotland itself, now under anglophile Protestant rule, ceased to be a threat. The way had been opened for the peaceful succession of James to the English throne thirty-five years later.

Foundation Myths

Behind the chequered story of Anglo-Scottish relations between Edward I's invasion in 1296 and James's accession lies another story that influenced the first at every turn, and that by no means reached its end in 1603 with the dynastic union of the two kingdoms under James VI/I. This is the story of how the peoples of the British Isles saw the territories they inhabited, and constructed narratives for themselves about their past, their present and their future.

Just as in the medieval Iberian Peninsula memories of Hispania and Visigothic Spain acted as a source of inspiration for the future, so also in medieval Britain a similar vision of lost unity helped shape the political agenda of later generations. King Arthur exercised a powerful hold over the medieval imagination, and the image of Arthur as king of all Britain permeated Geoffrey of Monmouth's enormously influential *History of the Kings of Britain* of the late 1130s.[29] The Galfridian legend, Geoffrey's account of Britain's origins, began with the great-grandson of Aeneas, Prince Brutus, who travelled to Britain after the fall of Troy, becoming the first king of the whole empire of Britain and the founder of an unbroken English royal line of kings, among them King Arthur.[30] In this Galfridian account, England and Britain were interchangeable.

Geoffrey of Monmouth's chronicle was one of those used by Edward I as he marshalled his claims to an imperial crown and sovereignty over Scotland. Since it could be shown that Arthur had ruled all the British Isles it was clear that the Scots were, and remained, vassals of the imperial English Crown.[31] In reality the appropriation of 'Britain' by the English long preceded Geoffrey of Monmouth and his optimistic inventions.[32] Traceable back to the tenth century, it was to remain a constant in England's approach to the other parts of the British Isles. Time after time those shadowy but glorious princes, Brutus and Arthur, would be deployed to justify English hegemony over Wales and Scotland, and even over Ireland.[33]

Medieval Spaniards, too, had their foundation myths. The great seventh-century scholar Isidore of Seville did much to popularize the concept of ethnic and national origins based on sacred scripture, thanks to his assertion that Europe had been peopled by the Japhetan descendants of Noah.[34] In his

History of the Goths he traced the Visigoths back to Tubal, the son of Japhet, and the supposed founder of Spain. In the ninth century, following the Islamic conquest of most of the peninsula, the Christian kings of Asturias in the unconquered northern part of Spain claimed direct descent from the legendary Pelayo, the son of the last Visigothic monarch – a claim that would be appropriated by the eleventh-century kings of León and Castile, who saw it as their mission to restore Christianity to the peninsula and reconstitute the empire of the Goths. This was a theme that would not only survive but flourish, perpetuated and embroidered in the chronicles sponsored in the thirteenth century by Alfonso X the Wise. These would allow Alfonso and his successors in the later Middle Ages to claim for the rulers of Castile hegemony over the entire peninsula, just as Edward I claimed hegemony over all the British Isles.[35] Alfonso de Cartagena in the fifteenth century would depict the Trastámara dynasty as the direct heirs of the kings of Visigothic Spain: 'My lord the king of Castile . . . not only descends from the kings of the Goths and from the royal houses of Castile and León, but also from all the kings of Spain; or, more properly, all the kings of Spain are descendants of his house . . .'[36] It was only a short step from here to the equation of Castile with Spain.

From the end of the fifteenth century the growing dominance of Castile in the life of the peninsula and in the minds of royal councillors did much to encourage this kind of thinking. The power of Castile, as the central and most populous region of the Iberian Peninsula, was already visible during the lifetimes of Ferdinand and Isabella, and it was soon to be reinforced by the acquisition of a transatlantic empire. The union of the Crowns did not diminish the essentially dynastic mentality of the two monarchs, and the New World of America uncovered by the voyages of Christopher Columbus was incorporated, not into the Crown of the newly united Spain but into the Crown of Castile. Although a number of Aragonese participated in the first stages of Spanish transatlantic expansion, the Indies were treated as a specifically Castilian conquest.[37] The new lands were to be governed by the laws and institutions of Castile, and the revenues and precious metals that would come from conquest and colonization would flow, at least in theory, into the Castilian royal treasury.

This acquisition of the Indies opened up almost unlimited prospects for an impressive expansion of Castilian power, even before it was reinforced in 1515 when a Castilian army conquered the south Pyrenean part of the kingdom of Navarre, and an ailing Ferdinand the Catholic incorporated it into the Crown of Castile. With little chance now of a renewed separation of the Crowns of Castile and Aragon, his decision made good sense: family and commercial ties were closer between Navarre and Castile than between

Navarre and Aragon.[38] Although the conquered kingdom was allowed to retain its institutional identity, the effect was inevitably to increase Castilian preponderance in the peninsula, and with it the tendency among Castilians to think of Castile and Spain as one and the same.

Finally, the weakening of Catalonia over the course of the fifteenth century did much to tilt the balance of power in the peninsula in favour of Castile, even if Catalonia's decline was to some extent offset by the economic vitality of Valencia.[39] The principality began the century not only as the dominant partner in the Catalan-Aragonese federation, but also as the mistress of the western Mediterranean. It was faced, however, with a combination of social, political and economic problems that would plunge it into crisis. In the aftermath of the Black Death the peasantry became increasingly vociferous in their demands to be freed of the 'evil customs' imposed on them by their feudal lords. The social question had already become serious when the Compromise of Caspe in 1412 brought to the Aragonese throne a dynasty with concerns distinct from those of its home-grown predecessor. The policies adopted by the Trastámaras led to a growing sense of alienation between the Catalan ruling class and the increasingly remote figure of the king. Tensions between Alfonso V (r.1416–58) and the Barcelona oligarchy induced him to take up residence in Valencia in preference to Barcelona, of which he was also the count, while his intervention in the affairs of Castile and his conquest of Naples in 1442 led to fears that he was subordinating Catalan-Aragonese interests to his imperial ambitions. After 1432 the Catalans would not see their count again.

The condition of the Catalan economy during the first half of the century remains uncertain, but in 1462 the peasantry, with its grievances still unaddressed, rose in revolt and the principality descended into civil war. Its neighbours and rivals, including its partners in the confederation, took advantage of its troubles to further their own interests. By the time Barcelona surrendered in 1472 to the forces of Alfonso's successor, John II (r.1458–79), continued population loss in the long aftermath of the Black Death had combined with social upheaval and civil war to destroy the foundations of Catalonia's earlier prosperity. John's son and successor, Ferdinand II the Catholic (r.1479–1504), would gradually restore a degree of social harmony and bring much-needed political stability to the principality, but it had lost out to its commercial rivals in the Mediterranean during the turbulent decades of the mid-fifteenth century, and it entered the new period of its history inaugurated by the union of the Crowns in a much weakened state.

The terms of the dynastic union ensured that Catalonia, like its partners in the Crown of Aragon, preserved its Constitutions – its laws and liberties – along with the institutions, the parliament or Corts and its standing committee, the Diputació or Generalitat, that were charged with their defence. In spite of this the principality inevitably felt overshadowed by its more powerful neighbour. By 1530 the Crown of Castile, including the Basque Country and Navarre, had just under four million inhabitants, or roughly the same number as England and Wales at the same time. Of the Crown of Aragon's population of 779,000 some 250,000 were Catalans – well under the figure for Scotland, which is estimated to have had between 500,000 and 700,000 inhabitants at the start of the sixteenth century. By the end of the century the Crown of Aragon had topped the million mark, and the Catalan population had risen to 360,000, but Castile, with its nearly six million, remained far ahead.[40] Castilian demographic dominance within the Iberian Peninsula went hand in hand with a growing political and cultural dominance, as Philip II succeeded Charles V in 1556 and chose Madrid as the permanent seat of his court in 1561.

Not surprisingly the Castilians, as the conquerors of the New World and increasingly dominant in the Old, displayed in their dealings with others all the arrogance of empire. A Catalan, Cristòfor Despuig, writing in 1557, complained that the Castilians had such a high opinion of themselves that they treated the rest of mankind like mud.[41] He also accused Castilian historians of failing to acknowledge 'the glory or honour of any Spaniard unless he is a Castilian', and of ignoring the achievements of the kings of Aragon and counts of Barcelona. Almost all Castilians, he claimed, 'are the same in wanting to use Castile as the name of all Spain'.[42]

The tendency of Castilians to equate Castile with Spain only served to reinforce what were already deep-seated fears among the peoples of the Crown of Aragon that a Castilian-dominated Crown and court harboured dark designs to suppress their treasured laws and liberties. Irritated by the resistance of the Aragonese Cortes, or parliament, of 1498 to her husband's requests, had not Isabel the Catholic herself said that 'it would be better to reduce these Aragonese by force of arms than put up with the arrogance of their Cortes'?[43] In the face of such threats it was natural that the Catalans, like the Valencians and the Aragonese, should cling tenaciously to their laws and liberties. It was equally natural that they should turn to the past, as the Scots turned to the past, for a narrative that would help protect them against the real or supposed designs of an overweening neighbour to undermine their national identity and deprive them of their rights.

The foundations of this narrative had already been laid in the fifteenth century. There had long been a tradition of great chroniclers in Catalonia, singing the glories of the early counts of Barcelona and the kings of Aragon.

But the extinction of the native dynasty in 1410, followed by the choice at the Compromise of Caspe of the Castilian Trastámaras as the new ruling dynasty and the subsequent descent of the principality into civil war, prompted a rethinking of the Catalan past in relation to that of Castile. It was natural to wonder where things had gone wrong. For future generations it all began at Caspe with the accession of a Castilian as the ruler of the Catalan-Aragonese federation – an event that would set in motion the nefarious process by which Catalonia would be deprived one by one of its ancient liberties. This made it essential to construct a narrative that would clearly differentiate the historical record of the Catalans from that of the Castilians, and would identify the special characteristics of Catalonia as a political entity.[44]

Much of this rewriting of the Catalan past would be done in the years around 1640 at the time of the principality's rebellion against the policies of the Count-Duke of Olivares and the government of Philip IV.[45] The polemicists and historians of the 1640s, however, drew heavily on the work of chroniclers, commentators and historians, who had struggled in the fifteenth and sixteenth centuries to provide a coherent narrative with only a few historical certainties to guide them. The part of the Pyrenean region that would become Catalonia lay in the marchlands between Muslim Spain and the Frankish realms, and one of the few certainties in a murky past was the recapture of Barcelona from the Moors in the year 801. But had the inhabitants of the region freed themselves from Moorish domination, as some alleged, or had freedom come as a consequence of their appeal to the Franks for help, in return for which they became part of the empire of Charlemagne and his successors? And if indeed they made a voluntary submission of sovereignty in return for Frankish protection, on what terms did they make it? Were the compacts then negotiated the true origin of Catalonia's famed liberties, as some argued, or did the compacts come later? In any event Barcelona and the surrounding region became part of Charlemagne's empire, but in the long run the Emperor's descendants proved unable to guarantee its protection, and at the end of the tenth century the counts of Barcelona renounced their vassalage. Much of the story of Catalonia's origins therefore revolved around the winning of independence from Muslim, and then imperial, domination – a story in which history was mixed with a heavy dose of legend.

In the fifteenth century it became important to counter Castilian claims to primacy over Hispania. As in Castilian historical writing, with its simultaneous recourse to the Bible and classical antiquity, so in Catalan historical writing Tubal, the son of Japhet, stood side by side with Hercules as the country's founder, with Cristòfor Despuig in the sixteenth century making assurance doubly sure by asserting that Tubal, on arriving in Spain, installed himself in the Catalan port-city of Tortosa. Yet the period of Carolingian domination was something of an embarrassment. Consequently, much was made of the independent origins of Catalonia and of a legendary Otger Cataló, who – as a counterpoint to Castile's warrior king Pelayo – was alleged to have won a great battle against the Moors. It was from him that the words 'Catalan' and 'Catalonia' were said to derive. With Castilian historians, however, claiming a dynastic and historical continuity reaching back to the Visigoths, and unbroken by that great point of rupture in medieval Iberian history, the Moorish conquest, Catalan chroniclers found it increasingly necessary to lay their own claim to the Visigothic heritage. Like the monarchs of Castile the counts of Barcelona came to be depicted as Goths, and 'Catalonia' was given a neo-Gothic etymology.[46]

It was probably only in the sixteenth century that Catalonia acquired the most durable of its foundation myths, and one that purported to explain the origins of the count-kings' heraldic device of four red bars on a golden field. According to legend, Wilfred the Hairy, who ruled Barcelona as probably its first independent count from 870 to 897, came to the aid of the Carolingian Emperor Louis the Pious in his battles against the Normans, and was rewarded with a grant of arms. When Wilfred was wounded in battle, the Emperor moistened his right hand with the count's blood and made four vertical stripes on his golden shield in recognition of his bravery.[47] The symbolic device would in due course provide the Catalans with their national flag, the counterpart of the saltire of St Andrew, the patron saint of the Scots, who was believed to have evangelized among their Scythian ancestors.

The fabrication or manipulation of the past for contemporary political purposes through legends like those surrounding Wilfred the Hairy was a common pursuit in medieval and Renaissance Europe. Monarchs and nobles needed the validation that came from being able to display genealogies that could be traced back to biblical times and the remotest periods of classical antiquity, and an army of chroniclers and historians were happy to oblige. Sometimes they built their arguments on the basis of genuine texts that might require creative embroidering. At others they fabricated their own sources or discovered convenient 'facts' where the available evidence left gaps they were unable to fill. This massive historical enterprise, blending history and myth and European-wide in its scope, was indispensable in furnishing monarchs with a battery of arguments that could be used to advance or uphold their territorial and jurisdictional claims against the arguments of their rivals. These were times in which antiquity conferred legitimacy and prestige.[48]

It was in the context of English claims to sovereignty over Scotland that Scottish chroniclers and historians developed their own narrative of their country's antiquity as an independent kingdom, which drew upon and finally displaced Pictish narratives of the kingdom's past. Sixteenth-century Scots were proud of their long line of monarchs – eventually calculated as forty in all – that allegedly stretched back to Scota, the daughter of an Egyptian pharaoh. It had long been assumed that her genealogy had been constructed around 1360 by that ingenious chronicler John of Fordun, but he now appears to have based his chronicle on earlier sources, the most notable of which was the *Gesta Annalia*, recently ascribed to Richard Vairement (Veremundus), the foreign chancellor of Alexander II's second wife, who seems to have finished writing it in 1285.[49] The genealogical information to be found in Veremundus and Fordun was later refined and elaborated by the imaginative humanist historian Hector Boece in his *History of the Scottish People*, published in Latin in 1527, and translated into the vernacular with adaptations nine years later.[50]

The legend told how Scota married a Greek prince, Gaythelos. The two of them, leaving Egypt with their followers before the pharaoh and his army were drowned in the Red Sea in pursuit of the Israelites, settled in the Iberian Peninsula. From here their descendants, carrying the stone of Scone as they travelled, moved to Ireland and then on to Scotland, where they defeated the Picts and took over the Pictish kingdom of Alba running north from the Firth of Forth. The Scots, arriving later than the Picts, could therefore trace their descent in an unbroken line from an Egyptian princess. This nicely checkmated Geoffrey of Monmouth's claims for an English hegemony over all Britain derived from the alleged British kingship of the Trojan prince Brutus, by giving the kings of Scots an ancestry far longer and more distinguished than that enjoyed by the English royal line. The legend had the added advantage of taking the Scots back to a biblical rather than a merely classical past.[51]

Peoples under threat from foreign aggression or domination were everywhere unearthing or fabricating evidence of this kind that would not only legitimate their resistance but that also served to strengthen the sense of their own distinctive identity. The same process was at work in societies where monarchs and their subjects found themselves in conflict, and especially in such countries as sixteenth-century France and Scotland where the conflict was exacerbated by the religious differences created by the advent of the Protestant Reformation. In order to save themselves from exile or death, dissidents in danger of persecution for heresy began searching for political and ideological weapons to justify resisting, and, if necessary, taking up arms against, rulers arrayed in all the panoply of kingship conferred on them by God.

In Scotland, Mary of Guise, as regent for her daughter, negotiated with some skill the double threat to royal power posed by religious and aristo-cratic rebellion in the so-called 'Wars of the Congregation', although her efforts would eventually be crippled by the withdrawal of French support. As she lay on her deathbed in July 1560, she knew that she had at least succeeded in saving the throne for her daughter, but she also knew that she had failed to halt the onward march of John Knox and his adherents. The Reformation parliament that met in Edinburgh in the month after her death, in casting off papal jurisdiction and abolishing the Mass together with other sacraments of the Roman Church, turned Scotland into an officially Protestant nation, removing it from the orbit of Catholic France and drawing it inexorably into that of Protestant England. Its newly adopted religion, along with its new political alignment, would gradually reshape the country over the following decades, while at the same time changing and renewing its self-image as it assumed the mantle of an elect nation that had entered, like the Children of Israel, into a special covenant with the Lord.[52]

The nineteen-year-old Mary Queen of Scots, no longer queen of France since the death of her husband at the end of that critical year, 1560, returned to her native land in the summer of 1561. Her religion clearly put her at odds with that of her Protestant subjects, but her upbringing in the French court did not help her come to terms with the challenge of governing a faction-ridden kingdom, while her disastrous marriages alienated one or other of the aristocratic factions and were hardly calculated to widen her appeal to a nation now beginning to pride itself on its godly ways.[53] Her forced abdica-tion in 1567, however, raised serious questions about the legality of the action taken against her, and required some form of justification.

This would be provided above all by that great humanist scholar George Buchanan, who became the ferocious tutor of Mary's child, the young James VI. In his *De jure regni apud Scotos*, published in 1579 but originally written to justify the queen's deposition twelve years earlier, Buchanan naturally drew on a radical European line of constitutionalist thinking, but also on his reading of the real or imagined history of his native Scotland, and particularly that of Hector Boece. But it was not only humanist historians who propagated the idea of Scotland as the free nation of a free people. By the time they were writing, the concept was firmly rooted in the popular imagination, and was popularized in the fourteenth and fifteenth centuries by works in the vernacular, and notably by John Barbour's verse romance, *The Bruce*, written in 1375 and kept alive by declamation.[54]

Monarchy to Buchanan was a form of elective government, and monarchs who broke the contract inherent in their coronation oath could lawfully be deposed. In effect his Scotland possessed an ancient constitution that subordinated its rulers to the laws of the community, although he was vague about the mechanisms by which that constitution operated. But Buchanan had at his disposal enough materials from the past to develop a theory of popular sovereignty that was conceived in purely secular terms and was sufficient to justify armed resistance and even, if necessary, tyrannicide. These materials, though, did not include, as might have been expected, the 1320 Declaration of Arbroath, with its implicit assertion of the notion of contract. This was a document that dissident Scottish nobles seem not to have invoked either now or earlier, and that only became generally available when the original Latin text was published in 1680. Even then it would not be until the twentieth and the early twenty-first century that it came to be seen as epitomizing the quintessential Scottish spirit.[55]

The notion of a contractual relationship between monarch and people invoked in its most radical form by Buchanan and widely deployed across sixteenth-century Europe, found its most famous formulation in the 'historic' Aragonese oath of allegiance, which was purported to have ancient origins but was in reality a contemporary invention: 'We who are as good as you swear to you who are no better than us, to accept you as our king and sovereign lord, provided you observe all our laws and liberties; but if not, not.'[56] In this instance, however, royal practice was to trump constitutionalist theory, as it failed to do in the realm of Mary Queen of Scots. In 1591–2, in response to an uprising in Zaragoza, Philip II sent an army into the kingdom and forced the Aragonese Cortes to adopt a number of changes designed to limit the degree of autonomy enjoyed under Aragon's ancient constitution.

Three years before this, in 1588, the Catalans had their own brush with royal power as the result of an attempt by the authorities to investigate the affairs of the Diputació. The clash prompted a flurry of literary activity that saw the elaboration of myths about the self-freeing of the Catalans from Muslim domination, the concept of Catalonia as a nation that had never been conquered, and the timing of the foundational compacts between the Catalans and their elected prince.[57]

In the light of the events of 1588 the Catalans naturally felt growing concern for the survival of their laws and liberties, and the concern was made all the greater by Philip's military intervention in Aragon and its consequences. Around the turn of the sixteenth and seventeenth centuries, therefore, it is not surprising to find Catalan chroniclers vigorously deploying all the historical arguments at their command in order to demonstrate the antique and sacrosanct nature of a constitutional system that they feared was under threat from the royal government in Madrid. Here there was no question, as there was in Scotland, of religious differences provoking political disagreement to the point of rebellion. The Catalans might take exception to some of the religious reforms that Philip II attempted to introduce, but while Scotland was re-imagining itself as a Protestant nation, a Catalonia exposed to the combined influences of Catholic Reformation and Counter-Reformation saw itself as a devoted daughter of the Church. According to Pere Gil, who wrote a geography of the principality at the turn of the sixteenth and seventeenth centuries, 'Catalonia is very inclined to the observance of piety, faith and the Christian religion.'[58] It was liberty, not religion, that was at stake, and it was to ensure the survival of their ancient liberty that the Catalans, like the Scots and the Aragonese, plundered the chronicles in pursuit of arguments to enable them to resist the encroachments of arbitrary power.

The principality, asserted its chroniclers, had traditionally enjoyed almost complete fiscal and judicial immunity, thanks to the laws of the Visigoths and the respect shown for those laws by the Frankish kings.[59] As with the Scots, Catalan society was one based on a compact – a concept that modern historians have called *pactismo* – and this contractual society was central to their image of their *pàtria*. Theirs was a fatherland uniquely blessed by God. It was their very own land, or *terra*, occupying its own well-defined territory, a land with a temperate climate and a fertile soil, bequeathed them by their forefathers, who had made it what it was. It had its own distinctive history and language, and above all, thanks to its cherished Constitutions, it was a land of the free.[60] 'The affairs of the Principality of Catalonia,' wrote a Catalan in 1622:

> are not to be judged by reference to those of other kingdoms and provinces, where the kings and lords are sovereign lords, with such power that they make and unmake laws and rule their vassals as they will ... The laws we have in Catalonia are laws compacted between the king and the land, and the prince can no more exempt himself from them than he can exempt himself from a contract ...[61]

This was a warning signal, uttered at the beginning of a new reign, that of Philip IV, whose accession to the throne in 1621 seemed to presage new and unwelcome changes to a principality that already felt itself under pressure from Madrid. His predecessor, Philip III, had only summoned the Cortes, or Corts, of Catalonia once, in 1599, and since then grievances had been accumulating without the possibility of resort to the parliamentary forum in which it was customary to press for the redress of wrongs. Philip had yet to visit the principality to take the oath sworn by all his predecessors to observe and uphold its Constitutions. Royal absenteeism – itself an inevitable characteristic of composite monarchies – was a long-standing source of complaint. The new prince not only showed no serious sign of intending to visit his aggrieved vassals and listening personally to their complaints, but was taking administrative actions, like appointing a new viceroy, which directly infringed the Constitutions he had not yet promised to observe.[62]

The dispute of 1622–3 between Catalonia, or, more accurately, the Barcelona oligarchy and the government in Madrid over the appointment of a viceroy before the king had taken his oath, pointed to the underlying problem that had bedevilled relations between the Crown of Aragon and its absentee ruler ever since the death of Ferdinand the Catholic. The late sixteenth century was the age of Jean Bodin, and the effect of Bodin's writings was to encourage and disseminate the assumption that sovereignty was indivisible. But in a composite monarchy like Spain since the late fifteenth century – a Spain increasingly dominated by Castile – where was the true source of sovereignty located?[63] This was a question that was also the subject of confusion and debate in the Great Britain created by the Anglo-Scottish dynastic union of 1603. In London and Edinburgh, just as much as in Madrid and Barcelona, dynastic union had implications and consequences that would prove equally unwelcome to all the parties involved. What, after all, was 'Spain', and what was 'Great Britain'?

Union and Dissension

In October 1604 James VI/I, overruling the objections of a parliament fearful that the historic kingdom of England would be swallowed up in a new and potentially monstrous body politic, altered his title by royal prerogative to that of 'King of Great Britain, France and Ireland'.[64] The term 'Great Britain' was not a new one. Just as 'Spain' – Hispania – was throughout the Middle Ages both a historical and a geographical expression used when referring to the Iberian Peninsula as a whole, the same applied to 'Great Britain'. Thirteenth-century writers influenced by the work of Geoffrey of Monmouth used *Britannia Maior* as a geographical term for the whole island of Britain; and the words 'this Nobill Isle, callit Gret Britanee' appear in the instrument for the proposed marriage of Edward IV's daughter Cecily to James III of Scotland in 1474.[65] James VI/I's appropriation of the term for the composite monarchy over which he now ruled, however, gave it a new, if at first unpopular, currency and launched it on what was to be a long and successful career. Yet the exact nature of this composite monarchy and of the relationship between its component parts was still obscure in 1603.

There was, after all, very little that was inevitable about the union that was now taking place, and in some respects the two kingdoms were further apart than in the thirteenth century before Edward I attempted in 1296 to assert his mastery by force of arms. The subsequent consolidation of Scotland as an effective working kingdom, together with its participation in the European international system, widened the gulf between the two countries. Matters were made worse by the insensitivity and brutality displayed in the English Crown's handling of its relations with its northern neighbour during the reigns of Henry VIII and Edward VI. Against this, the formal adoption by both kingdoms of Protestantism, even if in distinctive versions, had created a measure of shared interest, and with it the possibilities for the development of a more positive relationship.

Some voices had in fact been raised in sixteenth-century Scotland advocating union with its fellow kingdom, and not least that of the influential scholar John Mair in his *Historia Maioris Britanniae* of 1521. Rejecting the foundation myths of both the English and the Scots, he was keen to see a union for the common good of two peoples described by James III's secretary, Archibald Whitelaw, in 1484 as being 'bound together within a small island in the western sea'.[66] Mair's envisaged union was dynastic, the product of royal marriage alliances. In reality this was the only way in which union could now be achieved. Scotland might be the weaker of the two kingdoms, but centuries of indecisive conflict had shown that England had no possibility of achieving union through conquest. All that English aggressiveness had done was to reinforce the Scots' sense of themselves as a distinct and independent people. In Scotland, as in Catalonia, the effect of the aggressive behaviour of a more powerful neighbour was simply to strengthen a collective sense of the *patria*.

Even if some of their countrymen were capable of envisaging and embracing the concept of a united Britain, for most Scots the very word 'Britain' was associated with English claims to feudal overlordship and hegemony.[67] Not surprisingly, therefore, there was much discussion in Scotland of the impending changes and their implications. Many Scots were afraid that, once their king was in London and enjoying the fleshpots of England, they would never see him again. They were conscious, too, of their country's weakness and feared an eventual take-over by their more powerful neighbour. This made it important to insist, as did Sir Thomas Craig, that the union should be one of equals.[68]

The English, for their part, were no less wary of what lay before them. Over the centuries they had tended to assume that a king of England would one day incorporate Scotland within his imperial dominion. Yet now they saw the King of the Scots entering London in triumph to become their sovereign. This left a bitter taste in the mouth, and it was made all the more bitter by the sight of a swarm of James's countrymen descending on London with their eyes on court offices and household appointments. Difficulties of acceptance were compounded by the concept of undivided legislative sovereignty imbibed from Bodin. For the English, sovereignty was located in the English parliament and they found it hard to conceive of an English monarch ruling his three kingdoms as separate realms with separate parliaments. Consequently, their natural approach to union was to think in terms of outright conquest, as in Ireland, or of an incorporating union, as had happened with Wales, whereby the lesser power was subsumed in the greater. The notion of a genuinely composite monarchy was one they had yet to confront.[69]

Faced with so much opposition in both England and Scotland to the implications of union, James, in consultation with his judges, appointed Scottish and English commissioners in 1604 to negotiate the terms of a union settlement that could be presented to both parliaments. This was accompanied on both sides of the border by an outpouring of pamphlets and treatises by Scots and English alike.[70] The result was a debate both in print and in the respective parliaments that had no parallel at the time of the union of the Crowns in late fifteenth-century Spain.

The Spanish union had come about by stages. Isabella had succeeded to the throne of Castile five years before her husband succeeded to that of Aragon. Since the union was purely personal, with Juana, the eldest daughter to the royal couple, becoming Queen of Castile on Isabella's death in 1504 and Ferdinand remaining king of Aragon alone, uncertainty about the durability of the union was bound to linger as long as his second marriage left open the possibility of a separate heir for the Aragonese Crown. The uncertainty was not finally dispelled until Ferdinand's death in 1516, and it would take time for all parties to digest the long-term implications of a lasting union. As those implications grew increasingly clear over the course of the sixteenth century, natives of the Crowns of both Castile and Aragon began to reflect seriously on the character and perceived shortcomings of the arrangements by which their destinies had been joined.

Participants in the Anglo-Scottish debate were well aware of Iberian developments, which indeed helped to shape their thinking. They naturally looked to continental Europe for examples of union, like that between Poland and Lithuania, recently fortified by the Union of Lublin of 1569.[71] One precedent, and hardly a happy one, was to be found closer to home in the marriage alliance of Philip II and Mary Tudor in 1554, but commentators tended to dwell in particular on precedents within the Iberian Peninsula itself – precedents that could be used to display the union of realms in a light that was either positive or negative as circumstances dictated.[72]

The Spanish example was made all the more relevant by two recent events, both of which had major European repercussions: the Spanish-Portuguese union of 1580 and the revolt of Aragon in defence of its *fueros* (laws, customs and privileges) in 1590–1. In the words of Francis Bacon, when addressing the theme of 'union in name' in his *A Brief Discourse touching the Happy Union of the Kingdoms of England and Scotland*, 'the common name of Spain (no doubt) hath been a special mean of the better union and conglutination of the several kingdoms of Castile, Arragon, Granada, Navarra, Valentia, Catalonia, and the rest, comprehending also now lately Portugal'. On the other hand, as he also observed, Spain, along with other states and kingdoms, could serve as a warning of the consequences of imperfect union: 'it hath kept alive the seeds and roots of revolts and rebellions for many ages; as we may see in a first and notable example of the kingdom of Arragon ... Because it was not well incorporated and cemented with other crowns', the Aragonese 'entered into a rebellion upon point of their *fueros* or liberties, now of very late years'.[73]

For Bacon, a perfect union required not only 'union in name', something the Anglo-Scottish Union would now receive with the official adoption of the term 'Great Britain', but also the union of language ('both Your Majesty's kingdoms are of one language, though of several dialects'), along with the union of laws, manners and 'employments'. But, even while noting points of similarity between England and Scotland, he advocated proceeding cautiously. In particular, where law was concerned, 'it sufficeth that there be an uniformity in the principal and fundamental laws both ecclesiastical and civil'. The recipe for lasting union, or what Bacon called a 'perfect mixture', was, above all, time. An 'unnatural hasting thereof doth disturb the work, and not dispatch it'. A second prerequisite was that 'the greater draw the less'.[74] This, too, would need time and patience.

The king himself was a far more enthusiastic advocate of a 'perfect union' than the majority of his subjects on either side of the border, although his idealism would be tempered by a high degree of pragmatism, which may have reflected an early appreciation that the ideal far exceeded the limits of the possible.[75] The union that James VI/I envisaged was to be a truly British union, symbolized by the union flag combining the crosses of St Andrew and St George, which he ordered in 1606 to be flown on all royal and merchant ships.[76] His concept of Britain, however, did not involve the abandonment of the special characteristics of the two realms now united in his royal person, as the king made clear when defending his project against its opponents in a speech to the House of Commons in March 1607.[77] 'When I speake of a perfect Union, I meane not confusion of all things: you must not take from Scotland those particular Priviledges that may stand as well with this Union, as in England many particular customes in particular shires ... do with the Common Law of the Kingdome.'[78] On the other hand, as James went on to explain, he looked forward to 'such a generall Union of Lawes as may reduce the whole Iland, that as they live already under one Monarch, so they may all be governed by one Lawe'.

Although he was quick to praise the common law of England as 'the best of any Law in the world', the king was, he knew, treading on delicate ground. English common lawyers saw themselves as the vigilant custodians of the ancient constitution, and would pounce, like their Scottish counterparts, on any perceived infringement of historic rights and liberties. In principle there was likely to be more flexibility in the Scottish Faculty of Advocates than among the English common lawyers, since Scottish law by the time of the union was an amalgam of different elements. These consisted not only of Roman and canon law and parliamentary statute, but also included aspects of Norman feudal law closely resembling Anglo-Norman law. In consequence, Scotland's ancient constitution was an even more amorphous affair than that of England, and its historic underpinnings even more uncertain.[79] On the other hand, once union had occurred, the Scottish judiciary was likely to be much more inclined than in pre-union days to resist the encroachments of the English common law, which they feared would subvert little by little the ancient constitution and Scotland's fundamental laws.

James was well aware of the risks he was running in addressing the question of possible legal changes. What he wanted, he told the House of Commons, was not 'the abolishing of the Lawes, but only the clearing and the sweeping off the rust of them'; and even then he acknowledged that 'this is not possible to be done without a fit preparation'.[80] Uniformity between the legal systems of England and Scotland, rather than their fusion, was his goal.[81] But his speech failed to allay deep-rooted fears. The parliamentary session of 1606–7 displayed the depth of anti-Scottish sentiment at

Westminster, where members of parliament feared Scottish domination in English national life, just as the Scots feared English domination in *their* national life. To the Scots a federal-style union of equal and self-governing partners was the only form of union that would guarantee the continued existence of their kingdom. To the English, an incorporating union was the only acceptable one, and it had to be incorporation on English terms.

For the present, then, any amalgamation of the two countries' laws or parliaments was out of the question. So too was the amalgamation of their respective religious establishments. James had his fill of the Presbyterians in his years as king of Scotland, and it was a relief to find himself the head of the more docile Anglican church on his arrival in England. In religion, as in law, his aim was to secure a greater degree of conformity between the two kingdoms. In 1603 he intensified his moves against the Presbyterians in his northern kingdom by reviving the power of Scotland's two archbishops and eleven bishops and giving them control over the Presbyterian synods and Scottish church government.[82]

Between 1618 and 1621 the king went further, pushing liturgical changes, known as the Five Articles of Perth, through the Kirk's General Assembly in 1618 and then through the Scottish parliament in 1621 in an attempt to bring worship in Scotland more into line with Anglican ceremonial practices, including the practice, abhorrent to Presbyterian purists, of kneeling during communion. This Article aroused intense opposition, especially in the godly city of Edinburgh. Scotland's capital city regarded itself as the spiritual as well as the political and administrative capital of the realm, and was vigilant in seeking to prevent any deviation from correct religious practice.

In pressing ahead with his proposed reforms in the face of opposition from clerical ministers and their parishioners, from the Edinburgh city councillors and eventually from the members of his own Scottish Privy Council, James came close, by the time of his death in 1625, to provoking a major crisis in his northern kingdom. As it was, he left a dangerous legacy to his son and heir, Charles. Religious and political dissent were coalescing, as had happened in 1560 and in the 1580s and 1590s, and would happen again in 1637. An ecclesiastical policy intended to give the monarch the same degree of control over the Church in Scotland as in England threatened to subvert the fragile relationship between Church and State that James had established in his northern kingdom in the earlier years of his reign. It is clear that even for such an astute monarch the simultaneous government of two different kingdoms with two different forms of Protestant worship was a high-wire act, in which, as his son would discover, the danger of falling was never far away. As it was, James's repeated intrusions into a sphere that the

General Assembly regarded as its own left a legacy of resentment that would have a profound impact on Anglo-Scottish relations in the years following his death.[83]

With no incorporating union of his two kingdoms either possible or in prospect, the most pressing challenge facing James was to make the governance of his new composite monarchy work to the best of his ability. Here he faced practical problems similar to those with which Spanish monarchs had to grapple in the Iberian Peninsula and in the various component parts of Spain's composite monarchy, like the kingdom of Naples. In Scotland, as in the Crown of Aragon and now Portugal, prolonged royal absenteeism was a significant source of discontent, although a long history of royal minorities may have inured Scots to seeing little or nothing of their monarchs. James managed to return to his native land once, in 1617. It would be eight years after Charles I's accession to the throne before the new king made the journey to Edinburgh. In the British Isles, as in the Iberian Peninsula, the high costs of travel with a vast entourage were a deterrent to royal visits. Further heavy expenditure would be needed, too, to meet the deferred expectations of loyal subjects from whom the rays of the royal sun had for too long been withheld.

Spanish monarchs attempted to counter the deleterious effects of royal absenteeism by means of government through a number of councils, like the Council of Aragon, representing the interests of individual territories and meeting at court, while viceroys ruled the territories themselves in the absence of the king.[84] James took a different route. The Scots were adamant in their rejection of the idea that their kingdom should be governed by a Spanish-style viceroy or by a Lord Deputy, as in Ireland. Consequently there would be no viceroy in Edinburgh, and Scottish administration was left in the hands of the Scottish Privy Council meeting in the Scottish capital. The travelling distance between Edinburgh and London of around 400 miles was not very much more than that between Barcelona and Madrid, and one of James's first acts on becoming King of England was to establish a postal service between his two capitals. With letters taking around a week to pass between them, contact could be frequent, but in general James trusted his Scottish Privy Councillors to manage Scottish business without excessive intervention on his part.[85]

While James would add Scots to the English Privy Council, he chose not to create a single council comparable to the Spanish Council of State for general oversight of the various parts of his composite monarchy. He was also notably cautious in making appointments, excluding Scots from English judgeships and departments of state, and confining them to the

royal household, where he could dispense favours as he wished. In particular, numerous Scottish aspirants to offices in England were channelled
towards the royal bedchamber, where they could benefit from proximity to
the royal presence. As a result, the bedchamber became the nerve centre of
a patronage system linking an absentee monarch to his Scottish subjects.[86]

The English took umbrage when they saw Scots flocking to the court,
and feared, or professed to fear, that their country would be swamped by
this horde of hungry foreigners. In practice the numbers of Scots appointed
to official positions, even in the royal bedchamber, was relatively small,
although the English affected to think otherwise. The majority of Scots who
descended on London were ordered back to their own country once they
had been rewarded with pensions or cash for their services.[87] But were the
Scots, however unpopular, really foreigners once the two realms had been
united under a single monarch?

Similar problems of nationality had arisen in Spain following the union of
Castile and Aragon, and any attempts to resolve them were clouded in uncertainty. In the peninsula itself Castilians were determined to ensure that all
offices in the Crown of Castile were kept for themselves, and resisted every
attempt by Catalans, Aragonese and Valencians to break the Castilian hold on
court appointments. Not unnaturally the Cortes and the representative bodies
of the Aragonese territories responded in kind. To some extent, however, the
exclusionary policies followed in the peninsula broke down in the Indies.
Technically the American Empire belonged to Castile by right of conquest,
and there were continuing doubts as to whether inhabitants of the Aragonese
realms had the right to travel to, or settle in, the Indies unless they first
obtained Castilian naturalization. Yet in 1585 Philip II seems to have conceded
the existence of such a right when he issued a decree classing as foreigners,
and hence as being excluded from the Indies, all 'who are not natives of these
our realms of Castile, León, Aragon, Valencia, Catalonia and Navarre, and the
isles of Mallorca and Menorca, as belonging to the Crown of Aragon'.[88] This
would appear to leave the door open to the non-Castilian peoples of the
peninsula, with the exception of the Portuguese, who were specifically
declared in this decree to be foreigners. But well before this, legal restrictions
on the passage of inhabitants of the Crown of Aragon seem to have been
largely ignored, although if they took up residence they tended to be frozen
out of New World offices. Castilians had no intention of seeing their monopoly
of office broken on either side of the Atlantic, and the idea that Castilians and
Aragonese were all 'Spaniards' would only make slow headway.[89]

King James, too, wrestled with this question of nationality. Addressing
the topic of 'Naturalization' in his speech of 31 March 1607 to the House of

Commons, he upbraided members for their negative attitude to Scottish claims for acceptance: 'All you agree that they are no Aliens, and yet will not allow them to bee naturall.'[90] The English and Scottish commissioners who had worked out the terms of the union had drawn a distinction between the *antenati* – those born before James acceded to the English throne in 1603 – and the *postnati*, who, as subjects of the King of England, were held to be already naturalized under English common law. James was willing to accept the distinction and to exclude the *antenati* from English offices, while reserving his prerogative right to do as he wished. The Commons, however, rejected the ruling that the *postnati* were naturalized in the eyes of the common law and hence were automatically entitled to hold all offices in England. The alternative, as the Commons saw it, was an incorporating union in which the king's Scottish subjects embraced the English legal system – an alternative quite unacceptable to the Scots.[91]

In a collusive suit on the status of Robert Colvill, one of the *postnati*, the judges ruled that his condition as a subject of the king overrode any considerations based on nationality as determined by the kingdom of his birth. This was as far as the law could go. The notion of a common 'British' nationality, as envisaged by James, was plainly as alien to the English as was that of a 'Spanish' nationality to Castilians. He saw intermarriage between the nobility of his three kingdoms as a way of promoting union through the creation of a truly 'British' aristocracy, but although the presence of Scottish favourites and officials at his court inevitably led to increased contacts between English nobles and a select number of Scots, very few of these contacts led on to marriages, either during his reign or that of his son. Only three English peers married an Irish or a Scottish wife between 1600 and 1669. On the other hand, ninety-six Scottish peers or their heirs found English brides between 1603 and 1707, but many of these were second or third marriages of nobles who already had children through their earlier, Scottish, marriages. The numbers of aristocratic Anglo-Scottish marriages showed some increase after the 1707 Union, but James's dream of creating an integrated 'British' aristocracy would not begin to be realized before the nineteenth century. The Scottish nobility remained relatively closed, and the nobles of both kingdoms preferred on the whole to marry their own.[92]

The refusal, or inability, to think in genuinely 'British' terms – a refusal as common to the Scots as to the English – effectively blocked other initiatives that could help to bring the two kingdoms together, for example in the field of commercial relations. In Spain, following the dynastic union, the customs barriers between Castile and the Crown of Aragon stayed in place; and although Philip II abolished the customs posts between Portugal and

Castile in 1580 they were restored twelve years later, presumably because of the loss of revenue that had been incurred. The story in the British Isles was the same: in 1604 measures were taken to bring about commercial reciprocity between the two kingdoms, but in 1611 customs posts were reintroduced following complaints by Scottish customs farmers about the financial losses they had sustained.[93]

The Scots, however, were eager to participate in English overseas trading companies, but here they were met with adamant resistance, similar to that which frustrated the territories of the Crown of Aragon in any hopes they may have had of engaging in direct trade with the Indies – a trade over which Seville enjoyed an exclusive monopoly. In English eyes colonial ventures and the fruits of overseas empire must remain firmly in English hands. In 1621 James gave a grant to found a colony, New Scotland, in a region of the North American coast claimed by France, to Sir William Alexander, an enthusiastic proponent of a transatlantic empire in which the Scots would have a share. 'I think,' Alexander wrote in his *An Encouragement to Colonies*, 'that mine be the first National Patent that ever was so clearly bounded within *America* by particular limits upon the Earth.'[94] But his colony failed abysmally, partly because of French hostility but primarily because his compatriots showed very little interest in emigrating to North America.

There were good reasons for this. In 1607, following the flight of the rebellious Irish earls of Tyrone and Tyrconnell, the king, in his desire both to pacify and civilize the Irish and to promote his plans for a genuine unification of his kingdoms, issued orders for the establishment of an Ulster plantation, in which two-fifths of forfeited Irish land were assigned to English and Scottish settlers. In the first four decades of the century perhaps up to 30,000 Scots, many of them Lowland farmers, emigrated to Ireland, with consequences of enormous import not only for Ireland but also for the future of Scotland itself.[95] Scots had long been accustomed to emigrating, and were prepared to undergo many hardships in their search for a better life, but at this period in the seventeenth century prospects for emigrants looked far brighter in Ireland than in the North American 'wilderness'. The sea crossing, moreover, was incomparably shorter and safer.

The plantation in Ireland offered a rare opportunity for that blending of Scots and English on which James had set his heart. On acceding to the English throne he had dreamt of bringing about what he called a 'union of hearts and minds', or, as he put it in his 1607 speech to the House of Commons, 'a perfect Union of Lawes and persons, and such a Naturalizing as may make one body of both Kingdomes under mee your King'.[96]

But during the first decade of his reign he found himself thwarted at almost every turn. There was simply no meeting of hearts and minds, but merely dissension and mutual hostility as the English and Scottish parliaments entrenched themselves behind their respective ramparts.[97] In London there were street brawls between Englishmen and Scotsmen, fuelled by the negative images that each nation had of the other – the English as haughty and superior, the Scots as lazy, poor and grasping.[98]

By the end of the decade the notion of incorporating union was dead and buried, and James was shrewd enough to recognize this unwelcome truth. He could give a nudge here and a nudge there, but there was no prospect of forming 'one body' out of the two kingdoms in his own lifetime. His dream, however splendid, would not be realized then, and perhaps might never be.

CHAPTER 2

Rebellion and Its Aftermath
1625–1707/1716

Roads to Rebellion

Already by the time of James's death in 1625 there were growing indications that it would be hard to sustain the delicate equilibrium between the kingdoms of England and Scotland that he had struggled to achieve. On the English side there was contempt for the Scots who had taken up residence in the court, and resentment at the influence they wielded with the king. On the Scottish side there was a growing feeling that their monarch had been taken captive by the English, and a growing uneasiness in the Kirk about the direction being taken by his religious policies. Closer proximity had not brought increased mutual understanding. Nor was understanding helped by the recrudescence of violence on the Borders during the final years of the reign. In an attempt to bring peace to the lawless Border region, James had begun his reign by rebranding the Borders as the 'Middle Shires', where English and Scots would come together in amity as the frontier receded into memory. This dream, like so many of his dreams for closer union, came into conflict with harsh realities, as officials on both sides of the border tenaciously defended their separate jurisdictions; but for a time the border guard achieved some measure of pacification. Unwisely, however, James dissolved the guard in 1621, and although a new joint commission for the Borders was hastily established it proved unable to enforce the peace of earlier years. The failure was symptomatic of a more general decline in administrative effectiveness that went hand in hand with a decline in the power and prestige of the Scottish Privy Council. By the 1630s not only the Highlands but also the Scottish and English 'Middle Shires' had again become a disorderly region of banditry and feuding.[1]

In Catalonia, too, banditry had become endemic by the early seventeenth century. There had always been bandits and brigands in rural Catalonia and in its mountainous northern regions, as there had been in the Highlands and on the Anglo-Scottish borders. In Catalonia, as in northern England and Scotland, lawlessness fed on unemployment, hunger and misery, but public order declined in the principality during the later years of Philip II.[2] During the first two decades of the new century the breakdown of order became acute, with rural nobles employing armed bands to pursue their vendettas. Successive viceroys failed to bring the banditry and lawlessness under control, and it was only towards the end of the reign of Philip III that two strong-minded viceroys, the dukes of Alburquerque and Alcalá, succeeded in restoring some semblance of order. But they did so by ignoring or infringing the Catalan Constitutions, and thus succeeded in alienating important sections of the Catalan ruling elite. The relationship between the principality and Madrid was therefore already delicate when Philip IV came to the throne in the spring of 1621.

Within a few months of his accession the principality was plunged into controversy with the ministers in Madrid. Not only had the Catalans been accorded no sight of their monarch since 1599 but the new king had yet to take the traditional oath to observe the Constitutions, and had made it clear that pressing business made an immediate visit to Barcelona impossible. The delay raised the question of whether the viceroy could legitimately continue to govern in his name, and since the viceroy was the deeply unpopular Duke of Alcalá his enemies saw this as an ideal opportunity to be rid of him. The next two years witnessed a long and agitated debate, at once constitutional and political, in which the Diputació and the city government of Barcelona bombarded Madrid with petitions insisting on the contractual nature of the relationship between the Catalans and their prince – a relationship that they now believed to be under threat.[3]

Their vigorous reaction to the perceived infringement of their laws and liberties may be seen, at least in part, as a means of instructing a new ministry in the realities of governing a composite monarchy in which the monarch was expected to abide by the rules that defined his distinctive rights and obligations in each individual kingdom under his rule. At the same time the Catalan authorities were keen to make clear to Madrid how their list of grievances had grown during the long period which had seen no convocation of the Corts, an occasion that traditionally required the physical presence of the king. But behind all their assertions and complaints lay a gnawing fear that the Crown, under pressure from Castilians in high places, was planning to destroy Catalonia's freedom and subject the principality to Castilian domination and arbitrary power.

In the years that followed the dispute over the viceroyalty those fears intensified. It was not until 1626 that Philip IV came to Barcelona to take the long-delayed oath to observe the Constitutions and hold a meeting of the Corts. After much wrangling these broke up in acrimony without voting the grant requested by the king. The postponement of the royal visit, although not as long as that experienced by the Scots before Charles I's eventual arrival in Edinburgh in 1633, had increased the alarm over Madrid's intentions, especially since it was accompanied by disturbing reports of the plans being devised by the new king's favourite and first minister, the Count of Olivares, for the future government of Spain and the *monarquía española*.

Royal ministers had long been exasperated by the problems involved in governing Catalonia. As early as 1600 the Duke of Feria, at that time its viceroy, confided to his secretary that 'there is little use in keeping me in this province any longer because, thanks to these Cortes, no governor, however good, can keep the province in order, and no governor, however bad, can bring it to a worse pass than that to which it has already been brought by its own laws.'[4] There were always those in Madrid who would have liked to see the laws and liberties enjoyed by the peoples of the Crown of Aragon abolished, but judicial and practical considerations argued against such a drastic solution to the problem of governing a recalcitrant polity. After all, Philip II himself had been notably cautious in his response to the revolt in Aragon.

On assuming power Olivares naturally turned his attention to questions of government, and not least to those involved in the administration of a composite monarchy. In his 'Great Memorial', or secret instructions of late 1624 to his royal master, he put forward a series of proposals some of which are likely to have leaked out while he was still in power and which would lead nineteenth- and twentieth-century historians, and especially Catalan historians, to see him as bent on 'centralizing' and 'Castilianizing' the Monarchy.[5] At the heart of his proposals for structural change was the proposition that Philip should make himself 'King of Spain', rather than of 'Portugal, Aragon and Valencia, and Count of Barcelona', and 'reduce these kingdoms of which Spain is composed to the style and laws of Castile, with no differentiation in the form of frontiers, customs posts, the power to convoke the Cortes of Castile, Aragon and Portugal wherever it seems desirable, and the unrestricted appointment of ministers of different nations both here and there ...' These were more radical plans than those publicly advanced by James VI/I for the closer union of England and Scotland, although when Olivares allegedly went around murmuring *multa regna, sed una lex*, his words uncannily echoed similar sentiments expressed by James about his two kingdoms: 'as there is over both but *unus rex*, so there may be in both *unus Grex & una lex*' – one flock and one law.[6]

Any assessment of the motivation and intentions of both men needs to take into account not only the particular circumstances of the moment but also the political culture in which they were operating. On moving to England, James was confronted by a challenging new situation in which he was required to govern two kingdoms without offending the sensibilities of either, along with a third kingdom, Ireland. This forced him to play the political game largely by ear, but without sacrificing his fundamental aim of coordinating wherever possible their systems of secular and ecclesiastical government in ways that would facilitate the administration of Scotland and England, strengthen the fragile ties between their two peoples, and uphold and enhance the royal prerogative and royal authority in both. Olivares, on the other hand, faced the challenge of governing a long-established composite monarchy whose constitutional arrangements were fraying at the edges to the detriment of royal authority and to Spain's standing as the greatest power in Europe.

On coming to power in the early 1620s Olivares also faced a rapidly dete-riorating international situation, as a conflict that eventually metamor-phosed into the Thirty Years War broke out in central Europe. Hostilities were simultaneously being resumed with the Dutch Republic on the expiry of the twelve-year truce that had temporarily suspended attempts by Spain's army of Flanders over forty years to crush the revolt of the Netherlands. Renewed warfare on a number of fronts implied a massive increase in mili-tary and naval expenditure at a time when the economy of Castile, which had borne the brunt of taxation among the peninsular kingdoms over the past hundred years, was showing serious signs of strain, and when silver revenues from the Indies were substantially less than in the reign of Philip II.

Although James had his own financial difficulties he largely succeeded in keeping his kingdoms clear of war. The pressures imposed by a foreign policy designed to give his Stewart dynasty (henceforth to be called Stuart as it anglicized itself)[7] a higher continental profile and establish him as Europe's peacemaker, were therefore minuscule in comparison with those that confronted Olivares. If Spain were to retain its European hegemony and Philip IV be acknowledged as the greatest ruler in the world, it was essential in Olivares's eyes that all the kingdoms of the Monarchy should contribute to the common enterprise. This could only be achieved if they no longer exploited their laws, liberties and parliamentary institutions to block measures for mobilizing money and manpower across the *monarquía* to the benefit of all. The prime requisite, therefore, was to make Philip in practice what he already was in name, a true 'King of Spain'.

Olivares's desire, as expressed in his secret instructions to Philip, to 'reduce these kingdoms of which Spain is composed to the laws and style of Castile', would seem to justify contemporary suspicions and later assumptions that he was planning a progressive 'Castilianization' of the peninsula. The Scots entertained similar fears of a progressive anglicization of their laws and institutions when they heard James lavishing praise on the common law of England and expressing his wish for 'a generall Union of Lawes'.[8] Yet, in both instances, proposals for uniformity couched in terms of union were rather less drastic than they seemed at first sight.

For James, as for Olivares, the question of royal power was paramount, and both were concerned to reduce or eliminate differences between the kingdoms that impeded the effective exercise of the Crown's authority. Where institutional arrangements were concerned, this was more urgent in Spain, where the Cortes of the various peripheral territories were more intractable than those of Castile, than it was in Britain. Here the Scottish parliament, although since 1580 a more robust institution than in earlier times, was traditionally more amenable to royal requests for money than the English House of Commons.[9] Nor was a relatively impoverished Scotland in a position to make the kind of contribution to the Crown's revenues that might be expected of Portugal and the Crown of Aragon if their laws and institutional arrangements had not stood in the way. It was therefore natural that Olivares, faced by an acute shortage of funds, should wish to alter their system of government to make it conform more closely to that of Castile, where the Crown's fiscal requirements faced fewer obstacles.

In this sense, therefore, his aim was not so much to 'Castilianize' the Monarchy as to enhance the power of the Crown in kingdoms where the royal writ ran less freely than it did in Castile. In the circumstances their reduction to 'the laws and style of Castile' seemed the natural way forward. In Spain, however, as elsewhere in Europe, a clear distinction existed between 'justice' and 'government'. While a monarch had the right to introduce changes in government when they served the common good, 'justice', by contrast, was sacrosanct. Like his contemporaries, Olivares accepted this distinction as a matter of course. It was permissible to tamper with laws, liberties and privileges only when they were clearly prejudicial to royal authority and obstructed good government.[10]

Well aware that his plans for reform would run into resistance, Olivares hoped to sugar the pill by showing the non-Castilian kingdoms the benefits they could expect in return for some loss of their traditional privileges. In his Great Memorial he had written of the need to address their legitimate sense of grievance over royal absenteeism and their lack of access to appointments and court offices. His aim was to create a Monarchy whose constituent parts would all work together for the common good, and in which office-holders would be appointed without regard to their kingdom of origin. An immediate means of promoting this long-term aim was to persuade them of the advantages of a system for mutual defence. Olivares aimed to achieve this by means of a 'Union of Arms', a scheme by which every kingdom and province would raise a fixed quota of paid men ready to be called upon by the Crown when any part of the Monarchy came under attack. This, as he explained, would enable His Majesty's kingdoms to be 'all for one, and one for all'.[11] In 1626 he presented his plans to the Cortes of Aragon and Valencia, both of which were assembled in the Aragonese town of Monzón, and he and the king then moved on to Barcelona for a meeting of the Corts of Catalonia. In the Cortes of Aragon and Valencia, Olivares enjoyed only limited success, and none in Catalonia, where his proposed Union was seen as the prelude to a sustained attempt to subvert the principality's laws and liberties and make it as subject to the whims of an authoritarian ruler as Castile was assumed to be.[12]

The king's underlying intention, in the words of one of his ministers, was 'to familiarize the natives of the different kingdoms with each other so that they forget the isolation in which they have hitherto lived'.[13] Familiarization was a step towards the ultimate goal that Olivares had in mind, and one that he shared with James VI/I. For both men a real union of kingdoms and peoples could, in the end, only be achieved by bringing about James's 'union of hearts and minds'.[14] One device for achieving this was the promotion of intermarriage between noble houses of the various kingdoms. Here Spain had a century's head start over Britain. By the end of the sixteenth century the few existing Catalan titled nobles had married into the upper reaches of the Castilian nobility and had joined nobles from other kingdoms and territories of the Spanish Monarchy either at the court in Madrid, or serving in posts in one or other of their dominions or on diplomatic missions.

Intermarriage, in turn, tended to Castilianize these noble families and their descendants, a process exemplified by the history of the ducal family of Cardona since the reign of Charles V. Catalonia's principal noble in the first half of the seventeenth century, the Duke of Cardona, was nominally a Catalan and owned large estates in the principality, but his forebears had married into the Castilian aristocracy and he was Castilian in all but name.[15]

The reign of Philip IV (1621–65) saw increasing numbers of such marriages between the elite families of the different realms and territories of the Iberian Peninsula, Spanish Italy and the Netherlands, accelerating a process that had begun long before Olivares drove it forward in his bid to bring about a closer union of the king's dominions. To the limited extent that transnational aristocratic marriages were capable of promoting political integration, Spain's composite monarchy had achieved by 1700 a degree of integration of which James VI/I could only have dreamed.[16]

In presenting his plan for the Union of Arms through a system for mutual defence Olivares once again emphasized the need to end 'the dryness and separation of hearts' that had hitherto prevailed.[17] For him, as for James, the strongest bonds of all were the bonds of affection. This was to ask a great deal of peoples for whom the *patria* in the first instance meant their local town or region, and then, but much more vaguely, the larger polity to which they belonged.[18] Scotland, geographically divided between the Highlands and Lowlands, and the Northern and Western Isles, was hardly a single nation, and geographical division was compounded by a growing linguistic and cultural division. From the late fourteenth century, Gaelic, the language that had until then been predominantly spoken throughout Scotland, was receding into the clan society of the Highlands in face of the northward advance of 'Scottis', the Lowland Scots' version of English, a language increasingly regarded as the mark of civility and status.[19]

Geographical and linguistic divisions were equally sharp in the territories of the Crown of Aragon, which Olivares now hoped to incorporate into a more integrated Spanish Monarchy. After centuries of union, Aragon, Valencia and Catalonia were still in many respects strangers to each other, both politically and culturally. The Aragonese were Castilian-speaking, and while Castilian was making inroads, Valencians and Catalans, as also Mallorcans, continued to speak their own language. On top of these divisions, localism was rife throughout the Iberian Peninsula. How realistic, then, was it to expect that time-hardened barriers between Catalonia and Castile, or Scotland and England, could be broken down?

For James, as for Olivares, elevated to a dukedom in 1625 and henceforth known as the 'Count-Duke', kingship itself provided the essential bond of union. However great the diversity between the peoples they governed, and however negative the images they held of each other, they were all subjects of the same ruler. From the standpoint of James and of Philip IV's first minister, differences of nationality were subsumed within the loyalty owed by all subjects to a monarch shared by all of them. 'I am no *nacional*,' declared the Count-Duke on one occasion, 'that is for children.'[20]

On the other hand, subjects faced with a new round of taxes and unwelcome alterations to traditional customs and habits, were bound to regard with deep suspicion appeals to abandon ancient hatreds and unite for the common good. Not surprisingly, whether in Spain or Britain, royal initiatives for a change of attitudes fell on deaf ears. In both there was an instinctive opposition to anything that smacked of 'novelty'.

Novelty, or innovation, began in Scotland at the start of the reign of Charles I with relatively minor changes in the machinery of administration and justice. More dramatically, the new king ordered a sweeping revocation of all the gifts of royal and Kirk property that had been made to private individuals since 1540. It was usual for a monarch to reclaim usurped land at the beginning of a new reign, and part of the king's purpose was to make more adequate provision for ministers of the Kirk; but his action, taken with a minimum of consultation, was inevitably seen as a major threat to the nobility, who, over the course of the years, had been granted, or had appropriated, great tracts of royal and church land.[21] Since landowners would have to surrender the property in question and then receive it back on less favourable terms, the revocation was a useful fiscal device at a time when Charles was badly in need of funds. He had gone to war with Spain in 1625, and in 1627 the English Secretary of State, Sir John Coke, proposed, in direct imitation of Olivares's Union of Arms, that the king should build 'upon the same grounds of State as the Spaniards have built to unite his three kingdoms in a strict union and obligation each to other for their mutual defence when any of them should be assailed'.[22] The revocation of land grants could be used to provide funds for the raising of a Scottish contingent for this Union army. The resumption of alienated Crown lands figured, too, among the fund-raising devices under consideration in Madrid for financing the Count-Duke's Union of Arms. It was alleged that in Catalonia the Crown was losing 400,000 ducats a year to the nobility and gentry as a result of its repeated failure to recover 'usurped' lands.[23]

Opposition to his plans drove Charles into making a number of concessions, but the Act of Revocation created enormous resentment and did much to alienate the Scottish political nation from the king.[24] His alienation of his Scottish subjects was made all the sharper by his continuing failure to visit his northern kingdom. As Clarendon relates in his *History of the Rebellion*: 'The kingdom of Scotland generally had been long jealous that by the King's continued absence from them they should by degrees be reduced to be but as a province to England and subject to their laws and government, which it would never submit to'.[25] Although the word 'province' still seems to have been neutral in Catalonia at this time, whereas in contemporary Portugal, as in Scotland, it implied subordination, Scots, Catalans and Portuguese alike were afraid that they would be reduced by their more powerful neighbour to mere provincial status.[26]

When Charles did eventually arrive in Edinburgh in 1633 his visit did nothing to allay suspicions. As in Catalonia in 1626 and again in 1632, when the king returned to Barcelona for a new session of the Corts only to have them break down a second time without the granting of a subsidy, the Crown's efforts to raise money even through the normal parliamentary channels were not well received. The Scottish parliament, less obdurate than the Corts, had grown accustomed to voting extraordinary taxes, and approved them on this occasion, although resenting them as being as extortionate. In Scotland, as also in Catalonia, the failure or inadequacy of traditional sources of revenue compelled the Crown to resort to extra-parliamentary procedures, in this instance by increasing customs dues and the impost (duty) on wine.[27]

Yet if fiscal demands were a source of grievance in both Scotland and Catalonia and did much to offset the benefits expected from a visit by an all too absent monarch, fears in both countries over the growing pressures exerted by the state were compounded in Scotland by the king's alarming interventionism in matters of religion. In Catalonia the Crown's ecclesiastical policies were always capable of giving rise to tension, especially over such issues as the appointment of Castilian bishops to Catalan dioceses and the granting to non-Catalans of pensions drawn on ecclesiastical revenues.[28] There was, however, no parallel in the principality to the ambitious attempt of Charles I and Archbishop Laud to impose liturgical reform on the fiercely independent Scottish Kirk. The king's intentions had already generated great unease before his arrival in Scotland in 1633, and the opposition he encountered during the course of his visit seems only to have strengthened his determination to press ahead with his plans. In 1634, ignoring warnings from the Scottish bishops, Charles ordered them to make any necessary alterations to the English prayer book before he imposed it on the Kirk. Two years later, wading in where his father had reluctantly decided not to tread, he imposed a new book of canons embodying the highly controversial Five Articles of Perth. Then, towards the end of 1636, the Scottish Privy Council was instructed to issue a proclamation commanding the use of the new prayer book, now in the final stages of preparation.[29]

These measures – largely taken without consultation with Scottish clerical ministers and laity – for the closer alignment of the Kirk with the administrative structure and liturgical practices of the Church of England, inevitably stoked the fears, shared by many in England, that the king and his archbishop were secretly planning the restoration of popery in the British Isles. Coinciding as they did with growing discontent over the way in which Scotland was being governed, and with alarm at the authoritarian tendencies being displayed by the king, the measures were bound to provoke a strong reaction, not only in a political nation that was being progressively alienated from the royal government, but also among the populace at large. Ministers of the Kirk opposed to the new prayer book were meeting to plan their strategy, and on 23 July 1637, in what appear to have been well-organized demonstrations, the reading of the prayer book was met with protests and rioting in St Giles and other kirks in Edinburgh.

From this point events moved fast. Petitions were drawn up against the prayer book, numerous meetings were held, there was further rioting, and by the end of 1637 it was beginning to look as if Charles was losing control of his Scottish kingdom. In February 1638 a committee of nobles, lairds (lesser tenants-in-chief), burgesses and ministers drew up a National Covenant to 'maintain the ... true religion, and the king's Majesty'. The Covenant found an enthusiastic reception, especially in the Lowlands, and rapidly acquired vast numbers of subscribers.

While the imminent threat to the Kirk from Charles's ecclesiastical policies was responsible for the Covenant's widespread acceptance, its recourse to the instrument that, since John Knox's return in 1559 from his Genevan exile, had evolved into an established process of associating and signing under solemn oath, gave it a resonance that it would otherwise have lacked. Knox and his followers had enthusiastically embraced the biblical concept of a covenant between God and His chosen people, and in their eyes Scotland became a newly covenanted nation when in 1560 it liberated itself from the Roman yoke and adopted the Protestant faith. A national covenant with God involved a solemn act of religious association that may have held a particular appeal for a society in which ties of kinship and friendship had become formalized in the later Middle Ages in the practice of 'bonding' between lords and their followers in a compact of mutual obligation.[30]

The National Covenant of 1638, therefore, in recalling the Confession of Faith of 1581, which had been subscribed by the king, his councillors and by 'persons of all ranks', and then resubscribed in 1590, placed itself in a tradition that was both Calvinist and distinctively Scottish.[31] In the circumstances of 1638 it legitimized the resistance of a united Scottish nation to innovations in Kirk practice and discipline emanating from a government in London that had little understanding of Scotland and the Scots. In so doing it did much to provide Scotland, at this dangerous moment in its history, with a sense of collective identity that would long outlast the moment and would do much to shape its national self-image in the centuries ahead. Yet while the purpose of the document was religious, its political implications lay only just beneath the surface. Church and State might be kept rigorously apart in the Presbyterian worldview, but a covenanted nation also implied a 'covenanted king' – a monarch under contract – as Charles II would be forcefully reminded at his coronation ceremony at Scone in January 1651.

In spite of the existence of numerous examples, from the sixteenth-century Netherlands to early seventeenth-century Bohemia, of the danger posed to monarchical authority by the combination of religious and political dissent, Charles I was slow to react to the alliance of nobles and Presbyterians in his Scottish kingdom. It was not until June 1638 that he sent the Marquis of Hamilton to Edinburgh to negotiate with the covenanters, and he was not prepared to allow Hamilton to make serious concessions. In his eyes they were rebels, and he was already preparing to suppress resistance by force of arms. In November a General Assembly of the Kirk, meeting in Glasgow, set about reforming the Church. Among its reforms were the revocation of the Articles of Perth, the abolition of episcopacy and the deposition of the bishops. The king's army moved northward, and the First Bishops' War – a conflict that neither side wanted – began in March 1639, to be promptly concluded in June by the Treaty of Berwick.

The treaty was a victory for the covenanters, who had forced acceptance of their demands on the king. In order to pay for a new campaign to crush the Scottish rebels the humiliated monarch was compelled to summon a new parliament in England, the first in eleven years. The leaders of the English opposition shared with the Scots a deep distrust of Charles. The case for collusion was therefore obvious, and discreet contacts were made. When the Short Parliament met in April 1640 it showed no inclination to raise taxes to finance an English army for the invasion of Scotland. In spite of its refusal the king, advised by the Earl of Strafford and Archbishop Laud, was determined to press ahead with his plans for a campaign. The Scottish parliament, for its part, ratified the National Covenant and the acts of the 1638 Glasgow General Assembly, and passed a Triennial Act stipulating that a full and free parliament should convene every three years. It also set up a Committee of Estates to rule Scotland after parliament rose, rather along the lines of the standing committee of the Catalan Corts, the Diputació, and gave it powers to organize the kingdom's defences against the anticipated invasion.[32]

In August 1640 the Committee of Estates and the army officers decided to seize the initiative and invade England. Launching the Second

Bishops' War the Scottish army crossed the border on 20 August and, meeting with almost no resistance, easily secured the surrender of Newcastle a week later. The king, unable to raise troops to repel the invaders, called a great council of peers that met in York in late September 1640, which effectively forced him into summoning a new English parliament for early November. Under the terms of the Treaty of Ripon concluded in October between the king's representatives and the Scottish commissioners – terms even more humiliating to Charles than those of the Treaty of Berwick of the previous year – the Scottish army was to remain on English soil and be paid by the English until the English parliament met and peace negotiations could begin. In effect the Scots had handed a lifeline to the English opposition, and the Long Parliament would seize the opportunity to wrest the concessions it demanded of Charles and dismantle a regime that threatened England and Scotland alike with the loss of their treasured liberties.

While the drama of the Scottish rebellion was unfolding in the British Isles during the spring and summer of 1640, a comparable drama was unfolding in Spain – one in many respects very different but no less portentous in its consequences. After many years of tension and localized conflict between the two Crowns, France declared war on Spain in May 1635. In 1637, frustrated by the unwillingness of the Catalans to make the contribution to the war effort that he expected of them, the Count-Duke of Olivares tried to involve them more directly by planning a diversionary attack on Languedoc by an army based in the principality and containing a strong Catalan component.

As war came to the Pyrenean frontier region during the course of the following two years and the government in Madrid piled further pressure on the Catalans, tensions escalated between the Catalan authorities and the regime. Early in 1640, following the recovery by the royal army of the frontier fortress of Salses after a long and harrowing campaign, Madrid gave orders that the army should be billeted in the principality before campaigning was resumed in the spring. The billeting of the troops provoked numerous clashes between soldiers and the local population, and in the spring and early summer of 1640 rural Catalonia erupted in revolt. The rebels carried their message of defiance into the towns and on 7 June, Corpus Christi day, the *segadors*, or reapers, who had come into Barcelona to hire themselves out for the harvesting season, rioted and tried to set the viceregal palace on fire. The viceroy, the Count of Santa Coloma, a native Catalan who had become closely identified with Olivares and his policies, made his escape from the building, but was struck down by one of the insurgents as he struggled along the rocky beach in the hope of being rescued by a galley standing out to sea.[33]

With the viceroy dead and the principality in revolt, the ministers in Madrid, badly shaken by the turn of events, decided on a punitive action to restore order and bring the Catalans to heel. It was the same hard-line response as that of Charles I when confronted by the rebellious Scots, and turned out equally badly. In Spain, as in England, time was needed to assemble an army and move it into place. The delay during the autumn months of 1640 gave the Diputació time, under the charismatic leadership of Pau Claris, a canon of the Pyrenean diocese of Urgell, to prepare counter-measures against the anticipated attack. The principality was in a state of anarchy and the elite was deeply divided, but Claris and his fellow *diputats* were able to carry with them the city government of Barcelona and influential sections of the political nation as they struggled to maintain control.

In Catalan eyes France was the traditional enemy, but, realizing that the only long-term hope for the principality was to be found in French military assistance, the *diputats* secured in September 1640 a promise of help from Louis XIII and Richelieu, who had dangled before them the possibility of Catalonia's transformation into a republic under French protection. In a bid to ensure a wide range of support for their actions they also summoned an extraordinary Junta, or general meeting, of the Estates which came to include a strong element of popular representation in the form of the Third Estate. As divisions grew in the principality and the royal army drew closer to Barcelona, Claris appealed urgently to the French to come to the city's aid. The contractual character of the relationship between the principality and its prince provided ample arguments for the termination of the principality's allegiance to Philip IV. A meeting of the Estates on 16 January 1641 approved the transformation of Catalonia into an independent republic, but the French remained justifiably sceptical about the degree of Catalan commitment to a permanent dissolution of the ties that bound the principality to Philip IV and the House of Austria, and wanted something more. On 23 January 1641, with the Spanish army almost at the gates of Barcelona, Claris formally proposed to the Estates that the principality should place itself under the government of the King of France 'as in the time of Charlemagne, with a contract to observe our Constitutions'. The republic had lasted exactly a week.

Just three days later the Catalan-French defending force defeated the royal army on the hill of Montjuïc overlooking Barcelona. Catalonia was saved, but at the price of its transformation into a French protectorate. It remained to be seen whether Louis XIII of France would be any better a guarantor of Catalan liberties than Philip IV of Spain.[34] Madrid, therefore, like London, was confronted with an intractable rebellion in a peripheral territory – a peripheral rebellion that was promptly followed by a second, when a palace coup in Lisbon on 1 December 1640 caught the government by surprise. Like the Catalans, the Portuguese, exploiting the diversion created by events on the eastern side of the Iberian Peninsula, renounced their allegiance to Philip IV in the hope of ending their sixty-year union with Spain. But unlike the Catalans, they had a potential monarch-in-waiting, in the person of the Duke of Braganza, an aristocrat of royal descent, whom they proclaimed as John IV of the newly independent kingdom of Portugal. A few months later, in October 1641, London, too, was to be faced with its second peripheral rebellion, this time in Ireland.

For both Britain and Spain long years of conflict lay ahead. The Catalan revolt would end with the surrender of Barcelona on 13 October 1652 to the forces of Philip IV, who offered a general pardon and a promise that the principality's Constitutions would be respected. Portugal, on the other hand, finally won formal recognition from Spain of its newly recovered independence in 1668. The Scots, for their part, experienced a bewildering mixture of successes and failures before being defeated by Oliver Cromwell's army at the battle of Dunbar in September 1650. Subsequently they found themselves back in the regal union of the two kingdoms when Charles II, whom they had long since recognized as their monarch, was restored to the English throne in 1660.[35] In many respects, therefore, rebellion in both Scotland and Catalonia ended with a return to something very close to the constitutional situation of the pre-revolt years, although in both instances the conflict would leave deep scars, and memories of the events of those revolutionary years would become firmly etched into the national consciousness.

Although the Scottish rebellion had been provoked above all by the king's tampering with the governance and liturgy of the Kirk, this played into wider fears about the dangers to the kingdom's ancient traditions and liberties following the dynastic union of 1603. In this sense, even if there was no peasants' revolt in Scotland like that which precipitated the Catalan uprising of 1640, the origins of the two rebellions had much in common, in spite of the fact that rebellion in Scotland was not motivated, as it was in Catalonia, by war, and that religion was only a subordinate issue in the Catalan uprising, whereas it was central to the Scottish revolution.[36]

From the beginning the weaker partner in what was no more than a dynastic union was painfully aware of its vulnerability when it came under pressure from its more powerful neighbour. In the 1620s and 1630s that pressure became acute. The *patria*, with all its accumulated loyalties and memories, was in mortal danger, and the insurgents, whether peasants or covenanters, spoke for many more when they challenged the Crown's authority in a mass movement of protest. Their challenge gathered vital support, both idealistic and self-interested, from within the political nation. This support found expression in the ancient representative institutions of both countries – the Corts and meetings of the Estates in Catalonia, and parliament and the Estates of the realm in Scotland. In the eyes of the members of these institutions the prince had defaulted on his obligations under the terms of the contractual relationship that bound him to his people. But their responses to the king's refusal to abide by the contract took different forms, because of the very different circumstances of the two principal partners in the respective dynastic unions, Castile and England.

Although there was growing opposition to the Olivares regime in Castile, and the leaders of the Catalan revolt attempted to win the support of the Count-Duke's enemies by claiming to speak not only for themselves but for a Spain afflicted by his tyrannical government,[37] the opposition was weak and poorly organized. Moreover, the Cortes of Castile, although often an obstacle to the Count-Duke's plans, were politically ineffectual as a national rallying point for opposition when compared with the English parliament. If the revolt were to survive, therefore, the insurgents, lacking support in a Madrid which had little reason to love the Catalans, and without an equivalent of the Scottish army to protect them, had no choice but to seek, however reluctantly, the protection of France. The 1640 revolt became a separatist movement, but not by original intention. This was separatism under duress. Claris and his friends hoped as the insurrection spread that it would provoke the downfall of Olivares, and that this in turn would bring the king to his senses and be followed by the restoration of harmonious relations with his Catalan subjects. This hope would be frustrated. As for the establishment of an autonomous republic, it was true that, against all the odds, the Dutch rebels against Philip II had managed this, but the cards in mid-seventeenth-century Europe were heavily stacked against the Catalans achieving the same feat, and there is no evidence to suggest that Claris harboured this as his long-term ambition.[38]

In England, on the other hand, by the late 1630s the political and religious opposition to Charles's government was intensifying and gaining in credibility. The aims of his adversaries were similar to those of the Scots: to place such limitations on the king's power as would prevent him from governing as a tyrant. As a result, the Scottish rebels and the English opposition shared a community of interests that made their collaboration feasible.

Benefiting from the overshadowing presence of a Scottish army in the north, Charles's English opponents could turn to parliament and use it for the defence of the traditional English liberties.

By the 1640s, therefore, the dynastic union that had laid the foundations of Spain's composite monarchy appeared to be unravelling, as both Catalonia and Portugal chose the path of secession. In Britain's composite monarchy, by contrast, the events of 1639–41 had the effect of strengthening a union both recent and fragile, as Scots and English alike discovered that mutual necessity was more compelling than ancient antipathy. However, it was not yet clear whether the new conjunction of events would help to bring about the prospect of that 'union of hearts and minds' which James VI/I so loved to contemplate.

The Consequences of Rebellion

For both Spain and Britain the 1640s proved to be a decade of upheaval. The Catalan rebellion encouraged the Portuguese to follow suit, and the inability of royal forces to suppress either of the two revolts precipitated the downfall in January 1643 of the Count-Duke of Olivares after twenty-two years in power as the favourite and first minister of Philip IV. In this sense the revolt of the Catalans secured a prime objective – the overthrow of a hated and 'tyrannical' minister. On the other hand, in their struggle to save their laws and liberties they failed to secure the help of their partners in the Crown of Aragon, the Aragonese and Valencians, while Castile, the region of the peninsula most heavily burdened by war taxation, remained quies-cent.[39] As a result, the Catalans were unable to capitalize on the general discontent to rally the Hispanic realms to their cause, while Portugal's ener-gies were fully absorbed in preserving its own newly won independence. A rebellion, therefore, that its leaders hoped would bring relief to the entire Spanish body politic ended, as it had begun, as a purely provincial uprising – an uprising driven down the secessionist road by the necessity of securing the military assistance of a foreign government no more interested in the preservation of the principality's liberties than the government it replaced.

The palace coup that brought about the removal of Olivares from power, and Philip IV's announcement that he intended in future to rule without a minister-favourite, served to prevent a general implosion of royal govern-ment like that which occurred in the Britain of Charles I during these same years. The rebels therefore found themselves dependent on such help as the French could provide during the period of regency government and domestic turmoil that followed the deaths in quick succession of Richelieu

(December 1642) and Louis XIII (May 1643). As the principality became a battleground between the rival armies of France and Spain it also found that, in exchanging a Spanish suzerain for a French one, it had done little more than exchange one oppressive regime for another.

While Catalonia, on the margins of the peninsula, struggled with the fluctuating help of the French to keep its separatist movement afloat, the Scots found themselves, at least initially, in a much stronger position to influence the course of events at the very heart of the British composite monarchy. In setting out to assemble an army, the Scots, unlike the Catalans, who had shown little interest in military service whether in the king's armies or as mercenaries, could call on the numerous Scottish veterans of the continental wars for professional help.[40] Once their army had faced down Charles I's forces and invaded England with success, the covenanters were confident enough of their strength to pursue a policy of active intervention in the domestic affairs of the neighbouring kingdom.

Their opportunity came when Charles's parliamentary opponents turned to Scotland for help. The cause of religion, which had little bearing on the origins or the evolution of the Catalan revolt but was central to rebellion both in Scotland and in England, gave the Scots a powerful inducement to respond. After miraculously enabling them to achieve a religious and constitutional revolution at home, God had surely entrusted them with the solemn charge of coming to the aid of their persecuted English brethren and establishing the new covenanting dispensation throughout the British Isles. Not only would they restore England's trampled liberties, and assist in crushing the popish rebellion that broke out in Ireland in October 1641 but they would also confer on the Anglican Church the immeasurable benefit of Presbyterian church government.

This providential mission would also be an act of self-preservation, for if Charles were to gain the upper hand in England, Scotland's turn would be next and the covenanting cause would be lost. Beyond this, the current weakness of England offered a shining opportunity to transform the Union of the Crowns into something more than a mere dynastic union in which Scotland was no more than England's junior partner. The covenanters were seeking a stronger, not a weaker, union, and, unlike the Catalan revolt as it developed, there was nothing separatist about their movement.[41] They believed that the abolition of episcopacy and the imposition of the Presbyterian form of church government throughout the British Isles would do much to strengthen the bonds of affection between its peoples and so establish a closer Anglo-Scottish union. But this was a union *aeque principaliter*, which would now be properly based on true parity between the two kingdoms.[42] While Scotland and England would continue to govern themselves through their separate parliaments, the reform and renewal of British religion would be accompanied in the secular realm by an agreement for joint control of foreign and commercial affairs, and free trade between the two kingdoms.[43] This, in other words, was to be a confederal union with a holy imprimatur.

The Long Parliament had other ideas, both about church government and the nature of the union, but it desperately needed Scottish military intervention if Charles were not to emerge victorious in the English Civil War that broke out in August 1642. Wariness over Scottish demands made negotiations laborious, but in 1643 the Scots held the stronger cards, and in September the English negotiators for a Scottish alliance signed the Solemn League and Covenant, although surrounding the terms of the agreement with as much ambiguity as they could manage. At the same time, splits were opening up among the covenanters themselves. As the most committed among them pressed for increasingly radical reforms, the more moderate faction, which included many nobles and lairds, became alarmed. The most prominent figure in this faction was a man in conscious pursuit of glory, James Graham, fifth Earl of Montrose, who in 1640 had taken the lead in opposing the domination of the Scottish parliament and the Presbyterian cause by Archibald Campbell, head of the Clan Campbell and eighth Earl of Argyll. Biding his time, Montrose eventually broke with Argyll and moved over into the royalist camp. Created a marquis by Charles I and appointed Lord Lieutenant of Scotland, he raised an army in 1645 in defence of the king's cause and crushed the Covenant's forces in August of that year. But two months earlier Charles had been defeated by Cromwell's New Model Army at the battle of Naseby, and Montrose himself was subsequently defeated by the covenanting General Leslie, and forced to take refuge in Norway.

As the parliamentarians gained the upper hand and Cromwell's New Model Army carried everything before it, so the balance of power between the English and the Scots tilted once more in favour of the English. Scottish weakness was exposed in the spring of 1647, when the covenanters to whom Charles I had surrendered found it expedient to hand him over to the English army. Suspicious of the growing power of the Independents in the army and faced with English indifference or outright hostility to their plans, they saw their dream of a genuinely federal union of the two kingdoms slipping away. As Anglo-Scottish collaboration crumbled, the Engagers, a group of moderate covenanters who had made a secret engagement with Charles I to come to his aid, launched an unsuccessful bid to win the argument by sending an invasion force into England, only to have it routed by Cromwell at Preston in August 1648. In response to this disaster and those that followed it, an extreme Kirk party seized power in the General Assembly and the covenanting movement began to fragment.

Charles's execution in January 1649 and the abolition of monarchy in England ruptured the dynastic union of 1603 that had originally brought the two kingdoms together. Regicide of a monarch who, for all his faults, was of the Scottish royal line was an unforgivable act of English treachery. But although their king was dead, the Scots remained unwilling to abandon either the monarchy or the union. In open defiance of the Rump Parliament sitting in Westminster, the Covenanter Parliament proceeded to proclaim Charles, Prince of Wales, as ruler not only of Scotland but of all the British Isles. It refused him entry to Scotland from his continental exile, however, unless he agreed to the covenanters' programme of church government for Britain.

After the failure of an invasion of mainland Scotland by Montrose and his subsequent execution, the new monarch swallowed his reluctance to agree to the covenanters' demands and arrived in Scotland in August 1650. Facing pressure from the Scottish administration under the Earl of Argyll, he signed the Solemn League and Covenant, and was duly crowned at Scone on 1 January 1651 as king 'of Great Britain, France and Ireland'.[44] As far as the Scots were concerned, one Stuart monarch had succeeded another, and the Union lived on.

So too it did for the English, but not on Scotland's terms. Charles II's coronation at Scone posed a direct threat to the survival of the Commonwealth, and Cromwell, after reconquering Ireland with fire and slaughter, turned his attention to the Scots. If they had tried to export their revolution to England, the English would export *their* revolution to Scotland.[45] The high-handed behaviour of the Scots during the years of nominal alliance had not endeared them to the English, who, according to the Earl of Clarendon, had developed by 1647 'a great detestation of the Scots'.[46] The arrogant display of Scottish national sentiment found its equally arrogant English counterpart in the settlement that Cromwell imposed on Scotland following his victories over the Scottish army at Dunbar in September 1650 and over Charles II and a Scottish invading force at Worcester a year later.

With Ireland and Scotland at their feet the English were now in a position to reconfigure the relationships between the different parts of the British polity in ways that conformed to their long-held notions about the proper status of the Scots and the Irish in a united British Isles. The policy adopted by the Rump Parliament in its declaration 'concerning the Settlement of Scotland' over the winter of 1651–2 was for an incorporating union, in which all three nations would combine in a single Commonwealth.[47] While Ireland was a dependency and now happily restored to full English control, the Rump Parliament decided that Scotland was not to be treated as a conquered nation. It was, after all, a godly society, for all its misguided Presbyterian ways, and deserved to enjoy the many benefits that would come from incorporation into the English Commonwealth. Cromwell himself, echoing James VI/I, expressed a preference for making the two realms 'one nation'.[48] In the eyes of the English this required full incorporating union on essentially English terms. Where the Scots had been determined to maintain their own separate parliament, for the Rump Parliament an incorporating union between Scotland and an English republic could only take the form of a parliamentary union. Scotland's parliament, therefore, would disappear, and the Scots and Irish were each allocated thirty seats in the Westminster parliament.

Full incorporation would in principle enable the regime to impose on Scotland radical reforms such as the abolition of feudal tenure and the introduction of English law where 'matters of government', as distinct from matters of justice, were concerned.[49] In practice many of these reforms were watered down or abandoned during the years of the Cromwellian Protectorate.[50] It was hard enough, without embarking on English-inspired 'improvements' to a backward Scottish economy and society,[51] simply to restore a semblance of stability to a country where the Covenanting state had struggled to maintain control during the many years of turmoil.

General Monck's army of occupation successfully established order in Lowland Scotland, but in July 1653 the Earl of Glencairn raised the royal standard in the Highlands, and it took Monck two years to suppress Glencairn's rising of Highland chiefs and clansmen. After this it became possible to establish a Scottish Council and restore civilian government, but the Highlands remained what they had always been, a challenge to any Lowland government that sought to impose its own order. Nevertheless, Monck, the strong man of the regime, was persistent. With his troops spread through the Highlands, and troublemakers hunted down, captured and transported to Barbados, he achieved greater success than his predecessors in breaking down a warrior society and using a combination of force and favour to draw the Highland chiefs into the orbit of Edinburgh.[52]

In spite of Monck's imposition of order, the period of English rule was bedevilled by problems. There might now be an incorporating union, and the Scots be consulted over the introduction of new policies, but there was continuing uncertainty as to where, in the new order of things, power was located. Scottish notions of federal union had been dismissed out of hand, but both Commonwealth and Protectorate failed to hit on a satisfactory alternative system for governing in unison two disparate peoples whose mutual antagonism had been intensified by the events of the revolutionary years. Although the course of events between the late 1630s and the end of the 1650s compelled political leaders in England and Scotland to widen their horizons to include all Britain instead of only their segment of it, they also had the contrary effect of reinforcing the sense of distinctive national identities held by both.[53]

The English had emerged victorious in the war of the three nations. Their victory, followed by the military triumphs of the Cromwellian regime against the country's foreign enemies, inspired a renewed national confidence that too easily metamorphosed into the arrogance of power. God was English, and England now ruled supreme over Britain, as Providence decreed. The Scots, for their part, had savoured the fruits of victory but had also tasted the bitterness of defeat. This bitter-sweet experience brought home to them a stronger awareness of what, as a nation, they were, and yet also of what they were not. They had saved the Protestant cause in England but the Kirk had failed in its holy aim of establishing its own form of church government throughout the British Isles and Presbyterianism had lost out to the Independency espoused by the victorious English parliamentarians. This was a devastating disappointment, which inevitably drove the Kirk back on itself, and closely identified it with an exclusive Scottish nationhood.

The disappointment, was to some extent counterbalanced by the nation's success in consolidating its old liberties and securing new ones. During the years of turmoil the reform programme of the National Covenant had brought about a political and constitutional revolution.[54] As part of a move to curb the royal prerogative and prevent the arbitrary exercise of power by the Crown, the Triennial Act of 1641 stipulated that Scotland's parliament should be called into session every three years. It also secured for itself the power to ratify major royal appointments, including membership of the Scottish Privy Council and the Court of Sessions. The parliament and its committees were now in control of government, with taxation to be administered by the shires.

The effect of these reforms was to turn Scotland into a constitutional monarchy, in which sovereign power was moved from Crown to parliament.[55] When Charles II accepted the Covenant it was made clear to him that he was to be a monarch who ruled under contract. The Scottish rebellion, therefore, saved and extended traditional liberties based, like those of the Catalans, on a contractual relationship between a monarch and his subjects. Success, though, was tempered by a new sense of bitterness as the Scots were forced to recognize the superior military might of their English neighbours. Once in power General Monck gave evidence of the statesmanlike qualities that would enable him to engineer the restoration of the monarchy in 1660, but his army of occupation had made the English widely detested and had left a trail of grievances, above all in the Highlands, that would not be erased. As a result of twenty years of fluctuating achievement and failure Scotland emerged from the turbulent mid-century decades as a nation at once proud and aggrieved.

Consequently, when Charles II was restored to the English throne in May 1660 a genuine union of hearts and minds was even further away than when the civil wars began. The presence once again of a Stuart monarch on the thrones of both kingdoms seemed to signal a return to the style of union that had prevailed under Charles II's father and grandfather. Cromwellian union was dead and buried, to the extent that the Earl of Lothian could say in May that 'we must be a free Independent nation, brethren and Good friends ... under one soveraigne and Head, but no parte of England'.[56] In 1661 a restored Scottish parliament passed a sweeping Act Rescissory that annulled all legislation since 1633, thus effectively undoing north of the border the constitutional reform movement of the early 1640s.[57] Authoritarian kingship now replaced limited monarchy, the Earl of Argyll was arrested and executed in 1661 for his collaboration with Cromwell, and the nobility were cowed. A Scottish Council, a devolved committee of the English Privy Council, was set up in Whitehall to coordinate the policies of London and Edinburgh.

An age of reaction had opened as Scottish royalists seized the chances offered by the restoration of monarchy north and south of the border. Not surprisingly, all the old problems created by absentee kingship resurfaced. There were numerous tensions between London and Edinburgh and equally serious tensions within the Scottish political and religious establishment itself. Charles himself had no love of Scotland after his gruelling time there in 1650–1, but he retained a sense of gratitude to those Scots who had stood by him during those dark days, and in particular to John Maitland, one of the Engagers, who had been captured by Cromwell's forces after the battle of Worcester and later joined Charles in the Dutch Republic. The restored monarch appointed him Secretary of State for Scotland in 1660, and went on to create him Earl and later Duke of Lauderdale.[58] A clever and corrupt henchman, Lauderdale made the most of the king's not always reliable favour and was to dominate Scotland's political life for much of the reign. The Scottish Council was soon disbanded, and effective power was vested in the office of parliamentary high commissioner, a post held by Lauderdale between 1669 and 1678. Lauderdale's arbitrary and increasingly unpopular government gave him the appearance of a viceroy. Indeed when in 1681 the title of viceroy was mooted for James, Duke of York, who was to replace him, the proposal aroused so many objections that it had to be abandoned. Viceroys, the Scots asserted, were not for 'a free kingdom as Scotland is', but for conquered kingdoms, like Ireland or Naples.[59]

The change of regime had an even more dramatic impact on religion than on politics. Episcopacy was reimposed in 1661; the General Assembly of the Kirk, which had been abolished by Cromwell, was not allowed to resume its activities; and the Presbyterian form of church government, although allowed to continue, was subverted by placing the appointment of parish ministers in the hands of lay patrons. A third of them were ejected from their livings because of their refusal to accept episcopal governance, and were hounded and persecuted by government forces throughout the reign of Charles II as they sought to keep the covenanting flame alive by holding open-air 'conventicles'. Uprisings by extreme covenanters in south-west Scotland were brutally repressed in 1666 and 1679, but the Cameronians, the followers of the diehard Richard Cameron who was killed in a skirmish in 1680, continued their hopeless resistance. Not for nothing were the 1670s and 1680s known as 'the Killing Times', as troops were quartered on a sullen population and the civil authorities resorted to persecution and judicial torture to ensure political loyalty and religious conformity.[60] The Kirk, divided and split by two decades of triumph and disaster, would need time to recover both its confidence and its bearings.

In many ways the Restoration settlement in both Church and State would seem to have set the clock back to the 1630s, although in Scotland, as in England, the events of the 1640s had reinforced and consolidated the position of parliament in national life, however subservient parliament might be to the restored monarch. As he and his ministers were well aware, a general desire for a return to earlier and more stable times precluded the kind of drastic policy innovations that had characterized the reign of Charles I. Instead, during the years of Lauderdale and the Duke of York, the prerogative powers of the Crown were more subtly enhanced through a combination of politicking, patronage, corruption, and government by royal proclamation.

Much the same was true of the post-Olivares era in Spain. During the 1640s the forces of Philip IV slowly tightened the noose round the principality as the French, at war on several fronts and distracted by the turbulence generated by the Fronde, proved unable to save their disillusioned Catalan allies from increasingly probable defeat. As in 1640, peasants clashed with soldiers, although this time the soldiers were French and not Spanish. There were conflicts, too, between Catalonia's civil and ecclesiastical authorities and the French viceroys. In 1650 the plague that had swept northwards from Andalusia made its first entry into the principality and ravaged a demoralized population. The royal army, placed under the command of Philip IV's bastard son, Don Juan José de Austria, now closed in on Barcelona. Following the failure of French attempts to relieve the plague-ridden city, the municipal councillors and the *diputats* had no choice but to throw themselves on the royal mercy. On 11 October 1652, Barcelona made its submission on receiving the prince's promise of a general pardon for all but the most compromised Catalan adherents of France. Two days later, following the departure of its French and Catalan defenders, Don Juan José made his triumphal entry through the city gates.[61]

The surrender of Barcelona effectively marked the end of Catalonia's twelve-year secession, although not the end of hostilities on Catalan soil. For another seven years the principality would remain a theatre of war. The French still had their adherents among those sections of the population that retained an implacable hostility to the Castilians. These adherents of France, the so-called *miquelets*, fought alongside the French forces still campaigning in the principality and kept up resistance in the border regions. In 1659, however, the signing of the Peace of the Pyrenees finally brought to an end nearly twenty-five years of open war between the French and Spanish Crowns. Catalonia found itself at the mercy of the negotiators, and was among the principal losers from the long years of conflict. In accordance with the peace settlement a new frontier line, largely defined by the mountain barrier of the Pyrenees, was drawn between France and Spain.

The new frontier permanently sundered the principality from its two trans-Pyrenean *comtats* or 'counties', Rosselló and northern Cerdanya, with the tiny exception of the town of Llívia which remains a Spanish enclave in what today is France.[62] The Catalans had traditionally regarded the two counties as integral parts of their principality, even during the period that followed their conquest and annexation by the French in 1462. Once more united to Catalonia in 1493, when Charles VIII of France agreed to cede them to Ferdinand the Catholic, they shared its governmental and representative institutions. Yet relations were frequently tense between the capital of Rosselló, Perpinyà (the future Perpignan) and the city of Barcelona, to the point that in the 1620s Perpinyà launched an unsuccessful bid to free the counties from the principality's control.[63]

Nevertheless, the inhabitants of the counties were Catalan-speaking, and there was a constant traffic of people and goods between them and the rest of the principality, both by sea and over the mountain passes – a traffic that included a steady flow of immigrants from central and southern France in search of work in an underpopulated Catalonia.[64] The immediate effect of the Peace of the Pyrenees was to deprive Catalonia of a fifth of its population,[65] but there were also longer-term consequences. In the counties themselves there was continuing resistance to assimilation by the French, whose success in integrating them into France was for a long time only partially successful. There was continuous coming and going across what remained a highly porous border, and although the Crown gradually succeeded in instilling French language and culture into the elite, the majority of the population continued to speak Catalan. Spain, for its part, did not abandon hope of recovering the lost territory, whose inhabitants resented the imposition of new taxes by the French government and the damage inflicted by the constant movement and billeting of French armies during the Franco-Spanish wars of the second half of the century. Catalans themselves continued to mourn the loss of the counties, which for them remained essentially Catalan long after their inhabitants had become reconciled to the change of masters. Catalan nationalists of the twentieth and twenty-first centuries would not forget the presence of fellow Catalans on the other side of what is now a non-existent border.

After Barcelona's surrender, the future of Catalonia lay in the hands of Philip IV and his advisers, with promptings from Don Juan José, who had gained great prestige from his victory and would be named as viceroy a few months later. To a large extent the king's hands were tied by his promise, made in Lleida (Lérida) in 1644, that he would respect the principality's Constitutions if it returned to allegiance. This effectively ruled out any possibility of a return to Olivares's plans for the reduction of Catalonia to conformity with Castile, even if the new ministers in Madrid had been so inclined. But their prime concern was to pacify the principality and prevent further outbreaks of unrest that could only benefit the French. This suggested the importance of moderation, although the Council of Aragon, in a discussion on 14 November 1652 of the options to be placed before the king, drew a distinction between Barcelona and the rest of the 'province', as it described the principality. The city had been the head and heart of a rebellion that had shaken the Monarchy to its foundations and had encouraged the Portuguese, and subsequently the Sicilians and Neapolitans, to follow suit, and now that it had finally surrendered it should not be left unpunished for its sins.[66]

Faced with the options presented by the Council of Aragon, Philip IV chose to honour his promise and leave the principality's Constitutions untouched, but to bring the city of Barcelona under tighter military control. In line with the Council's recommendations, he also ordered an important change in the electoral procedures of the city council and the Diputació. Since the death of Ferdinand the Catholic in 1516 the Crown had played no part in selecting the names of candidates for office. These were placed in a bag from which they were drawn by lot. Under the new system all names were first to be scrutinized and approved by royal officials. The process of revision was to be annual, thus allowing the removal of any unacceptable names. In this way aspirants to office would know that they were, and remained, dependent on royal favour, and consequently would have every inducement to remain in line.[67]

While the principality retained its traditional laws and privileges under the restored regime of 1652, the effect of these changes to the electoral system was to make a significant section of the Catalan political nation dependent on the Crown as it had not been dependent in the pre-revolutionary years. The clock had therefore not exactly been set back to the 1630s any more than it had been in Scotland. In both societies carefully selected royal policies were directed towards the forging of a new consensus between the Crown and a political nation that had been scared by what had happened when popular fury was unleashed. Their overwhelming desire was for peace and order. If this was true of the Catalan elite it also held true of the post-Olivares regime in Madrid. With France presenting a continued danger, the ministers of Philip IV and of Carlos II, who succeeded to the throne on his father's death in 1665, took care to handle the principality with kid gloves.

Soft words, however, could not entirely hide the deep distrust of Catalonia that had taken root in Madrid. If the Catalans had rebelled once, they could rebel again.[68] The revolt of 1640 left a permanent legacy of bitter memories in the court, just as it did in Catalonia itself – a legacy that would have a lasting influence on the Crown's policies towards the Catalans. When Barcelona launched diplomatic overtures in Madrid in 1653–4, 1660–1 and again in 1675–6 for the full restoration of the measure of self-government enjoyed by the principality in happier times, it was firmly rebuffed.[69] Madrid, like London, remained wary of new outbreaks of violence in territories that were still only imperfectly under royal control.

Some of this violence was endemic in both societies, whether in the usual form of banditry in Catalonia or of clashes between the armies of rival clans in Scotland, but the breakdown of order during the years of rebellion had created conditions in which violence continued to flourish once peace was nominally restored. In Scotland it was increased by the resistance of diehard covenanters, who in 1666 assassinated the primate, James Sharp, archbishop of St Andrews, who was hated for his apostasy as a turncoat. Covenanter resistance was countered by the extreme violence of the troops sent to put it down, and their behaviour in turn generated reprisals from the householders on whom they were billeted.

In Catalonia, too, the billeting of troops had the same lethal consequences as at the end of the 1630s. As a frontier region the principality was exposed to all the tensions generated by the aggressive policies of Louis XIV, whose troops launched an invasion in 1684 and laid siege to Girona. The city was relieved and the French retreated, but the billeting of troops and the Crown's demands for campaigning contributions of money and men had the same effects as in 1640. The *diputats* clashed with the viceroy and, as in 1640, an impoverished and infuriated peasantry took the law into their own hands. Following a number of bad years the 1687 harvest was devastated by a plague of locusts. In October an uprising occurred in the town of Centelles when royal troops were sent to enforce a levy for their upkeep. As the uprising spread it escalated in 1688 into a massive rural revolt across the principality, with insurgents marching on Barcelona as in the spring of 1640. Although the rebellion, which came to be known as the revolt of the *barretines* after the caps worn by the peasants, was temporarily diffused, it flared up again in the following year, when France declared war on Spain and the viceroy, the Duke of Villahermosa, demanded a *donativo*, or 'voluntary' grant, to finance the army. Without a meeting of the Corts, which had not been convened since 1632, this was regarded, like the fiscal demands made by the Olivares regime, as a contravention of the Constitutions. Once again, as in 1640, the insurgents made contact with the French, who on this occasion failed to come to their aid. Again they descended on Barcelona and laid siege to the city, but Villahermosa had sufficient troops at his disposal to throw them back. He followed his success with fierce repression of the rebels.[70]

In reporting to Madrid on what he called 'the state of the province', Villahermosa was damning in his account of the rebel leaders, who, he alleged, had succeeded, at least for a time, in persuading the population that they were fighting for 'the freedom of the principality', when their real aim was to hand it over to the French. He also wanted an end to a practice that had arisen in response to the demands of war, of convening in Barcelona meetings of notables. Such meetings, in his view, represented a direct threat to the authority of the Crown.[71] Although the viceroy's harsh policies found supporters not only in Madrid but also in the principality, the government of Carlos II held back. While the revolt of the *barretines* confirmed its worst fears about the innately rebellious instincts of the Catalans, the war with France suggested the continuing need for caution. Moreover this time, unlike 1640, the Catalan elite did not support the rebels and was anxious to demonstrate its unshakeable loyalty to the Crown. As in Scotland, royalist policies, together with fear of a repetition of the tumultuous 1640s, had brought about a degree of convergence between the interests of the elite and the royal authorities. The composition of the elite, too, was changing, as the alterations to electoral procedures allowed new individuals and groups, among them merchants who had made their money from provisioning the royal army, to enter the lottery for offices and climb the social ladder.[72]

Yet suspicions on both sides remained deeply entrenched, and as the war with France continued, the inability of the royal army to defend Catalonia from French invading forces was a source of mounting exasperation in the principality. The Catalans, who had for so long feared the overwhelming power of Castile, were now the victims of the weakness to which Castile had succumbed after the upheavals of the 1640s. Although the Castilian economy showed some signs of recovery after 1680, and the royal government gave high priority to Catalonia as the outer bastion of Spain, an under-resourced royal army proved incapable of halting the French advance. Moreover the government itself was weak and increasingly divided, with faction-fighting intensifying over the looming problem of succession to the Spanish throne as the health of the childless Carlos II deteriorated. In Catalonia viceroys followed one another in bewildering succession as the military situation worsened. Between 1695 and 1697 the French army occupied a large part of the principality, and captured Barcelona in August 1697 after a two-month siege. It was only the international peace settlement at Ryswick that autumn which brought about its withdrawal.

Carlos II died on 1 November 1700, leaving his throne, in his last will and testament, to Louis XIV's grandson, Philip, Duke of Anjou. Carlos's thirty-five-year reign has tended to be seen as a period of *neoforalismo*, or respect for the *fueros*, laws and privileges of the non-Castilian regions of the peninsula.[73] Yet in so far as the Crown respected the Catalan Constitutions this seems to have been less out of conviction than out of fear of a repetition of 1640 and the belief that there were less confrontational means of gaining its objectives. The refusal of the political nation and urban Catalonia to join the revolt of the *barretines* suggests that this belief was not misplaced.

A post-revolutionary generation had come to maturity – a generation that seems to have been more outward-looking than its predecessor and more conscious of the advantages that could be derived from a fuller commitment to the Spain of the House of Austria and its global Monarchy.

Here Catalonia was able to build on the achievements of the preceding hundred years. Since the middle of the sixteenth century important transformations had been occurring in the principality's economic life. The small coastal and inland towns in the general area of Barcelona were becoming the centre of an increasingly urbanized network as their populations grew in response to new commercial possibilities and the expanding demand for Catalan textiles in the domestic and overseas markets. At the same time, there was a growing colony of Catalan merchants in Seville and Cadiz, anxious to participate in trade with the Indies, to which they exported Catalan agrarian products, textiles, and metal and glassware.[74] Significantly, when the Flemish consul in Cadiz, who had jurisdiction over foreign merchants, asserted that the Catalans, with a language of their own, fell within his remit, they protested that, as vassals of the Spanish Crown, Catalans 'are, and are called, Spaniards, since Catalonia is indubitably Spain'.[75]

Even if 'Spain' may here have been intended more as a geographical expression than as a national concept, the response of the Catalan merchants in Cadiz indicates that they felt themselves to be members of a larger community than Catalonia alone, a community formed by a common allegiance to a shared monarch. This wider awareness was not simply inspired by their desire to break into the transatlantic trade. The second half of the century, again building on the work of previous generations, saw an upsurge of commercial and industrial projects in the principality, all of them bearing the imprint of contemporary mercantilist thinking. Catalan projectors, or promoters of economic projects, like those in the circle round Narciso Feliu de la Peña, the author of a famous treatise, *Fénix de Cataluña* (1683) – a book dedicated to Carlos II, whom he would later describe as 'the best king Spain has had' – set their projects for the resurrection of a debilitated Catalan phoenix within the context of the economic space constituted by Spain and its European and American possessions.[76] Their concerns pointed to the need for more active Catalan intervention in Spanish political life if they were to command success. When Don Juan José marched twice on Madrid, in 1669 and 1677, with the intention of seizing power and instituting a programme of reforms, he enjoyed widespread support in the Crown of Aragon. It was from here that he launched his bid for power, although Catalan support seems to have been more passive than active when compared with that given by the Aragonese.[77] Reform at the centre of government, however, was clearly essential if Catalonia were to reap the economic benefits of fuller participation in the Spanish Monarchy, and Feliu and his friends turned for help to the Junta de Comercio, the Committee for Trade set up at court by Juan José in 1679 with the idea of stimulating the economic regeneration of Spain.[78]

At the same time, the principality, under constant pressure from France, needed all the financial and military assistance it could wring out of Madrid. This meant that there was continuous interaction between Barcelona and the court, and specifically with the Council of Aragon, from which Catalonia could expect to receive a more sympathetic hearing than from councils dominated by Castilians and the high nobility. Yet all the time disillusionment was growing as Madrid failed to provide the amount of help that the principality needed, while viceroys infringed the Constitutions in their attempts to sustain the war with France.

The weakness of the Diputació since 1652 and the unwillingness of the Crown to convene the Corts suggested the need for alternative ways of filling the institutional vacuum. As the Duke of Villahermosa had reported, a new body had emerged, the Conferència dels Tres Comuns (the Three Commons), which began as an assembly of notables, drawing its strength from a renovated noble Estate, but also including ecclesiastics and members of the Barcelona civic elite. The Three Commons effectively took over some of the traditional functions of the Diputació by speaking out in defence of the Constitutions and the interests of the principality. Towards the end of the century, in the climate of general uncertainty created by the question of the dynastic succession, it evolved into an almost permanent committee composed of two members apiece of the Diputació, the Barcelona city council and a renovated and revitalized Braç (Estate) of nobles. It was this committee that in practice would control and direct the principality's policies in the opening years of the new century during the War of the Spanish Succession.[79]

The Three Commons were, at best, an *ad hoc* solution to the problem of defending the principality's interests against the intrusive policies of royal ministers, who had a very different set of priorities. In this respect Scotland was better served than Catalonia. It had its own unicameral parliament, although this, while convened three times by Charles II and once by James II, was only in session for half the period between 1660 and 1689.[80] In spite of its many inadequacies it at least provided a forum for discussion and could address matters of national concern. It had, too, the great advantage of possessing a vigorous counterpart in the English parliament, whereas in

Spain the Cortes of Castile ceased to be summoned after 1665 and lapsed into desuetude. The existence of parliaments both north and south of the border provided an additional channel of communication between Edinburgh and London. As in 1641 this enhanced the possibilities of collusion between opposition forces in the two capitals against an unpopular minister, in this instance Lauderdale.[81]

Those members of the Scottish and English parliaments who had not succumbed to royal influence clearly shared a common concern in the preservation of constitutional monarchy at a time of creeping authoritarianism at home and aggressive authoritarianism abroad in a continent increasingly dominated by Louis XIV. The dangers were greater in Scotland than in England because of the wholesale unscrambling in 1661 of the constitutional revolution of the 1640s. The impoverished Scottish nobility, still licking the wounds it had suffered during the civil wars and all too pleased to let itself be bought by Charles II's ministers, was in no position to champion the cause of liberty. The Scottish legal profession, on the other hand, was in much better shape. Many of its members had studied in continental universities, especially in the Dutch Republic, and it included in its ranks such learned figures as Sir James Dalrymple, Viscount Stair, author of *Institutions of the Law of Scotland* (1681). Drawing alike on Scottish custom and on continental and humanist theory and practice, the profession consolidated during the Restoration period the distinctive legal system and culture that was to constitute a significant dividing line between Scotland and England in the centuries that followed the incorporating union of 1707.[82]

The cultural vitality and growing social prestige of the legal profession made the Faculty of Advocates an influential presence in Scottish political life. Inevitably the debates among the lawyers over the degree to which the monarch was subject to the law, and whether this meant a relatively vague fundamental law or one based on custom, played into the general concern about the encroachment of the royal prerogative on personal and collective liberties. In addition to anxiety over the exercise of the royal prerogative, other major issues were provoking rising concern. These ranged from the restrictions imposed on Scottish trade by the English Navigation Acts to the new taxes levied to pay for England's unpopular wars with the Dutch, and the threat to property rights created by the quartering of troops.[83] Such issues prompted insistent demands that parliament should be a regular constitutional fixture rather than a body whose summoning and prorogation were dependent on the whim of the monarch. For all the irregularity of its sessions, the Scottish parliament, while all too often supine, was nevertheless capable of vigorous protest when sufficiently aroused.

As in Spain, anxieties became acute as the royal succession rose to prominence as the dominant issue in both England and Scotland. The Exclusion Crisis of 1679–81 raised the bitterly divisive question of whether the Roman Catholicism of James, Duke of York, should debar him from succeeding to the throne of England as his brother's heir. The Crisis had immediate implications for Scotland and for the Union of the Crowns. To remove his brother from the heated political atmosphere of London, Charles sent him to Edinburgh as parliamentary commissioner in succession to Lauderdale. Between 1679 and 1682, when James took up residence with his own court in Edinburgh, the Scots could almost forget that they remained the subjects of an absentee king, and the Edinburgh town council took advantage of his arrival to commission portraits of Scotland's mythical forty monarchs for Holyrood House.[84] James used his time in Scotland to win popularity, and to build a strong following not only in the Lowlands but also in the Highlands, where his harassment of the staunchly Presbyterian ninth Earl of Argyll and his Campbell adherents secured him many supporters among the clansmen.[85] His efforts were rewarded in 1681 when the Scottish parliament passed under his presidency a Succession Act asserting the indefeasible right of hereditary succession to the Scottish throne in spite of James's adherence to the Church of Rome.[86]

The Act served as a warning shot across English bows that Scotland had its own royal line and that when Charles II died it was perfectly capable of going its own way. But the Act did nothing to resolve the latent issue of religion. On the accession of James II/VII in 1685 the Earl of Argyll landed in Kintyre from his foreign exile to lead an insurrection in support of the Duke of Monmouth's rebellion in England. The rebellions were put down with relative ease and both leaders were executed. Yet if James acceded to the thrones of both kingdoms without serious difficulty, there was an obvious incompatibility between his ecclesiastical supremacy and the anti-popery legislation passed by their parliaments. The actions of the new monarch only served to bring the incompatibility into sharper relief.

Emboldened by the failure of Argyll's rebellion, James seems to have regarded Scotland as a useful laboratory for trying out measures that could later be extended to England to improve the situation of his fellow Catholics and enhance the prerogative powers of the Crown.[87] Parliament appeared passive and the Kirk cowed. In the circumstances the king felt able to favour Roman Catholics in making appointments to positions of authority and to press ahead with his plans for introducing liberty of conscience, which would bring relief to his co-religionists as well as to non-Episcopalians among members of the Kirk. His policies, however, aroused mounting disquiet. Failing in 1686 to persuade the Scottish parliament to legislate in favour of freedom of conscience, James resorted to the royal prerogative in the following year to issue a general edict of toleration.

The combination of James's religious policy with his resort to the prerogative united against him broad swathes of the political and religious establishment in Scotland as in England.[88] He was patently overstepping the bounds of his constitutional authority. As William of Orange mounted his bid for the British throne, prominent Scots came out in his favour. These included the tenth Earl of Argyll, whose grandfather had been executed by the order of Charles II and his father by order of James II. They also included Sir James Dalrymple of Stair, the pillar of the legal establishment, who would mastermind Scottish opposition to the monarch. Public opinion, too, had moved strongly against James, motivated especially by widespread hatred of the Church of Rome in a country where professed Catholics amounted to 2 per cent of the population at most.[89] When William of Orange issued a separate Declaration for Scotland, promising to 'free that kingdom from all hazard of Popery and Arbitrary Power', and 'settle a parliament to redress grievances',[90] he could count on strong popular sentiment in his favour. As James moved his army southwards to counter what he saw as the greater threat of attack, anti-popish riots, more violent than those in England,[91] broke out in Edinburgh and elsewhere. This was a widely supported revolution at elite and popular levels alike.

Succession Crises

James's flight to France in December 1688 gave rise to a mixture of rejoicing, foreboding and widespread relief. His departure appeared to have resolved the twin issues of religion and the succession, but only, as it soon transpired, at the price of recasting both in a different form, while revealing new divergences between England and Scotland.

The Glorious Revolution of 1688–9 transformed the political and religious landscape in all three British kingdoms. It salvaged the dynastic succession of the Stuarts by bringing James's daughter Mary to the throne, but in granting to her Dutch husband William equal title to the throne it handed power to a monarch determined to involve the British Isles in his epic struggle to save the liberties of Europe from being crushed by Louis XIV. As a result, for almost the whole of the next quarter of a century, political life in Britain as in Spain was played out against a background of war – the Nine Years War of 1688–97, and the War of the Spanish Succession from 1701 to 1714.

The Convention Parliament of January 1689 in England and the Scottish Convention of Estates that assembled in March handled the sudden departure of James II/VII in different ways. Whereas the Whig-Tory compromise in England preserved a fig leaf of constitutional continuity by declaring that James had abdicated and left the throne vacant, the Scottish Convention, dominated by Whigs and Presbyterians, was in no mood for compromise. As it assessed the rival claims to the throne of James on the one hand and of William and Mary on the other, the contractual nature of Scottish kingship lay at the heart of the unfolding political debate, although contractual arguments were not taken to extremes. In early April the Convention passed a resolution that James, whose legality as monarch was anyhow open to question through his failure to take the Coronation Oath, had forfeited his right to the throne through his actions as king. He had subverted the 'fundamental constitution' of Scotland by turning it from 'a legall limited Monarchie to ane Arbitrary Despotick Power'.[92] The Convention's resolution, in making a reality of that 'fundamental constitution', amounted to a full-scale rejection of divine right monarchy.

A few days later, following the example set by the English in drawing up a Bill of Rights, the Convention issued a Claim of Right, putting forward a series of demands that harked back to the political revolution of the early 1640s, which had been overturned when the monarchy was restored. Parliaments should be held frequently and give their assent to the raising of supply; the royal prerogative should no longer be able to override the law; the Lords of the Articles, the committee that had been revived in 1663 for the management and control of parliamentary business, should be abolished, and all committees were to be chosen by parliament itself; no Roman Catholics should succeed to the throne or be appointed to public office; and prelacy should be abolished.[93]

There remained the problem of legitimizing allegiance to William and Mary, which was largely sidestepped by treating it as a *fait accompli*, since James was adjudged to have forfeited the throne. After the new monarchs had taken the Coronation Oath in April 1689, the Convention of Estates was formally turned into a parliament from which the bishops were excluded. It reassembled in the spring of 1690 to consider William III's request for taxes to pay for his continental wars. The legislative process was assisted by the willingness of the new king to garner support by agreeing to the restoration of Presbyterian church government. The Presbyterians took full advantage of their opportunity, and after legislating for the return of the traditional apparatus of Kirk government under the General Assembly, parliament went on to abolish lay patronage. Thanks to Presbyterian dominance over parliamentary proceedings, even the limited form of toleration conceded to dissenters under the English Toleration Act of 1689 would therefore have no counterpart north of the border. The principal victims of this intransigence, other than Roman Catholics, were Scotland's Episcopalians. These worked hard to court High Church English Tories over the next fifteen years in the hope of overturning the Presbyterian establishment, but their efforts were in vain. As Presbyterianism became definitively established in one country while the Anglican Church retained its commanding position in the religious and political life of the other, a lasting divide came to separate the two kingdoms.

Yet the Revolution Settlement had also created points of convergence. Whereas in Ireland the continuing loyalty of the Roman Catholic population to James II persuaded William III to force the island into submission by a war of conquest, in Scotland a consensus formed around a settlement engineered by the political and religious establishment but also drawing on popular support. James still had his loyal adherents, especially in the Highlands and the north-east Lowlands, and these were rallied by John Graham of Claverhouse, Viscount Dundee. But after his death at the battle of Killiecrankie in July 1689 the insurgents lacked effective leadership and the rebellion was slowly but harshly suppressed. Nevertheless, loyalty to James remained strong, and it was reinforced by the adherence of Episcopalian clergymen who had been ejected from their parishes. The terrible events of these years, among them the most terrible of all, the Massacre of Glencoe in February 1692 – an atrocity that did more than anything else to entrench the intense form of Stuart loyalism that came to be known as Jacobitism, along with hatred of the Earl of Argyll's Clan Campbell in the Highlands – left a store of memories that would haunt the country for generations to come.

For the moment at least, however, the time of the Jacobites had passed, but as the kingdom moved gingerly towards the closer union with England that international politics and the succession question were forcing upon it, Scotland remained a deeply divided society. Strict covenanting Presbyterians, exulting in their triumph, might claim to speak for the Scottish nation, but theirs was an exclusive rather than inclusive vision of the nation, and many were left outside. The fault line already present in Scottish society but hardened by the events of the 1690s would have long-lasting consequences for Scottish nationalism. While the Scots as a people were proud of their distinctiveness as a historic nation, the continuance of this fault line would make it difficult to bridge the many divides – between Presbyterians (of differing stripes) and Episcopalians, Hanoverians and Jacobites, Highlands and Lowlands – that impeded the construction of a coherent image of Scottish nationhood capable of commanding general assent at a time when the Anglo-Scottish relationship was being subjected to unparalleled review and revision.[94]

Whether or not they welcomed the prospect, the Scots found themselves in the 1690s being drawn inexorably into England's orbit and William III's grand Protestant design. The new political reconfiguration created by the events of the Glorious Revolution had the effect of reviving proposals unsuccessfully advanced under Charles II and James for a closer Anglo-Scottish union.[95] William's managers in Scotland brought forward fresh proposals, but it was the aspiration after economic union that primarily interested the Scots. For them, closer union meant free trade across the border and would address the deeply resented consequences of the Navigation Acts – legislation that, at least nominally although not always in practice,[96] had excluded Scottish merchants from England's overseas trading networks. The English, on the other hand, were interested first and foremost in settling the succession question. Once the Scots had done what was expected of them, English interest in closer union waned. Free trade without an incorporating union was simply not on the English agenda.

Having achieved their Revolution, however, the Scots were not disposed to play second fiddle to the England of William and Mary. The disappearance of the bishops from Scottish political life and the abolition of the traditional managers of parliamentary business, the Lords of the Articles, brought about an institutional revival of the Scottish parliament. With the clerical estate no longer represented, the gentry acquired additional influence, while the larger shires were given greater representation.[97] William and his ministers were to find that the parliament was no longer as amenable to direction as in earlier times, and from 1689 until the Union of 1707 it became heavily engaged in the political and economic affairs of the nation. Those years were to set Scotland's future direction.

The 1690s were to be a period of acute economic hardship for Scotland, aggravated by Britain's involvement in the Nine Years War. The conflict closed off Scotland's profitable French market and disrupted trading links with other continental states. More devastating still was a series of harvest failures between 1695 and 1699, which brought famine in their train and a heavy fall in population. The loss of population through high death rates was increased by mass migration, largely to Ireland but also to the West Indies and America, where the Scots had already settled in Nova Scotia, East New Jersey and South Carolina.[98] The combined effect of mortality and emigration was to reduce the population by perhaps 13 per cent to a figure of just over a million at the end of the century.[99] With its seriously under-developed economy relative to England, Scotland was ill-equipped to confront its devastating agrarian and commercial problems. Yet these years of disaster also saw determined attempts by the Scots to escape from their poverty trap. Around 1680 they began to feel the seductive power of England's culture of 'improvement', and the 1690s would be a decade of ambitious – indeed excessively ambitious – schemes for a national economic revival.[100]

The incorporation by the Scottish parliament of the Company of Scotland in 1695, originally an Anglo-Scottish joint-stock venture for trade with Africa and the Indies, was an attempt to emulate the commercial success that had laid the foundations of English prosperity. But behind it lay a larger vision, which saw in the Company a chance to free Scotland from excessive dependence on its more powerful neighbour and carve out economic and political space for itself alongside other European states. Scotland, after all, was an 'imperial crown', a sovereign state,[101] with the right to promote its own vision of an empire that was based, unlike that of the English, on free and open trade.

The plans for the Company were partly inspired and insistently promoted by an economic projector, William Paterson, who persuaded its directors in 1696 to establish a strategically placed trading post between the Atlantic and the Pacific oceans, at Darien on the isthmus of Panama. This was Spain's area of influence, and William III had no wish to antagonize an important ally in his war with France. The hostility of English trading companies and the king's angry rejection of a scheme that cut across English political and commercial interests led to the withdrawal of English inves-tors and compelled the Scots to continue the project on their own.[102] They did so with enthusiasm, and speculative mania took hold. In the words of Sir Walter Scott: 'Not even the Solemn League and Covenant was signed with more eager enthusiasm. Almost every one who had, or could command, any sum of ready money, embarked it in the Indian and African Company; many subscribed their all.'[103] The consequences were catastrophic.

The Darien expedition of 1698, followed by a second expedition in 1699, ended in disaster in March 1700 when the embryonic colony was forced to surrender to a Spanish blockading flotilla. The financial losses – £400,000, or nearly two and a half times the estimated value of Scotland's exports and at least four times the annual revenues of its government – were enormous. The disaster had a devastating impact not only on Scottish pockets but also on Scottish morale. In the face of English indifference or outright hostility what future did Scotland have? Yet along with the defeatism there was a sense of outrage at the way in which William had treated his Scottish subjects. Theirs was an independent sovereign kingdom, and his behaviour had been an affront to Scotland's sense of itself. Hurt pride and indignation would make Scottish politicians more prickly in their dealings with Westminster at the turn of the century, but would also encourage new thinking about the best way forward – thinking that was at its most creative in the writings of that acute observer of the Anglo-Scottish political scene, Andrew Fletcher of Saltoun.[104]

As an intensely patriotic Scotsman and a lover of liberty, Fletcher was throughout his life a vigorous defender of the integrity of the Scottish parliament, but at the same time he was well aware of the extent to which the future of his homeland was intimately bound up with that of England. In that sense he epitomized in his person and his writings the perennial dilemma of Scottish patriots.[105] Both as an observer and, at times, as a member of the parliament, he engaged in a permanent juggling act as he sought to adjust what he saw as the best interests of his native land to the opportunities and limitations created at any given moment by constantly shifting events in England and continental Europe. In 1700 the course of events in both was dramatically altered by two royal deaths, that of William, Duke of Gloucester, and Carlos II of Spain.

The death in July 1700 of the Duke of Gloucester, the only surviving child of Princess Anne, threw open the whole question of the future succession to the English and Scottish thrones. If the young son of the exiled King James were excluded on the grounds of his religion, the immediate line of Stuart succession would come to an end following the death of the future Queen Anne. A few months later, in November, the death of Carlos II, the last Spanish Habsburg in the male line, created another, more immediate, succession problem, and one that involved the fate of all Europe. In accepting the terms of Carlos II's final will, in which he left Spain and all its possessions to Philip, Duke of Anjou, Louis XIV appeared close to establishing a French universal monarchy. Once again William III rallied his coalition in defence of the liberties of Europe and launched the War of the Spanish Succession – a conflict that also became the war of the English Succession when Louis, on the death of James II in September 1701, publicly recognized his son James Edward as James III, King of England, Scotland and Ireland.

In the composite monarchies of Britain and Spain disputed royal succession raised questions of allegiance that went to the heart of the relationship between their component parts. In Britain's composite monarchy the decision was relatively clear-cut. The Jacobites had been crushed in Ireland and

Scotland, and it was impossible in the circumstances to countenance a Roman Catholic on the Scottish throne. Popery and tyranny were now firmly equated with one another in the consciousness of the English and Scots alike, and Louis XIV's behaviour, and not least his persecution of the Huguenots, had driven the lesson home. On the other hand Fletcher was among those quick to realize that the succession question, along with England's requirements for the waging of a continental war in which the Scots felt little involvement and would once again be disruptive to their trade, created useful bargaining chips in their dealings with Westminster and Whitehall.

Their determination to deploy these bargaining chips was strengthened by anger at the unilateral action of the English parliament in passing the Act of Settlement of 1701, under which the succession to the English throne on the death of Anne would pass to Sophia, Electress of Hanover, and her heirs. Since the Act made no mention of succession to the Scottish throne, the legislators seem to have assumed that the other component parts of the British composite monarchy would fall meekly into line. While this proved to be true of the Irish, it was asking too much of the Scots, whose kingdom, as they insisted, was not, like Ireland, constitutionally subordinate to the English Crown, whatever arguments English polemicists might put forward to the contrary.[106]

Before William III's death in March 1702 his fears for the survival of the Union of the Crowns after the death of his successor, Queen Anne, led him to recommend a closer union, but his own ministers showed little interest in the proposal, and this was not a message to which the Scots in their present mood of anger and exasperation were prepared to listen. Anne herself was a persistent advocate of closer union, and commissioners were appointed by both sides to discuss the issues at stake, but the Court party in the Scottish parliament was unable to impose its wishes. In the new parliament elected in the spring of 1703, which included Fletcher among its members, the ministry lost all control of the proceedings, to disastrous effect. The parliament went on to approve an Act of Security. Its purpose was to ensure a Protestant succession on the death of Queen Anne, but to exclude the House of Hanover unless the English parliament showed itself prepared to make concessions. Under the terms of the Act the Scottish parliament was to meet within twenty days of the death of Queen Anne and choose an heir who was both of the Scottish royal line and a Protestant.

The passing of the Act of Security created a major constitutional crisis for Britain's composite monarchy, with the two kingdoms now set on a collision course. As seen by Bishop Burnet, 'a national humour of rendering themselves a free and independent kingdom did so inflame them, they seemed capable of the most extravagant things that could be suggested to them'.[107] But had not Scotland always been 'a free and independent kingdom', except during the period of Cromwellian rule? As the two parliaments faced each other and the war of words intensified, closer union had never seemed further away than in 1703–4. In March 1705 the English parliament countered with an Alien Act which, if implemented, would effectively turn Scots into foreigners. By its terms, if the Scottish parliament did not settle the succession question by Christmas Day, Scots would be declared aliens in England, and a prohibition would be placed on trans-border trade in Scotland's major exports of coal, cattle and linen. By now it was becoming painfully clear to the parliaments of both kingdoms that, if they were not both to fall into the abyss, the moment had come to decide.[108]

The Moment of Choice

In this same year, 1705, the Catalans, too, faced a crucial choice, and one that was directly related to Britain's participation in the War of the Spanish Succession. On 14 April 1701 the Duke of Anjou made his ceremonial entry into Madrid as Philip V of Spain. The first stages of the dynastic transition from the Habsburgs to the Bourbons went smoothly, and in September the new king set out on a visit to the Crown of Aragon, where he duly swore to observe the Catalan Constitutions and convened the Corts in Barcelona. There was expectation on both sides, and, in spite of clashes between the Corts and royal ministers, an impressive amount of legislation was accomplished and Philip was able to bring the session to a formal conclusion in early January 1702 – the first time that this had happened since 1599. He duly confirmed the Constitutions, and met a long-standing Catalan demand for the establishment of a tribunal to consider any alleged case of their contravention. The Corts, for their part, voted a substantial subsidy, and the Catalans were given much of what they wanted, including some of the commercial privileges for which Feliu de la Peña had long been lobbying, such as the right to form a trading company and to send two ships a year to trade with America. They were unsuccessful, however, in their attempt to achieve two important demands: an end to billeting and to the new electoral procedures introduced in 1652. Yet, on balance, when the king left Barcelona for Naples three months later to visit his Italian possessions, the Catalans could feel satisfied with what had been achieved, while Philip could feel that in heeding his grandfather's advice to treat the Catalans with care he had negotiated a potentially difficult situation with success.[109]

The success, though, was to prove short-lived. During the king's nine-month absence from the peninsula the Bourbon succession, which at first seemed to have been effected with a minimum of domestic trouble, began to be questioned both in Castile, whose nobility resented the presence of French officials and their challenge to old ways,[110] and in the Crown of Aragon. Although the king was given a triumphant welcome in Barcelona in December 1702 on his journey home from Italy to Madrid, the misery and devastation created by French aggression over the past two decades had intensified traditional Catalan hatred of France and the French. In September 1703 the Austrian Habsburg claimant, the Archduke Charles, second son of the Emperor Leopold I, was proclaimed King of Spain in Vienna. With a rival candidate on the scene who enjoyed Anglo-Dutch military and naval support, divisions began to open in the peninsula between supporters of the Bourbons, who soon came to be called *felipistas*, and the pro-Austrian *austracistas*, who favoured a Habsburg succession.

In January 1704 Philip compounded his troubles by appointing as viceroy of Catalonia Don Francisco Antonio Fernández de Velasco, already a deeply unpopular figure because of his failure to defend Barcelona against the French in 1697. His high-handed behaviour on assuming office involved him in repeated clashes with the Catalan authorities. His attitude contrasted sharply with that of Prince George of Hesse-Darmstadt, who had helped defend Barcelona in 1697 and who between 1698 and his dismissal by Philip in 1701 served as the last Habsburg viceroy.[111] Darmstadt was therefore an obvious intermediary between the Archduke, the allied coalition and the Catalan *austracistas*. In Lisbon he joined the Archduke, who had arrived in the Portuguese capital in March 1704 to launch his bid for the Spanish throne, and he went on to lead the Anglo-Dutch fleet in a failed attempt to capture Barcelona that May. The city did not rise in the Archduke's support as he had hoped, but Velasco's government was doing his work for him. The number of the Archduke's adherents in the principality grew rapidly, in spite of Velasco's success in dismantling a pro-Austrian conspiracy; and in the Treaty of Genoa of June 1705 the English committed themselves to military support of the Catalans in return for Catalan recognition of the Archduke as King of Spain.

In August the allied fleet, under the command of the Earl of Peterborough, appeared off Barcelona, while the Diputació and the city council waited on events. After a first attack in which Darmstadt lost his life, Peterborough began his assault on Barcelona on 9 December, aided by a popular uprising in the Ribera district of the city. Following his surrender Velasco was given protection by the English, thus avoiding a repeat of the terrible events of

Corpus Christi 1640 when the Count of Santa Coloma met his death at the hands of the insurgents. In the negotiations with the victorious allies the Catalan authorities asked that the Archduke should observe their Constitutions, and in particular the privileges conceded them by Philip in the Corts of 1701–2. The Archduke arrived in Barcelona shortly afterwards and convened new Corts, which would sit from 5 December 1705 to the end of March 1706. These would confirm the privileges approved by Philip and extend them to include further guarantees of civil liberties as well as an end to royal control over elections to the city council and the Diputació.[112]

The contrast is striking between the welcome given by the Catalans to Philip V in 1701 and their satisfaction with the outcome of the 1702 Corts, and their rebellion against their legitimate ruler three years later. The reasons for what ultimately proved to be a disastrous choice have given rise to much historical debate,[113] and cannot be understood in a purely Catalan context. The determination of the Emperor, William III and the Dutch to prevent Spain and its empire from falling into the hands of Louis XIV, and the arrival of the Archduke Charles in Portugal, which ranged itself with the allies, turned the War of the Spanish Succession into a Spanish civil war. At the beginning of Philip's reign Versailles was dictating policy in Madrid, and this created a swelling tide of resentment in the court. Groups of grandees began conspiring against the new regime and in 1704 a plot was uncovered in Granada to proclaim the Archduke as king.[114]

The physical presence of the Archduke in the peninsula created an alternative focus of loyalty for the disgruntled and the dissatisfied. The allied military and naval forces operating on his behalf displayed their strength when they seized Gibraltar in 1704, and made landings on the eastern coast of the peninsula, capturing Barcelona and the city of Valencia at the end of 1705. The Archduke's prospects therefore appeared promising, and, with his forces preparing to invade Castile from Portugal, there were good reasons for reconsidering a possibly premature acceptance of a Bourbon monarch who looked all too much like a French puppet. But it is open to question whether the Catalans would have taken the decision they did if the allied fleet had not dominated the western Mediterranean and appeared off their coast.[115]

With the advance of the allied forces in the east of the peninsula the territories of the Crown of Aragon moved into the Archduke's camp, although with varying degrees of enthusiasm.[116] Much of the population seems to have been neutral, but, for all the outward respect paid by Philip to the constitutional arrangements of Catalonia and Aragon, his conduct failed to banish fears that his ultimate intention, together with that of Louis XIV, was to bring about their abolition. The suspicion of the ruling elites in the Crown of Aragon that a Bourbon dynasty would sooner or later replace contractual with authoritarian kingship was bound to influence their calculations, although they were divided as to whether a French Philip V or an Austrian Charles III represented the safer option when weighing the balance of probabilities for the likely outcome of the contest.

The special circumstances of Catalonia, however, tended to tilt sentiment in the principality, perhaps more strongly than elsewhere, in favour of a Habsburg succession. French aggression in the 1680s and 1690s had left an open wound. The clergy were loud in their denunciations of French troops for profaning churches,[117] and the French capture of Barcelona in 1697 was neither forgotten nor forgiven. Castile and France were almost equally distrusted, and Velasco's brutal government of the principality had reawakened all the old suspicions surrounding the long-term aims of Castilian ministers and the new government in Madrid. By the spring of 1705 an insurrection against the Velasco regime had taken hold in the plain of Vic, and it was the leaders of this insurrection, the so-called *vigatans*, who on their own initiative and without authorization negotiated the Treaty of Genoa with Queen Anne's representative, an English merchant resident in Barcelona, Mitford Crowe. The principality, therefore, was already in turmoil when the allied expeditionary force arrived to promote the Archduke's cause by supporting their uprising.

After two centuries of Habsburg rule the Catalan elite knew, by and large, where it stood with the House of Austria. As a result, the nobility and an increasingly assertive bourgeoisie had reason to think that their privileges, along with the liberties of Catalonia, were likely to be in safer hands if entrusted to the Archduke rather than to his Bourbon rival, in spite of Philip's compliant behaviour during his stay in Barcelona.

It was true that the agreements reached by Philip V and the Catalan representatives in the Corts of 1701–2 included potentially valuable commercial privileges. Yet the Barcelona patriciate and the Catalan mercantile class may well have felt that alliance with England and the Dutch Republic offered them better long-term prospects. While Dutch and English merchants were installing themselves in Catalonia, the French were busily moving to secure control of Spain's Atlantic trade, and the imposition of protectionist policies by France for the benefit of its own industries would mean the exclusion of Catalan textiles and other products from the American market. It was therefore natural for a Catalan business and commercial community which was flexing its muscles, like the Scottish commercial community that threw itself into the Darien scheme, to look to the Archduke for a better deal than the one negotiated with Philip V.

The Corts held by the Archduke in 1705–6 held out the prospect of important new commercial benefits. Feliu himself, under Dutch and English pressure, had moved away from a protectionist stance. His move underlined the divisions within the Catalan business community between those who wanted protection for Catalan woollen and silk textiles, and those, especially in a flourishing port town like Mataró along the Mediterranean littoral, who favoured free trade.[118] The Anglo-Dutch model, however, held great attractions for all parties. England and the Dutch Republic had apparently found the elusive key to national prosperity, and there was no reason why Catalonia, sheltered by their alliance, should not become equally prosperous and dynamic if it enjoyed the same kind of liberty as these two flourishing states. The Archduke's government seemed to offer a guarantee of this, and the resulting vision of a free, open and prosperous Catalonia giving a pioneering lead to the regeneration of Spain was seductive.[119]

While it was the elite that piloted Catalonia towards adherence to the Archduke, whether for self-interested reasons like the protection of its privileges, or for the salvation of a venerated constitutional system, or for the commercial prospects it offered, there was also substantial popular support in 1705 for the decision they took. The peasantry had suffered deeply at the hands of the French, and virulently anti-French parish priests had no hesitation in reminding them of their sufferings. Moreover, peasants and urban artisans alike had a sense of Catalonia as a historically free society, and although divisions would open up in the years after 1705, there seems at the time to have been a fair degree of consensus in the principality, even if some of that consensus came from a willingness to acquiesce in the rule of whichever candidate held the upper hand.[120]

The choice, therefore, was made, and, in making it, the Catalans placed themselves irrevocably in the hands of foreign powers. Their fate was tied to that of the allied armies, and at first their prospects looked promising. In 1706 the Archduke's forces captured Madrid, and it appeared that Philip's cause was lost. But a year later the commander of his army, James II's illegitimate son, the Duke of Berwick, turned the tables at the battle of Almansa, which left Valencia and Aragon at the mercy of his forces. From the moment of his overwhelming victory in April 1707 Philip looked safe on his throne. That same year he seized the opportunity of the alleged rebellions of Aragon and Valencia to proclaim the *Nueva Planta*, or new system of government, which stripped them of their traditional laws and liberties.[121]

Yet appearances were deceptive. In the spring and summer of 1710 the allies won a string of victories in Aragon over the Bourbon forces, and once again advanced on Madrid. Philip V fled his capital, which the Archduke re-entered. But the population gave him a hostile reception, only a few nobles came over to his side, and military supplies ran low. Deciding to return to Barcelona, he ordered his demoralized army to retreat to Aragon, and Philip returned in triumph to Madrid in early December.

As the remaining regions of the Crown of Aragon fell to Philip's advancing forces the principality was left standing alone. It was now dependent on the increasingly fragile support of foreign powers which were growing weary of an apparently interminable war and had their own interests to safeguard. The writing was now on the wall for the Catalans, although it would be another four years before their tragedy ran its full course. When it did so in 1714 with the surrender of Barcelona to the forces of Philip V, the resulting settlement would be imposed by force of arms on a conquered nation. In this it differed profoundly from the settlement reached between the Scots and the English in the year of the battle of Almansa – a settlement that had been under serious negotiation since 1705, when it finally became clear to both parties that neither could live without the other.

For all their mutual distrust, the imperatives driving Scotland and England to settle their disagreements were strong.[122] Overshadowing the discussions of 1705–7 was the great international conflict. England could not countenance the prospect of France placing the Jacobite Pretender on the throne of an independent Scotland; Presbyterian Scotland could not contemplate with equanimity the prospect of a Roman Catholic monarch and, with it, the certainty of war with its English neighbour – a war that it was bound to lose. If the achievements of the Glorious Revolution were to be preserved, both sides had come to the conclusion that this demanded a closer political union, although there were some suggestions, particularly among those who gave special weight to Scotland's economic future, that it might fare better as an eighth province of its strongest trading partner, the Dutch Republic, than as England's junior partner.[123]

The debate for the most part, however, revolved around the union with England. As such, it would not be a debate between nationalists and unionists, but one fought over the particular nature of a new political union. Should it be an incorporating, a confederal, or a federal union? An incorporating union, as proposed by the English Union Commissioners in 1702–3, would mean the end of Scottish independence and the Scottish parliament. In Scotland, not surprisingly, federal or confederal union were the preferred options, but even incorporating union – the most extreme of the options – had its Scottish supporters, who believed that the mutual benefits to both kingdoms would outweigh the disadvantages.[124]

But the Scottish parliament made it clear that it would not negotiate under duress, and insisted that the English parliament must repeal the Alien Act before serious discussions could begin. When Westminster unexpectedly conceded the point, the road to a revised form of union lay open.[125] After three months of meetings during the spring and early summer of 1706 the Union Commissioners of the two kingdoms agreed the outlines of a Treaty of Union. This, as the English commissioners insisted, must be an incorporating and not a federal union of equal and autonomous partners. In return, the Scots would achieve their two principal objectives, unrestricted free trade and navigation within the United Kingdom and its overseas 'plantations', and security for the Presbyterian Church.

The proposed treaty had then to be piloted through both parliaments, starting with the Scottish, where its acceptance was by no means a foregone conclusion. Following the reading of the articles of union in October 1706, angry protests erupted both inside and outside parliament. Pro-unionist politicians were denounced as traitors in the streets of Edinburgh and dragoons were sent to put down riots in Glasgow.[126] Nevertheless, a combination of coercion, bribery and persuasion won the day for the ministry, whose most effective bribe of all is likely to have been the bail-out offered to the 1,320 subscribers to the Company of Scotland.[127] The 'Equivalent', as it was called, was exceptionally generous, not only indemnifying the subscribers for their losses in full, but also granting them annual interest payments of 5 per cent. Since a substantial part of the Scottish political elite – nobles, lairds, merchants and members of the professional classes – had invested heavily in the Darien scheme, and had suffered disastrous losses as a result of its catastrophic failure, the government's offer proved irresistible. Opposition to the Union in the Scottish parliament crumbled as the 'Squadrone Volante', with its twenty-five votes, succumbed to the inducements and pressures emanating from the court. On 16 January 1707, with a few minor amendments, the parliament ratified the Treaty of Union by 110 votes to 67.

In February the treaty was recommended in a speech from the throne to the English parliament, where it was attacked by the High Tory leaders because of its recognition of the Presbyterian Church as the church of Scotland. According to the Earl of Nottingham the treaty destroyed 'the very constitution of England'.[128] But it enjoyed the support of the Whigs and the pro-government Tories, and was passed by both houses of parliament without difficulty. On 1 May 1707 Great Britain, now sanctioned by statute, came formally into existence. Queen Anne went to St Paul's to give thanks for the greatest victory of a victorious reign, but an Edinburgh correspondent wrote to the Earl of Mar that 'the first tune of our music bells this day is *Why should I be sad on my wedding day*?'[129]

On 29 June 1707, a few weeks after the Anglo-Scottish Union came into effect, Philip V, capitalizing on his army's victory at Almansa, decreed the abolition of the laws and privileges of the kingdoms of Aragon and Valencia. The two kingdoms, according to the decree, had failed in their duty of obedience. Justifying his action on the grounds both of his possession of absolute dominion and the legitimate rights of conquest, the decree continued: 'I have therefore deemed it appropriate, both for this reason and also because of my wish to reduce all my kingdoms of Spain to a uniformity of laws, usages, customs and tribunals, governing them all equally by the laws of Castile ... to abolish and derogate entirely ... all the said *fueros*, privileges, practices and customs hitherto observed in the said kingdoms of Aragon and Valencia ...'[130] Commenting on the decree, the Count of Robres, an Aragonese noble then living in Barcelona, circumspectly observed that, in the view of some, a better way for the king to have achieved the unity of his kingdoms would have been to follow the example of the Anglo-Scottish Union, under which the names of 'English' and 'Scots' were subsumed into 'Britons' and their two parliaments into a single parliament of 'Great Britain'. Then it should have been left to time, the indispensable prerequisite of unity, to do its work.[131]

From the moment of Philip's decree the Catalans could be in no doubt of the fate that awaited them if the Archduke's forces were defeated. Although the immediate effect of the publication of the imposition of the Nueva Planta in the two neighbouring kingdoms was to stiffen the determination of the pro-Habsburg *austracistas* to resist, it also sharpened the dividing lines in Catalan society. As Philip's forces advanced deeper into Catalonia, the *austracistas* tightened their repressive measures against the pro-Bourbon *felipistas*, growing numbers of whom took refuge in Bourbon-held territory. But it would be simplistic to see the *austracistas* as the champions of contractual government while the *felipistas* favoured an 'absolutist' approach. Just as in Scotland, where the principal dividing line was not between unionists and non-unionists but between those with differing views over the style of union that offered the best guarantee for the preservation of national identity and the promotion of national prosperity, so in Catalonia the division was over means rather than ends. Patriotism was far from being the exclusive preserve of one party rather than of the other.[132]

There were numerous reasons for moving into a particular camp. Many of the older nobility, in particular, detached themselves from the Habsburg cause, antagonized by the policy of the Archduke in lavishly bestowing titles of nobility on his supporters, many of them social *parvenus*. They also felt that, in a polity where disorder had become endemic and 'liberty' was all too prone to degenerate into licence, a Bourbon monarch offered a better long-term prospect of political and social stability. Philip V, moreover, was the legitimate ruler and there had always been traditionalists in the Crown of Aragon, like the Count of Robres, who respected him as such and remained loyal to him, although no doubt gravely disillusioned by his abolition in Valencia and Aragon of the laws and liberties he had taken a solemn oath to observe. The Catalan Church, too, was divided. The Habsburgs, who were famed for their religious devotion, had given the clergy many exemptions and immunities. When in 1709 Philip V broke with the papacy over its decision to accept the Archduke's claim to the Spanish throne, a largely *austracista* secular clergy turned on members of the religious orders, whom they regarded as disloyal.[133] Consequently, as the Bourbon and Habsburg armies battled over Catalan territory and left devastation in their wake, Catalonia's struggle began to acquire some of the characteristics of a civil war, but one in which neither side was satisfied with the available options. Many *felipistas* were dismayed by the king's draconian treatment of Aragon and Valencia, while the *austracistas* became disillusioned when they saw that the Archduke's government, in spite of a number of populist measures, appeared as ready as that of the Bourbons to trample on treasured laws and liberties in its efforts to sustain a faltering military effort.

Although the Archduke had momentarily reoccupied Madrid in 1710 before the tide turned again, the international situation was steadily moving against the Catalan cause. Britain was growing war-weary, and the victory of the Tories in the parliamentary election of 1710 had brought to power a party that was determined to bring the conflict to an end. Its opportunity came with the sudden death of the childless Emperor Joseph I in April 1711, and the resulting succession of his brother, the Archduke, to the imperial throne as the Emperor Charles VI. The union of Spain and Austria beneath a single monarch was no more acceptable in the eyes of the British and the Dutch than that of Spain and France. Each held out the prospect of universal monarchy which the coalition had originally been formed to prevent. Without the support of the maritime powers Charles was in no position to continue the struggle for long.

The facts of war and of international politics were moving inexorably against him. The British forces in Catalonia were starved of funds by the Tory administration. The second Duke of Argyll, John Campbell, son of Archibald Campbell, the tenth earl, who had been raised to a dukedom in 1701, had been sent to Spain in 1711 as ambassador to the archduke and commander-in-chief of the British forces, mostly, it seems, to get him out of the way. Earlier John Campbell had played a critical part in the negotiations over the Anglo-Scottish Union as the queen's commissioner to the Scottish Estates, where he had shown a ruthless determination to advance the court interest.[134] He then fell out with the ministry, which needed his support and that of his adherents, the so-called Argathelians, but found it difficult to keep such an imperious and temperamental magnate in harness. The duke's great ambition, apart from promoting his extensive family interests and supporting the Presbyterian cause for which his grandfather and great-grandfather had given their lives, was to win glory on the battlefield. Unfortunately Catalonia in 1711 offered little chance of this. He arrived to find his troops close to mutiny, and the Tory ministry that came to power in 1710 had no intention of reinforcing his army at a time when the Archduke's cause looked increasingly hopeless and ministers were scheming to make peace with Louis XIV. The often uneasy relationship between the Archduke and the Catalans had anyhow placed the duke in a difficult political position, and he probably felt no great distress in leaving Barcelona to its fate when he gave orders in November 1712 to evacuate the British army to the British-controlled island of Menorca.[135]

The remaining European powers were now moving towards a general settlement, and Philip's renunciation of his rights to the French throne that month cleared the road for progress in the negotiations under way in Utrecht. As the plenipotentiaries edged towards the treaty that was eventually agreed on 11 April 1713, Catalonia, which was not represented at the peace conference, was left waiting to learn its fate. The Tory administration, while making sympathetic noises, was quite prepared to break Britain's solemn promise to the Catalans if this was a necessary precondition for peace. The Emperor, for his part, although pressing Philip to respect the Catalan Constitutions, decided that the time had come to evacuate his forces from the principality, and urged the Catalans to reach a settlement with the king before it was too late.

The prospect of imminent defeat by the royal army sharpened the already deep divisions in the Catalan body politic between the partisans of negotiation with the Bourbon commander in the hope of saving the Constitutions, and those who wanted to fight to the end.[136] At a tense meeting of the Estates on 30 June those who favoured resistance narrowly carried the day, thanks largely to the votes cast by the representatives of Barcelona and other municipalities. Meanwhile, Philip's forces made their final dispositions for the capture of the city and the implementation in the principality of the 1707 decree. By the beginning of 1714 Catalonia was largely occupied by an army of 55,000 men, and much of the resistance was reduced to Barcelona and its region. In the words of one of their British supporters 'they now see themselves beset on every Side, Destruction threatens them, and they seem to be at the Point of being sacrific'd to the Resentment of an angry Prince'.[137] The partisans of resistance still harboured faint hopes that their former allies would change their minds and come to their rescue, but to no avail. By late July 1714, 40,000 soldiers encircled the city, which was defended by a mere 5,000 men, most of them members of the militia companies formed by the guilds. For the next few weeks the starving population held out, but on 11 September, after prolonged bombardment had opened numerous breaches in the city walls, the Duke of Berwick's army launched a final assault. Rafael Casanova, the city's head councillor, had no choice but to make a formal surrender. The siege that had lasted for a year and three months and had seen extraordinary acts of heroism by the inhabitants, had finally come to an end.

The principality now lay at the mercy of Philip V, and repressive meas-ures were quick to follow. The Barcelona city council was dissolved, many of the leading *austracistas* went into exile or joined the Emperor in Vienna, and 900 houses in the city quarter of the Ribera were demolished to make way for the construction of a large fortress, the Ciutadella, to ensure that Barcelona would in future be kept under strict royal control. The princi-pality had fought for its liberties, in what may in retrospect seem like a quixotic struggle. But when it made its fateful decision in 1705 the outcome was by no means clear, and the king's subsequent suppression of the *fueros* of Aragon and Valencia pointed clearly to the fate that awaited it if the Bourbons should prevail.

Whether, in the long run, the Archduke Charles would have been more sympathetic than Philip V to the liberties of the Crown of Aragon is open to question. His record as Emperor suggests that a more benign approach to particularism than that of the Bourbons was far from assured, and exiles from the Crown of Aragon were among his closest advisers in planning an incorporative union of Spain's former Italian possessions into the territo-ries under his rule.[138] But during their years of resistance Catalonia's *austra-cistas* could look upon themselves as champions of liberty, fighting for freedom and a constitutional form of government not for the principality alone but for all Spain.[139] Now, with the triumph of the Bourbons, the forces of 'despotism' had prevailed; and, as Philip V took his time between 1714 and 1716 to determine the exact system of government to be established in Catalonia, there was every reason to fear that Madrid, in pursuance of the grand design of Olivares nearly a century earlier, was about to reduce the principality to uniformity with 'the style and laws of Castile'.[140]

CHAPTER 3

Incorporating Unions
1707–1789

Forms of Union

The Anglo-Scottish Union of 1707 and the Nueva Planta of 1707–16 were both incorporating unions, in the sense that they incorporated Scotland and the Crown of Aragon respectively into a larger polity, 'Great Britain' in the first instance, and 'Spain', or the *nación española*, as it came increasingly to be called, in the second. The methods by which the incorporation was brought about were, however, very different. So, too, were the forms taken by the two incorporating unions, and the nature of the new and larger polities that emerged from the process. Yet, for all the differences, there were similarities, both in the character of the incorporating unions and in their long-term consequences, although these consequences would be subject to differing interpretations, depending on time, place and national sentiment, right up to the present day.

The union of England and Scotland was presented as a Treaty of Union between two sovereign kingdoms that had the same queen, but which in future would also share a single parliament and a single flag. Like all treaties it was the result of negotiation, even if the negotiation was conducted under a duress felt more strongly by the Scottish than the English commissioners – although these too were subject to their own pressures, generated by the war with France and particularly by the issue of dynastic succession. In Spain, on the other hand, the Crown of Aragon was subjected to a settlement imposed by a victorious monarch, who stigmatized its peoples as rebels, and who took it for granted that their rebellion gave him the right to determine their fate. The Nueva Planta decree of 29 June 1707 abolished, at least nominally, the laws and privileges of the kingdoms of Valencia and Aragon.[1] Issued precipitately, and without close consideration as to how it was to be implemented, the decree was the outcome of discussions in Philip V's cabinet, where the president of the Council of Aragon argued in vain that 'prudence' should be given priority over 'innovation'.[2]

If its details were still uncertain, the intention behind the decree was clear. Its immediate inspiration came from Paris, which was currently dictating the policies of Madrid, using as its instrument the French ambassador to the court of Philip V, Michel-Jean Amelot. Louis XIV was adamant that his grandson's victory at Almansa in 1707 gave him the opportunity to 'establish his authority there in an absolute form and to extinguish all the privileges that provide a pretext for those provinces to exempt themselves when they are called upon to contribute to the necessities of the State'.[3] The term 'Nueva Planta' did not in fact appear in the decree itself, but came to stand for the 'new plan' of government established in the territories of the Crown of Aragon, initially by the abolition of the *fueros* of Valencia and Aragon, and then by a series of measures introduced between 1711 and 1716. By this last year Catalonia and Majorca were also included in the reforming decrees.[4]

Although in theory the Nueva Planta was intended to make the government and the legal systems of the Crown of Aragon uniform with those of Castile, in practice full uniformity proved impossible to achieve. From the beginning, modifications turned out to be necessary. Discrepancies crept in, or had to be allowed, between Castilian practices and the new regulations introduced with excessive speed in Valencia and Aragon. Yet in spite of the discrepancies and modifications, the forcible introduction of the new system in these two kingdoms was brutal, and had a major impact on the lives of their citizens. The experience of Catalonia, however, while no less drastic in its impact, differed in some respects from that of its two neighbours.

This was partly because, by the time Philip's advisers came on 9 October 1715 to issue the decree extending the Nueva Planta to the principality, their experiences in Valencia and Aragon had made them aware of some of the realities involved in attempting to introduce blanket measures of reform. As a result, nearly two years elapsed between the surrender of Barcelona in September 1714 and the implementation of the new measures outlined in a royal decree signed on 9 October 1715, and confirmed by a second decree dated 28 May 1716. During those twenty months much thought was given in Madrid to the exact shape that the proposed new system of government should take in the principality. Some ministers felt that the Castilian system of law and government was not well adapted to the realities of Catalonia or to the character of its inhabitants, who, in the words of one of them, José Patiño, were 'so passionate about their *patria* as to lose all sense of reason; and they speak only their native language'.[5]

The circumstances leading up to the surrender of Barcelona were also different from those accompanying Philip's victory at Almansa. A war-weary Louis XIV was no longer the fierce advocate of root-and-branch reform for Spain that he had shown himself to be six years earlier. The allies, for their part, while no less war-weary, still felt some obligation to salvage what they could from the wreckage of a Catalonia that had fought alongside them through good times and bad. The British negotiators at Utrecht therefore used their bargaining powers to extract some limited concessions from their Spanish counterparts. Article XIII of the Anglo-Spanish treaty, as agreed in July 1714, stipulated that the Catalans should be given a general amnesty and be left in full possession of 'their properties and honour'. This was the best they could manage, given Philip's adamant refusal to let the Catalans keep their historic rights and liberties. He did, though, agree to an amnesty, while conceding to Catalonia the grant of all those privileges, including the privilege of similar access to civil and ecclesiastical offices, enjoyed by his Castilian subjects – a concession that Catalans, traditionally contemptuous of what they regarded as Castile's lack of true liberty, were unlikely to see as compensation for the loss of their Constitutions. In the period following the accession of George I in 1714, however, his Whig ministers made efforts to recoup something of what their Tory predecessors had sacrificed. Their efforts eventually succeeded in wresting from Philip permission for the principality to retain its civil law, or, as Philip expressed it in a letter to his grandfather, 'those customs of the region that relate purely to private relationships'.[6]

The Nueva Planta as introduced into Catalonia therefore resembled the 1707 settlement in Scotland in preserving the old legislative system in matters of private right. Regardless of other considerations, this reflected in both instances the practical impossibility of bringing about a genuine unification of disparate legal systems. Even where the will existed, early modern states simply lacked the necessary resources and mechanisms of control.[7] Justice and government were firmly separated in the mentality of the age, and the retention of private law in Scotland and Catalonia indissolubly tied the new constitutional order to the old, in spite of the innovations brought about by incorporating union. The extension of the Nueva Planta to Catalonia therefore meant the transfer from Castile of certain institutions such as the Castilian-style Audiencia, the captaincy-general, and *corregidores* for purposes of local government, but these were inserted into the principality's well-established juridical and institutional framework. Yet there was a fundamental constitutional difference between the incorporating union imposed on Catalonia and the Anglo-Scottish Union of 1707. Under the new system, Catalonia lost the effective form of representation it had possessed for centuries. Not only was its traditional legislative forum, the Corts, abolished, but the principality found itself incorporated into a larger political entity in which the king was effectively above the law. Although a number of cities in the Crown of Aragon were given seats alongside those of the Castilian cities in the Cortes of Castile, which now in effect became a Spanish institution, the Cortes had ceased to be a dynamic assembly, and would meet only on rare occasions and for largely formal purposes in the eighteenth century. This, then, was little more than an empty gesture.

Scotland, by contrast, although losing its own parliament, now formed part of a new, politically (and religiously) pluralist parliamentary monarchy, based, unlike Bourbon Spain, on the principle of consent. While the kingdom of Ireland kept its own parliament, the kingdom of Scotland would be represented in the House of Commons of the reconstituted British body politic by forty-five shire and burgh commissioners, while sixteen elected Scottish peers would be added to the House of Lords. London might have supplanted Edinburgh as the political and administrative centre of their universe, but at least the Scots still had a forum, however inadequate, in which to express their discontents and lobby for their interests. The Catalans, it was true, were now represented in the Cortes, and the inclusion of representatives of the Crown of Aragon turned the Cortes into a Spanish, as distinct from a Castilian, institution, just as the coming of the Scots to Westminster had transformed the English parliament into a British parliament. Yet the political impotence of the Cortes can scarcely be said to have given a meaningful voice to the Catalans. Even the principality's traditional channel of communication with Madrid, the Council of Aragon, disappeared when the Nueva Planta was introduced. The task of governing the peninsular territories of the Crown of Aragon was now shared between the Council of Castile and the secretariats of state. Under the new Bourbon regime, these took over many of the functions previously exercised by the councils.[8]

Although the Scots had succeeded in maintaining their form of church government and their legal system under the terms of the Union, they remained uneasy on both counts. The Church of Scotland enjoyed the assurance that it would not suffer interference from a predominantly Anglican parliament, but there remained several reasons for concern. The

Presbyterian form of government had been restored only a few years earlier, in 1690, and the Kirk still felt itself to be vulnerable and exposed. On the one hand it was faced by the hard-line remnants of the Covenanting movement, the Cameronians. On the other, living as it did under the shadow of the Jacobite threat, it remained preoccupied with the danger from Rome. Its fears were by no means groundless. The Old Pretender made a bid for the throne in 1708 and again, with a better chance of success, when John Erskine, Earl of Mar, launched his uprising in 1715.

Jacobites and papists were not the only danger. This was an age when religious orthodoxy was being eroded, and heresy seemed rampant. Yet if church discipline was now needed more than ever, it stood at risk of being undermined by the Toleration Act of 1689, and subsequently by two pieces of parliamentary legislation in 1712 specifically directed at religious life in Scotland: a Toleration Act and a Patronage Act. The first of these granted freedom of worship to Scottish Episcopalians as long as they prayed for the reigning monarch, while the second restored the appointing powers of lay patrons, typically the lairds, to vacant parishes and church offices. Both these acts subverted the Act for the Security of the Protestant Religion and the Government of the Church, passed by the English parliament in November 1706, which was intended to meet the Kirk's objections to an Act of Union by placing a protective barrier around the Presbyterian system of church governance. Not surprisingly, a newly aggrieved Kirk felt itself under threat from real or imagined encroachments by Episcopalians and from a hostile Anglican Church establishment, which had its own fears that the Treaty of Union would strengthen the hand of the English dissenting community.[9] The fears of Scottish Presbyterians that the Act of Union would enhance the possibility of a creeping anglicization of the Scottish Church seemed all too likely to be realized.

Increased anglicization also seemed to threaten Scotland's legal establishment. Under the Union, English common law stopped at the border, and the kingdom's legal institutions and judiciary remained in place. But the House of Lords, which was seen as unsympathetic to Scottish law, now became the ultimate court of appeal. The Act of Union also set up in Scotland a Court of Exchequer on the model of the English Court of Exchequer, with the purpose of ensuring uniformity in the regulation of trade, customs and excises between the two kingdoms. This court could be considered something of a Trojan horse, since, although its jurisdiction was carefully circumscribed, it introduced into Scotland elements of English law and procedures. The fact remained, too, that while existing Scots laws continued to be in force if they did not contravene the terms of the

Treaty of Union, the British parliament retained the power to alter them if necessary.

In practice, there were few major reforms to Scots private law in the eighteenth century, other than the abolition of military tenures and heritable jurisdictions following the Jacobite rebellion of 1745, but there were latent fears of creeping anglicization as Scottish lawyers found it necessary to increase their knowledge of English law. On the other hand, Scottish law, with its basis in civil law, had always been open to outside influences, and closer acquaintance with the English system brought about a realization that in some respects the common law provided a model that improved on what Scottish law had to offer. For jurists in the age of the Scottish Enlightenment, who saw the old Scottish feudal system swept away in the legal reforms of 1747–8, it was not difficult to equate anglicization with the general modernization of Scottish society to which they aspired. As a result, by the end of the century the two systems had drawn closer to each other, although the continuing independence of Scotland's legal system was by now solidly established.[10]

With its law, its system of local government, its religion and its universities left in place, post-Union Scotland retained a large measure of its pre-Union administrative, and even political, autonomy, and would continue to maintain it well into the nineteenth century. It had, however, been incorporated into a Westminster parliamentary system in which the mass of Scotland's population could feel little or no involvement, following the reduction of Scottish constituencies from 159 to 45, and the assimilation of the 45 Scottish members and the 16 representative peers (soon to become dependable government voters) into the management politics of the age of Walpole – an age in which group interests took precedence over party affiliation.[11]

On the other hand, management politics had their advantage where the government of Scotland was concerned. As successive ministers proved quick to realize, this was best left to the Scots themselves, as long as they remained subordinate to London. The contrast was stark between the loose administrative structure of post-Union Scotland, with its heavy dependence on the management of patronage, and the system of government imposed by the Nueva Planta on eighteenth-century Catalonia. In many respects the principality was treated as occupied territory, and for the rest of the century a royal army of between 20,000 and 30,000 men was garrisoned on Catalan soil, with Barcelona transformed into a major military base.[12] A vast urban area was demolished to make way for the construction of the oppressive new citadel, the Ciutadella, which came to overshadow the city. The fortress, which successive generations saw as a symbol of absolutism and oppression, would only start to be demolished as a result of unilateral and unauthorized action by a municipal Junta in 1841.[13]

There was also a major territorial reorganization. The royal government in Madrid swept away the old administrative structure and divided the principality into twelve *corregimientos*, modelled on the administrative divisions of Castile. Unlike the Castilian *corregidores*, though, the majority of those appointed in Catalonia were military men, many of them retired officers, and this practice would be continued into the nineteenth century.[14] Almost all of them, too, were non-Catalans: 160 between 1717 and 1808, as against a mere 13 who were Catalan by birth.[15] *Corregidores*, as the essential links between the central government and local administration, wielded enormous authority, and the appointment of non-Catalans on such a scale reflects the determination of Madrid to control and hispanicize a province that had for too long, in its view, been a law unto itself. As for municipal government, members of city and town councils would in future be appointed by the Audiencia, except in Barcelona, whose twenty-four *regidores* were to be royal nominees.[16]

The Bourbon government also seized the opportunity to introduce radical new fiscal measures into a territory that Madrid had always regarded as failing to contribute its fair share to the royal finances. Without abolishing the principality's old taxes, most of them indirect, it imposed, from 1 April 1716, a new tax, the *catastro (cadastre)*, as part of its plan to bring tax contributions in the Crown of Aragon into line with those of Castile. Catalonia's new tax, arbitrarily fixed by the Crown, was to be shared out among the *corregimientos*, and was to be levied on property and revenues from land, on personal incomes derived from professional activities, and on mercantile and business enterprises. The nobility, the clergy, royal officeholders and members of the military were in principle exempted from personal contributions. In practice the government greatly overestimated the principality's tax-paying capacity, at a time when it was emerging from a long war and when the billeting of a large standing army imposed heavy additional burdens on householders. Between 1720 and 1726 the *cadastre* brought in no more than 40 per cent of the anticipated return.[17] The initial figure had to be reduced in the face of continuing protests, but the *cadastre*, often hailed as a rational and modernizing fiscal device that helped stimulate the principality's economic development, now appears to have been an arbitrary and inequitable form of imposition. The sums to be levied moved upwards over the course of the century, leaving the mass of the Catalan population with a fiscal burden that has been calculated as double that which fell on Castilian taxpayers.[18]

Just as, after the signing of the Anglo-Scottish Union, Scottish coins had to be called in and weights and measures standardized between the two countries,[19] so the movement for fiscal uniformity between Castile and the Crown of Aragon was accompanied in 1719 by measures designed to bring about monetary unification. In practice it would be several decades before provincial rights to mint coinage were entirely abolished, while a unified system of weights and measures would be slow in coming.[20] Joseph Townsend, travelling through Spain in 1786–7, reported that 'in Catalonia ... accounts are kept in livres, sols, and deniers'.[21] The aim of the Bourbon regime, however, was gradually to weld together these formerly disparate regions into a single centralized unit.

The process of welding was also designed to include the principality's cultural life. Catalonia at the end of the seventeenth century possessed five universities, although only the University of Barcelona enjoyed some prestige. All five were now abolished, to be replaced by a single new university. This was located well away from Barcelona in the small, impoverished town of Cervera, which had come out in favour of the Bourbons, and which Philip V wished to reward for its loyalty.[22] The move, partly designed to prevent the concentration of politically subversive students in the major urban centres, was strongly but vainly resisted by the old university towns. The new university was intended to be a centralizing institution in the Bourbon style, serving the interests of the state and holding a monopoly on the publication of textbooks.[23] In the event, the fractious nature of its origins and the remoteness of its location helped to ensure that it would never enjoy more than a half-life. Cervera was not the type of university to promote the kind of intellectual revival that would give eighteenth-century Catalonia its equivalent of the Scottish Enlightenment.[24]

The Nueva Planta extended its reach beyond the principality's cultural arrangements to include regulations affecting its language. The language and culture of Castile had already made substantial inroads among the Catalan elite well before the coming of the Bourbons, just as English had tended to replace the Scottish vernacular as the language of literary Scotland by the turn of the seventeenth and eighteenth centuries; and even in the Gaelic-speaking Highlands the majority of the principal chiefs had become bilingual in English and Gaelic.[25] Yet inevitably, the imposition of Bourbon rule gave a strong impetus to the process of linguistic and cultural castilianization in Catalonia, Valencia and Majorca. Henceforth, Castilian was to be the official language of public administration in the principality, and its use was made compulsory in all lawsuits brought before the Audiencia.

Yet while the regime clearly hoped that Castilian would in due course replace Catalan, and took a number of steps in this direction, it was unable to go much further. At a time when governments did not automatically equate language with nationality, pressures for the standardization of language in Spain, as elsewhere in pre-revolutionary Europe, were less likely to come from the state than from clerics who found it hard to communicate the fundamental tenets of their faith when they were unable to speak the language of their flock.[26] In Catalonia the parish clergy naturally spoke the language of their parishioners, however much Castilian-born bishops might object to the use of the vernacular. Since the enforcement of linguistic uniformity on large populations was anyhow beyond the capacity of the state in this period, it is not surprising that Catalan remained the language of daily life for the mass of the population, and that notarial and business documents continued to be drawn up in Catalan well into the nineteenth century.[27]

According to a 'memorandum of grievances' submitted to the Crown in 1760: 'Here a distinctive language is spoken; and although in the cities and principal towns there are many people who understand and speak Castilian, rural folk, in spite of everything, neither know how to speak it nor do they understand it.'[28] In the cities and towns, on the other hand, higher education, much of which was in the hands of the Jesuits, had helped create a bourgeoisie that had come to look down on Catalan as a plebeian language, 'rough and uncultivated.'[29] As mental horizons widened, new generations naturally turned to books published in Castilian to follow the latest results of European scientific and rational inquiry. Taste, fashion and growing commercial contacts with other parts of the peninsula all drew members of the urban middle and upper classes increasingly into the linguistic and cultural orbit of Castile.[30] In 1768 the government of Charles III felt able to go further than its predecessors, and ordered, in a decree partly directed to ending the use of Latin in civil and ecclesiastical tribunals, that henceforth all primary and secondary education should be conducted in Castilian. The purpose, it explained, was to 'extend the general language of the Nation to bring about its greater harmony and closer reciprocity'. The decree was not in itself a prohibition on the use of Catalan, and the extent of its success remains unclear.[31]

In any event, Catalan survived as the commonly spoken language, although replaced by Castilian where necessary or where it seemed appropriate. It would not, however, become the language of high culture and jurisprudence until the twentieth century. For Salvador Sanpere i Miquel, the leading Catalan positivist historian of his age and the author of a study published in 1905 on 'the end of the Catalan nation', the survival of Catalan was critical for a proper assessment of the events of 1714.[32] He saw the disaster of that year as marking the culmination of a process under way for two centuries or more – the process whereby a Castilian dynasty, in pursuit of the absolutist ideas that were common to European monarchs of the period, sought to undermine and eventually destroy the contractual system of government developed in medieval Catalonia. While recognizing that this system was far from perfect and that seventeenth- and early eighteenth-century Catalonia was a divided society, he saw Philip V as completing the subversion of a political system possessing 'essentially democratic institutions'.[33] The reign of Spain's first Bourbon ruler would therefore seem at first sight to mark the end of the Catalan nation. In the view of Sanpere, however, 'a people lives as long as its language lives'.[34] What was destroyed, then, was not the Catalan nation, but a long-standing political order that embodied the notion of liberty as enshrined in a reciprocal relationship between the ruler and the ruled.

Yet Sanpere's nineteenth-century linguistic nationalism was largely alien to the thinking of those Catalans who fought to stave off victory by Philip V and his army. They did not equate the survival of their language with the survival of their *pàtria*, nor would they have seen linguistic survival as a cause for hope for the future. What they had lost was the Catalonia of the Constitutions. In its place a political system was being imposed that was arbitrary and authoritarian, and depended on military power to ensure compliance with its edicts. As the forces of absolutism emerged victorious from the conflict, they had no doubt that Castile was imposing on Spain long-cherished plans for centralized government from Madrid.

How far were they right? In practice, the changes brought about as a consequence of the war were not as clear-cut as the enemies of the new regime feared or supposed. There is no doubt that the intention of the Bourbons was to replace the 'horizontal' Spain of the House of Austria with the top-down government of a 'vertical' Spain, in which administrative orders issued from the centre were transmitted to the regions.[35] While, at least in general terms, the territories of the Crown of Aragon now became part of this 'vertical' Spain, this was not true of the kingdom of Navarre or the three Basque provinces of Álava, Guipúzcoa and Vizcaya, all of which had sided with Philip V. These continued in possession of their traditional laws, liberties and assemblies, while Navarre also remained what it was under the Habsburgs, a kingdom with its own parliament, or Cortes.

Nevertheless, the new dynasty did move to bring about economic integration of these territories with other parts of Spain by decreeing in 1717 the transfer of the internal customs barriers to the ports. But its plan failed. Following protests and uprisings in the Basque provinces, the Crown retreated in 1722 and restored the inland tolls. For the time being at least, Madrid's hopes of establishing a Spanish common market and some kind of fiscal union had to be abandoned. The Spain of the *fueros*, or the 'exempt provinces', as they came to be called, lived on in the north of the peninsula, with the result that the country became an asymmetrical state. Under the rule of the Bourbons the Basque provinces and Navarre would cling proudly to the institutions and immunities evolved during a past that had suffered no rupture as a result of the war and its aftermath. The Catalans, by contrast, could only look back regretfully on a past that was gone, and adjust as best they could to a future that was fraught with uncertainty.[36]

In all this there were profound differences between the Spain of the Nueva Planta and the Great Britain created by the Anglo-Scottish Union. This was a state that possessed some of the characteristics of the 'vertical' monarchy of the Bourbons, in the sense that the organs of government were centralized in London. The Scots, however, retained some control over their fate through their parliamentary representation in Westminster; and Hanoverian Britain was at least in part a 'horizontal' monarchy, in so far as a significant degree of self-government remained in Scottish hands.

Yet there is no denying that the Union represented a decisive break with the past. Until 1707, Scotland had been, with the brief interruption of the Cromwellian Protectorate, an independent kingdom since the remote past, even if that independence had to some extent been abridged by the dynastic union of 1603. For centuries it had possessed and enjoyed all the appurtenances of a European state, no less 'sovereign' than England, Sweden or France, in that it accepted no external right of interference in its political and institutional life. In this respect pre-Union Scotland has better claims to be regarded as a 'complete State' than Catalonia before the Nueva Planta, for which this title has been claimed.[37] The principality of Catalonia, after all, had been from the twelfth century onwards part of a wider political grouping, the Crown of Aragon, and for all the influence it exerted at many moments over the affairs of the Crown, it cannot convincingly be described as a 'complete' or 'sovereign' state in itself, however strong and well developed its institutional and fiscal arrangements. Even before the late fifteenth-century union of the Crowns of Aragon and Castile it was less of a sovereign independent state than medieval Scotland.

In 1707 the kingdom of Scotland, or its governing class, chose to sacrifice that independence for the benefits, real or imagined, that a closer union with its neighbour could bring. Of those benefits, economic integration was the one most coveted by the Scots. Union with England could be expected to link their country to an economy more buoyant than their own, and open the door to the colonial and overseas trading opportunities that they had unsuccessfully sought in the ill-fated Darien project. Yet once the Treaty of Union was signed, the prospects of union bringing about dramatic economic growth were still far from certain, and an incorporating union would have consequences for Scottish society that could no more be foreseen than those that awaited Catalonia in the aftermath of the Nueva Planta.

The Impact of Incorporating Union

For the Scots and Catalans alike, the events of the early eighteenth century marked the end of the old political order. The Catalans, faced with the harsh imposition of the Nueva Planta, had no option but to salvage what they could from the past, and make the best of such opportunities as integration into an authoritarian Bourbon state could offer them. For the Scots, by contrast, integration into a transformed British state was less immediately disruptive. The Union negotiated with the English by the Scottish political establishment might be deeply distasteful to many or most Scots, but post-Union Scotland retained enough of the past to be able to move forward into the eighteenth century relatively unchanged, but with the possibility of a higher degree of political and social stability than it had possessed during the turmoil and upheavals of the seventeenth century.

Yet in the years immediately following the Union, this greater degree of stability seemed far from assured. Where the Catalans were left after 1714–16 with diminished reasons for hope, the story of Scotland in the post-Union years was one of disappointed expectations. Disillusionment began with the failure to establish satisfactory administrative arrangements for the smooth functioning of the Union – a failure for which Scots themselves bore the larger responsibility. The political influence of the house of Argyll was challenged by the political grouping of the Squadrone, which had played an important part in securing the passage of the Union Treaty. The outcome of its machinations for short-term electoral purposes was the abolition in 1708 of the Scottish Privy Council, which had traditionally served as the executive government of Scotland and as the channel of official communication between Westminster and Edinburgh. The Squadrone argued that a Scottish Privy Council was no longer needed, since the jurisdiction of a post-Union British Privy Council included Scotland; but it was motivated by the knowledge that, as long as a Scottish Privy Council survived and was dominated by the Squadrone's opponents in the Court party, its pickings from the Union settlement would be slender and the influence of its adherents in Scotland limited.[38]

The fall of the Whig Junto in 1710 and its replacement by a Tory administration in which the Lord Treasurer, Robert Harley, soon to be created Earl of Oxford, was the dominant figure, changed the political situation in Scotland as in England, but not quite in the way that the members of the Squadrone had hoped. Navigating between High Tories and Whigs, and between the rival factions of the Squadrone and the Duke of Argyll, Oxford hoped to rule above faction by keeping power in his own hands and relying on the information of agents and informants. But the disappearance of the Scottish Privy Council created a power vacuum that made his task much harder.

In addition the Earl of Oxford initially decided not to appoint a Secretary of State for Scotland in order to help him maintain close personal control over Scottish affairs. But in 1713, as he became increasingly dependent on Scottish parliamentary votes to shore up his own position in a faction-ridden administration, he revived the secretaryship, having come to recognize the need for a formal channel through which Scots could apply for offices and honours. In a bid to avoid becoming dependent on the Argyll interest he chose the Earl of Mar, a court placeman on whom he could rely, to occupy the post. But the death of Queen Anne at the beginning of August 1714 brought about a political revolution. The new monarch, George I, replaced a Tory ministry tarred by the Jacobite brush with a Whig administration and dismissed Mar from office.[39]

It was becoming clear that the Union had not led to improvements in the governance of Scotland, while the involvement of the Scots in British political life was heightening Scottish faction feuds now that the stakes, and the potential pickings, were so much higher. There was disillusionment, also, over the failure of the Union to bring, as if by magic, the expected economic benefits. The continuing disruption of Scotland's commercial links with the continent as a result of the long war with France was a source of growing hardship. At the same time, England's protectionist policies and the imposition on Scotland of the bureaucratic apparatus of its customs and excise system were damaging to Scottish trade and introduced the Scots to an unaccustomed and unwelcome degree of rigour in the collection of customs dues. Nor did the opening of England's overseas markets to Scottish merchants compensate for the loss of their European markets, since their lack of capital prevented them from investing in the colonial and overseas trade on the scale that the Union's advocates had hoped. The opening of these markets to the Scots was in any event incomplete. The very first session of the new British parliament created by the Treaty of Union enshrined the monopoly of the East India Company across the British Isles. Although they were now citizens of a nominally United Kingdom this effectively excluded natives of Scotland from participating in England's Asian trades other than as employees of a company that remained a purely English, and London-based, corporation.[40]

One of the attractions of the Union was the promise by the Westminster government to provide compensation to shareholders in the Darien Company for their loss of capital through payment of the Equivalent.[41] Although wagon-loads of coins were sent north and deposited in Edinburgh Castle, payments in fact tended to be delayed and compensation was often slow in coming.[42] Nobles and lairds, and especially those who had lost heavily in the mania, were originally keen advocates of closer union, but were among those who felt particularly aggrieved by the course that events were taking. This included the grant of additional authority to Justices of the Peace, which the nobles and lairds interpreted as the first move in a grand design to undermine their extensive territorial jurisdictions.[43]

There would be outrage, too, when it transpired after the Tories' election victory in 1710 that peers newly ennobled as British peers would not, as they had assumed, enjoy an automatic right to join the sixteen Scottish peers in the House of Lords. The Earl of Oxford was anxious to reward James Douglas, fourth Duke of Hamilton, for his electoral support, and in 1711 secured him the British title of Duke of Brandon. But when it came to Hamilton taking his seat in the House of Lords, a close partisan vote in the Lords in December of that year refused to recognize his right to sit among them. The vote was seen by the Scots as a national humiliation, and it would only be just over seventy years later, in 1782, that the decision was reversed.[44] True integration between the two kingdoms, even at the elite level, still had a long way to go.

For all their discontents the leading nobility had made no move in 1708 to support 'James VIII', the Old Pretender, when a French invading fleet had brought him within sight of the Scottish coast. In 1715, however, the situation was very different. A Hanoverian, not a Stuart, now sat on the British throne, and he commanded no natural loyalty among his Scottish subjects. His accession, and the downfall of the Tories, had transformed the political landscape. Although Scots nobles and gentry hastened to express their loyalty to George I, the accumulation of grievances and an undercurrent of resentment emboldened those who found themselves out of favour with the new regime.

The Scots Tory peer, the Earl of Mar, became the self-appointed spokesman for the discontented. Now that the Tories were excluded from power, perhaps for ever, and the Kirk had welcomed a Protestant Hanoverian succession, it was the Jacobites and assorted Episcopalians who could claim to be the sole true keepers of the national flame. There were pockets of Roman Catholics in Scotland who would naturally be inclined to support an exiled prince of their own religious persuasion, but many Episcopalians in the conservative north-east of Scotland were also strongly Jacobite, having failed to secure an Episcopal Church in the Union settlement and finding themselves excluded from the terms of the Toleration Act of 1712 by their refusal to pray for the reigning monarch. Jacobite sentiment was strong, too, among the clan chiefs and gentry of the Grampian region, but the Earl of Mar's bid to tear up the Union resonated far beyond the Highlands, extending all across the Lowlands north of the river Tay. Only southern Scotland could be counted upon to remain more or less loyal to the Hanoverian regime in the event of an uprising. Westminster's insouciance in the face of such a threat, and its failure to take adequate defence measures until Mar raised the banner of revolt, gave his rebellion a fair prospect of success. In November 1715 his military incompetence led it to defeat.[45]

The failure of the rebellion was a shattering blow to the Jacobite cause, and correspondingly a political gift to the Whig ascendancy, which could denounce the Jacobites as the treacherous tools of the papists and the French. In 1709 an act of parliament had extended England's savage treason laws to Scotland, but in the aftermath of the uprising the rebels were treated with relative leniency. The Whigs had no desire to replicate in Scotland Judge Jeffreys's Bloody Assizes of 1685. Forty rebels, including two peers of the realm were executed, and 638 prisoners were transported to the Caribbean and North America, but many prisoners either escaped or were released without trial. Although rebels were condemned to the loss of their estates, forfeiture proved to be a complex process, obfuscated and obstructed by legalistic manoeuvring.[46]

The inability of James Edward Stuart to inspire his adherents in the course of his brief and unhappy appearance in Scotland in 1715–16 did not augur well for the future of Jacobitism, although he had yet to realize that he would be spending the rest of his life in continental exile. He was still a useful pawn in the hands of England's foreign enemies, and was preparing to make another bid for the throne when a Spanish invasion fleet set sail from Cadiz for the British Isles in 1719, only to be dispersed by a storm off Corunna. The few Spanish soldiers who finally reached Scotland received no local support.[47] The wounds left by the defeat of the '15 were still too raw, the relative clemency of the government's response to the rebellion was yielding its first results, and potential supporters lacked confidence in the ability of James Edward and his continental allies to organize a successful invasion.

Yet the political situation remained volatile, and in Scotland the Squadrone and the adherents of the Duke of Argyll battled for pre-eminence and sought the Scottish secretaryship for their own nominees. By 1718 the Squadrone had entrenched themselves in the Scottish administration, but with the Argathelians, the followers of Argyll, contesting their every move. The Squadrone, however, found themselves confronted by an increasingly formidable opponent in the robust figure of Sir Robert Walpole, the Norfolk squire who came to dominate both the House of Commons and the court, and finally battled his way to the top when he was appointed First Lord of the Treasury and Chancellor of the Exchequer in April 1721. The Walpole era had begun.

Walpole, like Oxford before him, was anxious to keep close personal control over Scottish affairs, but in order to break the Squadrone's hold he turned to the Argyll faction as a necessary counterweight. By supporting the faction in contested elections he secured for Argyll some two-thirds of the Scottish members of parliament, giving himself in the process valuable voting fodder in the House of Commons.[48] The alliance with Argyll served Walpole well during the early years of his administration, but in 1725, when he was confronted with Malt Tax riots in Glasgow in response to his attempts to tighten fiscal control over Scotland, he resisted the temptation to lean too far in Argyll's direction; he disappointed Argyll's younger brother, the Earl of Ilay, by not giving him the Scottish secretaryship and deciding instead to abolish the post. Walpole preferred to entrust Scottish affairs to the two remaining secretaries of state, Charles Townshend and the Duke of Newcastle, the latter of whom became largely responsible for the management of Scottish business.

With the disappearance both of the Scottish Privy Council and the Scottish secretaryship of state, the post of Lord Advocate, the senior Scottish law officer, acquired additional influence. As before the Union, much of the governance of Scotland was managed by the Lord Advocate and the central courts of justice, working in conjunction with a system of local government in which English-style Justices of the Peace had been given powers equal to those of their English counterparts following the suppression of the Privy Council. Yet the Lord Advocate was only a partial substitute for a secretary of state, although for Walpole the exercise of patronage was the best way to keep the Scots in line. At the same time it was essential for Sir Robert Walpole's system of governance that neither Scottish faction should be allowed to win absolute dominion nor secure control of patronage for itself.

While making Argyll's brother, Ilay, responsible for keeping the peace in Scotland and promoting the government interest, Walpole kept him on a tight rein and ensured that he took his orders from London.

Ilay kept the machinery of Scottish government running smoothly. Like his master, he successfully survived the change of monarchs following the death of George I in June 1727, and attained his greatest influence in the early years of George II. Yet inevitably, as Walpole's man, Ilay came to share in Walpole's growing unpopularity, and was similarly tarnished by the allegations of corruption that swirled around the minister. Ilay's relationship with his irascible elder brother was never easy, and Argyll, who had moved into the anti-Walpole camp, broke with him in 1739–40. In 1742 Walpole fell from power, and, with his fall, Ilay, although keeping his offices for life, lost his management of patronage. A year later he succeeded his brother as the third duke, and, from 1742 until his sudden death in 1761, he dedicated his energies to his many intellectual concerns and to the improvement of the vast Argyll estates, although retaining his political interests and at times intervening actively in support of the ministry when called upon to provide it.[49]

As was made clear by the Glasgow Malt Tax riots of 1725 and the Porteous Riots in Edinburgh in 1736 over a case involving smuggling, many Scots deeply resented the policies and practices of the Westminster government. Moreover, the presence of an alternative monarch over the water injected an additional element of uncertainty into the Anglo-Scottish relationship, even if for a time the political dominance of Sir Robert Walpole seemed to carry everything before it, and the Hanoverian succession looked more secure with every year that passed.

After the imposition of the Nueva Planta, Catalonia was more quiescent than Scotland, but if it did not exactly have its '15 rebellion, for one moment it came close. The crushing defeat of 1714 might seem to have decided once and for all the fate of the *austracista* adherents of the Habsburgs, but the repression that followed defeat and the imposition of the new form of government sparked a guerrilla war against the new regime in years that were marked by harvest failure and widespread misery. An alliance of the great powers antagonized by Philip V's ambitious plans to recover his lost Italian territories offered the *austracistas* some hope that the verdict of Utrecht might yet be reversed, and in 1719 a rebellion broke out under the leadership of Pere Joan Barceló, nicknamed 'Carrasclet'. The rebels demanded a restoration of the Constitutions and an end to the *cadastre*, but foreign support proved as fickle as it was for the Jacobites. The allied powers failed to send help, and the revolt was soon put down. Yet in spite of the regime's success and further repression, clandestine resistance lingered on, even after the Emperor Charles VI and Philip V ended their war in 1725.[50]

Even though rebellion had been defeated at home, Catalan and Aragonese exiles in Vienna, like their Jacobite counterparts in Rome, still cherished hopes that the tide would turn,[51] but, unlike the Jacobites, the *austracistas* had no candidate-in-waiting for the throne. In their Catalan homeland, memories of life under the House of Austria began to fade as a new generation came to maturity, and even the more recent horrors of war and repression receded into the background with the passage of time. Lacking a figurehead, the *austracista* cause in Catalonia was unable to command the widespread support that Jacobitism still enjoyed in Scotland. Nor did it have the kind of regional base and potential recruiting ground that the Highlands could provide.

Both before and after the Treaty of Union the Highlands of Scotland were a world unto themselves. This was an impoverished region in which clan chiefs were dominant, lawlessness was endemic, and in which perhaps a third of the population was still Gaelic-speaking in the early eighteenth century in spite of an increasingly vigorous campaign to eradicate the Gaelic language and culture. Inhabitants of the Lowlands regarded this as a barbaric region, badly in need of the civilizing process, while the Kirk saw the language of the natives as a serious impediment to the inculcation of true religion. Fearing that, if left to themselves, both the Highlands and the north-east could all too easily relapse into popery, it set up in 1709 a Scottish Society for the Propagation of the Gospel in an attempt to improve the schooling of a benighted people.[52]

No government, either before or after the Union, had managed to impose its will on a part of Scotland that was still, in effect, semi-autonomous, and could only be managed through the use of local supporters working within the clan system. It was thus that the Campbells had risen to their position of predominance. In the opening years of the eighteenth century their hereditary chief, the Duke of Argyll, owned some 500 square miles of rent-paying lands, and was the overlord of chiefs and landholders whose estates in Argyll and western Inverness-shire covered 3,000 square miles.[53] In throwing in his lot with the Whigs and with the Hanoverian succession the second duke had made himself indispensable to the Westminster government, but had also driven the clan enemies of the Campbells into the opposing camp – one in which a combination of High Toryism, Episcopalianism and patriotic sentiment could easily slip into active support for the Jacobites.

Even after the events of 1715 and 1719, therefore, Jacobitism continued to be a latent threat in the Highlands, and in the mid-1720s Walpole woke up to the need to pay the region some attention. The first essential was to create a stronger military presence. General Wade was authorized to raise six Highland Companies, establish barracks and forts, and embark on an ambitious programme of military road-building that would help to break down the physical isolation of the region and allow a more rapid response if trouble arose. Belatedly recognizing that an enhanced military presence was not itself enough, the government even made an annual grant of £1,000 for schools in the Highlands.[54] Lowland society had become increasingly aware that only cultural and social transformation could solve the problems of endemic lawlessness in the Highlands and eliminate the danger of a Jacobite revival. The message had at last got through to Westminster, although it was not heard for very long.

In reality the transformation was already under way, although more as a result of native Scottish efforts than of any action by the government. Anglicization and the urge for improvement were not confined to the Lowland aristocracy and gentry, but had also affected the Highland aristocracy, including some, like the Earl of Mar himself, who came out in support of the Jacobite cause in 1715. Many Highland gentry had served in wars on the continent, and their horizons had been broadened by foreign travel. It is not, therefore, surprising to find improving landlords among them.[55] Yet improvement, for all its potential agrarian benefits, also meant social dislocation, as developments on the Argyll estates were to show.

The second duke, an enthusiastic improving landlord, was always in need of money, and enthusiastically set about revolutionizing the system of land tenure on his properties. When 'tacks', or leases, fell vacant they no longer went automatically to clan followers, but were auctioned off to the highest bidder, who would pay a substantially raised rent. The old tacksmen found themselves displaced, to the detriment of old-style clanship and vassalage. By the time of the second duke's death in 1743 the social disruption caused by his treatment of his tenants was so serious that his brother and successor, the Earl of Ilay, took immediate steps to reverse it and restore Campbells to their holdings. But by then the damage had been done. Loyal clan families had seen their lives broken, or at least seriously disrupted, as tacksmen were changed from chiefs and military leaders into gentlemen farmers with insecure possession of their land. Others moved away, some of them emigrating to the colonies. As a result, the political and military influence wielded by the ducal house over a large area of the Highlands was gravely weakened just at the time when it would most be needed.[56] In July 1745 Charles Edward Stuart, on board a French vessel, landed in the Outer Hebrides, and went on to raise his standard at Glenfinnan in Inverness-shire on 19 August.

The government was totally unprepared for this unexpected turn of events, in spite of the fact that it had been aware of French invasion plans for some time. The very month of the Young Pretender's landing, the fourth Marquis of Tweeddale, in whom the secretaryship of state for Scotland had been temporarily revived after the fall of Walpole in 1742, wrote confidently that 'there is little ground to be alarmed for any Insurrection'.[57] Tweeddale's appointment, made at the request of the Squadrone, had split the Scottish administration, and his observation shows how out of touch he was with Highland affairs. As a supporter of the war on the continent he had allowed Scotland to become denuded of the relatively few troops stationed in the country on the grounds that they were needed for foreign service. The country's defence force now numbered fewer than 4,000 men, the majority of them unseasoned. In facing, in the person of Charles Edward, an impetuous and dashing leader, who came with no army of his own but never doubted his ability to rally his countrymen, both the government and its forces were hopelessly slow to react.

Charles Edward's optimism was not entirely misplaced. Westminster, with the usual mixture of arrogance, carelessness and neglect that it tended to display in its dealings with Scotland, was deeply unpopular, even among those who were not of the Jacobite persuasion. Although the Presbyterian clergy, the burghs, and the Lowlands in general, with the exception of the north-east plain, were hostile to the prince's cause, their lack of enthusiasm for the current regime gave him an initial advantage. With the support of convinced Jacobites and a group of Highland chiefs who could call out their clan followers, some 5,000 in all,[58] Charles Edward was able to take Edinburgh and make his spectacular advance into England almost unopposed. Then he seems to have lost his nerve and failed to push beyond Derby. It was only a question of time before a panic-stricken government recovered its confidence. At Culloden on 16 April 1746 the prince's band of hungry and ill-equipped Highland followers had no hope against the firepower of the well-provisioned government forces, including many Scottish soldiers, who were rushed northwards under the command of the virulently anti-Scottish Duke of Cumberland.

This time, in contrast to 1715, the government would take no chances. Its response was similar to that of the Bourbon government of Philip V in Catalonia between 1714 and 1721. The counter-insurgency measures taken by Cumberland, and the savage repression that followed his victory, were designed to break the power of the Highland clans once and for all. Cumberland established himself at Fort Augustus in the heart of the Highlands; a commanding new Fort George was built north-east of Inverness as part of the process of remilitarization; the clans were disarmed; and the wearing of Highland dress and the playing of the pipes were prohibited. The most far-reaching and effective of the measures taken against the clan system, however, was the Heritable Jurisdictions Act of 1747 that abolished most of Scotland's feudal jurisdictions from March 1748, in spite of the article in the Act of Union that guaranteed their survival.[59] Neither this nor the counter-insurgency measures were fully effective, but in the second half of the century the Highlands would slowly but steadily be integrated into a Scotland that had embraced with growing enthusiasm the notion of improvement.

The abolition of heritable jurisdictions, although driven by the determination to deal with the problem of the Highlands, can be seen as part of a wider design in the aftermath of the '45 to make the administration of Scotland more uniform with that of England and to ensure a greater degree of governmental control. Unlike the Nueva Planta, the Heritable Jurisdictions Act cannot be dismissed as simply the unwanted imposition of an alien legal structure on a prostrate land. The Scottish legal profession, always so prominent in Scottish public life, had long regarded the country's private courts as archaic and prejudicial to justice. The nobility, for their part, may have benefited from the possession of hereditary powers over their tenants, but by now their outlook was sufficiently anglicized to make them uneasy over the continuation of a semi-feudal system that could be seen as holding the country back.[60]

Where the old structures of landownership and inheritance were swept away in Scotland, they survived in eighteenth-century Catalonia in spite of the advent of a Bourbon administration eager to tighten its grip on a rebellious land. In Scotland, the government viewed the principal challenge to its authority as the clan system of the Highlands – a view amply confirmed by the Jacobite rebellions. It therefore became essential to uproot those features of Highland society that encouraged lawlessness and instability, and made it possible for clan chiefs to raise private armies. It was true that rural Catalonia, especially in the mountainous area of the Pyrenees, had a record of banditry and lawlessness comparable to that of the Scottish Highlands, but it was the cities and towns, and above all Barcelona, which had shown themselves the most fervent supporters of a system of rights and liberties that Madrid had traditionally regarded as conducive to anarchy and rebellion.

Catalan towns, like the Scottish burghs, were largely under oligarchical control in the sixteenth and seventeenth centuries. Although their systems of government included a popular element, power in Barcelona and other towns was concentrated in the hands of a hereditary class of 'honoured citizens', together with members of the professional classes, like lawyers and physicians. To these were added a growing number of honoured citizens of royal creation as the seventeenth century advanced.[61] By suppressing city councils, like Barcelona's famous Council of a Hundred (the Consell de Cent), and making the new magistrates, or *regidores*, appointees of the Crown or the Audiencia, the Bourbon administration broke the power of the old municipal oligarchies. It then had to find reliable figures for civic appointments. In a society infused by notions of social hierarchy the regime naturally turned to members of the landholding nobility and gentry to occupy posts from which many of them had hitherto been excluded by municipal rules and regulations. The first half of the eighteenth century therefore saw a progressive aristocratization of Catalan municipal government.[62]

Although in 1716 the Crown seized control of the lands and lordships of *austracista* nobles, with the passage of time many of these nobles were quietly reintegrated into Catalan society and into civic and public life, just as happened with their Jacobite counterparts in post-1715 Scotland.[63] Meanwhile, in deference to the social order, the seigneurial regime in the countryside was left untouched, and ecclesiastical and lay landlords continued, unlike Scottish landlords after 1748, to enjoy jurisdictional rights. At the end of the century, therefore, Catalonia was still a society with many seigneurial and feudal remnants. Some 55 per cent of the population remained subject to seigneurial justice administered by baronial courts exercising civil and criminal jurisdiction. As peasants and their lawyers contested baronial rights, the barons sought to defend them by appealing to royal justice.[64]

The financial weight of the feudal burden imposed on the rural population, however, remains uncertain. When added to the *cadastre* and other royal taxes, seigneurial dues could consume a significant portion of a peasant's income, but commutation into cash payments of dues collected in kind tended to reduce the proportion over the course of the century. Many peasants, too, could claim 'usufructory' rights, handed down from generation to generation under the form of lease known as emphyteusis that gave tenants and their heirs substantial security of tenure in return for a continuing obligation to farm the land and to pay ground rent and certain feudal dues. Landlords might contest their rights in the royal courts, but the fifteenth-century Sentence of Guadalupe, by which Ferdinand the Catholic had brought the peasant uprisings to an end, had led to the creation of a class of substantial peasant farmers. Nominally feudal tenants, these peasant farmers had effectively come to treat their landholdings as their own. Living in their *masies*, or farmsteads, they were to be the driving force behind the great movement of agrarian improvement and expansion of the eighteenth century.[65]

In Scotland and Catalonia alike, incorporating union had inevitably brought about important political and administrative changes to the old order. Resistance to those changes proved to be stronger and more long-lasting in Scotland than in Catalonia, partly because of the Highlands question and partly because military coercion – a constant in the life of the principality – was almost non-existent in Scotland before the 1740s. Yet in both countries, resistance went hand in hand with a sometimes grudging but often willing acceptance of the new status quo. The loss of what, until the early eighteenth century, had been at least relative independence, was to a greater or lesser extent offset by gains in other directions. The sheer fact of disruptive change can itself stimulate new ways of thinking, and by the middle years of the century both Scots and Catalans were developing their own creative responses to the challenges and opportunities that incorporation into new-style polities were bringing in their train.

New Opportunities

Between the 1720s and the early nineteenth century, Scotland and Catalonia both experienced a number of dramatic transformations. Among the most striking was the growth in the number of their inhabitants. Scotland's population around 1700 numbered a little over a million. A contemporary estimate for the 1750s put the figure at around 1,265,000 (about half that of Ireland), and thereafter, in spite of significant emigration, there was continuous and accelerating growth. The census of 1801 gave Scotland a population of 1,608,000, as compared with a population of some twenty million for England and Wales. By 1821, Scotland's population had risen spectacularly to just over two million. The statistics for eighteenth-century Catalonia have been much debated, but a population of possibly 700,000 in 1717 may nearly have doubled over the course of seventy years to reach 1,200,000 in 1787, in a total Spanish population of over ten million.

If almost every region registered growth, the increase was uneven: in Scotland, from the second half of the century, the central belt saw the largest population increase, and in Catalonia the west and south. In both countries much of the increase was concentrated in the towns. A Scotland that was among the least urbanized countries in seventeenth-century Europe came fourth in the league table by 1800, thanks to dramatic increases in the previous few decades, with the number of Glasgow's inhabitants rising from nearly 32,000 in 1755 to almost 84,000 in 1800, and those of Edinburgh from 57,000 to nearly 82,000 in the same period. In Catalonia, Barcelona's coastal region and hinterland had been the scene of precocious urbanization in the later sixteenth and early seventeenth centuries, and population density in the towns of this region is estimated to have risen from 11 inhabitants to the square kilometre in 1553 to 22.2 in 1707.[66] Urban growth accelerated in the eighteenth century. By 1787 the number of Catalan towns with more than 5,000 inhabitants at the start of the century had risen from four to fourteen, and Barcelona had tripled its population to over 100,000, making it substantially larger than eighteenth-century Edinburgh.[67]

Urbanization came late to north Britain in comparison with the Barcelona littoral. The later eighteenth century, however, saw a dramatic spurt in Scotland, even by continental European standards of the period, although the England of 1800 remained more urbanized than Scotland.[68] But if urbanization was widespread in eighteenth-century Europe, the Castilian interior of the Iberian Peninsula remained outside the trend. The exception was the national capital, Madrid, whose population grew over the course of the century from around 115,000 to 180,000, as compared with Barcelona's 100,000.[69]

As with urbanization, the economic growth and social and cultural changes experienced by eighteenth-century Scotland and Catalonia fit into a wider, European, pattern. Both had become by the end of the century exceptionally dynamic societies, with domestic conditions and an external projection that stood in marked contrast to their situation a hundred years earlier. The obvious question is the degree to which the remarkable changes they underwent over the course of the eighteenth century can be attributed to their fuller incorporation into the larger political units constituted by Great Britain and Spain. There can be no clear-cut answer to the question of whether, after the first years of dislocation and disruption had passed, incorporating union was more beneficial than the possible alternatives either to the well-being of the inhabitants of Scotland and Catalonia, or to the long-term national development of the two countries. It can never be known what would have happened if, at the beginning of the eighteenth century, they had permanently broken away from the larger units to which they had until then been fairly loosely attached, and, like Portugal in the 1640s, made their own way in the world as independent states.

During the negotiations that led to the Treaty of Utrecht in 1713, at a time when the situation of the anti-Bourbon resistance movement had become desperate, Catalonia's representatives in London and The Hague, harking back to Pau Claris's plans for independence in 1640, urged on the allies the case for a free Catalan republic as a possible option if the great powers were to give up the fight.[70] In their earlier rebellion Catalans had taken the success of the Dutch as an example of how economic potential could be realized from small beginnings and in highly adverse circumstances.[71] With its prosperity based on its global outreach and the industriousness and entrepreneurship of its inhabitants, the Dutch Republic remained a potent model for early eighteenth-century Europeans, and not least for the Catalans.

The agrarian, industrial and commercial advances made in Catalonia before the conflicts of the 1690s and the War of the Spanish Succession suggest that confidence in the principality's economic future was not misplaced. At a time when Castile was still suffering from acute monetary fluctuations, the Catalan monetary system was stable, and this stability had laid the foundations for economic growth. The rural economy, benefiting from the demographic recovery that followed the mid-century plague, was showing a renewed vitality, assisted by a growing demand, both in northern Europe and Spanish America, for wines and brandy produced in the Penedès and the region around Tarragona. In spite of French competition, the rural textile industry, as distinct from that of Barcelona, was enjoying success with its new draperies, and the smaller port towns along the Mediterranean coast had grown in size and wealth on the strength of their importation of commodities for Barcelona and their export of the agrarian produce of the Catalan interior. Merchants, with their eyes on the domestic Spanish market and the Indies trade, were organizing themselves into companies based in Barcelona, Mataró and other Mediterranean ports, and creating a business community with an increasingly influential voice in the principality's affairs. It was in this promising environment that Feliu de la Peña and his circle dreamed up their grand projects for the economic revival of Catalonia and Spain.[72]

Although two decades of war interrupted this story of economic growth, the groundwork had been laid for the impressive development of the Catalan economy of the middle and later years of the eighteenth century. The same holds true of Scotland. The famine years of the 1690s, like the warfare that ravaged Catalonia in the same period, interrupted but did not wipe out the gains made in the decades since the Restoration. There were parts of Scotland, and not only in the Lowlands, where improvements had been made both in methods of cultivation and in tenancy arrangements, giving leaseholders greater security and thus making possible the development and consolidation of a class of substantial tenant farmers, comparable to the farmstead peasants – the peasants of the *mas* – of rural Catalonia. Increasing demand in the towns, and especially Edinburgh, encouraged the growth of a market economy, and at least before the crisis years of the 1690s,

Scotland was producing enough food not only to feed itself but also to generate a sufficient surplus to allow the export of grain to the continent. Cattle on the hoof were being exported to England from the 1660s,[73] and by 1700 the English market for cattle, sheep, linen, coal and salt accounted, in value, for 40 per cent of Scotland's foreign trade.[74]

Scotland's commercial networks, like those of Catalonia, were disrupted by the continental wars of the late seventeenth and early eighteenth century, and investment in large-scale commercial ventures was hampered in both nations by the shortage of capital, exacerbated, where Scotland was concerned, by the Darien disaster. Growth had remained patchy in spite of the economic advances of the later seventeenth century, and the economies of both countries were vulnerable when they emerged from the upheavals and dislocations caused by war and incorporating union. Both had begun the process of redirecting their trade towards newer and potentially more profitable markets – the English market for Scotland, the wider Iberian market for Catalonia – but in both instances they came up against protectionist policies that limited their success. Equally, both countries, in their search for new overseas markets, were turning towards the expanding economies of the British and Spanish Atlantic, but were finding difficulty in inserting themselves into pre-existing and firmly regulated trading networks.

It is hard to see how, in the circumstances, they could have overcome these economic problems if they had tried to do so on their own. Scotland was being inexorably drawn into the economic orbit of England and the English Atlantic, while an independent Catalonia would have found it difficult to avoid becoming economically and politically dependent on the English and the Dutch, just as eighteenth-century Portugal, even though possessing an overseas empire, could not avoid being transformed into a British satellite. For the Scots and the Catalans alike, exclusion from the larger political unit to which they were geographically attached would certainly have meant more restrictions on access to the markets they needed for survival.

In both instances, therefore, the economic benefits of incorporating union would seem to have been substantial, although the individual and collective skills, resources and commitment of Scots and Catalans would be needed if those benefits were to be fully reaped. With the groundwork in both societies laid in the seventeenth century, both rose to the occasion in the eighteenth. In Catalonia, as the agrarian economy shifted towards viticulture in response to a rising demand from peninsular and external markets, that century saw a fivefold increase in the revenues of those who either owned land or held favourable leaseholds.[75]

The structure of rural life, which left the indivisible inheritance of the *mas* – the farmstead – in the hands of a single heir, encouraged agrarian improvement, while compelling the younger sons, the *fadristerns*, who received a monetary compensation in return for their exclusion from the inheritance of the family property, to make their living in Barcelona or elsewhere. Agrarian profits were ploughed into trade as well as into the land, and then from the 1740s, when trade was again disrupted by war, into calico printing and cotton production, which would lay the foundations of Catalonia's future industrialization.[76] Across Catalonia during the course of the eighteenth century a new, dynamic entrepreneurial class, drawn from families of artisans, shopkeepers and substantial peasantry, was emerging – a class energetically engaged in building and extending family businesses with a view to the expanding peninsular market, and which identified itself increasingly with the rest of Spain.[77]

It was in this century that the Catalans, shedding some of the negative images that had accumulated around them, acquired their reputation as industrious workers – 'the most hard-working of all the peoples of Spain', as they were described in 1747.[78] Cohesion was given to Catalonia's social structure by the strong sense of family relationships, which saw the heir to the family patrimony supporting the entrepreneurial activities of younger sons who would not forget their obligations to him and to the family home after making their money in trade or manufacturing. In this way, too, close ties were maintained between town and the country.[79] Yet by no means all the economic achievements of eighteenth-century Catalans can be ascribed to their close-knit family relationships and their own individual efforts. They also profited from intervention by the Bourbon state, in the form of protective legislation in 1717 and 1728 that provided the initial opportunity for import-substitution, just as they profited from concessions to Catalan manufacturers granted by a central government increasingly concerned to promote Spain's economic recovery.[80]

These and other concessions led to a growing acceptance of the Bourbon regime by the territorial, mercantile and business elite, and also by those lower down the social scale, like shopkeepers, artisans and small peasant farmers, who had benefited from the new-found political stability.[81] Inevitably there were important disagreements with Madrid, not least over the role of guilds and of private enterprise in manufacturing. Catalans regarded both as fundamental to their successes, whereas royal ministers had more *dirigiste* ideas for the attainment of economic growth.[82] Yet there was sufficient identity of interests between Barcelona and Madrid for Antoni de Capmany, the great Catalan economic thinker and writer at the turn of the later eighteenth and early nineteenth centuries, to be happy to speak of Bourbon Spain as his 'nation' – a nation of which his native Catalonia, his *pàtria*, formed an integral part.[83]

Yet, in comparison with what was happening in the British Isles, Catalonia can hardly be said to have been integrated into an especially dynamic economic complex. It is true that in the late seventeenth century the economy of the interior saw the beginnings of Castilian recovery from its long stagnation, and it showed further signs of improvement over the course of the eighteenth. It is true, also, that the peripheral regions of the peninsula, like Catalonia itself, were displaying a new vitality, and that the government in Madrid was taking active measures to encourage agrarian, commercial and industrial development. There were important changes, too, in social attitudes, as local and regional societies – most notably the 'Societies of Friends of the Country' (Amigos del País) – were founded to promote improvements and economic growth.[84] Yet the government was constantly obstructed in its reforming efforts by entrenched opposition to its projects and by its inability to impose its policies on a peninsula poorly integrated in its economy and in its transportation networks, in spite of the administrative reforms initiated by Philip V. The defeat of its attempts to impose a common external tariff on all Spain, with the resulting need to restore internal customs barriers between Castile and the Crown of Aragon to compensate for the difference between Catalan and Castilian external tariffs, was symptomatic of the problems that it faced.[85]

Unlike Catalonia, eighteenth-century Scotland was hitched to an economy in full expansionist flow. Rising production and national income, generated by major agricultural improvements and growing overseas trade with the colonies, had created by the middle decades of the century a prosperous and increasingly self-confident society. While the inclusion of Scots within the British protectionist system undermined their traditional North Sea and continental trades, the permanent opening of the English market offered them exciting opportunities, and they showed themselves ready to seize them. With many Scottish merchants firmly established in London, and others active in the colonies, confidence was well justified. Memories of the liquidity crisis of the 1690s were receding, and the risks of investment were now substantially reduced.

It was not only the merchant community that benefited from the more benign economic environment. Scottish landowners had been catching up with the English in their enthusiasm for agricultural improvement, and in 1723 a 'Society of Improvers in the Knowledge of Agriculture' was founded in Edinburgh. Highland farming continued to present many difficulties, but the numerous improvements made in Lowland farming in the first half of the century were followed in its second half by a transition to more intensive farming, encouraged by increased commercialization and higher levels of investment. The result was an agricultural revolution.[86]

Initially, the advent of Union proved more problematic for industrial than agricultural development, leaving a real possibility that Scottish manufactures would wither, and that post-Union Scotland would be relegated to the status of a mere supplier of food and raw materials to the English market. The woollen industry was hard hit by English competition, and the all-important linen industry was not only subjected to new levies but was also hampered by defective techniques that made it uncompetitive. But it received a stimulus from the Bounty Act of 1742 which, by offering a bounty on the export of British linens, encouraged exports to the American colonies, where there was a strong demand for coarse linen.

The future, however, lay, as it did in Catalonia, with cotton manufacture, which would develop out of the linen industry. From small beginnings in the 1730s, cotton production was revolutionized by the advent of water power in the late 1770s and the coming of mass manufacture with the opening of the New Lanark mills in 1786. The factory system had arrived in Scotland, preparing the way for the future industrial revolution and the emergence of an industrial proletariat.[87] There were some parallels here with the industry's development in Catalonia, where spinning machinery, copied from England, was introduced in the 1790s, although small-scale production units survived much longer in Catalonia than Scotland, and the break with artisanal production, when it came in the 1830s and 1840s, was correspondingly more dramatic.[88]

In a range of industries – iron manufacturing, wool, pottery, glass-making – eighteenth-century Scottish manufacturers, unlike Catalan entrepreneurs, benefited from their proximity to a more advanced economy than their own, and could draw on more advanced English methods and on English expertise. It was two English entrepreneurs, John Roebuck and Samuel Garbett, who founded the famous Carron ironworks in south Stirlingshire in 1759.[89] Above all, proximity was translated, at least from the 1740s onwards, into a high degree of incorporation into a British commercial system more comprehensive and efficient than that of Spain, where controls and customs dues continued to hamper effective integration. Without the Union, Scottish exports would have run into an English tariff wall. Without it, too, they would probably have lacked the encouragement of bounties like the Bounty Act for linens of 1742.[90]

Along with access to an English market characterized by high consumer demand, Scottish merchants and businessmen enjoyed the supreme advantage, denied their Catalan counterparts, of easy geographical access to the fast-growing markets of colonial America. The Clyde ports were ideally placed for engagement in the British Atlantic trade. Scottish merchants had been infiltrating this trade on a casual basis since the seventeenth century, but from the 1720s their intervention became increasingly organized, and Scottish ports were soon vigorously competing with the west-coast ports of England. By methods both open and clandestine, Scots merchants forced their way into the tobacco trade with the southern mainland colonies. By the 1760s Glasgow, with sailing times to British America two to three weeks faster than those from the English Channel ports,[91] had become the tobacco capital of Britain's Atlantic economy. The massive trade in tobacco imports and re-exports brought an inflow of capital needed for further investment, and helped shift the balance of the economy from the east to the west coast of Scotland. It also stimulated the growth of other Scottish industries besides linen, as Scots merchants built up a network of transatlantic contacts, and used them to provision the West Indies and the mainland colonies with Scottish goods.[92]

Participation in an expanding Atlantic economy was as enticing a prospect to the Catalans as it was to the Scots, but they were faced with greater obstacles in achieving it. As long as Cadiz was the sole emporium of the Spanish Atlantic trade, it was primarily through that city that Catalan merchants had to operate. Although Cadiz and its merchant Consulate still maintained its monopoly, wartime conditions during the War of Jenkins's Ear (1739–48) led to a first loosening of restrictions. British naval blockades and attacks on Atlantic shipping forced the Crown to suspend the transatlantic convoys and allow 'registered ships' to make the crossing on their own. The convoys to the Mexican viceroyalty of New Spain were restored once the war was over, but the lifting of restrictions had given Catalan merchants in Cadiz an opportunity to increase their exports to the Indies of Catalan wines, brandy and other products, and to install agents in the major Spanish American ports.[93]

In 1756 Madrid, anxious to increase revenues from the Indies trade, authorized the founding of a chartered company, the Royal Company of Barcelona, to trade with designated Caribbean ports, but the company, underfunded and poorly managed, was not a success and came to a virtual end in the 1780s. Catalan family firms wanted greater freedom of action than a monopolistic company could afford, and preferred to take advantage of reforming measures, starting in 1765, that were intended by the ministers of Charles III to promote economic growth and thus assist a hard-pressed royal treasury. The 1765 decree allowed for the first time direct trade by individually registered ships sailing from Barcelona and eight other Spanish ports to the West Indies. More American ports were added in succeeding years, and small colonies of Catalan merchants established themselves in major port cities like Havana, Vera Cruz, Cartagena and Buenos Aires. These reforms culminated in the famous *comercio libre* decree of 1778, by which thirteen Spanish ports, including Barcelona, were confirmed in, or granted, the right to trade directly with Spain's 'empire of the Indies'.[94]

Comercio libre was far from being a system of 'free trade' in the modern understanding of the term, but it broke the transatlantic commercial monopoly enjoyed by Cadiz, in effect allowing a select number of Spanish ports a limited share in the trade. Once merchants from Barcelona and the Catalan coastal towns secured a firm foothold in the Indies in the years after 1765, they were well positioned to ignore or circumvent obstructive regulations, and participate, legally or illegally, in such profitable fields of activity as the sugar and slave trades.

Permission for direct trade with America was clearly an important step towards the expansion of Catalonia's regional economy, but Barcelona did not have the advantages enjoyed by an Atlantic port like Corunna. To some extent, though, the relative disadvantage of its geographical location was offset by a number of assets. Barcelona was now the hub of a well-integrated regional economy, with a strong agrarian sector and a growing industrial base. Catalonia's exports to the rest of the peninsula and to other parts of Europe of wine, spirits and dried fruits, along with textiles and other manu-factured goods, had provided its businessmen with capital for investment in agriculture, industry and trade. It possessed well-established family firms and a flourishing mercantile community, supported by a commission for trade, the Junta de Comercio, established in Barcelona in 1758. It had also built up a network of national and international contacts and had acquired growing experience of American trading conditions. Where Cadiz had become the prisoner of vested interests created over time, Barcelona, as a relative latecomer to the Atlantic trading system, enjoyed a greater degree of flexibility and more room for manoeuvre.

The capacity of Catalan merchants and entrepreneurs to adjust to the new opportunities was reflected in the increase in Catalan agricultural and industrial exports to the Indies and the consequent inflow of American silver for reinvestment in the local economy. It was also reflected in the impressive growth of the shipbuilding industry in the dockyards of Barcelona and the

Mediterranean littoral, mirroring the growth of shipbuilding in the Clyde ports in response to Scotland's entry into the economy of the British Atlantic.[95] Yet in spite of these advances, Catalonia in the mid-1780s still had only a minimal average share, 4.34 per cent, of Spain's exports to the Indies, and its transatlantic trade was heavily weighted in favour of agricultural produce rather than the products of its textile industry, which were still of insufficient quality for a demanding American market.[96]

Some at least of the difficulties experienced by Catalan merchants in establishing themselves in Spain's transatlantic empire were, however, not so much a consequence of Catalan failings as of long-standing weaknesses in the Spanish Atlantic system. For all Madrid's protectionist regulations, Spanish industry had long shown itself unable to provide manufactured goods of the quality, or in the quantity, required by an expanding Spanish American market. Inevitably the gap had been filled by Spain's foreign rivals, who had been infiltrating the Atlantic trade from the early seventeenth century, and used the Caribbean islands and points along the coastline of mainland America to engage in massive smuggling. In the face of this competition from cheaper and more readily available foreign manufactures, it was difficult for any region of Spain to break into the American market for industrial products in the way that Scotland was able to break into the markets of the West Indies and Britain's North American settlements.

Scottish merchants were able to take greater advantage of the possibilities because they now formed part of an empire that possessed the naval power to enforce its protectionist policies, and was more commercially oriented than that of Spain. The regions covered by this empire were vastly extended by the string of British victories in the Seven Years War of 1756–63, many of them won with the help of Scottish regiments. Following the old Scottish tradition of military service in foreign parts, Scots officers and men were to be found spread across the globe, whether in the service of the East India Company, or stationed in the Caribbean and the mainland American colonies. Between 1777 and 1800 the Highlands alone produced twenty line regiments for the British Army.[97]

The reordering of the British Isles after the Revolution of 1688–9 and the Treaty of Union of 1707, and the reorganization of Spain following the Nueva Planta of 1707–16, brought benefits as well as costs to peoples who, following the changes, found themselves enclosed more tightly within state structures that the majority viewed as alien. That general reordering also brought costs and benefits to the state structures into which they were incorporated. The later seventeenth and eighteenth centuries witnessed the development of a European-wide phenomenon, the emergence of 'fiscal-military' states – monarchies possessed of greater military and naval capacity than their predecessors and an enhanced bureaucratic outreach.[98] Eighteenth-century Britain and Spain were fiscal-military states on an imperial scale. They needed huge resources to build up and maintain the armies and fleets required for imperial defence, and to meet the multifarious costs involved in administering and running distant overseas possessions.

The most obvious device for meeting the rising costs of the state was to generate more income by raising the level of taxation and improving and extending tax-raising systems. This was the policy pursued in the Crown of Aragon following the imposition of the Nueva Planta. But some regions were simply too poor to sustain higher tax levels over any length of time, and early eighteenth-century Scotland, to a greater extent than Ireland, fell into the category of the impoverished. Neither, however, was capable of supplying substantial monetary surpluses on a reliable basis.[99] Yet there were other ways to extract resources from societies in which money was scarce, and one of the most valuable was the exploitation of their manpower. Eighteenth-century Scotland, like Ireland, could offer this in ample measure, providing officers and men for British armies, and settlers for its colonies.

The Scots, unlike the Catalans, had long been a migrant people. They had moved in large numbers into Ireland in the seventeenth century,[100] and had begun settling in America even before the Union. Now, as participants in a worldwide empire, the range of possibilities that lay before them was enormously expanded. Immigrants from the British Isles to North America had a good chance of being able to pursue their craft or trade in the growing cities of the Atlantic seaboard, or of settling and cultivating the nominally 'vacant' land of Indian peoples who could either be marginalized or pushed deeper into the interior of the continent. Immigrants to Spain's 'empire of the Indies', on the other hand, found themselves competing for jobs in cities with increasing numbers of white, mixed-blood and Indian inhabitants, and their opportunities for the acquisition and settlement of land lay mostly in the empire's expanding borderlands.

It was only with the 1765 decree and the advent of *comercio libre* in 1778 that inhabitants of the eastern regions of the Iberian Peninsula began to move to America in significant numbers.[101] Even then, however, the majority of the Catalans who crossed the Atlantic did so as merchants or factors of commercial enterprises, or else as members of the religious orders. Once there, they inserted themselves into existing Catalan networks and went about their business, but showed little inclination to settle permanently in America, and kept in close contact with the homeland to which they hoped one day to return. Growing numbers of Scots, by contrast, were willing to make a new home for themselves overseas, although Scottish emigration to America began on a really large scale only after the ending of the Seven Years War in 1763. Ten years later, writing his account of his tour of the Hebrides with Dr Johnson, James Boswell noted 'the present rage for emigration'.[102]

Statistics are very uncertain, but perhaps 30,000 Scots, or 500 a year, emigrated to America between the beginning of the eighteenth century and 1763. Some 40,000 went to the mainland colonies between 1760 and 1775; and another 5,000 in the war-torn period between the end of the American War of Independence and the turn of the new century, giving a total of 75,000 migrants to mainland America for the century as a whole. Immigrants came from both the Lowlands and the Highlands, with the Highlanders tending to emigrate as whole communities and staying together after they reached North America. Here they would concentrate in certain regions, like Nova Scotia, the Upper Hudson valleys and North Carolina, where they could pursue their former rural activities of farming or cattle-rearing. Yet although Highland emigration has enjoyed much of the historical limelight, the number of Lowland emigrants seems to have been substantially higher, in spite of some spectacular figures for emigration from the Highlands between 1773 and 1776.[103]

Many of the emigrants, particularly from the Lowlands, were skilled workers or tradesmen, and large numbers were drawn to settle in those areas of America where Scottish communities already existed. Others were the counterparts of the Catalan *fadristerns* – younger sons of laird, or gentry, families with no inheritance prospects at home. Many of these families found themselves in trouble as the structure of Scottish landholding changed during the course of the eighteenth century. At the start of the century only about half of the 9,500 or so of the country's landowners had the right to inherit or sell the land they possessed, and as the century advanced the great landowners ruthlessly tightened their grip and extended their territorial control. Subjected to such heavy pressure, those without inheritance prospects looked for ways of escape. In the decades of relative European peace after the ending of the War of the Spanish Succession, the traditional outlet for the ambitious and the dispossessed – military service on the continent – no longer provided the opportunities of earlier times. Now, though, the expansion of the British fiscal-military state appeared to offer a whole range of glittering possibilities for impoverished Scots. Not all, by any means, planned to leave their homeland forever. Merchants, soldiers and seamen were, by the nature of their vocation, people on the move.

Others saw in mainland America or the West Indies, and in service with the East India Company, glittering possibilities for making a quick fortune, and not a few would return home as wealthy nabobs or as absentee West Indian planters.[104]

Most of them, however, would need initial help. Here the natural instinct of the Scots to give each other a helping hand came into its own, as also did the inclusion of Scotland in a generalized British system of outdoor relief. As prime minister, Walpole used the many patronage opportunities both at the heart of empire and in the overseas territories to tighten his ministry's hold over Scottish political life. Already from the 1720s Scots were appearing in India. By the end of the century their presence in the subcontinent would be all-pervasive, whether as servants of the East India Company or as officers and soldiers in the fourteen regiments – seven of them Scottish – garrisoning the Indian provinces. Walpole was quick to see the immense patronage potential of the East India Company, on which he could easily bring governmental pressure to bear. He needed political stability in Scotland, and, at Westminster, the votes of Scottish members of parliament. Scotland's needs dovetailed neatly with his own. While the Earl of Ilay, later the third Duke of Argyll, would manage Scottish politics and patronage for the Prime Minister, he in turn would make sure that the Scots were well placed in the queue for East Indian bounty.[105]

Later in the century Henry Dundas, Solicitor General, Lord Advocate and Keeper of the Signet, fulfilled much the same functions as Ilay. His high-level connections with successive administrations gave him unrivalled opportunities for influencing overseas appointments, although, on becoming a commissioner of the Board of Control of the East India Company and in 1793 its president, he was careful to avoid accusations of excessively favouring his compatriots for Indian posts. Successful applicants were likely to owe more to Warren Hastings, 'Scotland's Benefactor' and India's predator, than to Dundas.

The Scotsmen appointed to high office in India, or to governorships in the West Indies, would in turn appoint fellow Scots to lesser administrative posts that offered useful opportunities for gainful employment.[106] In the early stages of a dazzling political career Dundas himself enjoyed the patronage of the first Scot to become a British prime minister, the Earl of Bute. It was probably to Bute, also, that a serving naval officer, George Johnstone, owed his unexpected appointment in 1764 to the governorship of the newly acquired British colony of West Florida. The Johnstones, a Dumfriesshire family of eleven siblings whose members treated the world as their oyster, were only one of the many Scottish families to benefit, both directly and indirectly, from imperial opportunities. In the 1730s and 1740s seven Johnstone brothers left their homeland for foreign parts, and embarked on overseas careers, whether as military and naval officers, merchants, East India Company servants, or plantation and slave owners in the West Indies. Later, two of their sisters travelled to India.[107]

Mortality rates were high for those who hoped to make a fortune in the West Indies or the Indian subcontinent, but the potential rewards for the survivors were huge, whether they carved out careers on their own or signed up to syndicates. Richard Oswald and Alexander Grant, for example, joined Scottish associates in acquiring an African slave factory at Bance Island at the mouth of the Sierra Leone river. With their profits from the slave trade, members of the syndicate were able to cash in on the plantation economies of the West Indies and engage in lucrative land speculation in the mainland colonies.[108]

The life stories of the Johnstones and of Oswald and Grant provide vivid personal evidence of the way in which the British imperial state became embedded in regional and local Scottish society, with effects at many different social levels. Yet they also show how their activities served the interests of the imperial state. This was a two-way relationship from which both parties stood to gain. The empire acquired the services of capable military and naval officers, merchants and administrators who extended its influence and global effectiveness. Those who served it, on the other hand, were offered opportunities for gainful employment of a kind that was not available at home, along with the chance of profits on a scale of which they could scarcely have dreamed.

Overseas family connections and experiences enriched Scottish life at many levels. It made even those who never left home better informed about distant worlds. It brought exotic new commodities to their homes, like the Indian muslins sent back to the Johnstones, and, in the process, had a transforming effect on the family's attitudes and sensibilities. Above all, the vast profits that accrued to those who made a success of their overseas activities allowed them to enrich their families back home, to buy new estates or expand old ones, and to commission or acquire country and town houses built in the neo-classical style that Scottish architects, most notably James Gibbs and the Adam brothers, did so much to make fashionable throughout the British Isles.

These kinds of possibilities were rarely open to eighteenth-century Catalans, for most of whom the association with empire was at best very marginal. In 1760 the Catalans were complaining that the promise made in the Nueva Planta of reciprocity in appointments to civil and ecclesiastical office had not been kept, and that the best positions in the Crown of Aragon were being taken by Castilians.[109] In the circumstances there was little chance of Catalans securing high office in the Spanish imperial bureaucracy, although Manuel de Amat y Junient, the younger son of a Catalan noble family, crowned a military career in Europe and North Africa with his appointment as Captain-General of Chile and then as Viceroy of Peru – a post he held for an unprecedented fifteen years, from 1761 to 1776. Here he made the most of the numerous opportunities for which a posting to Lima was notorious. On his return to Barcelona he built for his young wife the handsome palace of the vicereine (the Palau de la Virreina) on the Rambla out of the fortune of five million pesos he allegedly amassed during his lengthy tenure of office.[110]

If the doors to overseas service were largely closed to Catalans, the opportunities provided by empire and the expansion of the imperial bureaucracy did much to reconcile a significant cross-section of Scottish society to the Union by integrating Scottish men and women into the wider economic, social and cultural community of Britain and its overseas possessions. Yet closer integration did not automatically promote that 'union of hearts' which James VI/I had longed to bring about more than a century before. On the contrary, the dynamism and opportunism of the Scots, their success in running off with the spoils of empire, and their growing visibility on the streets of London, set alarm bells ringing. In the early 1760s an upsurge of virulent anti-Scottish English nationalism found expression in the obloquy heaped on the unhappy person of Lord Bute. It was manifested, too, in the famous incident at Covent Garden, recounted by Boswell, when two Highland officers, returning victorious from the capture of Havana, entered the theatre only to be greeted with cries of 'No Scots! No Scots! Out with them!'[111] The Scots, it was felt, were getting above themselves, and the very extent of their contribution to what was no longer an English but a common British enterprise was beginning to rankle.

As the Scots were discovering, to Boswell's indignation, losses as well as gains were involved in joining this common British enterprise. The derision and dislike they were liable to encounter south of the border raised troubling questions. These questions, although at the deepest level touching on the nature of Scottishness, were primarily related to Scotland's place in post-1707 Britain and the ways in which the Union could be used to improve Scottish civil society and free it from the shackles of a feudal past.[112] This was a burning issue in the eighteenth century because of the historic existence of two Scotlands, the Lowlands and the Gaelic-speaking Highlands, which had given Scotland its central foundation myths of Scota and the ancestry of the Scottish royal line.[113]

Lowland Scotland failed to develop an alternative founding myth of its own, leaving the legends that swirled through the mists of the Gaelic Highlands to hold undisputed sway. Yet although Highlands and Lowlands were to become fused in the historical imagination into a single Scottish *patria*,[114] the Lowlanders had long been accustomed to thinking of the Highlands as a savage region different from themselves. Consequently, ever since the Reformation they had sought to extirpate its barbaric customs, and instil among its inhabitants their own culture, language and values.

The values were those of Presbyterianism. The culture was that of the nobility, the gentry and the professional classes of the burghs – a culture heavily marked by proximity to England, and one that had long interacted with English lifestyles and manners. Intermarriage between the higher nobility of the two countries since the Union of the Crowns, a growing tendency to give the children of Anglo-Scottish marriages an English education, and the conscious attempt of sections of the ruling elite to 'improve' their homeland by emulating English tastes and fashions, had all contributed to the anglicization of parts of Scottish society. Yet instead of being embraced by their English neighbours, Scots who travelled to, or settled in, England could find themselves cold-shouldered. Even their language – the 'Scots' that they were so careful to differentiate from the barbaric Gaelic of the Highlands – gave rise to mockery. The popularity of elocution lessons for the teaching of correct English pronunciation was testimony to an underlying anxiety about what it meant to be Scottish in the post-Union era.[115]

Was Scotland to be no more than a political and cultural appendage of its more powerful neighbour? Belonging and yet not belonging, eighteenth-century Scots were faced with the dilemma of every 'provincial' society. At once proud of their history and accomplishments, and yet uneasily aware of being looked upon by the dominant society as in some way inferior, they struggled to disprove the allegation of inferiority and to locate themselves as equal partners in a changed relationship. This was a challenge that was also faced by eighteenth-century Ireland, and by the increasingly self-confident colonies of British America. It was faced, too, by the no less 'provincial' society of eighteenth-century Catalonia as it struggled to find its place in a Spain dominated by Castile.

The Scots had the advantage over the Catalans of being actively involved in the construction of a global empire, and one that defined itself not as English but as British. It was as the Scottish members of a British Empire rapidly outpacing that of Spain – an empire that could take pride in its unique blend of freedom, religious tolerance and commercial enterprise – that they would be able to make their mark in the world.[116] They were British, but not

English, while still remaining patriotic Scots. The options available to eighteenth-century Catalans were less immediately attractive. Although Antoni de Capmany might refer to Spain as his 'nation',[117] it is difficult to determine the degree to which his compatriots actually thought of themselves as 'Spaniards', although there were strong indications by the later eighteenth century that many of them were on their way to doing so.[118] In reality 'Catalan' and 'Spanish' were no more incompatible as descriptors of loyalty than 'Scottish' and 'British'. Yet, at least before the Napoleonic invasion in the early nineteenth century, 'Spain' remained a more abstract entity than 'Britain', and one primarily associated with the efforts of the Bourbons to construct from their administrative capital a united nation out of its fragmentary parts.[119]

Degrees of Enlightenment

When asserting their equality of status with English men and women in the British national enterprise, Scots in the 1760s and early 1770s could point to Scotland's new-found prosperity and to the dramatic improvements in the agrarian economy made in recent years. At this rate they would soon be able to abolish the stigma of backwardness long attached to them – a stigma that had threatened to condemn them to permanent subordination. By the second half of the century they could even lay claim to a degree of superiority, at least when it came to the life of the mind. In the space of four or five decades their nation had become for all Europe a beacon of cultural and intellectual enlightenment.

If the 'Scottish Enlightenment' can be dated from the publication of the first major philosophical works of Francis Hutcheson in the 1720s,[120] the groundwork had been laid well before the Union of 1707. Scotland possessed an educated professional class that was not confined to lawyers, but included medics, clerics and university professors. Its five universities offered students a generalist teaching in the arts, but had also set up specialist chairs in such subjects as mathematics, medicine and law even before 1700. Study and travel on the continent, and numerous personal and cultural connections both with continental Europe and with England, had exposed it to outside influences that helped to counteract the rigidities of a narrow Presbyterian outlook. As early as the 1660s university teachers were discussing the ideas of Descartes and Galileo, while Newton acquired a keen group of Scottish adherents in the years following the publication of his *Principia Mathematica* in 1687.[121]

Yet the closer approximation to England brought about by the Union undoubtedly gave a new impetus to the development of enlightened thinking in a Scotland that already had a strong indigenous tradition in branches of medicine, mathematics, historical writing and the law. Union expanded and facilitated the process of cultural and intellectual interchange between the two countries, introducing, where it had not already existed, a dash of emulation to the response of the Scots to an increasingly dominant English culture.[122] It also signalled new paths that were there for the taking. In particular, the notion of improvement so eagerly embraced by the Scots opened the way for them to develop the science of political economy that was to be central to their Enlightenment. David Hume and Adam Smith between them were to illustrate the dependence of modern society on material improvement, offering their own recipes for the continuation of social and economic progress.[123]

There was, however, another way in which Union is likely to have encouraged the process of Enlightenment. The very fact of Scotland's political relegation to provincial status provided an inducement not simply to emulate the English but to shine in alternative fields of endeavour. Since the start of the century, Edinburgh, like Barcelona, had become a former capital city, and a puny rival to London, which was more than ten times its size.[124] With the city no longer the seat of a separate parliament, its political life, so vibrant in the years leading up to the Union, experienced a deadening at both the elite and the popular levels. In what had become a closed political system managed from London, the elite now looked to the metropolis to resolve internal conflicts and provide the order and stability for which it craved.[125] Yet, although it had lost its political centrality, Edinburgh possessed the intellectual and cultural resources to overcome the creeping sense of inferiority and achieve a compensating status as a cultural capital with its own distinctive style.

Here its very location worked to its advantage. It was sufficiently far from London to avoid being swamped by the culture of the metropolis. As late as 1763 only one regular stagecoach travelled between London and Edinburgh, and the notoriously uncomfortable journey took two weeks.[126] Although Edinburgh society looked to the London newspapers for much of its information, and kept a close eye on changing metropolitan tastes and fashions, its relative isolation left it with space to cultivate a distinctive cultural and intellectual life of its own. Members of the nobility and the professional classes, spurred by a determination to prove to themselves, as well as to others, their nation's continuing worth in the competitive environment created by the Union of 1707, joined together in clubs and voluntary associations that would promote national improvement, and provide a forum for the debating of issues of philosophical and literary concern. The

Philosophical Society of Edinburgh was founded in 1737, while the Select Society, of which David Hume was one of the founders in 1754, became the principal forum for the discussion of politics, economics, morals and the arts. Such societies were not confined to Edinburgh but were imitated by other leading towns. Glasgow had its own Literary Society, founded in 1752, and Aberdeen a Philosophical Society in 1758.[127]

Nothing can wholly explain the emergence in a single society, and sometimes even in a single city, of a cluster of figures of genius and creative talent such as that which occurred in the Edinburgh and the Scotland of the 1760s and 1770s – the Scotland of David Hume and Adam Smith, of the social theorists Adam Ferguson and John Millar, the historian William Robertson, the engineer James Watt, the physician William Cullen, and the polymath Lord Kames. In many respects, however, the environment can be seen as unusually propitious for innovative thought and action. This was a society with a long tradition of learning and of respect for the life of the mind. The law, the Church and the universities provided an institutional base on which talented individuals could build their careers without excessive dependence on intrusive patronage. The social and intellectual elite was small and homogeneous enough for easy and relatively harmonious personal contacts within a face-to-face society; and while religion continued to exercise a powerful hold over that society, the Moderates, who now controlled the General Assembly of the Kirk, were sufficiently well established to allow for the relatively unfettered pursuit of rational and scientific inquiry. Finally, the constant and creative tension between provincialism and cosmopolitanism, between indigenous traditions and practices and innovating ideas from England and continental Europe, created a climate that proved conducive to ways of thinking that transcended conventional boundaries.

With the construction from the 1760s of its New Town, graced by regularly traced streets and fine squares, Edinburgh gained an appearance appropriate to its newly acquired status as one of the intellectual capitals of enlightened Europe. The city's expansion in the later eighteenth century transformed its urban geography, altering, although more slowly, the social distribution of space, as members of the upper and professional classes began to move northwards, abandoning their crowded Old Town tenement houses for the comforts of polite living in handsome New Town residences. The contrast was sharp with contemporary Barcelona, in spite of the urban improvements that were under way by the 1770s. These included the building in 1753 by a military engineer to a grid-iron design of Barceloneta, a waterfront suburb intended to provide cheap housing for artisans and dock-workers, and the transformation of the clogged and filthy watercourse of the Rambla along the medieval edges of the city into what would in time become the city's principal avenue. Yet the city remained encased and constricted by its ring of medieval walls, a city closed in on itself and hopelessly overcrowded until the eventual demolition of the walls in the 1850s and 1860s made it possible to engage in serious town planning and massive urban expansion.[128]

This densely populated city, however, was as proud as Edinburgh of its historic pre-eminence, and no less determined to maintain its position as a national centre in the changed circumstances of the eighteenth century. Faced, like Edinburgh, with the challenge presented by relegation to provincial status, Barcelona did not follow Edinburgh's example by becoming a capital of learning and the arts. Its Acadèmia de Bones Lletres, founded in 1729 for the study of Catalonia's history, was a servile and ineffectual body.[129] Nor did the city produce any prominent figure of the European Enlightenment, with the possible exception of the historian and political economist Antoni de Capmany, whose compilation of documents and innovative ideas about the sources of the principality's economic prosperity and progress during the Middle Ages did much to shape the Catalans' image of themselves as a commercial and industrious people.[130]

The later part of Capmany's career was spent in Madrid, where from 1770 he was a member, and subsequently secretary, of the Royal Academy of History. It was as a member of this Academy that Capmany sat on a commission to examine and revise a translation of one of the great works of the Scottish Enlightenment, William Robertson's *The History of America* (1777). Although Robertson was notably impartial in his treatment of Spain's record in America, this proved to be a fruitless exercise. The commission's favourable report was overturned, publication of the Spanish edition was suspended, and circulation of the English edition was prohibited throughout Spain and its empire.[131]

There are a number of possible reasons for Barcelona's absence from the list of the leading cultural centres of the age. In spite of a late seventeenth-century renewal of interest in scientific and rational inquiry, particularly in court circles and the peripheral regions of the country,[132] Spain in general lagged notoriously behind other parts of Europe in accepting or promoting the ideals of the Enlightenment. Although Bourbon ministers were keen to promote reformist ideas and practices by founding academies and encouraging the societies for economic improvement springing up across the peninsula, much of the country remained resistant to change. The Church, the Inquisition and state censorship, while pursuing distinctive agendas of their own, all placed obstacles in the way of free-ranging inquiry, impeding the development of cultural and intellectual diversity and the toleration of dissent. The fate of Robertson's *History*, which, for all its impartiality, was condemned in Madrid for its alleged anti-Spanish bias, was characteristic of the problems faced by foreign and Spanish authors alike.[133]

If Catalonia were to develop an interest in Enlightenment thinking, it would therefore have to look beyond Spain itself. Castile was in no position to serve, as England served for Scotland, as a leading repository of new ideas and a spur to innovation, although it did act as a publishing centre for Castilian translations of foreign works deemed acceptable by the Spanish authorities. Among these publications, economic treatises held an obvious appeal for a society that was similarly being attracted by the concept of improvement, although some decades later than Scotland. In the light of his travels in the peninsula in 1786–7 Joseph Townsend could report that 'the seeds of improvement have again been sown in this country . . . In the northern provinces of the peninsula, and in Catalonia, the people are the most industrious . . .'[134] But access to European works on political economy was not always simple. In 1790 the Inquisition banned the publication of a French translation of Adam Smith's *Wealth of Nations*, 'because beneath a captious and obscure style, it favours toleration in point of religion and is conducive to naturalism'. Later that year the government overruled the Inquisition's censure, and in 1794 a Spanish translation made directly from the English original was published in Valladolid, although with the omission of some passages touching on religion.[135]

While eighteenth-century Catalans showed more interest in technical and utilitarian investigation, especially in the field of medicine, than in philosophical inquiry,[136] the country was unlikely to reaffirm its sense of national identity by means of intellectual innovation in the manner of Scotland. It could, however, achieve much by devoting itself to industry and enterprise. 'We can agree,' wrote Francisco Mariano Nifo in 1761–2, 'that if everyone in Spain were as active as the Catalans, they would all contribute usefully to the wealth and augmentation of the State.'[137] The idea of helping to bring about the renovation of Spain by making it more like Catalonia was one that became increasingly attractive to the eighteenth- and early nineteenth-century Catalan elite. To offer an example for others would indicate the unique place of Catalonia within the Spanish community of peoples, and would help complete its recovery from the sense of humiliation and loss that came with the Bourbon victory and its relegation to provincial status.

There was also a strong element of calculation at work. Catalan merchants had benefited from the liberalization of the American trade, while manufacturers were well aware that the nascent cotton industry needed the protection that only Madrid could provide. Joseph Townsend expressed his outrage at the Spanish ban on the import of Manchester cottons, 'against which there appears a peculiar enmity in this government'. 'This prohibition,' he scathingly continued, 'is now meant to favour a company of monopolists in Catalonia, who pretend to manufacture enough, but cannot produce one-tenth of the national demand ...'[138] Townsend's comments were a sign of the times. By the end of the century the mutual interests of government and the Catalan business community had done much to close the gap between Barcelona and Madrid, and testified to the development of a partnership advantageous to both.

It remained to be seen whether enhanced cooperation of this kind would be sufficient to dispel the old distrust. Would the Catalans be willing to abandon that passionate attachment to their *pàtria* which, in the eyes of José Patiño, had made them 'lose all sense of reason'?[139] Would Madrid be willing to abandon its punitive and oppressive policies, and give Catalonia space to breathe inside the Spanish 'nation' now in the process of construction? Old suspicions were not easily set aside, nor old enmities forgotten, even in the more benign British environment of the eighteenth century. James Boswell's outrage at the audience's reaction to the entry of the two Highland officers into the Covent Garden theatre suggests something of the tensions that lay beneath the surface of the Anglo-Scottish relationship.[140] 'My heart warmed to my countrymen, my Scotch blood boiled with indignation. I jumped up on the benches, roared out, "Damn you, you rascals!", hissed and was in the greatest rage ... I hated the English; I wished from my soul that the Union was broke, and that we might give them another battle of Bannockburn.' Boswell quickly recovered from his indignation and went on to enjoy the opera, but memory had shown itself to be a powerful force. The Romantic movement that swept the continent at the close of the century would give memory new wings.

CHAPTER 4

Nations and States
1789–1860

Dual Patriotism

The French Revolution and the Napoleonic Wars had a profoundly trans-forming impact on Britain and Spain alike. In both countries the fear of revolutionary contagion put a brake on reforming initiatives and ushered in a period of repressive governmental measures designed to prevent the subversion of the state by radicals infected by dangerous revolutionary ideas. In the wake of the French Revolution both countries became embroiled in war with revolutionary France, initially as allies. For Britain, this would mark the beginning of some twenty years of global warfare that would finally end in 1815 with the allied victory over Napoleon at Waterloo. While the conflict was enormously costly and placed heavy strains on the country's social fabric, a victorious Britain emerged from the war as the most advanced industrial society in Europe, the dominant player on the international stage, and the undisputed master of the seas.

For Spain, however, the story was very different.[1] Charles III died in December 1788. With the outbreak of the French Revolution some seven months later, his inept son, Charles IV, found himself trapped in a hopeless dilemma. Bourbon France was Bourbon Spain's natural ally, while, in the eyes of Madrid, a commercially dominant Britain remained, in spite of the loss of its seventeen North American colonies, the natural enemy and a continuing danger to the integrity of Spain's empire of the Indies. On the other hand, the Revolution, after overthrowing the Bourbon monarchy in France, had come to pose a direct threat to the established European order. Charles IV, as a help-less observer of the fate that overtook his cousin, Louis XVI, naturally regarded this threat as both dynastic and personal. Having jettisoned the last ministers of Charles III and entrusted power to Manuel Godoy, the young guards officer who had won the queen's favour and then his own, he swallowed the pill and joined with Britain and other European powers in a coalition designed to check the advance of the Revolution beyond the frontiers of France.

The war that broke out in the spring of 1793 was one for which Spain was hopelessly unprepared. Across the country the population rallied behind the regime in a great wave of patriotic and anti-French sentiment which suggested that the concept of Spanish nationhood that monarchs and ministers had tried to inculcate since the advent of the dynasty had become something more than a Bourbon dream. Yet if the people were ready to take action, the army was not. Catalonia and the Basque provinces were vulnerable to French attack, and in 1793–4 memories of the events of 1640 and 1705 did much to shape the policies of both Paris and Madrid towards the Catalans. The French, expecting a spontaneous Catalan uprising on the model of 1640, sent an invading army across the frontier, while the Madrid government, congenitally distrustful of the Catalans and burdened with an enormous debt, hesitated to send troops and arms to their assistance. Its lack of confidence proved to be misplaced. The Catalans mounted a strong resistance that received only belated and ineffective support from Madrid. Although the French succeeded for a time in occupying much of northern Catalonia, their forces had been beaten back by the time Spain and France made peace in July 1795.

The war, however, only aggravated a serious financial and economic situation both in Catalonia and in Spain as a whole, which was now suffering the beginnings of what would become a succession of crop failures and food shortages. The saturation of the American market had already created among Catalan exporters a loss of confidence, and the war of 1793–5 undermined it still further. But the struggle against revolutionary France was only the prelude to a series of disasters that would culminate in catastrophe in 1808. After Spain's weakness had been painfully exposed by its failures in the war, Godoy performed a volte-face and signed a treaty of alliance with the French in August 1796 at the palace of San Ildefonso. The agreement placed Spanish troops and ships at the disposal of the French, and in effect converted Spain into a satellite of France. The war with Britain that followed was a disaster for Spain. Its fleet was defeated at the battle of Cape St Vincent, and the British naval blockade of Cadiz disrupted the transatlantic trading system, creating further difficulties for Catalan exporters, while also depriving the government of the American revenues on which it depended for survival.

Although Charles IV and his queen received a rapturous welcome when they visited Barcelona in 1802,[2] the two wars with Britain, of 1796–1802 and 1804–8, coming on top of the war with revolutionary France of 1793–5, compounded the general misery of these years, and led to growing discontent over governmental mismanagement and Godoy's erratic leadership. In October 1807 Godoy yielded to pressure from Napoleon to allow French troops to march across Spain to invade Portugal, England's ally. The king's son, Ferdinand, the Prince of Asturias, was actively plotting against the favourite, and on 17 March 1808 Godoy was the target of a riot at the palace of Aranjuez orchestrated by the prince. In the wake of Godoy's overthrow and imprisonment a bewildered Charles IV abdicated in favour of his son. On 3 March French forces under the command of General Murat moved into Madrid, and the next day Ferdinand received an ecstatic welcome on entering his capital. But if he now thought that he possessed all the attributes of power, he was promptly disillusioned. Napoleon had other ideas for the future of Spain. He packed Ferdinand off to Bayonne to join his parents in exile, and forced the new monarch, like his father, to abdicate. The Bourbons' involuntary abdication was followed by the installation of Napoleon's brother, Joseph Bonaparte, on the Spanish throne.

On 2 May 1808, the celebrated *dos de mayo* immortalized by Goya, the population of Madrid rose against the French. As the Spanish state imploded, one province after another followed the example of the inhabitants of Madrid in what became a countrywide movement for the salvation of the nation.[3] With royal authority gone, juntas sprang up across Spain to fill the power vacuum and coordinate resistance. In Catalonia, which had experience of setting up juntas in the earlier struggle against France in 1793, a Junta Superior was organized in July 1808. This in turn elected representatives to a Junta Central for Spain as a whole.[4]

The creation of the Junta Superior meant that, for the first time since 1714, Catalonia had a semi-autonomous government of its own, although one that was deferential to the decisions of the Junta Central. From the start the Junta Superior was overwhelmed by the double challenge of stemming the French invasion and halting the breakdown of order in the principality. The popular uprising, although directed against the French, was also aimed against local and municipal authorities that had remained passive in the face of the invasion. As in the uprising of 1640, the insurrection became at least in part a movement of protest against the dominance of the privileged classes. Wartime conditions gave peasants the chance to embark on a wave of anti-seigneurial protests against landowners who had prospered from rising agricultural prices in the closing decades of the eighteenth century and who had simultaneously been attempting to extract higher dues from their tenants. In the words of the inhabitants of Falset: 'We have no king, so we don't have to pay.'[5]

Although a regular Spanish army was mobilized to fight the French, much of the resistance movement, in Catalonia as elsewhere, took the form of guerrilla warfare. The Junta Superior appointed a Captain-General for Catalonia, and attempted to assemble an army. But there was strong popular opposition to forcible recruitment. The traditional, and much preferred, form of armed local resistance in the province was the local call to arms, or *sometent*, while bands of *miquelets*, half-soldiers, half-guerrillas, sprang up in 1808, as in previous Catalan insurrections.

Yet neither in Catalonia nor in the rest of Spain were organized troops or guerrillas able to hold back the French invaders, and within two years almost all Spain had fallen under French control. In the face of the inexorable French advance the Junta Central was forced to take refuge, first in Seville and then in Cadiz, where the British fleet provided protection for this last outpost of the legitimate Spanish state. A regency government acting on behalf of the exiled Ferdinand VII now replaced the Junta Central as the nominal executive.

Although conservatives and radicals who had taken shelter in the city were deeply divided, there was a perception that the Cortes held in late medieval Spain were truly authentic parliamentary bodies in a way that their successors, undermined by the authoritarian rule of the Habsburgs and the Bourbons, were not. This view gained widespread currency through the writings of the great legal historian, Francisco Martínez Marina. Initially a supporter of the newly installed reformist French regime, Martínez Marina subsequently joined the ranks of the liberals and became a deputy in the Cortes of Cadiz. His historical and critical study of the legislation of the kingdoms of Castile and León, published in 1808, was followed by his *Theory of the Cortes*, then circulating in manuscript and finally published in 1813. The constitutionalism embodied and expounded in his works assumed different forms at the hands of historians and jurists from the different provinces and regions of Spain, but it had a profound impact on the politics of the moment. There was general agreement that the time had come to revive the ancient Cortes of the Spanish kingdoms as they were thought to have existed before they succumbed to the arbitrary power of the Crown. A newly summoned Cortes would confer historical and national legitimacy on any future government and would map out a direction for the country once the French had been expelled.[6]

The Cortes, composed of deputies elected from all parts of Spain and many parts of Spanish America, duly assembled in Cadiz in September 1810 under the presidency of the elderly and eminent Catalan jurist, Ramon Llàtzer (Lázaro) Dou i Bassols, professor of canon law and chancellor of the university of Cervera and an admirer of the writings of Adam Smith.[7] It took time for many of the deputies to reach the city, but at its largest the Cortes numbered 304. Of these, twenty-one were from Catalonia, some of them representing the entire province and others individual cities.[8] The first action of the Cortes was to proclaim, as against the traditional principle of sacrosanct monarchy, the revolutionary principle of the sovereignty of the nation, with the French concept of the 'nation' preferred to the North American concept of the 'people'.[9] From the start bitter divisions arose between conservatives and radicals, but the outcome of the debates was a liberal and reformist document, the Constitution of 1812, which took its place alongside the Constitution of the United States and the French Constitution of 1791 as the third of the great constitutions of the western world. As an exercise both in state-building and nation-building, the Constitution of Cadiz aspired to transform Spain and its empire into a constitutional monarchy on the British model while incorporating the revolutionary ideals of popular representation and national sovereignty that had found expression in the American and French Revolutions.

Catalan involvement both in the War of Independence against the French and in the process of constitution-drafting in Cadiz can be seen as the reflection of what has been termed 'dual patriotism'.[10] In rising up against the French, Catalans took to arms, not for the first time, to defend their *pàtria*, their homes and hearths, against their traditional enemy, France. Some of them cherished a deep hostility to Castile and Castilians, but they also saw themselves standing shoulder to shoulder with their brethren across the length and breadth of Spain and America in defence of king, religion and the *nación*, a word that they sometimes used of Catalonia in place of the more common *patria*, but by which they also meant the collective national community of Spain.[11]

Similarly, the Catalan deputies in the Cortes of Cadiz, while fully aware of their obligations to their homeland, also saw themselves as participants in a wider project: the reconstruction of a Spain urgently in need of reform and modernization. In this they were following in the steps of supporters of the reformist projects of Charles III's ministers and they aspired to renovate Spain by instilling Catalonia's distinctive virtues into the nation at large.[12] This was the programme that had been advocated in the 1770s by the now elderly historian and economic thinker Antoni de Capmany, who was himself one of the Catalan deputies in the Cortes. The American and French revolutions, however, had injected a new and dynamic element into the equation by identifying the movement for liberty and reform with the idea of a community as an expression of the will of its people, and as a living organism endowed with its own unique characteristics. The new spirit was captured by Capmany in a violently anti-French polemic, *Centinela contra franceses*, which he published shortly after Napoleon's troops had entered Madrid in the spring of 1808.

Saluting the popular uprising against the army of occupation, Capmany wrote: 'You have now shown the world that the people is the nation ...' For Capmany that nation was Spain, and all its peoples were Spaniards. At the same time he was anxious to emphasize the power of regional sentiment to combat the French. 'What,' he asked as he contemplated the French invasion, 'would have become of Spaniards if there had not been Aragonese, Valencians, Murcians, Andalusians, Asturians, Galicians, Extremadurans, Catalans, Castilians etc.? Of these small nations is composed the mass of the great Nation', Spain.[13]

Inevitably there were moments when the embryonic concept of Spain as an authentic national community came into conflict with more traditional notions about the Catalan *pàtria*. Such moments were especially liable to occur when questions relating to the legislative and administrative unification of Spain were discussed. In its 1810 instructions to the deputies the Catalan Junta Superior, while using carefully crafted phraseology, made it clear that the common good of Spain should take precedence over regional and provincial considerations, although these were to be borne in mind where appropriate. The deputies, it stipulated, should 'recognize the political advantages that would come from making legislation and the rights of all the provinces of the Monarchy uniform, so that it should not remain a body composed of heterogeneous parts once the present crisis is over'. On the other hand it stated that 'when the plurality are not in favour, or when insuperable obstacles prevent this salutary measure from being implemented, in such cases Catalonia should not only keep its present privileges and *fueros*, but also recover those which it enjoyed when the august House of Austria occupied the Spanish throne, since the incalculable sacrifices it is making in defence of the nation make it fully worthy of the recovery of its prerogatives'.[14]

The Junta's instructions reveal the tension at the heart of the 'dual patriotism' professed by the dominant groups in Catalan society: a tension between their sense of identification with the Spanish nation that was still in process of construction and which it was their duty to help build, and their desire to preserve the distinctive character of their own nation or *pàtria*. As the instructions indicate, there was even a wistful hope that the *pàtria* might be allowed to revert to the form of constitutional government it had enjoyed during the two centuries of Habsburg rule. The liberties – and the liberty – lost in 1714 remained a potent reminder both of what had been lost and of Catalan distinctiveness. Yet, for all the expressions of nostalgia for a Catalonia that was dead and buried, the language being spoken by the Catalan deputies to the Cortes of Cadiz was the new language of liberal nationalism and popular sovereignty. When they spoke of the 'nation' they were overwhelmingly speaking not of Catalonia but of Spain. Spain was the nation-state to which they owed their allegiance, and the Catalan distinctiveness in which they took legitimate pride was for them subsumed into their Spanish nationality.[15]

Nevertheless there was continuing debate about the form that the Spanish nation-state should take. When the administrative unification of Spain came under discussion in the Cortes, one of the Catalan deputies, Felip Aner d'Esteve, gave expression to his Catalan patriotism in arguing against the provincial reorganization that was being proposed. He did not want to see the old provinces carved up, or joined to others that had different customs and spoke a different language. 'Nobody,' he asserted, 'is capable of making Catalans forget that they are Catalans.'[16]

The words of Aner d'Esteve point to the difficulty of holding a balance between the claims of the local *pàtria* and the totality of the Spanish nation. For Capmany, a personal friend of Lord Holland and well acquainted with the Whig thinking of the Holland House circle,[17] it was the English who had found the answer. Medieval England, like the medieval Crown of Aragon, had pioneered a constitutional system that protected the community and the individual from the exercise of arbitrary power. But whereas in Spain that constitutional system had been eroded by the government and finally abolished in 1714–16, England had succeeded in preserving its freedom from the assaults of a centralizing monarchical power. In so doing, it had managed to evolve a system of government that made possible the country's striking economic and political development without the sacrifice of its ancient liberties. Taking the medieval Crown of Aragon as its inspiration and contemporary Britain as its model, Spain could follow a similar route.[18]

While the *liberales*, who formed a well-organized minority in the Cortes, tended to favour a uniform system of law and government as offering the best chance of national progress, the competing claims of centralizing uniformity and regional particularism left hearts and minds divided. The liberals themselves were divided between conservative reformers, like Capmany and Aner, and those who were genuinely committed to the cause of liberalism. Their day would not come until the revolution of 1820 that followed the transformative upheavals brought about by the years of war in Spain and Spanish America, and the emergence of a new liberal generation in the European mould. In the end, the highly controversial question of administrative reorganization was put on hold. It was not until 1833, following the death of Ferdinand VII and the advent of a regency government which included amnestied liberals, that the historic regions of the 'sovereign nation' – Aragon, Catalonia, Valencia, Galicia – would be replaced by new ones organized along the lines of the French administrative model. Catalonia itself would be allowed to keep its territorial borders, but was artificially divided into four separate provinces: Lérida, Barcelona, Gerona and Tarragona.[19]

For liberal-minded reformers like Capmany who were devoted both to their own *pàtria* and to the concept of a united and progressive Spain, the dilemma inherent in dual patriotism could be acute, but this did not deter them from remaining faithful to their double loyalty. The same was true of later eighteenth- and early nineteenth-century Scots. Like their Catalan counterparts the elite members of Scottish society can similarly be seen as proponents of dual patriotism, but the circumstances in which they upheld it were very different from those prevailing in Spain, and, as a result, involved a lesser degree of inner conflict. Where the Spanish state was driven to collapse by poor governance, massive indebtedness, and finally by foreign invasion and occupation, the British state, rebounding from the loss of its American colonies, was projecting a new image of power. Its acquisition of an Indian empire, its industrial development, its growing commercial and naval dominance, pointed to a story of success with which the Scots were happy to associate themselves. As inhabitants of what it was now fashionable to call 'North Britain',[20] they had become heavily engaged in the imperial project, and had proved, both to themselves and others, that they could at the same time benefit from, and contribute to, the modernization of Britain.

The fashion for 'improvement' had already transformed the face of South Britain, and was now well on the way to transforming that of North Britain also. Sir Walter Scott, who had imbibed in Edinburgh the ideas of the Scottish Enlightenment about the progressive stages of civilization, wrote glowingly in 1814 of the massive transformation that had already occurred:

> There is no European nation which, within the course of half a century, or little more, has undergone so complete a change as this kingdom of Scotland. The effects of the insurrection of 1745, – the destruction of the

patriarchal power of the Highland chiefs – the abolition of the heritable jurisdictions of the Lowland nobility and barons, – the total eradication of the Jacobite party, which, averse to mingle with the English, or adopt their customs, long continued to pride themselves upon maintaining ancient Scottish manners and customs, commenced this innovation. The gradual influx of wealth, and extension of commerce, have since united to render the present people of Scotland a class of beings as different from their grandfathers, as the existing English are from those of Queen Elizabeth's time.[21]

It was not difficult, therefore, for many Scots to develop a loyalty that extended beyond their borders – a loyalty that embraced a common British imperial project, along with a British state that rested on firm constitutional foundations and gave the Scots a space they could still call their own. On 1 May 1807, at a grand ball held in Edinburgh to commemorate the centenary of the Union, the pipers played such patriotic tunes as 'Rule Britannia', 'Hearts of Oak' and 'God Save the King'.[22] For all its defects, a union that in earlier years had seemed a recipe for disaster could now, a century later, be celebrated as a model of enlightened self-interest. This made it possible to think of Great Britain, both north and south of the border, as a successfully united nation-state. When elaborate theories of racism came to be developed in the nineteenth century the notion of union could be further extended to embrace not only the successful union of two states, but also a union of peoples who shared a common ethnic stock.[23]

A developing British patriotism, however, did not preclude the survival of a strong sense of Scottish national identity that was made all the stronger by the early stirrings of the Romantic movement. Beneath the capacious mantle of British patriotism, English and Scottish patriotisms were in effect mutually reinforcing, since the emphasis on what the two nations shared tended also to highlight those features that differentiated them. The Highlands long remained outside the evolving British narrative, but they figured prominently in the version of a glorious Scottish past nurtured by the Jacobites. Although the Jacobite reading of Scotland's history came to be partially absorbed into the larger British story, the names of William Wallace and Robert Bruce, which it did so much to immortalize, were potent reminders of the struggles and triumphs of the old Scottish kingdom.[24] The extraordinary popularity of James Macpherson's poems of Ossian suggests that, in an age of transition from the Enlightenment to Romanticism, the sense of loss could itself be satisfactorily contained within an unfolding narrative of success.[25] The feeling of loss can also be seen as providing a valuable form of compensation. An invented or romanticized past helped to meet the emotional needs of a society that, in its own eyes, had responded to the call of reason by choosing the path of progress.

The choice was less clear-cut in Spain where it was hard to associate a broken regime with a trajectory of progress, and where the situation was further complicated by the French occupation. Joseph Bonaparte came to the Spanish throne with reformist intentions, and many, especially among members of the bureaucracy and the professional classes, were prepared to collaborate with the new regime, either for opportunistic reasons or because they believed that it offered the best hope of continuing Charles III's programme of reform from above.[26] Denounced as traitors by Spanish *patriotas*, these *afrancesados*, as they came to be called, found themselves in a particularly delicate position in Catalonia. This was the first province to be occupied by the French and the last they were to leave, although guerrilla forces compelled their troops to pull back, and from 1810 only two enclaves, Barcelona and its surrounding region, and Girona-Figueres, were effectively under French control.[27]

At an early stage of the French occupation of Barcelona the magistrates of the Audiencia, the supreme Catalan judicial tribunal, had already fallen foul of the French authorities, and had either fled or been arrested, to be replaced by others chosen by the French. By the start of 1810 Napoleon had decided to treat Catalonia differently from the other Spanish provinces and annex it to the French Empire. In pursuance of this policy, General Pierre Augereau, the military commander from January to May 1810, although himself in favour of a gradualist approach, began the process of introducing civil institutions into Catalonia that were modelled on those of France. In March he proclaimed in Girona the establishment of a separate government for the province and the rebirth under French auspices of the Catalan *pàtria*. He was soon recalled, to be followed by officials prepared to move faster along the road that led to the full assimilation of the region, purging recalcitrant Catalan officials and implementing in full the French judicial system.

Their moves to bring about uniformity, however, soon clashed with reality, and nowhere more sharply than over the question of language. In a despairing bid to win over the population it was decided in 1812 that Catalan should take its place beside French as the regime's official language. The plan soon had to be dropped because of resistance by the Audiencia. By a supreme irony, the magistrates asked for business to be conducted in Castilian, which, they insisted, was now their natural language of government.[28] The linguistic question in Catalonia has never lent itself to an easy solution.

Some *afrancesados*, like Tomàs Puig, a well-travelled and wealthy lawyer with Enlightenment views who became Augereau's right-hand man in Girona, saw in Napoleon's plans for a separate Catalonia an opportunity to preserve the province's distinctive identity, and perhaps even to reverse the measures implemented under the Nueva Planta. But his collaboration with the French did nothing to endear him to a fervently anti-French Catalan population, for whom the exiled Ferdinand VII was Spain's only legitimate ruler. Nor did his assertive brand of Catalan patriotism suit Napoleon, who in 1812 effectively annexed Catalonia to his empire.[29]

There were reform-minded elements in the British Isles that similarly found themselves at odds with the policies and practices of the government, although they were spared the additional problems of loyalty that the French occupation created for reformist Spaniards who aspired to build a progressive state and nation. The English parliamentary reform movement of the 1760s and 1770s attracted some attention in Scotland, where the minute size of the electorate left it wide open to corruption and manipulation. As in England, however, it was the early stages of the French Revolution that encouraged the development and diffusion of more radical ideas. On the occasion of George III's birthday in June 1792 there were three days of rioting in Edinburgh, followed by a series of popular riots and protests across the country, although the extent to which these were an expression of radical popular sentiment remains unclear.[30] Meanwhile, Societies of the Friends of the People, more populist than the English model on which they were based, were springing up across Scotland.

As a frightened government began to clamp down on real or suspected dissidents, public opinion became increasingly polarized. The fear of violence encouraged the Scottish political nation to line up behind the repressive policies of the prime minister, William Pitt, and of Henry Dundas, whom he appointed his home secretary in 1792. Escalating repression made it hard for radical societies to secure a foothold in Scotland. The voices of opposition were weakened, too, by the loyalism of a Scottish press that faced stiff competition from English newspapers now reaching North Britain in substantial numbers. In 1794 Dundas established an administrative structure of Lords Lieutenant in a bid to reinforce the coercive powers of government. Traditionally the government had been afraid to place arms in the hands of the Scots, and it had refused to allow the formation in 1757 of a Scottish militia at the time of the revival of the English militia – a disparity that offended Scottish pride although there were sharp divisions within Scotland itself about the desirability of establishing a Scottish national militia.[31] But in 1796 a French fleet appeared off Bantry Bay in

Ireland. Fears of a French invasion led the government to rush through parliament a Scottish Militia Act, only to provoke a cascade of anti-militia riots.[32] The Scottish populace, like its Catalan counterpart, displayed a visceral dislike of compulsory military service.

Although Tory governmental measures like the Militia Act had the effect of alienating growing sections of Scottish opinion, there was to be no Scottish equivalent of the Irish rebellion of 1798. The Irish, unlike the Scots, had kept their own parliament. The congenital distrust of Irish Roman Catholicism by a fiercely Protestant British state, however, meant that the Irish enjoyed far less control over their own institutional and domestic life than the Scots, who possessed a much greater degree of self-governance as a result of the provisions in the Treaty of Union allowing them to keep their own courts, Church and universities, while also leaving their burghs and heritable jurisdictions untouched. Although its economy had grown, Ireland had also missed out on the transformative development that did so much to reconcile the Scots to the Union, while the island's festering griev-ances and sharp religious divisions conspired to create an explosive situa-tion that had no parallel in Scotland. Rebellion was followed by violent repression that only served to stoke nationalist resentment. The incorpo-rating union of 1801 that brought Ireland into the British parliamentary state left a country torn between the aspiration to enjoy the benefits of closer integration into the British national community and the desire to achieve a larger measure of control over its own destiny.[33]

Nevertheless, the British parliamentary system gave the peripheral peoples of the United Kingdom – the Welsh, the Scots and now the Irish – opportunities to secure for themselves a degree of room for political manoeuvre that did not exist for the peripheral peoples of Spain until new Liberal constitutions in the 1830s led to a lasting revival of the Cortes as a national institution; and even then its effectiveness as a representative body was by no means assured.

Under the terms of the Treaty of Union, Scotland was represented in the British parliament by its quota of sixteen representative peers and forty-five MPs (one-twelfth of the total number). During the course of the eighteenth century the Scottish presence in the House of Commons was enhanced by that of several Scots who had English family connections and sat for English constituencies. There came to be more Scots, too, in the House of Lords following the reversal in 1782 of the 1711 decision to bar the fourth Duke of Hamilton, and any future Scottish peers holding post-Union English titles, from sitting in the upper house. The success of the petition by the seventh Duke of Hamilton, which in effect recognized that Scottish peers, with their increased wealth and importance, were in reality the equals of their English counterparts, had important political and social consequences. Scottish peers in growing numbers now lobbied for English peerages, allowing Dundas to exploit their craving for English honours by using his patronage to tighten his hold over the Scottish nobility.[34] These developments, especially when followed in 1801 by the inclusion of twenty-eight Irish peers in the House of Lords, had the additional consequence of encouraging the emergence of an integrated and truly British aristocracy of the kind that James VI/I had been so anxious to create.

Yet in spite of these changes English members of both houses of parliament heavily outnumbered those from the peripheral nations, to a degree far beyond anything warranted by the relative size of their respective populations. England's population in 1801 was five times larger than that of Scotland, but there were ten times more English MPs than Scottish, and the Great Reform Bill of 1832 did nothing to alter the balance.[35]

With such an overwhelming English superiority it might have been expected that parliament would become an instrument in ministerial hands to anglicize the British Isles. Yet in practice no such policy was pursued on any systematic basis. Although during the eighteenth century there was some ministerial and parliamentary intervention in Scottish affairs, particularly in the wake of the 1745 Jacobite uprising, the total amount of Scottish legislation was so small as to suggest that, on the contrary, Westminster had no great interest in meddling in Scotland's domestic affairs as long as the country remained quiet. Yet even where the governance of England was concerned, the eighteenth century was not a great legislating century for other than local bills. The lack of specific legislation for Scotland is not in itself, therefore, evidence of deliberate neglect.

In any event, the Scots, sheltering behind their own institutions, were happy to be left largely in charge of their own business, and so had little inducement to initiate new laws in Westminster. But when some new economic measure or tax proposal came before the Westminster parliament that affected Scottish interests adversely, as happened with the Malt Tax in 1725, Scottish MPs were quick to band together to resist it. Although in this instance they were finally compelled to accept 'the best of a bad bargain in this hard case', the habit of acting as a group in defence of Scotland's 'national interest' became well established over the course of the century. Even if the Scottish lobby often failed to win its case, it was sufficiently vociferous to force ministers, who were accustomed to treating Scottish MPs as political cannon fodder, to take its protests into account.[36]

Following the inclusion of Irish MPs in the House of Commons in 1801, the first half of the nineteenth century saw an increase in domestic legislation specific to Scotland, although not on the scale of legislation for Ireland. In part this was because the Scots themselves, benefiting from the experience of sitting in a parliament made up of representatives of all four British nations, picked up ideas that could usefully be appropriated for the management of their own domestic affairs. As this occurred, the administrative systems of the different constituent parts of the United Kingdom began to move more closely into line with each other, but what remains striking is the absence in Westminster of purposefully pursued integrating policies of the kind that Madrid sought to implement in its bid to transform Spain into a more unitary state.

Union in Britain was union by association and imitation, rather than union imposed from above, and already by the turn of the eighteenth and nineteenth centuries this informal process was showing signs of working. The determination of the Scottish elite and Scotland's intellectual establishment to buy into the British project is not the only indication that the creation of a British national community was becoming a reality. The more radical elements in Scottish society showed themselves as well aware as the Scottish establishment that their nation belonged to a wider political and social community than one confined to their own region of the British Isles. In the years following the outbreak of the French Revolution, English, Scottish and Irish radical groups and societies made contact with each other, offering advice and mutual support. The English reformers helped to inspire the Scottish campaign for parliamentary reform in the 1790s; the London Corresponding Society, which included among its members Scottish radicals living in London, was a genuinely British institution; and the United Irishmen were influential in the formation of the United Scotsmen in 1797.[37]

There were parallels here with contemporary developments in Spain. The response of the traditionalists to the ideology of the French Revolution and Napoleonic aggression strengthened the sense of a national community in Spain as in Britain. Meanwhile, a similar broadening of horizons also occurred among Spanish reformist elements who looked to the principles of the Revolution for their inspiration. Like their British counterparts, they were eager to build a progressive nation-state, although one whose religion, in the words of the Constitution, was to be 'perpetually Catholic, Apostolic, Roman', thus uniting the elite and the people in an all-embracing national community.[38]

In both countries, as across all Europe, the events of the revolutionary and Napoleonic era had the effect of pitting ancien régime societies, with their hierarchies and corporations, against the new ideologies created by the American and French revolutions. Governments might adopt authoritarian responses to the challenge of the new, but they would struggle to return the genie to the bottle. Many of those who had formerly thought of themselves as the subjects of monarchs were now beginning to think of themselves as citizens, and were discovering a new solidarity as members of emerging civic societies that were becoming bolder, and more insistent, in demanding a representative form of government and the recognition of their rights. Newly emerging social groups, thrown up by the wars and by the early stages of industrialization, were jostling for places among the ranks of the old or were making their own bids for social influence and political power. Francisco Javier Castaños, a Peninsular War hero appointed Captain-General of Catalonia at the end of the war, was shocked by the changes that had taken place in Barcelona over the last half century. Fifty years earlier merchants had aspired to enter the ranks of the nobility and wear a sword. Now nobody carried a sword and the prefix *Don* was everywhere to be found: 'In the space of half a century people have adopted totally different opinions and now it seems they despise everything they formerly made a show of appreciating.'[39]

Changing attitudes and opinions made for volatile societies. It was not easy for governments to maintain control in the face of the new social and cultural realities as urban populations expanded and a growing bourgeoisie began to clamour for the enjoyment of their presumed rights. The new causes of the revolutionary era – liberalism, regionalism, nationalism – were proving dangerously seductive. Faced with these challenges, a political and social establishment consisting of Crown, Church and landed aristocracy that had no intention of relinquishing its hold on power, came to realize that repression alone was an insufficient response. The context of political debate and action was changing, and all the parties involved had to adjust to the change.

New demands would lead to violent confrontations, most notably in the liberal and national revolutions that swept across Europe in 1848, and repression often seemed the easiest response. Yet mutual accommodation offered a better chance of conflict resolution in the longer term. The European establishment turned out to be resilient and flexible enough to incorporate members of the new classes who themselves were all too eager to join it, while also conceding political ground at moments when demands for change became irresistible, as in Britain with the passage of the Great Reform bill in 1832. This form of rearguard action met with marked success. Whether in Britain, Spain or Europe as a whole, the dramatic story of revolutionary and frequently violent change would be accompanied by the less dramatic but no less compelling story of the persistence into the twentieth century of the Old Regime and its traditional hierarchies.[40]

In this dual process of confrontation and accommodation, the nature and the concept of the state were also changing in response to the new realities. The Napoleonic Wars had massively increased the tributary and manpower requirements of Europe's fiscal-military states. The national and imperial rivalries of the new age would reinforce those requirements, and with them the state's centralizing aspirations. Simultaneously, governments had somehow to absorb, assimilate and manage the domestic pressures created by the economic and social demands of societies in the early throes of industrialization, and by the new-style nationalism – linguistic, ethnic and historicizing – of regions and communities now embarking on the intoxicating process of self-discovery.

The context in which the dialogue between central governments and regional and provincial communities had traditionally been conducted was therefore undergoing a profound transformation. Advocates of the new nationalism of the Romantic era had to consider how best to advance their cause. Was it better to engage in politics at the national level in the hope of influencing the central administration, or concentrate on fostering national consciousness in their own communities? If the two could be combined, which should be given priority? A dilemma of comparable complexity confronted governments faced by evidence of a surging nationalism. Was it possible to tolerate new nationalist demands without risking the unity of the state – a question that would be raised with particular acuteness in the multi-national and multi-ethnic Austro-Hungarian Empire?[41] How far could the state fashion, in the manner of the eighteenth-century Spanish Bourbons, a national loyalty that transcended regional and ethnic loyalties, and in the process neutralize them? And could the construction of a centralizing and integrating state of the kind demanded by the new domestic and international realities of the nineteenth century be reconciled with insistent claims for the recognition of diversity?

Every European state had to grapple with such questions, but the challenge was especially acute in Spain where a new state had to be built on the ruins of the old. The Cortes of Cadiz had time to do no more than lay the groundwork when Ferdinand returned in triumph in 1814 and promptly rejected the Cadiz Constitution. His reactionary behaviour opened a period of authoritarian government that drove many of the reformers into exile and was only briefly interrupted in 1820 when troops commanded by Colonel Rafael de Riego, who were being dispatched to Buenos Aires as part of an expeditionary army for the recovery of Spain's rebellious American possessions, mutinied in Cadiz. Riego's uprising inaugurated what was to be known as the liberal triennium of 1820–3. Liberal hopes were dashed, however, in 1823 by the intervention in support of Ferdinand VII of an invading French army nicknamed the Hundred Thousand Sons of St Louis,[42] acting under the mandate of a Quadruple Alliance of Britain, France, Austria and the Netherlands, all fearful of the contagious potential of liberal triumph in Spain.

The French invasion allowed Ferdinand to resume his former style of government. Yet the battle lines had been drawn. Riego's mutiny drew its legitimacy from the Cadiz Constitution to which the king had refused to swear allegiance – a Constitution that, in the words of Riego's proclamation, was a 'compact between the monarch and the people, the foundation and incarnation of every modern nation'.[43] A country governed by the rule of law, a nation in which every citizen possessed both rights and duties, was the concept of Spain enshrined in the Constitution of Cadiz and embraced by nineteenth-century Spanish liberals. Over the next century and more they would struggle against the more reactionary elements in Spanish society, and also amongst themselves, to realize their vision.

In Britain, too, the Napoleonic wars and their aftermath inaugurated a period of reaction, although the liberal reformist element, fortified by its representation in parliament, was better placed to win long-term effective power than its Spanish counterpart. Wartime conditions had failed to stifle the movement for parliamentary reform, and an article published in 1808 in the *Edinburgh Review*, founded six years earlier by a group of young Scottish reformist lawyers, praised the national uprising in Spain against the forces of Napoleon, and seized on the event to call for reforms across the British Isles.[44] Scottish institutions seemed to many Scots to be even more corrupt and less representative than their English counterparts. Scottish popular radicalism took wing in the immediate post-war period, and its advocates made common cause with English parliamentary reformers, appealing to the shared constitutional inheritance of both countries as they campaigned for radical reforms for the British nation as a whole. In the struggle for liberty Wallace and Bruce stood shoulder to shoulder with John Hampden and Algernon Sidney, the seventeenth-century English heroes of resistance to the arbitrary exercise of power.[45]

Post-war distress was to be found throughout the British Isles, and not least in the weaving and textile communities of Scotland, and the distress was compounded by the harsh fiscal measures introduced by a post-war government committed to reducing the crushing national debt. The

Peterloo Massacre in Manchester in August 1819 was followed by riots in Glasgow and Paisley in September – riots that led the government to concentrate more troops in potential trouble spots amidst fears of a general rising. The radicals drew encouragement from the news of Colonel de Riego's mutiny in Spain and the inauguration of the liberal triennium. The 'radical war' that broke out in Scotland in April 1820, however, was stamped out almost before it had begun. It left behind a trail of twenty-four capital convictions and three executions, but it seems that it was only in the second half of the twentieth century that the events of 1820 began to assume anything approaching a prominent place in the national memory. In September 2001 a member of Scotland's new assembly introduced a contested motion that the assembly should recognize 'the sacrifice of the three 1820 martyrs, who were hanged and beheaded in the 1820 uprising, which fought for social and economic justice, workers' rights and an independent Scottish parliament'.[46] National memory, as always, is selective, and heavily conditioned by time and circumstance. At the end of the twentieth century both of these had come to favour a populist brand of nationalism.

Radicalism might be suppressed in Britain and Spain alike, but liberal reformism lived on, waiting for an opportune moment for its voice to prevail. In Spain there was no chance of this during the terrible ten years of the *década ominosa* – the 'infamous decade' – between the overthrow of the liberal government in 1823 and the death of Ferdinand VII in 1833. The prospects of success were considerably stronger in England and in the Scotland of the *Edinburgh Review*, which enjoyed great national and international influence in promoting and maintaining the cause of moderate reform.

In both Britain and Spain, as across much of Europe, a fundamental question hovered over the process of creating unified nation-states. How much space should they allow to the constituent parts of their respective national communities? In Britain the issue was raised in an acute form by the Irish rebellion of 1798. In Spain the debates in the Cortes of Cadiz highlighted the difficulty of reconciling particularist interests with the model of a national unity that was eagerly sought. This was a question that defeated conservatives and liberals alike. In Britain the issue of religion obstructed the finding of a solution to what would come to be known as the 'Irish question'. In a Spain where the cause of liberal reform identified itself with centralization, Catalans and Basques struggled to find or renew a degree of autonomy inside a unitary state in process of reconstruction. Their struggle was both helped and hindered by constant and sometimes violent changes of regime.

In neither country was the cause of closer integration helped by the attitudes and opinions of influential sections of English and Castilian society. Amongst the English there was an arrogance of empire, well exemplified in Scott's *Waverley* by Colonel Talbot, 'a man of extended knowledge and cultivated tastes, although strongly tinged . . . with those prejudices which are peculiarly English', and which made him disdainful and contemptuous of Scottish peculiarities.[47] The Peninsular War had given the military a new prominence in Spanish life, and among the military in particular there was a feeling that the Catalans were congenitally unruly and needed to be kept under strict control. This was coupled with a more generalized sense that, as they moved towards securing a monopoly of the national market, these were a people who were simply out for themselves. Catalan reaction, already apparent in the 1830s, was that the province was being subjected to deliberate discrimination and that hostile Castilian officials were treating it as if it were a colony.[48]

It is of the nature of dual, or multiple, loyalties that their coexistence demands a constant process of rebalancing in the light of competing pressures and changing circumstances. For much of the time the process of rebalancing is instinctive, and it is only at certain moments and in response to a particular and often unpredictable configuration of events that the strain becomes so great as to force the jettisoning of one loyalty at the expense of the remainder. Even then, this does not necessarily lead to a permanent rupture. Circumstances change; individuals come and go; and compromises are sought and perhaps attained, leading to the restoration of the old balance or the achievement of a new one.

By the early nineteenth century dual patriotism had taken root, at least among the ruling elites, both in Scotland and in Catalonia. Forward-looking Catalans like Capmany rejected 'provincialism', or anything that smacked of federalism, as threatening the unity of the Spanish nation.[49] The two national communities of Scotland and Catalonia, however, would take very different paths over the course of the century as they grappled with the consequences of industrialization and sought to affirm their distinctive identities in a political and economic environment much less favourable to consensus in Spain than in Britain.

Industrialization and Its Consequences

Massive Scottish participation in the construction of the British Empire from the middle of the eighteenth century onwards did much to reconcile Scots at many levels of society to the fact of Union. It also strengthened their dual patriotism as loyal members of the new British state that had been created in 1707 and also as loyal Scots who could take a justifiable pride in a national contribution to Britain's international power and overseas expansion out of all proportion to the size of their population. Catalans, on the other hand, had only just begun to take full advantage of the opportunities afforded them by the growing consumer market of Spain's empire of the Indies when the implosion of the Spanish state under the impact of the Napoleonic invasion was followed by the independence movements that engulfed one after another of the American viceroyalties. The attempt of the restored monarchy of Ferdinand VII to recover Spain's American possessions failed abysmally. By 1830 its once great overseas empire was reduced to Cuba, Puerto Rico and the Pacific colony of the Philippines. The fragmentation of Spanish America into eleven, and later sixteen, independent republics, did not in itself preclude the continuation of strong commercial contacts with the former empire, as was shown by the experience of the British after the United States won their independence. But in the turmoil of the civil wars and independence movements of the 1810s and 1820s, British and American merchants made such heavy inroads into Spain's traditional American markets that there was no chance of displacing them.

The three remaining colonies would prove to be valuable possessions – Cuba and Puerto Rico as major producers of sugar, tobacco and coffee, and the Philippines in providing access to Asian markets[50] – and during the nineteenth century Catalan businessmen would exploit their resources to impressive effect. The shrinking of the American market, however, made it all the more important that they should recover the privileged position they had enjoyed in the Spanish domestic market before the events of the Peninsular War opened it to foreign, and particularly English, competitors.[51] Catalan factory owners therefore directed their energies to lobbying Madrid for the protection of their textiles and other manufactures in the hope of shielding themselves from foreign competition behind high tariff walls. Protectionism, they argued, would lead to the modernization of the Spanish economy by creating a strong domestic market for home-produced industrial goods.

Their demands brought them into conflict with the urban elite of Madrid. The capital had always been a centre of mass consumption thanks to the presence of the royal court, and of bankers, merchants, government officials and their families, and had become all the more so as a result of its eighteenth-century growth. By the early nineteenth century its policies were in the hands of an 'agro-commercial oligarchy' composed in part of great absentee landowners with close social and economic ties to the elites that ran the towns of the Castilian interior and southern Spain. The members of this Madrid oligarchy, now emerging as a dominant force in national politics,[52] had no wish to pay more for their foreign goods. Along with the import merchants of the port cities of the south they therefore strongly supported free trade in manufactured products. Consequently, lobbyists for Barcelona and the Catalan industrial community risked alienating influential sectors of Spanish society with their vigorous advocacy of protectionist policies on foreign manufactures.

In spite of the problems and disagreements of the post-war years, the Spanish economy enjoyed a gradual revival, aided by the reorganization of state finances and the introduction of annual budgets in the 1820s. Ferdinand's regime, for all its reactionary character, introduced some significant modernizing measures, most notably the creation in 1832 of a Ministry of Development (*Fomento*) with a wide range of competencies, including public health, road and canal building, the gathering of statistics, and internal and foreign trade.[53] Irrespective of the nature of its particular regimes the centralizing state was consolidating itself in Spain, as in the other nations of nineteenth-century Europe.

The economic revival gathered pace after the death of Ferdinand VII in 1833 and the replacement of his authoritarian government by a more liberal regime that proved relatively favourable to tariff legislation. It was in the 1830s and 1840s that the Catalan business community forged the alliance with the government that was to prove so critical for its relationship to the Spanish state. It was during these years, too, that the introduction of steam power led to the modernizing of the Catalan textile industry. Heavy investment in manufacturing by entrepreneurial dynasties like the Güell, who had made their fortune in the Cuba trade, led to an impressive diversification of the Catalan economy during the middle decades of the century as it moved into a wide range of consumer goods. By the 1860s Catalonia had established itself as one of Europe's most dynamic industrial regions. Not only did it dominate the Spanish domestic market but it was also well integrated into the international trading system.[54]

At the heart of this industrial society was the manufacturing and port city of Barcelona, the hub of a rapidly growing regional network of smoky industrial towns like Manresa, Terrassa and Sabadell. By 1850 it was the second largest city in Spain with a population of some 175,000, as compared with Madrid's 281,000. By the end of the century the number of its inhabitants had nearly caught up with the capital's 540,000.[55] But the two cities differed sharply in environment and character. Madrid was no centre of manufacturing, and depended for its food supplies on the surrounding agricultural region and the urban network of the Castilian interior. Unlike Barcelona it had no access to the sea, and had to rely on primitive overland transport until the coming of the railways in the years after 1860.[56] Unlike Barcelona, too, its power was essentially political and administrative, and it was through administration and political patronage that it struggled to integrate the different regions of Spain into the unified polity that it was trying to recast in the light of modern needs.

The economic dynamism of nineteenth-century Barcelona therefore had no parallel in Madrid, although Madrid consolidated its position as the financial capital of Spain in the 1850s when the national bank originally founded by Charles III in 1782 was remodelled under the name of the Banco de España. By the mid-nineteenth century Barcelona was coming to be seen, in contrast to Madrid, as a 'European' rather than a 'Spanish' city, although in practice it had developed a multitude of commercial and personal ties across an Iberian Peninsula on which it was largely dependent for its economic prosperity.[57] It was, however, distinctively 'European' in experiencing the kind of urban and social problems that rapid industrialization was bringing to other European towns and cities. While an increasingly affluent upper middle class was consolidating its social position as a powerful bourgeoisie, a large and depressed industrial proletariat was beginning to make its presence felt. Wages were low, living conditions were appalling, and chronic overcrowding was at best mitigated by the belated demolition of the old city walls in the 1850s and 1860s.[58] Epidemics, like the cholera epidemics of 1834 and 1854, when Barcelona lost 3 per cent of its population to the disease, periodically swept through crowded urban tenements; and a city that was no stranger to unrest witnessed a growing radicalism and outbursts of Luddite-style destruction of machinery, including a dramatic arson attack which burnt down the model new Bonaplata textile mill in 1835.[59]

There was much that Barcelona shared in common with Glasgow, a city that already had a population of over 250,000 inhabitants in the 1830s, compared with Barcelona's 175,000, although both cities would pass the half a million mark during the last decades of the century.[60] A close comparison of Scottish and Catalan industrialization has yet to be undertaken,[61] but the profound impact of industrialization on Glasgow and the Clydeside during the first half of the nineteenth century was comparable to its impact on Barcelona and its hinterland. The 1830s were a critical decade for the industrialization of Scotland, as of Catalonia,[62] but both, with their long tradition of rural and urban production of cloths and linens, had a promising proto-industrial record. Both, too, had experienced a significant population increase and growing urbanization in the eighteenth century, and achieved major agricultural improvements in response to the demands of expanding market opportunities. While eighteenth-century Catalonia saw an impressive development of viticulture in particular, Lowland and Highland Scotland underwent an agricultural revolution over the later eighteenth and early nineteenth centuries.[63] As connections between town and country multiplied, industrial and agricultural transformation went hand in hand, although Scotland and Catalonia both remained predominantly rural societies, at least until the middle of the nineteenth century. In Scotland, agriculture and domestic service were still the largest employers of labour in 1851.[64]

In both countries commercial capital had done much to bring about the massive changes underway by the middle decades of the nineteenth century. Barcelona's merchant families invested heavily in the new industrial developments; later eighteenth-century Glasgow, the tobacco capital of the British Atlantic economy, had its 'tobacco lords', who, in common with its sugar lords, lived in prosperity, bought up country estates around the city, and, like their Barcelona counterparts, invested in any developments where it looked as if money was to be made.[65] It was the interaction of trade, agriculture and industry over many decades that created, both in Scotland and Catalonia, an environment favourable to economic transformation, although in both countries success ultimately depended on the capacity of entrepreneurs to make the most of such opportunities as lay open to them. It also depended on the existence of a labour force sustained by a stream of rural immigrants into the towns, many of them coming down from the Highlands, or, in Catalonia, from the mountainous northern region, while in Scotland large numbers of Irish immigrants provided a steady external supply of cheap labour.[66]

The economic diversification of Scotland and Catalonia in the late eighteenth and early nineteenth centuries is testimony to the adaptability of their merchants and businessmen, and their willingness to take risks. Catalonia lacked a powerful landholding aristocracy, which in Scotland was active in providing capital investment in new enterprises, including the construction of the roads and canals that would do much to reduce the costs of transport and link the eastern Lowlands with Clydeside. Each country, however, had seen the emergence of a new business and professional elite, drawn primarily from the middling ranks of society, both rural and urban.

Many members of the mercantile elite of Glasgow had spent some time at the city's university, and in Glasgow, as in Edinburgh, there was a vigorous urban culture of clubs, coffee houses and debating societies.[67] In Catalonia it was only in 1837 that the university of Cervera, with a mere 137 students, was finally closed, and its teaching faculties were transferred to Barcelona, where there had been no university since the Bourbons shut it down. The education of the city's elite had for the most part been left to the religious orders, particularly the Jesuits. Like Edinburgh and Glasgow, nineteenth-century Barcelona saw the creation of new social and cultural centres, notably the Ateneu Barcelonès, founded in 1835, which would become the seed-bed of Catalan liberalism and romanticism, the Ateneu Català, founded in 1860, and the theatre of the Liceu, dating from 1837, whose splendid new building, opened with much pomp ten years later, was to become the heart of Barcelona's musical life.[68]

The Liceu, with its concerts and its operatic performances, was regarded as the preserve of the elite, but musical education would become an important form of civic education for the working classes from the 1850s. It was then that Josep Anselm Clavé, a musician who was a republican activist and had been gaoled for his participation in the Barcelona uprisings of the early 1840s, began to organize an extremely successful movement for the founding of choral societies. These became enormously popular, spreading across Catalonia and including in their repertoire Catalan folk songs that Clavé had found in the course of his researches, along with songs of his own composition written for them in Catalan.[69] It was in this period, too, that the elaboration and promotion of the long and measured *Sardana* of the Ampurdà region gave the Catalans a dance form that became a symbol of their national spirit.[70]

Even if Catalonia failed to develop a serious equivalent of the Scottish Enlightenment, the growing strength of the professional classes and the cultural and intellectual environment they created for themselves encouraged the development and consolidation of a relatively open-minded and outward-looking bourgeoisie. Just as the bourgeoisie of the Scotland of Sir Walter Scott had its partisan divisions between Whigs and Tories, so the Barcelona bourgeoisie was made up of liberals and conservatives; but, as in Scotland, both groups, while proud of the distinctive characteristics of their own communities, saw themselves as loyal members of the larger polity. Where the Catalan bourgeoisie stood at a serious disadvantage to its Scottish counterpart was in having to navigate its way through the persistently turbulent waters of national politics. In Britain, the great Reform Act of 1832, effectively inaugurating in Scotland a period of Whig and Liberal ascendancy that lasted until the end of the century, brought about much needed change without plunging the country into civil strife. Spain, by contrast, failed over many decades to achieve lasting political stability, and this failure had profound implications for the relationship between Catalonia and the Spanish state.

The first of the military *pronunciamientos*, many of them of a liberal character, that would punctuate the political life of nineteenth-century Spain, occurred with Riego's mutiny in 1820. Hostility to the new liberal regime that followed his uprising was nowhere stronger than in large areas of rural Catalonia. This was currently suffering from a deep agrarian depression that especially affected the most dynamic sector of the rural economy, viticulture.[71] The new tax measures hit a peasantry already struggling to pay their seigneurial dues to landowners who stood to benefit from the government's agrarian reforms. The parish clergy took the lead in whipping up support for what became in 1822 an insurrection in the name of Church and King across large areas of northern Catalonia and through the vine-growing region of the Camp de Tarragona. As in the Napoleonic wars, peasants mobilized, juntas were formed, and the uprisings assumed a political complexion when a so-called 'regency' was established at Urgell by anti-constitutional royalists. With constitutionalist families fleeing to Barcelona and other safe havens, Catalonia was plunged into a form of civil war.[72]

Government troops managed to bring the various Spanish insurrections under control, even if guerrilla warfare by gangs made up of bandits, disgruntled soldiers and embittered peasantry continued in the province. In 1827 Ferdinand VII paid a visit to Catalonia, where ultra-royalist volunteers called *Malcontents* had risen in arms against a royalist regime they regarded as being too soft on the liberals. The *Malcontents* included army officers and soldiers who were left with nothing when the war was over, along with former liberals who had been Ferdinand's supporters but were disappointed when he failed to give them their expected rewards.[73] More royalist than the king himself, they even entertained plans for replacing Ferdinand on the throne with his younger brother, the infante Don Carlos. The cries of 'Long live Carlos V', heard in Vic and other Catalan towns, were the first ominous hints of the emergence of a Carlist movement that was to tear Spain apart during the middle decades of the century. The fact that many Catalans, especially those living in agrarian regions, were willing to mobilize under the reactionary banners of king and Church points to the width of the gulf separating rural Catalonia from Barcelona and the industrializing towns of the Mediterranean littoral. But this traditional Catalonia was no less Catalonia than the modernizing Catalonia of Barcelona and its hinterland. Its very traditionalism has all too easily led to its airbrushing out of today's nationalist historiography, bent on equating the Catalans with the progressive and the modern. But its omission distorts the picture and leaves a significant piece of the story untold.

Ferdinand's presence, combined with military repression, brought the 'war' of the *Malcontents* to an end within a few months.[74] Although he was well received when he entered Barcelona, bringing with him a decree that guaranteed protection of the Catalan textile industry, his visit had little in common with that paid by George IV to Edinburgh six years earlier. Where the appearance of a tartan-clad king in his northern capital could be seen as a symbolic act of reconciliation between the Crown and Highland Scotland, Ferdinand's visit to Catalonia was the prelude to a new and savage round of repression. In a bid to clamp down on dissent by liberals and ultra-royalists alike, he appointed a crazed royalist, the Count of España, as Captain-General of Catalonia, and gave him full freedom of action. The consequences were disastrous. For five years the count terrorized the province, hunting down indiscriminately those accused of promoting disorder. In so doing he massively alienated the young from the royalist cause and converted Barcelona into a bastion of liberalism.[75]

Although the liberal triennium of 1820–3 had ended in failure it gave a powerful impetus to the liberalism that had attracted growing numbers of the professional classes of Barcelona and other major towns, and extended it to merchants and members of the business community, artisans and shopkeepers.[76] A climate had been created that would make Barcelona one of the capitals of Spanish liberalism in the middle decades of the century – a liberalism that could draw on the growing strength of civil society in this period.

On the other hand, the very fact that the liberal regime had been overthrown in 1823 heartened the forces of political and ideological reaction, headed by the Church and the landowners. The cause of the traditionalists was further assisted by splits among the liberals, whose record in government during their three years in power was itself tarnished by violence and repression. When Ferdinand VII died in 1833 he left his widow, María Cristina de Borbón, in charge of a regency government that would rule Spain for ten years until the king's three-year-old daughter, Isabel II, officially came of age. During the regency the splits among the liberals intensified, leaving them divided between *moderados* and *progresistas*, who would struggle for control of the government in the years ahead.

Further complications were added to the Spanish political scene when Ferdinand's younger brother Don Carlos claimed the throne for himself on the grounds that female succession was barred by the Salic law. As a result, the year of Ferdinand's death saw the outbreak of the first of the three Carlist wars that would divide the country and periodically disrupt its political life between 1833 and 1876. The Carlists, acting in the name of the Catholic unity of Spain and its 'legitimate' king, Don Carlos, rose in revolt against the regency government of María Cristina. The queen regent was left with no option but to entrust power to the liberals, who seized the opportunity to embark on a massive disentailing and transfer of Church lands and property in 1835–6 – a transfer that did much to consolidate the power of traditional landowning elites while bringing into their ranks *nouveaux riches* who were all too happy to imitate their lifestyles. The liberals followed up this measure by introducing a radical new Constitution in 1837, although one that, in spite of the attack on Church property, preserved the privileged position of the Church in Spain.

In placing herself in the hands of the liberals María Cristina could draw on the support of the army, which viewed itself as the defender of constitutional legality. Her generals, however, had great difficulty in repressing the insurrection of the Carlists, who were well embedded in the Basque provinces, Navarre and the more rural parts of Catalonia, especially central Catalonia and the Pyrenean region. The continuing resentment of the inhabitants of this still impoverished Catalonia – oppressed peasants, agricultural labourers, artisans and small shopkeepers – found an outlet in a Carlist movement that stood for traditional values and the defence of a Church that felt itself to be under siege.[77] The war, which lasted for seven years, was immensely destructive, claiming some 150,000 casualties before it ended with the victory of the government forces in 1840.

Five years earlier, in the summer of 1835, a wave of anticlericalism swept Catalonia, provoked by the activities of the Carlists and inflamed by liberal agitators. Great monasteries like those of Ripoll and Poblet were sacked, and in Barcelona crowds raced through the streets, burning and gutting the convents, although leaving the parish churches intact. A few days later the Bonaplata textile mill was burnt down. Not for the first time in Barcelona's history discontented workers and the teeming, impoverished populace of an overcrowded city had made their voices heard.[78]

A frightened bourgeoisie struggled to restore order, although with little help from a government preoccupied by the war with the Carlists in the Basque provinces. As in the period of the Napoleonic invasion, juntas sprang into life, and during the final years of the war the province was effectively left to its own devices. Once again, therefore, it experienced a period of semi-autonomous government after the emergence of a Junta in Barcelona that called for the restoration of the old Crown of Aragon. As elite elements recovered control, a Central Superior Council composed of central and regional authorities assumed the leadership of the province.[79]

The effect of the eventual victory of government forces over the Carlists was to seal the alliance between the liberals and the army, but it also marked a period of military intervention in Spanish political life. This began when the most successful of María Cristina's generals, General Espartero, encouraged by the Progressives, forced her out of the regency and assumed its powers himself.[80] But his authoritarian behaviour progressively lost him support. Barcelona turned against him, and in the autumn of 1841 an irate populace, encouraged by Progressive city councillors, began tearing down parts of the hated Bourbon fortress of the Ciutadella stone by stone. As the protests and disorder continued, Espartero sought to recover control in December 1842 by ordering his troops to bombard the city from the castle of Montjuïc, causing immense damage. In the following year, as support for his regency government dwindled, Espartero was ousted from power by Generals Narváez and O'Donnell. But protests in Barcelona by workers and shopkeepers over a new city tax escalated into an insurrection, known as the *Jamància*, or pastry-cooks' revolt.[81] The unrest only stopped when the new military governor of Barcelona, Brigadier Joan Prim, a Catalan and a monarchist, bombarded the city into submission.

The 1843 overthrow of Espartero's regency government set the scene for an era in which Narváez and O'Donnell, together with a politically resurrected Espartero, changed places in bewildering succession as heads of government for Isabel II. They held centre stage for twenty of the twenty-eight years between 1840 and 1868, when a coup led by General Prim forced the abdication of a queen who had persistently meddled in politics. Over the same period there were at least thirty-two changes of government.[82]

For all the instability of Spanish political life during these years, a quiet revolution was belatedly transforming a country in which areas of subsistence economy now coexisted with regions in the rapid process of economic modernization, with the industrial belt of Catalonia in the lead.[83] There might be *pronunciamientos* and attempted, or successful, coups d'état, but the general trend over this period was towards the construction of a state based on the ideas of national sovereignty and constitutional government promoted by a growing number of members of the upper middle classes, like those of Barcelona, who espoused the doctrines of a European-wide liberalism. This modernizing state was based, like other western European states, on an evolving parliamentary system. In this system the Moderates – increasingly the conservative and neo-Catholic wing of the liberals – held power for all but two years between 1845 and 1868.

The strongly liberal Constitution of 1837, which a weakened monarchy had no choice but to accept, was not a mere replica of the Cadiz Constitution. Sovereignty, as in 1812, was shared between Crown and people, but the people were this time to be represented by a bicameral Cortes composed of a Senate and a Congress of Deputies. When in 1845 a new, more restrictive Constitution replaced that of 1837 the Senate was transformed into a chamber entirely nominated by the Crown. The 1845 Constitution also reduced to a mere 0.8 per cent the size of an electorate that the 1837 Constitution had enlarged to 2.1 per cent, and which had risen to some 5 per cent of the population by 1845. This compares with an electorate of 3.3 per cent of the United Kingdom's population following the passage in 1832 of the parliamentary Reform Act.[84] In post-1845 Spain, as in mid-century Great Britain, electoral reform lagged far behind the rise of an industrial working class, and the mass of the population remained without a political voice. In Spain in 1869, however, in the wake of the 1868 revolution, universal male suffrage, originally embodied in the Cadiz Constitution, would be reintroduced. It would be withdrawn in 1878 but was re-established in 1890. It came to Great Britain only in 1918.

In Scotland, where radicalism could lay claim to a proud record of protest, large crowds demonstrated in favour of parliamentary reform in the early 1830s. The Scottish Reform Act of 1832 brought Scotland under the English electoral regime and in so doing extended the country's pathetically small franchise among the middle classes. The electorate was increased from a mere 4,500 to 65,000, and the Act made significant improvements in the working of the electoral system, but failed to meet the needs of a rapidly changing society.[85] As in England it left the working classes without a vote and led them to seek alternative forms of expression. But trade unionism was weakened by the collapse of the cotton spinners' strike of 1837, and the availability of a constant supply of cheap labour continued to hamper the growth of unionism throughout the nineteenth century. As late as 1892 only 20 per cent of the working Scottish population were trade union members – half the number of those in the major industrial cities of England and Wales.[86]

The Chartist movement of 1838–43, with its demand for working-class political representation and radical reform of the state, drew crowds of supporters in Scotland as in England, especially among weavers, artisans and disaffected members of the middle classes. Following the failure of the movement, however, industrial workers did not resort to violent mass protest or revolutionary activity. Scotland's brand of Protestantism had instilled in working-class culture, and especially that of the skilled work-force, a puritanical ethos that viewed self-education, self-improvement and temperance as a more acceptable response than revolutionary upheaval to the harsh conditions of daily life.[87]

In mid-century Scotland there would nevertheless be strikes and street protests, like the Glasgow riots of 1848, but nothing on the scale of the violence that periodically took over the streets of Barcelona and other Catalan industrial centres. While the contrasting responses may in part be attributable to the different religious and political cultures of the two work-forces, it seems likely that differences in the nature and extent of state inter-vention do more to explain the contrast. While the state certainly deployed its coercive power in Scotland, knowing that it could count on the support of the property-owning classes,[88] there was not the generalized brutality of repression that scarred Catalan public life. The captains-general of the various Spanish regions possessed a wide range of powers, and while some showed themselves willing to engage in constructive dialogue with trade and workers' associations like the influential Society of Cotton Weavers, others had no scruples in deploying those powers forcefully.[89]

As Espartero's bombardment of Barcelona in 1842 made clear, the resort to military force was an all too easy option, although it took three years to suppress a new wave of rural unrest known as the War of the *Matiners* of 1846–9. In 1855 a general strike of textile workers was called when the new Captain-General, General Zapatero, dissolved illegal trade associations and placed mutual help societies under military control. Zapatero quickly earned his nickname as the Tiger of Catalonia. His execution of the presi-dent of the Society of Barcelona weavers on a trumped-up charge provoked the assassination of the president of the Industrial Institute of Catalonia in reprisal. Zapatero responded with a campaign of repression, which drove the strikers back to the factories at bayonet point, left many dead in the streets, and alienated factory owners and workers alike.[90]

The government did nothing to stop the bloodbath. The combination of governmental inaction at the centre with governmental overaction in Catalonia had the inevitable effect of widening the gulf between Barcelona and Madrid. In Victorian Britain no gulf of comparable magnitude sepa-rated Edinburgh and London, which tended to leave the Scots very much to their own devices. In large measure the Scotland of the *laissez-faire* middle decades of the nineteenth century, although nominally under the control of the Home Office from 1827, managed its own affairs. The Lord Advocate, as the senior law officer, ran much of the day-to-day business, in company with a series of boards or commissions that had been set up in Edinburgh, like the Court of Exchequer, the Board of Excise and the Board of Police. A 'police system' of local authorities, created by legislation in 1833, gradually extended its powers over local affairs and became increasingly interven-tionist, but this was interventionism run by the Scots themselves, and in that sense very unlike the interventionism displayed by Madrid and its local representatives in Catalonia.[91] Where the Catalans were therefore constantly inveighing against 'centralization',[92] and responded to pressures from Madrid by emphasizing with a growing stridency the uniqueness of their own history and culture, the Scots felt less need to be assertive about their distinctive heritage. Instead, they were happy to endorse, as Britons who happened to be Scots, a 'unionist nationalism' that offered sufficient space to accommodate both their inheritances.[93]

As a result of the willingness of the Westminster government to keep Scotland on a loose rein, and of the equal willingness of the Scots to embrace a unionist ideology that fully accepted the concept of a United Kingdom of free and equal peoples, the tensions between London and Edinburgh, although they existed, were far fewer than those to be found in the Barcelona-Madrid relationship. These tensions were now being exacerbated as elements of the Catalan working class, radicalized by the behaviour of the factory owners and the savagery of military and civil repression, began to turn their backs on trade associations and on peaceful protest. In an attempt to redress their grievances they started resorting to direct action and to the kind of anarchist violence that would bring terror to the streets of Barcelona as the century drew to a close.

Frightened by growing manifestations of popular violence, the propertied classes had no choice but to look to the government for help, however inadequate its response. This locked them into the Spanish nation-building project with which they had identified themselves since the middle decades of the eighteenth century. Yet whereas the English and Scottish elites were in substantial agreement as to the kind of nation they inhabited and envisaged, this was far less true of their Spanish counterparts. Sharp differences of opinion prevailed over the concept of the Spanish nation and Catalonia's place within it, and nation-building itself still had a long way to go.

National Narratives

Nations need symbols, and flags and national anthems are among the most evocative symbols of national identity. The Union Jack, devised in 1606 as a regal flag, became the 'ensign armorial' of Great Britain following the Union of 1707, and acquired its current form in 1801, when the British-Irish Union added the red saltire of St Patrick to Scotland's blue saltire of St Andrew. At around the same time 'God Save the King', sung lustily on public occasions since 1745, began to be spoken of as Britain's 'national anthem'.[94] In Spain, Charles III gave orders in 1785 that his navy should fly a red-yellow-red 'national flag'. This became a symbol of resistance to the Napoleonic invasion, and the liberals subsequently adopted it. The Carlists, however, chose to fly the white flag with the cross of Burgundy, which dated back to the reign of the Emperor Charles V. Although the government officially adopted the red and yellow flag in 1843, it was only in 1908 that orders were given to fly it on all public buildings. A Spanish national anthem had an even more chequered career. Again it was in 1908 that the eighteenth-century royal march, the 'Hymn of the Grenadiers', finally acquired official status, but only as a tune that has never been accompanied by words.[95]

The uncertainties over flag and anthem hint at the difficulties involved in realizing the Bourbon dream of turning Spain into a centralized nation-state – a dream carried over into the nineteenth century by those who drafted the 1812 Constitution in the Cortes of Cadiz. Liberal governments of the middle decades of the century picked up the baton, and adopted a raft of measures designed to create a strong government and bring uniformity to a country which, like other continental countries, lacked the cohesion required to conform to the new contemporary standards. Reforms of central and local government reduced the level of provincial autonomy by stripping the provincial *diputaciones* of much of their power; a paramilitary national police service, initially intended to keep order in rural Spain, was established with the creation of the Guardia Civil in 1844; and the judicial system was reformed with the introduction in 1848 of a criminal code. In 1844 the finance minister in General Narváez's administration, Alejandro Mon, introduced a uniform tax system that provoked widespread provincial discontent, not least in Catalonia, which found itself deprived of its relative fiscal advantages.[96]

Measures were also adopted that might help to unify a disparate population both culturally and linguistically, with Castilian being promoted as the language of the state. Three years of conscription into the army were made compulsory in 1833, but the measure does not seem to have been very rigorously enforced, with the result that military service was less successful than it was in France in creating a linguistically unified nation. A national system of secondary education was introduced in a bid to reduce the appallingly high national rate of illiteracy, while university reforms included the granting to the University of Madrid of the exclusive right to award doctorates. The centrality of Madrid to national life was further emphasized when the development of a more professional bureaucracy brought a requirement that all candidates for office should take their examinations in the capital. Geographically, too, Madrid's dominance was reinforced as it became the hub of the national rail network under construction in the 1850s and 1860s.[97]

The assertion of Madrid's position as the national capital reflected the continuing evolution of Spain into a centralized nation-state, very much in line with other European states of the period. The state, in Spain as elsewhere, was becoming more bureaucratic, more interventionist, and consequently more intrusive into the lives of its citizens. The effect of this process during the course of the nineteenth century was to change the rules of the political game. If the state was demanding more of the people, the people, who had been taught to see themselves as sovereign, were in turn demanding more of the state. As taxpayers they expected the provision not only of law and order at a level that would ensure their personal security, and a judicial system that would deliver impartial justice, but they also looked to the state to give them fair access to the growing number of facilities at its command. These included posts in an expanding bureaucracy, both central and local, and in the army and the fleet – positions that it was increasingly expected should be filled on the basis of merit rather than of social status or place of origin. Moreover, imperial states with colonial possessions, like Britain and Spain, also offered valuable commercial opportunities overseas, together with enticing career prospects for the adventurous, the ambitious and the needy.

The existence of these enlarged patronage opportunities raised the stakes in the negotiating process between governments and the governed, while making the capture of government by one political faction or another increasingly rewarding. Yet much depended on the capacity of states with modernizing intentions to function effectively, and here Spain during the first sixty or seventy years of the nineteenth century stood at a serious disadvantage to Britain. Weak finances meant a weakened state, and Spanish state finances took time to recover from the impact of the Napoleonic wars and the loss of most of its American empire.[98] On top of this, sudden changes of regime led to a lack of sustained commitment to well-intentioned reforms. As the history of nineteenth-century France shows, Spain was by no means unique among its European contemporaries in experiencing bouts of political and social instability, but the resulting confusion was compounded by the Carlist wars that disrupted civil life, distracted governments and drained national energy.

The nineteenth century for Britain, by contrast, was a century characterized by a high level of domestic peace and rapidly growing prosperity. These conditions allowed its governments to move at a measured pace, reforming or holding back as circumstances and competing political philosophies dictated. Yet the general trend was unmistakable. As on the continent the state would become more dominant as the century progressed. This growing dominance would find expression in the expansion of state revenues, the massive growth of the civil service, and an increasing tendency towards interventionism by the government. These developments would have important consequences for the relationship between the constituent parts of the United Kingdom.[99] Until then, Scotland and Ireland, benefiting from the relatively relaxed attitude of Westminster, continued to possess a substantial measure of semi-independence.

It was easier for Westminster to adopt a relaxed approach to other constituent parts of the United Kingdom than it was for Madrid to do likewise in a nominally unitary Spain. In spite of the impressive industrial growth of Glasgow and the Clydeside, Scotland was never central to the economic development of a Britain in which England enjoyed economic as well as political preponderance. In Spain there was no such conjunction of economic and political power. Economic power was located in Catalonia, and specifically in Barcelona and its region. Political power was located in Madrid.

This disjunction had momentous implications for Spanish politics and society. Catalonia was a major source of wealth and revenue generation for all Spain. As the most industrial part of the country it was also at the forefront of economic and social change. Madrid could therefore not afford to neglect the province or let it slip beyond its control. Movements that took root in a Catalan civil society in process of rapid transformation – republicanism, syndicalism, anarchism and nationalism – were likely to affect, or infect, the rest of the Spanish body politic. It was a portent of things to come that the textile workers' strike in Barcelona in 1855 escalated into the first strike of workers across Spain.[100] Not surprisingly, governments were convinced of the need to keep a close oversight on developments in Catalonia and be ready to intervene when they felt it to be necessary. Consequently, social and political developments in Barcelona impinged at numerous points and with increasing frequency on national politics. Whether they liked it or not, Catalonia and Madrid were locked in a tight but often uncomfortable embrace. Madrid might bring administrative and military pressure to bear on the province, but Catalan industrialists could operate behind the scenes to influence the shaping of government policy, while the Cortes provided Catalan deputies with a forum in which to campaign for regional or sectional interests. The development of Barcelona's industrial strength on the one hand and Madrid's growing administrative dominance on the other therefore involved a constant, if often tacit, bargaining process that raised the relationship of centre and periphery to a level of complexity far above that of the pre-industrial era. It also had major implications for Spain as a whole. Other peripheral regions, and especially the Basque provinces as they followed Catalonia down the road that led to industrialization, had the Catalan example before them, and a similar incentive to become involved in the political game that was being played in Madrid.

The various liberal regimes of mid-nineteenth century Spain were ill-equipped to cope with the growing complexities of the relationship between the central government and regions engaged in reaffirming and expanding their own sense of identity. They were regimes that aspired to imitate the centralizing French model of the state but lacked the means to do so, and consequently were all too prone to make the worst of every world. Continuous political instability, endemic corruption, especially at the local level, and political and administrative inefficiency all hampered their efforts. They could not afford to appear weak, but neither did they have the strength to assert a convincing dominance.

Although Spain's liberal state enjoyed the backing of the army, its generals found it hard to assume the mantle and the outlook of politicians, and their natural instinct for discipline and order led them to adopt measures that alienated those elements in society whose image of Spain was of a pluralist rather than a unitary nation. The very articulation of the state, running as it did from north to south rather than from west to east, also stood in the way of constructive dialogue with at least some of the regions. Basques and Andalusians had always been more prominent in the central administration than Catalans and Valencians, and had used their position at the centre of government to construct clientage networks that linked Madrid to their respective provinces. The result, not surprisingly, was that the capital showed itself especially sensitive to the requirements of Andalusian landowners and Basque businessmen. By contrast, the Catalan business community, in its anxiety to preserve the protected status of its industrial products in Spain's domestic market, too often appeared as a supplicant knocking at the door.[101]

The difficulties encountered by the Catalan bourgeoisie in projecting itself on the Spanish national stage underline the extent of the growing differentiation between the eastern, urbanized, regions of industrial Spain and the more traditional Spain of the interior and the south, although it had its liberal pockets, not least in the intellectual circles of Madrid. Following the loss of America and the consequent reduction of a formerly Atlantic-wide *nación* to the Iberian Peninsula,[102] it was far from certain whether the narrative of a unitary state and a unified Spanish nation could accommodate the ideas and aspirations of the more developed regions of the Spanish periphery. Yet, at least until the middle decades of the century, potentially contradictory attitudes and aspirations were held together by the overarching narrative of the epic struggle to free Spain from French control.[103]

The years of French invasion and occupation made the struggle against foreign invaders central to the story of the emergence of a sense of Spanish national identity; and the further that memories of the struggle receded into the past, the greater the number of myths clustering around it.[104] Although this was a story in which every region could claim a share, the victory of the *miquelets* at El Bruc, near Barcelona, in June 1808, and the defence of the besieged city of Girona that August, made it especially strong in Catalonia. The Aragonese, too, could point to the defence of Zaragoza as an example of popular resistance to the French. These and other stories of heroism fed into the grand narrative of a national uprising of all the peoples of Spain against an invading army.

Yet the narrative of heroic struggle against foreign invaders had a particular relevance for Castile, where it took its place in a long tradition running from the protracted resistance of the Celtiberian city of Numancia when confronted by the overwhelming forces of the Romans, to the glorious achievements of the reconquest of the Iberian Peninsula from its Muslim occupiers. This narrative, beginning with the fight-back launched by Don Pelayo from the mountain fastnesses of early medieval Asturias, and culminating in the capture of Granada by Ferdinand and Isabella, left little space for the non-Castilian contribution to the forging of the Spanish nation.

The Romantic medievalism of the early nineteenth century, by idealizing the political and institutional history of the kingdoms of Castile and León, also allowed Castile a prominent place in a constitutional reading of the evolving national narrative. If the deputies to the Cortes were to construct a liberal and constitutionalist Spain, they needed to demonstrate that all medieval Spain, including Castile, possessed parliamentary institutions as vigorous as those of France and England. They could then argue that constitutionalism, although subverted by the Crown in the sixteenth and succeeding centuries, was integral to the nation's formation and identity.[105] This depiction of Spain's medieval past as the golden age of its representative institutions made it easier to approximate regional historiographies to the historiography of Castile.

Catalans, caught up in the European enthusiasm for the works of Walter Scott, romanticized their own Middle Ages as the period in which they won their liberties – liberties that had lasted longer than those of medieval Castile. For this reason it could be argued that inhabitants of the territories of the Crown of Aragon, with their more recent experience of contractual monarchy and representative institutions, were ideally placed to work alongside Castilians in shaping the future of Spain. This was the view of Antoni de Capmany, and it encouraged the first generation of Catalan Romantic historians to delve more deeply into the Crown of Aragon's medieval history. The histories they wrote still contained many of the old myths, but acquired a more solid documentary basis following the publication of some of Catalonia's early chronicles and the first systematic exploitation of the vast resources of the Archive of the Crown of Aragon. The direction of the archive was entrusted in 1814 to a conservative liberal, Pròsper de Bofarull, whose family would manage it up to the twentieth century.[106]

Like their Catalan counterparts, the middle and professional classes of early nineteenth-century Scotland also found it possible to identify with a narrative that primarily reflected the historical assumptions of the stronger partner. At first sight this seems surprising, given the success of medieval and sixteenth-century Scottish historians in constructing their own ingenious, if largely mythical, narrative of Scotland's national past. Their construction, however, proved unable to survive the scrutiny of eighteenth-century scholars. Thomas Innes (1662–1744), a Jacobite whose years in France exposed him to the bracing winds of French historical scepticism, demolished to devastating effect the myths of the ancient Gaelic origins of Scottish constitutionalism.[107] For their part, the thinkers of the Scottish Enlightenment, in promoting the theory of the four stages of human progress, challenged old assumptions about the unbroken institutional continuity of the Scottish past and relocated the origins of Scotland's laws and institutions in the Middle Ages. This made possible a closer convergence of Scottish and English history. No longer Celtic but Gothic, Scotland's medieval polity began to look not so very different from the Gothic polity that the Normans brought to England.[108]

Although the heroic figures of what would later come to be known as the Wars of Independence[109] retained their place in the Scottish national pantheon, the similarities between the medieval histories of the two sister kingdoms made it possible for the Scots to appropriate Magna Carta as a fundamental charter of freedom not only for the English but for all the peoples of Britain. They were also compelled to acknowledge that in some respects the pre-Union English polity was more advanced than their own. Its parliament, for instance, was historically more impressive than its Scottish counterpart, reaching a higher stage of development and thus paving the way for the glorious constitutional achievement of the Revolution settlement. The English had also succeeded in abolishing feudalism, whose survival in Scotland into the eighteenth century was a source of embarrassment to Scottish jurists. Such considerations made it more comforting to reconceptualize Scotland's past as forming part of a wider, British, narrative of liberty and progress, instead of clinging to a narrative that was both obsolete and restrictive. But there was one essential qualification. The narrative had to be Scottish as well as English, just as the essential qualification for Catalan and other regional historians was that Spain's national history should be written as the history of all the peoples of the peninsula, instead of being presented as no more than the history of Castile.[110]

Even if the two histories, Scottish and English, could move in unison rather than being integrated into one single narrative, there remained awkward questions about the uniqueness of Scotland's distinctive national identity and how to preserve it. Sir Walter Scott might evoke the romance of Scotland's past, but in the struggle between head and heart that made him the great historical novelist that he was, it was the head that won when he contemplated the present.[111] The past was over and done with for those who, like him, saw the Union as standing for the future. It is symptomatic of the state of mind exemplified by Scott that there was no call for the restoration of the old Scottish parliament. After all, the British parliament had shown itself to be a true bastion of liberty. Equally, Scotland's legal heritage, that traditional symbol of the country's distinctiveness, looked less unique once it had been found to share the Gothic origins of the English common law. Trial by civil jury was introduced in Scotland in 1815, and although there were continuing fears of the anglicization of Scottish law, legal nationalism would not arise in any serious form before the twentieth century.[112]

It was around the Kirk as a uniquely Scottish institution that national sentiment traditionally coalesced. But the Church of Scotland now spoke with not one but several voices. Internal dissension, that perennial feature of Scottish Presbyterianism, was made all the more acute by mounting disquiet over Church–State relations. The origins of the disquiet lay in the perceived subversion of the Kirk's right to freedom from secular intervention, in contravention of the terms of the 1707 Union. It was now intensified, however, by the changes that had taken place in England's relationship with Ireland since the union of 1801, culminating in parliament's approval of Catholic Emancipation in 1829–30. With fears of creeping Catholicism on the increase, old disagreements over intrusion by the state acquired fresh bitterness and came to a head in 1843 when the Disruptionists broke away from the Church assembly and founded the Free Church of Scotland.[113]

As traditional loyalties were called into question, the emotional void left by the disappearance of an independent Scotland had somehow to be filled. An obvious and continuing focus of loyalty presented itself in the form of a British nation whose empire owed so much to the courage, energy and endurance of thousands of Scottish men and women. Catalans had less reason to identify themselves with an empire-building enterprise in which they had played so small a part, and still less now that Spain's overseas empire was largely lost. The great exception was the Catalan commercial and business community, which paradoxically profited far more from Spain's three remaining overseas colonies in the nineteenth century than it had profited from its now defunct empire of the Indies.[114] But other Catalans may have identified themselves less with the Spanish nation-state as they contemplated the effects of what all too often seemed to them the oppressive policies of Madrid. In compensation, it was natural to rally round those regional practices and institutions that helped define them as a people.

One such institution was Catalonia's 'foral law', the part of the legal system that had survived the catastrophe of 1714–16. The principality's marriage and inheritance laws, which made it possible for a testator to leave an entire estate to a single heir, were regarded as central to the survival of the family, the foundational unit of Catalan life. In the popular imagination loyalty to the family, as a coherent and functioning entity, lay at the root of the nation's long tradition of liberty and was the source of its prosperity. Not surprisingly, then, the Catalan legal profession raised an outcry in 1851 when Madrid, dismissing the laws as retrograde, sought to promulgate a civil code heavily influenced by the Code Napoléon.[115] For all their concerns about creeping anglicization Scottish lawyers did not have to face an onslaught of this kind.

For the time being the proposed codification was put on hold, and it was only when the government resumed its moves for the creation of a general legal code during the last two decades of the nineteenth century that the defenders of Catalan civil law began actively to espouse the cause of Catalan nationalism. They did so at a time when other members of the liberal professions were moving in the same direction.[116] By that time the defence of Catalan jurisprudence had become no more than one among several components of a more general movement for the assertion of a sense of national identity.

Long historical experience, magnified by Catalonia's treatment at the hands of the government and its provincial agents between the 1820s and 1840s, lay behind the increasingly outspoken Catalan political nationalism of the late nineteenth century. But the political nationalism was fed by a cultural nationalism that reached back to the age of the Romantic movement, when Catalan intellectuals and scholars, like their contemporaries elsewhere, rediscovered the nation as an organic community with its own distinctive traits. As the Scottish example showed, there was no inevitability about the metamorphosis of Romantic cultural nationalism into a fully fledged political movement. A sentimental Jacobite tradition might nurture a sense of defeat, or help inspire the idealization of the Highlands in the Victorian imagination, but it had little to contribute to the political debate of the times.[117] In Catalonia, by contrast, Romantic revivalism came up against contemporary realities that moved it, if only by degrees, in a political direction.

Along with history and law, Romantic revivalism venerated religion and language as the symbols of a people's identity. Although in Scotland, as in England, Protestantism was central to the nation's image of itself, its effectiveness as a source of national cohesion was diluted by doctrinal pluralism and sectarian rivalries of a kind that did not trouble a uniformly Roman Catholic Spain. Yet while Spanish nation-building drew heavily on the Church's monopoly of worship and belief, it was a monopoly that still left room for variations, both regional and local. Catalans could lay claim to their own unique sacred space in the famous Benedictine abbey of Santa María, set amidst the serrated rock formations of Montserrat in Catalonia's pre-coastal mountain range and within easy distance of Barcelona. In a nineteenth century imbued with Romantic sentiments that embraced mountain landscapes like those of the Highlands, the abbey of Montserrat, famed for its precious image of the 'Black Virgin', became a potent symbol of Catalan national identity.[118]

Language, too, raised problems for Scots anxious to affirm their national distinctiveness. After the long and hard battle fought by the civil and ecclesiastical authorities to eradicate Gaelic as the tongue of a barbarous and benighted Highlands,[119] a reversal of direction was out of the question. Gaelic could not be the language of a Scotland that had turned its back on barbarism and advanced to a new and higher stage of civilization. Lowland Scots, or Lallans, was a different proposition, but it had been in decline as a literary language since the end of the sixteenth century, and during the eighteenth century growing numbers of Scots were turning to English as the language of refinement. Lexicographers might pore over the ancestry of Lowland Scots, and Walter Scott's *The Antiquary* might display its rich variety, but there was no denying that its origins lay in Old English. It could hardly, then, be used as convincing evidence of a distinctive Scottish identity, although some might claim that Scots was the purest form of what was now the shared language of the British nation. As with history so with language, it seemed that Scottishness had a tendency to merge into a general Britishness.[120]

Catalan, on the other hand, is a Romance language distinct from Castilian and it continued to be spoken by all sections of society. As the language of the people its origins attracted the attention of intellectuals and writers keen to uncover Catalonia's national roots. In 1815 Josep Pau Ballot published the first Catalan grammar. There had always been broadsheets, popular romances and works of devotion published in the vernacular, but Bonaventura Carles Aribau's 'Ode to the *Pàtria*', published in 1833, set a precedent for the writing of patriotic poems in Catalan that would be followed by a cluster of Romantic poets like Joaquim Rubió i Ors. Their poetry, and other publications of the 1830s and 1840s, marked the beginnings of the recovery of Catalan as a literary language, although one confined to a few rarefied forms, most notably poetry and plays. It was a process that reached a climax in 1859 with the institution of annual 'floral games', the *Jocs Florals*, in imitation of competitions among medieval troubadours, at least as imagined in the nineteenth century.[121]

The revivalist movement, however, reflected the interests and preoccupations of a small cultural elite. Even the members of that elite, while valuing Catalan for its popular origins, did not question the position secured in specific areas of Catalan life by Castilian, the national language of Spain, and would often use Castilian when writing to each other. Although the Romantics had given Catalan a new and more sophisticated literary dimension, as a written and a spoken language it continued to coexist and interact with Castilian as it had in the past, with the two languages catering for different needs and situations. The same person would speak Castilian in certain circumstances and Catalan in others, although Castilian as the language of public life enjoyed a higher status. It was only in the 1860s that the first serious attempts were made to extend the use of Catalan beyond a limited and refined literary sphere.[122]

The revival of Catalan by the Romantics of the first and second generation did not imply or involve any distancing from Spain as the nation to which Catalans owed their allegiance, although it may be tempting to view it retrospectively in this light. It is striking, too, that literary and historical publications of this period make notably little mention of the fall of Barcelona in 1714, which was to form the centrepiece of the twenty-first-century campaign for independence, not least because the tercentenary came at a time when radical nationalists were pushing the Catalan regional government along the road that would lead to its unilateral declaration of independence three years later. Such publications tended, rather, to dwell on a romanticized Middle Ages and an idealized rural Catalonia.[123] In this respect they resembled publications appearing in Scotland during the first half of the nineteenth century, which were similarly imbued with Romantic medievalism and idealized the Highlands, both past and present. Yet around 1860 Romantic revivalism in Catalonia acquired an intensity not paralleled in contemporary Scotland, widening into a full-blown revivalist movement that was first given the name of the 'Renaissance', or *Renaixença*, in 1864.[124]

This deepening and broadening were partly a natural continuation and expansion of the Romantic revivalism of the preceding decades, and had the comforting effect of providing an alternative image of Catalonia to that of a society in the throes of rapid industrialization. But they were also a response to the growth of political and administrative pressures from Madrid – pressures resulting from the desire to build a stronger and more centralized Spanish nation-state. The pressures were reflected, too, in the deployment of a Spanish historical narrative that heavily emphasized the contribution of Castile to the making of Spain.

In the middle years of the century this Spanish national history, although liberal in its origins, began to reflect the growing divisions within the liberal camp. The Moderates drew much of their strength from the Madrid-based network of landowning families that dominated the Castilian interior,[125] and although the two groups of Moderates and Progressives had much in common, the Moderates were more conservative, and less European, in outlook.[126] During the ten unbroken years in which the Moderates held power between 1844 and 1854 the divisions between the two wings of liberalism widened and factionalism intensified. In producing the new Constitution of 1845 the Moderates were turning their backs on reforming measures introduced by the Progressive faction. This faction was responsible for the whole-scale secularization of Church property in 1837, a radical reform that prompted a strong neo-Catholic reaction, especially in Moderate circles.

Church and State were formally reconciled in the Concordat of 1851, but the expulsion of the religious orders and the wholesale stripping of the Church's assets had opened deep wounds. The resulting bitterness could only fortify an already existing conservative narrative that placed at the heart of Spain's national history the adoption of Catholicism by its Visigothic monarch Recaredo in the year 587, and the centuries of struggle to preserve and uphold the faith.

This reading of the Spanish past was not confined to Castile. In Catalonia it found an ardent advocate in Jaume Balmes, the most influential Catalan conservative thinker of the nineteenth century. Although a patriotic Catalan who saw it as his duty to persuade the socially conservative Catalan bourgeoisie to adjust to the challenges of an industrializing society, Balmes was strongly imbued with the sense of Spain as a nation defined by its religion. He was also adamant in his warning that Spain's hard-won national unity must not be put at risk by precipitous regional reactions to contemporary events. 'Without dreaming of absurd projects of independence, unjust in themselves and made unrealizable by the European situation', as he wrote in

1844, he memorably advised his Catalan compatriots not to be carried away by 'blind provincialism' or forget that 'Catalans are also Spaniards'.[127] But the conservative interpretation of the Spanish past that he espoused was not automatically centralist in its orientation. It was an interpretation that resonated strongly with the Carlists, who would deploy it in the defence of a politically reactionary romantic regionalism against the centralizing aspirations of the state.[128]

While the Catalan bourgeoisie was deeply devout, and the *Renaixença* was suffused with religious sentiment, growing clerical obscurantism in the 1850s and 1860s, together with the association of a discredited monarchy with the forces of conservative reaction, progressively alienated the more liberal sections of Catalan society. Many members of the Catalan bourgeoisie held to the top-down narrative of the creation of Spain as a unitary nation-state elaborated by successive Liberal regimes. They therefore accepted the fifteenth-century union of the Crowns of Castile and Aragon as a necessary phase in the building of the nation from the centre, just as many Scots accepted the 1707 Union with its transfer of powers to Westminster as essential to national development. Yet a strongly conservative narrative revolving around the creation of national unity by a centralizing state and an all-embracing Church inevitably jarred with Catalans of a progressive turn of mind and encouraged them to develop their own alternative approach.

Denouncing the 'centralization' pursued by successive Madrid governments, they pointed to the history of the Catalan *pàtria* as the story of a continuous struggle for liberty. Centralization, as they saw it, was placing Catalonia, and all Spain, in a straitjacket.[129] When they depicted Catalonia's history as one of a never-ending struggle for freedom, Catalan Romantic historians of the second generation were less shackled by inhibitions than nineteenth-century Scottish historians who tended to ignore or reject those aspects of their national past, like the survival of feudal institutions, that now caused them some embarrassment. Since Scottish constitutionalism was now successfully merged with a more English-based constitutionalism, there was little demand for the teaching of a distinctively Scottish history when new chairs of history were established in Scottish universities in 1876.[130] Catalan historians, by contrast, felt free to indulge to the full their pride in the achievements of a medieval Crown of Aragon that had created a far-flung Mediterranean empire and had been in the forefront of medieval Europe's struggle for liberty and representative government.

In 1846 Antoni de Bofarull, Pròsper de Bofarull's nephew and the author of poems and plays celebrating famous episodes from Catalonia's past, published a patriotic account of the 'Deeds and Memories of the Catalans'.[131]

In the 1840s and 1850s Víctor Balaguer, another member of Barcelona's literary elite and himself a progressive liberal who went on to hold ministerial appointments in Madrid, linked the history of the principality specifically to the land itself in a succession of works devoted to its beauties and its architectural heritage. He then produced between 1860 and 1863 an enormously influential five-volume *History of Catalonia and the Crown of Aragon*.[132] These and other Romantic historians of the second generation were animated above all by the desire to recover Catalonia's distinctive historical identity. This made them more critical of the fifteenth-century Union of the Crowns than members of the generation caught up in Spain's struggle against the forces of Napoleon. For them, the election at the Compromise of Caspe in 1412 of a member of the Castilian ruling house to govern the lands of the Crown of Aragon, and the Union of the Crowns that flowed from that fateful choice, had indeed produced the beneficial result of creating a united Spain. Yet it also inaugurated a long period of decadence for Catalonia and the progressive loss of its medieval liberties. As Balaguer complained, Spain's story was too often told from the standpoint of Castile, and this, he wrote, was 'a grave error. Spain is a composite of different nationalities. What a few centuries ago were kingdoms and nations, today are provinces.'[133]

This alternative, decentralized, reading of the history of Spain meant not only the exaltation of Catalonia's medieval past as the history of liberty, but also the placing on pedestals of two figures identified with heroic resistance to Castilian domination: Pau Claris, the defender of Catalonia's liberties in the 1640 revolt, and Rafael Casanova, the city councillor who had led Barcelona's doomed struggle against the Bourbon army in 1714.[134] In 1863 Barcelona's city authorities asked Víctor Balaguer to suggest names for the streets that would criss-cross the large new area for urban development opened up by the recent demolition of the city walls – an area that came to be known as the Eixample, or 'enlargement', based on a plan drawn up by a Catalan engineer, Ildefons Cerdà. The actual process of enlargement was delayed by endless disagreements between Barcelona and Madrid over attempts at governmental interference, and it was no doubt a source of gratification to the city's inhabitants that Balaguer's choice of street names should primarily have commemorated people, places, institutions and events that served as reminders of the principality's glorious past. Pau Claris and Rafael Casanova both had streets named after them, as did the old City Council of a Hundred (the Consell de Cent), the Diputació and the Corts, all abolished by the Bourbons. Streets were named, too, after the different kingdoms and territories of the medieval Crown of Aragon and the warriors whose heroism and daring had given its inhabitants their Mediterranean empire. Gestures were also made to heroic episodes drawn from Spain's national past like the resistance of Numancia to the Romans, but the Eixample acted above all as a route-map through Catalonia's history.[135]

The *Renaixença* was the literary, linguistic and historical recovery of a lost Catalan *pàtria* that was idealized in the process. While expressing a sense of loss, it also constituted a search for identity by a people proud of their achievements, both in the past and the present, but uncertain about the place that belonged to them in the new Spanish nation-state. The construction of Barcelona's Eixample, in looking to the future while using street names to anchor itself in the past, typified the ambivalence that ran through Catalan society in the mid-nineteenth century. Spain and yet not Spain, different but yet the same, a Catalonia undergoing unprecedented change in the space of two or three generations naturally displayed signs both of confidence and fear. Its business elite was, and knew itself to be, painfully dependent on Madrid for the protection of Catalonia's industry; its expanding bourgeoisie still saw itself involved in the Spanish national project, although with growing doubts. Its industrial workers and artisans, many of them living in abject poverty, were restless and prone to sporadic acts of violence that frightened the propertied classes and left them wondering where to turn. There was here a dangerous mixture of interests and emotions that pointed a nation in search of itself towards several different paths. The *Renaixença* testified to the creativity of this society, but also to the deep uncertainties that gave creativity an edge.

Mid-nineteenth-century Scots were less obsessively concerned with the possible loss of national identity and the recovery of their past, primarily because they fitted more comfortably than contemporary Catalans into the larger political association of which they formed a part. Empire and industrialization were bringing unprecedented prosperity to their country, although Scots, too, like the Catalans, were experiencing the social dislocations that accompanied rapid industrial growth.

In so far, therefore, as a Scottish *Renaixença* existed – and 'Renaissance' seems a term unsuited to the description of Scotland's cultural life in the middle decades of the nineteenth century – it was less inward-looking than its Catalan counterpart, and was more an affirmation of a successful present than a paean in praise of a regretted past. As elsewhere, ballads and folklore might be its stock in trade, and statues be raised in honour of national figures like Robert Burns, but its most visible symbols were the great building projects of the age, from the Scottish Baronial castles that paid lip service to the medieval past, to the magnificent town halls that testified to the nation's present prosperity and its confidence in the future.

In contrast to the relationship between Catalonia and Madrid, the British state was conveniently remote from Scotland's day-to-day concerns, and a host of voluntary associations occupied the intermediate space between state and citizen.[136] A series of articles written in the 1850s for the *Diario de Barcelona* expressed admiration for the capacity shown by the British to organize themselves into voluntary associations and thus create a civil society for themselves, contrasting this with the French centralizing model that was blighting local initiative in Spain. Catalans should follow the example set by the British.[137]

The number and vitality of Scotland's many associations testified to the strength of its determination to maintain an active civic life that would preserve the nation's character and its distinctive values. Awareness of, and pride in, national distinctiveness was deeply rooted in this vibrant mid-nineteenth-century Scotland, and if the twenty-three-year-old Robert Louis Stevenson is representative of his compatriots, it became all the sharper as they travelled south. In 1873 he wrote from Suffolk to his mother of his gratitude at living in Scotland, and went on as follows:

> I cannot get over my astonishment – indeed it increases every day, at the hopeless gulph that there is between England and Scotland, and English and Scotch. Nothing is the same; and I feel as strange and outlandish here, as I do in France or Germany. Everything by the wayside, in the houses, or about the people, strikes me with an unexpected unfamiliarity; I walk among surprises, for just where you think you have them, something wrong turns up.[138]

Scottish civil society, however, operated within the structure of the imperial nation-state to which the country belonged – a nation-state that, for its part, gave Scottish nationals unparalleled opportunities to make their imprint on a wider world. For the time being, at least, the competing claims of nation, state and empire coexisted in ways that worked to the advantage of all three. Yet, as with Catalonia, the rapidly accelerating pace of social and economic change would require adjustments on all sides to the necessarily uneven relationship between a people possessed of a proud sense of their own distinctiveness and a nation-state that claimed their full allegiance as citizens.

CHAPTER 5

The Call for Home Rule
1860–1975

Grievance and Redress

A sense of grievance can easily become all-consuming. Grievance was no stranger to nineteenth-century Scots and Catalans as they contemplated the nature of the relationship between the central government and themselves. Unequal unions inevitably encourage in the junior partner a feeling that the stronger party fails to understand it and ignores its concerns. Every indication of neglect – or, even worse, of deliberate ill-treatment – every misunderstanding, and every perceived or actual slight, is set alongside others in the storehouse of collective memory. As memories accumulate they create a mentality of victimhood that goes looking for some fresh grievance to add to the store. In a famous leading article of 4 December 1856 *The Times* unkindly described Scotland as 'manifestly a country in want of a grievance'.[1] It was not entirely wrong.

Catalonia and Scotland, however, from the seventeenth century onwards, did in fact have many good reasons to feel aggrieved. *Greuge* – 'grievance' or 'affront' – was a word frequently to be heard on Catalan lips. Among eighteenth- and nineteenth-century Catalans there lurked a memory of the oppressive policies of Olivares that had led their countrymen to revolt in 1640. To this were added the rawer memories of the repression that followed the surrender of Barcelona in September 1714 and the abolition of the principality's Constitutions, followed by the harsh periods of martial law under the government of successive captains-general. The collective memory of Scotland, shaped by its medieval Wars of Independence and its frequently unhappy experience of English behaviour both before and after

the dynastic union of 1603, had at its forefront the repression that followed
the uprisings of 1715 and 1745, the suppression of Highland culture,
and the continuing tragedy of the Highland clearances.

On the other hand incorporating union had brought benefits to both
countries, even if these were not always acknowledged or even obvious. The
disaster of 1714 may or may not have administered a salutary shock to the
Catalan psyche, but the eighteenth century had been a period of undeniable
growth and prosperity for the principality, which took advantage of expanding
domestic and imperial markets to lay the foundations of the commercial and
industrial society that emerged in the course of the nineteenth century.
Scotland, for its part, gained from the Union of 1707 full membership in
what was rapidly becoming a dynamic political, commercial and imperial
enterprise. This had allowed it to develop its native talents and ingenuity to a
point where it was able to take its place as one of the great success stories of
nineteenth-century Europe. It undoubtedly seized with both hands the
opportunities that came its way, but it is hard to imagine that Scotland would
have enjoyed such success, or that the success would have taken the form that
it did, if it had remained outside the British imperial project.

Yet grievances rankled and by the final decades of the nineteenth
century were leading to demands for major changes in the existing political
and constitutional systems of both Spain and Britain. In view of the turbulence of mid-century Spanish political life it is not surprising that Catalan
demands for change were more urgent and insistent than those of the Scots.
The reinvigoration of a sense of Catalonia's regional identity within the
Spanish nation-state by the historical and literary researches of the writers,
scholars and folklorists of the *Renaixença* – all diffused through the medium
of plays, novels and articles in the press – had created a mental environment
conducive to the advancing of political demands where this seemed appropriate. There were, moreover, some suggestive contemporary models for
those who were seeking a way forward. In Europe, Giuseppe Mazzini had
shown how the spirit of popular nationalism could be aroused to great
political effect. On the other side of the Atlantic mid-nineteenth-century
Cuba, where Catalan merchants and industrialists possessed extensive
economic interests, had embarked on a long period of revolutionary agita-
tion, first in pursuit of autonomy within the Spanish imperial polity, and
then of independence.[2]

The term 'Catalanism', hitherto confined to a cultural movement, began
to acquire serious political overtones during the course of the so-called
'Revolutionary Sexennium' of 1868–74, which began with the overthrow of
the Isabelline monarchy by the Catalan General Prim, went on to witness

the proclamation of the first Spanish Republic in 1873, and ended with the restoration of the monarchy under Isabella's son, Alfonso XII, in 1874.[3] These six years, culminating in the transient triumph of republicanism, brought all the political and social contradictions of Spain to the surface. They were also years that saw the emergence of new forces in Spanish political life, and an upsurge of fresh thinking about the ordering of the Spanish state. For the first time, Catalans were seriously represented in the Madrid government, with ten of them appointed as ministers in this period, as against three in the reign of Ferdinand VII, and six in that of his daughter. This was to be only a fleeting success. No more than five Catalans would hold ministerial appointments between 1875 and 1902, during the first twenty-seven years of the Restoration monarchy – years of two-party dominance, instituted by Cánovas del Castillo, when Conservatives and Liberals, each supported by massive patronage networks, took turns in holding power. Of 183 ministers between 1902 and the proclamation of the Second Republic in 1931, 13 would be Catalans. By contrast, of British prime ministers alone, six of the eleven between 1868 and 1935 were Scots by birth or origin.[4]

The 1868–74 sexennium and its failure were to prove critical for the transformation of Catalan cultural regionalism into political nationalism. For a brief moment, Catalans found themselves at the centre of high politics in Madrid. The leader of the Progressives, General Prim, a native of the Catalan town of Reus, engineered the coup that overthrew the Isabelline monarchy, but his tenure of power, which was under constant assault, was brought to an abrupt end by his assassination in December 1870. In the spring of 1873, after the collapse of a new monarchical experiment under Amadeo of Savoy, attempts were made to set up a Federal Republic. The leader of the Federal Republicans, and the man whose philosophy inspired the Federal movement, was Francesc Pi i Margall, one of the four presidents of the short-lived first Spanish Republic, two of them Catalans.

Pi's presidency in the summer of 1873 lasted for just over a month. The Republicans were divided, and their programme proved far too visionary; but, both before and after his brief appearance at the heart of Spanish political life, Pi was the standard-bearer of a movement and an ideology that enjoyed a wide appeal. In equating republicanism with federalism, which in earlier years had been an unacceptable concept because of the dangers it posed to Spain's national integrity,[5] his message resonated strongly in Catalonia, where it attracted the support of members of an increasingly large and politically conscious middle class, and of a working class with a greater sense of solidarity than was to be found elsewhere Spain.

But he and his followers failed in their ambition to generate a mass popular movement in support of their cause.[6]

Yet they were putting forward answers, even if often impractical ones, to a long-standing question that would not go away – the question of the best form of state for a country that contained within its borders a number of historic regions and communities. The question was by no means unique to Spain, and indeed was also implicit in the constitutional and administrative structure of the United Kingdom. In nineteenth-century Spain, however, it had a particular urgency because the state was functioning so badly. The Liberals of the Cortes of Cadiz had inherited from the reformist ministers of Bourbon Spain the concept of a strong central government, and left this as their legacy to succeeding generations. In the three decades preceding the revolution of 1868, successive Liberal regimes sought, although with very mixed success, to build up the power of the state at the centre, and in so doing succeeded in antagonizing many of those whom they sought to embrace in a grand national project.

Those regions or parts of Spain that resented the heavy hand of Madrid had two possible options by way of response. One was to demand a reorganization of the state along the federal lines advocated by Pi i Margall, and a second was to seek a form of home rule within a more or less centralized state. While Pi was himself a doctrinaire liberal, an important practical precedent for this second option had been set by the British North America Act of 1867, which made Canada a self-governing entity within the British Empire.[7] The war in Cuba, breaking out in 1868 and brought to a temporary close ten years later by a proposal from the Spanish authorities for a form of autonomy that came to nothing, showed that home rule, as a possible solution to the problems of Spain and its overseas possessions, was at least an option deserving of serious consideration. A third possible option, independence, which was won by Cuba in 1898 after a bitter struggle against a colonial regime that had united broad sections of society against it, was barely contemplated in the Spain of the later nineteenth century.

The Cuban conflict, shaped until the abolition of slavery in 1886 by the attitude of a rich planter class that looked to Spain to defend it in the event of a slave revolt, touched Catalonia closely. Cuba, after all, was a major market for Catalan manufactures, and Catalan businessmen and merchants had made a massive contribution to the development of the island's sugar and plantation economy. It had also become a second home to Catalan immigrants of modest origins, who had set up their own small businesses as artisans or shopkeepers, but stayed in touch with their homeland. The impact of events in Cuba was therefore felt not only in the Catalan financial and commercial world, but also at a personal and emotional level in many Catalan families. If the question of Cuba played a dominant part in Spanish political life of the time, it is not surprising that it also cast an especially heavy shadow over the Catalonia of the later nineteenth century. It also had a belated but curious by-product when a Catalan nationalist who had returned from Cuba invented in 1915 a Catalan separatist flag, the *estelada*, which introduced alongside the red bars on a gold background of Catalonia's traditional flag, the *senyera*, a white five-pointed star in a blue triangle inspired by the flags of Cuba and Puerto Rico. A hundred years later the *estelada*, taken up by the partisans of secession, would be fluttering from the balconies of numerous municipal and private buildings.[8]

While independence had a few devotees, the great majority of Catalans saw their native country as an integral part of Spain, and for many of them some form of federation had an obvious appeal. For federalists, a centralizing government in Madrid meant authoritarianism and military repression, bureaucratic inefficiency and political corruption. A degree of autonomy, whether in the form of federalism or home rule, promised to tackle these ills at source by reducing the extent of the power exercised from the centre. In proposing a fundamental reordering of the structure of the state it also tapped into a widespread desire for the political and economic regeneration of Spain.

Catalans were in no doubt that they were the best equipped of all the peoples of Spain to bring this regeneration about. In their eyes regeneration meant making Spain over in the image of Catalonia, and this in turn required the restoration of the kind of contractual relationship between ruler and ruled that had once existed in the Crown of Aragon. Such a relationship, they believed, would liberate forces capable of transforming Spain's backward economy. Proud of their commercial and industrial achievements in the face of constant discouragement, their self-image was that of a practical, industrious and pragmatic people, universally known for what they called their *seny*, or practical common sense. It is not surprising that, in keeping with this image, modern Scottish philosophy should have found an appropriate home in Barcelona, where from 1837 it was promoted in the city's restored university by its first professor of 'Ideology and Logic', Martí d'Eixalà, and later established on firmer foundations by his successor, Xavier Llorens i Barba. The empirical doctrines of the Edinburgh School were well calculated to appeal to a people of *seny*.[9]

Federalism, republicanism and regeneration might be the order of the day, but when the Federal Republicans were finally installed in government in 1873 they failed disastrously, in part because of bitter divisions between all-out federalists and those who were afraid that intransigent federalism would result in the break-up of Spain. Their short and precarious tenure of power served to discredit their cause, and the restoration of the monarchy in 1874 made it clear that their moment had passed. A frustrated Pi i Margall, although remaining the leader of a minority republican faction, devoted himself increasingly to the exposition of his federalist theories in speeches and print.

Although the republican cause might be lost, Pi and his followers believed that the federal system they had been unable to establish was the only viable alternative to the centralized nation-state. In 1876 Alfonso XII approved a new Constitution for Spain, now once again a monarchy. Introduced by Cánovas del Castillo this Constitution was carefully designed to lower the political temperature by incorporating a broader section of the middle classes within the oligarchical political structure that would run the state from Madrid. In that same year Pi published *Las nacionalidades*, a book that was to become the bible of Spanish federalism.

Surveying the contemporary international scene in his opening chapters, Pi expressed his opposition to great unitary nations, and asked whether the recent unification of Germany and Italy had really been worth so many calamitous conflicts. For him true unity could not be artificially imposed, whether by monarchical or religious power, but could only be achieved through a voluntary federation. Spain had been united by the use of force, and this had produced disastrous consequences. Nevertheless, in spite of the efforts of the central state, 'there survives in Spain not only a diversity of laws but also of languages', and an infinite variety of customs.

The only solution, in Pi's opinion, was for all the peoples of the peninsula, including the Portuguese, to join forces to form a federal republic. While each of its constituent parts would enjoy autonomy, the autonomy must be kept within bounds. His answer to the argument that federalism would lead to 'the dissolution of the *patria*', was that 'the nation asserts itself vigorously in the minds and hearts of all Spaniards . . . What people or province has ever shown a tendency to separate itself from Spain – not even the Basque provinces, with their unequalled autonomy . . .?'[10] Although he claimed that even the so-called 'cantonalist' or regional uprisings of the summer of 1873 in south-eastern and southern Spain did not lead to bids for independence, it was hard to escape the conclusion that the anarchy they unleashed did not augur well for the prospects of a federal state.

Much of Pi's federalist programme for Spain, and ultimately for all Europe, was remote from reality, and his ideas failed to generate the mass popular enthusiasm he had expected. But, for all the flaws in his proposals, he was grappling with a fundamental problem relating to the structure of European nation-states, which was all the more challenging if, like Britain and Spain, they were also imperial powers with overseas colonies. Most, in some form or other, were still composite in character, made up as they were of disparate peoples and regions, many of them reluctant to comply with the demands of remote central governments.

Spaniards like Pi i Margall were not alone in their preoccupation. Scotland, too, had its federalists or partial federalists. One of these was Frederick Scott Oliver, a Liberal Unionist. In a series of letters to *The Times*, published late in 1910 as a book entitled *Federalism and Home Rule*, Oliver, who was deeply exercised by the Irish question, advocated a reform of the British Constitution in a federalist direction. Like Pi i Margall, he was impressed by the success of a federal United States, but rejected the term 'federalism' for his proposed constitutional reforms. These entailed a devolution of power to four 'national parliaments' in England, Scotland, Ireland and Wales. Like the parliaments of Britain's overseas dominions, these would be subject to the supreme authority of the Imperial Parliament at Westminster. This, he explained, 'is not a process which . . . can be correctly called Federalism. It is something a great deal safer. It is also something which is a great deal easier to bring about. The right word is Delegation.'[11]

Federalism in its full manifestation did not have much appeal in the British Isles at this time, while Pi i Margall's response to the challenge of establishing what he called 'unity in variety'[12] was too imprecise and abstract for many of his followers. The most dynamic of these was Valentí Almirall, who, although a federalist, was more interested in the fate of Catalonia than in any theoretical reorganization of Spain. Imbued with the spirit of the *Renaixença*, and disillusioned by the failure of the Republic, Almirall set out to promote Catalan regionalism as a political cause. In 1879 he founded the first daily newspaper in Catalan, the *Diari Català*, and in 1882 set up a Catalan cultural and political Centre, the Centre Català. In effect he was turning his back on the politics of Madrid, and in his book, *Lo Catalanisme*, published in 1886, he insisted on Catalonia's unique national character, which he contrasted with the impulsive and authoritarian character of Castile. It was Castile's assertion of hegemony over Spain that had drained life away from the provinces and was responsible for the country's decay.[13]

Almirall's Catalan particularism, for all its emotional identification with his Catalan *pàtria*, still looked outwards as well as inwards. The salvation of Spain, he believed, could only come from a synthesis between 'the generalizing spirit of Castile and the analytical spirit of the regions that constituted the old Aragonese federation'. This alone would make possible 'a new organization of the state which can lead us to a different political and social style of life and raise us in the eyes of cultivated nations'.[14] But if Almirall, like Pi i Margall, was still thinking in terms of the entire Hispanic community, he was also anxious to make the government aware of the nature and extent of Catalonia's discontents. In 1885, at a moment when plans for a commercial treaty with Great Britain threatened the protected position of Catalan manufacturers in the domestic market, and when Catalonia's 'foral law' was again under attack from Madrid,[15] Almirall drew on all shades of Catalan opinion to organize what came to be called a 'Memorandum of Grievances' (*Memorial de Greuges*), for personal presentation to Alfonso XII. In the memorandum he seized the opportunity to expound his ideas about the historical evolution of Spain, and the disastrous consequences of its unification by Castile.

Although the king was encouraging when greeting the Catalan deputation sent to Madrid to present the memorandum, it was given a hostile reception by the capital's political circles and by the press. Not surprisingly, the deputation received an enthusiastic welcome on returning home, and the large print run of the memorandum did much to disseminate Catalanist ideas among the province's population at large.[16] Almirall, however, found it increasingly difficult to hold his movement together, and he never succeeded in turning his Catalan Centre into a real political force. Pressure came from the left, which was hostile to the conservative administration in Madrid, and from the strongly Catholic conservative right. He also failed to win over businessmen, industrialists and rural landowners in a period of impressive economic growth, duly celebrated by the holding in Barcelona in 1888 of a grand Universal Exhibition to which Almirall objected.

The 1888 exhibition was intended to put Barcelona on the European map as one of the great industrial and commercial centres of the continent. In this year, which also saw the foundation in Barcelona of the socialist trade union, the UGT (Unión General de Trabajadores), Barcelona's formidable mayor, Francesc Rius i Taulet, was determined, against all the opposition, to make the world aware of his native city's importance. With the support of Liberal Prime Minister Práxedes Sagasta of Spain, and of Conservative and Liberal members of the local elites with ties to the business community, he would showcase Barcelona as the motor of Spain's economy. He would also reveal it to the world as a progressive European metropolis, whose modernity was reflected in the great process of urban renewal then under way and in the new public monuments under construction. The exhibition was opened by Sagasta, who spoke some words in Catalan in the presence of the queen regent, María Cristina de Austria, accompanied by her infant son, Alfonso XIII. The concluding speech was delivered entirely in Catalan by

Marcelino Menéndez y Pelayo, the great Catholic polymath who held a chair in Spanish literature at the University of Madrid. Even the language of the Catalans, it appeared, was now accepted and approved, and María Cristina went on to attend the *Jocs Florals*, of which she was proclaimed the queen.[17]

In spite of Almirall's diatribes against an exhibition that seemed to him a waste of money, it drew large crowds, especially from within Spain itself. His opposition to the exhibition did nothing to endear him to the business community, many of whose members disapproved of his anticlericalism and were distrustful of his liberal and republican ideology. In addition they were too dependent on the maintenance of good relations with the government to run the risk of undermining the relationship by embracing Almirall and his ideas, and they were anxious to ensure Catalonia's place in the vanguard of Spanish national regeneration. This depended on close cooperation with ministers in Madrid. Almirall's opposition to the exhibition, on the other hand, may in part have been motivated by the desire to hold the government at arm's length.[18]

As Almirall's movement fragmented, the Catalanist cause found a new and more persuasive advocate in Enric Prat de la Riba, a lawyer, like Almirall and so many of the professionals involved in the literary and cultural *Renaixença*. Prat de la Riba was a major driving force behind the 'Bases of Manresa' (*Bases de Manresa*), a programme that emerged out of the deliberations of an assembly held in the Catalan city of Manresa in 1892. This was in effect a programme for home rule and it shaped the Catalanist political movement that would eventually triumph with the advent of the Second Republic in 1931. It envisaged Catalonia as an autonomous region within the Spanish state, with its own parliament as the supreme legislative authority. All administrative posts were to be filled by Catalans, and Catalan was to be the language of government.[19]

At a time when Catalan regionalism was acquiring a political dimension, and when Basque demands for the restoration of fiscal exemptions lost in 1839 were assuming a stridently nationalist tone, regional aspirations were also becoming a burning issue in British political life. At the end of 1885 the intractability of the Irish question and the increasingly assertive character of Irish nationalism converted Gladstone to the cause of Home Rule. Although Ireland was his prime concern, his new political stance was bound to resonate strongly in Scotland. The close ties between Ireland and Scotland, and especially western Scotland with its heavy Irish immigration, meant that any major change to the terms of the Anglo-Irish union, like the disestablishment of the Irish Church in 1869, had immediate consequences for the Anglo-Scottish relationship.

The 1707 Union had set out the terms that were to govern the relations between the state and the Presbyterian Church. These terms were now brought into question as a majority of the Free Church, under the impact of the new Irish measure, came out in favour of disestablishment for Scotland also. It was a striking example of how the priority that Westminster insisted on according the Irish question impinged on Scotland's domestic affairs. Resentment was mounting, and this became yet another in the lengthening list of Scottish grievances.[20]

As early as 1853 an Association for the Vindication of Scottish Rights had been founded, in response to a growing feeling that the Union of 1707 was not working well. At its first Glasgow meeting the president of the new Association, the Earl of Eglinton, evoked 'great applause' when he told his audience: 'We love our English brethren, and we are proud to be associated with them in an empire on which the sun never sets – but we are Scotchmen still. We glory in the triumphs of a Marlborough, a Nelson and a Wellington, but may we not look with pride to the achievements of a Wallace and a Bruce?'[21] The mixture of pride and defensiveness is palpable.

While disclaiming any desire to dissolve the Union, the Association wished to 'obtain that justice for Scotland which the Union promised, which the English promised; but which we have not yet received.'[22] Resenting the failure to give Scotland its fair share in the disbursement of public funds, the Association wanted more Scottish MPs at Westminster, and a separate Scottish administration headed by a restored Scottish Secretary. In practice, Scots were largely running their own affairs at all but the top administrative levels, as the Catalans were not. In spite of this, successive London governments were thought to be either intervening too much, thus introducing a creeping form of centralization, or else intervening too little, as when the government did not come to the help of the Highlands when the potato crop failed in 1846–7.

The list of real or imagined grievances was long, but the Association failed to win the support of leading figures in the dominant Scottish Liberal Party, and was wound up after only three years of existence. Further discontent, however, was fuelled not only by the question of Church disestablishment but also by such measures as the Scottish Education Act of 1872, which abolished the old parochial school system and established a Scottish Education Board located in London rather than Edinburgh. Although the Act brought the benefits of compulsory universal education to Scotland, and demands for change in the Scottish educational system came from within Scotland itself, it was attacked for diluting the Scottishness of Scottish education, long a source of national pride.[23]

Early in 1884 resentment over London's management, or mismanagement, of Scotland's affairs prompted a fresh attempt by leading members of the Scottish political, social and administrative establishment to recover the political initiative. A mass 'National Meeting' in the Free Assembly Hall in Edinburgh demanded the creation of a separate Department of State for Scotland.[24] Lord Salisbury's conservative government responded by reviving the office of Scottish Secretary of State, although without giving the holder cabinet rank, and by establishing a Scottish Office in Whitehall. Although the Reform Act of 1884 increased the number of Scottish MPs to seventy-two, and made substantial progress towards establishing adult male suffrage, the sense that Scotland was being short-changed persisted, and was enhanced when Gladstone launched his Irish Home Rule Bill in April 1886. Scots failed to understand why the Irish should be rewarded for their rebelliousness with the prospect of a parliament of their own, while loyal partners to the Union like themselves and the Welsh were promised no such reward.

Gladstone's offer of limited Irish home rule in 1886 split the Liberal Party, which had always been an uncomfortable coalition of old Whigs and new Liberals. On the one hand it led to a breakaway movement of Liberal Unionists whose belief that the Union was in danger induced them to make common cause with the Conservatives, and finally to amalgamate with the Conservative Party in 1912.[25] On the other hand it prompted a second group of dissident Liberals to set up a Scottish Home Rule Association, with a programme for the restoration of a Scottish parliament in Edinburgh – a proposal reluctantly embraced by Gladstone, who came round to the idea of Home Rule for Scotland in 1888. In spite of denunciations of the Home Rulers as separatists bent on the destruction of the British monarchy, the Association's programme was in practice very moderate, especially when compared with the Catalan programme for autonomy that would be outlined in the Bases of Manresa of 1892. It offered no challenge to the sovereignty of the Westminster parliament, showed no interest in the reorganization of Great Britain along federal lines, and was primarily directed towards giving Scotland more efficient and accountable government.

The support of the hierarchy of the Liberal Party for the cause of Scottish Home rule was tepid, and it took the creation in 1900 of a youth movement within the party, the Young Scots Society, to inject new vigour into the cause by making home rule a *sine qua non* for social reform. In view of the resistance of an English-dominated Conservative Party to confronting the grave social challenges of an industrial society, Scottish self-government appeared the obvious way to achieve this. The Young Scots made it clear, however, that they had no wish to dissolve the Union, but instead asked for 'all-round devo-lution' – Frederick Scott Oliver's 'delegation' – within a 'Home Rule Empire'.[26]

The fortunes of the Scottish Home Rulers, both before and after the emergence of the Young Scots, proved to be closely tied to those of the movement for Irish Home Rule. They waned with the defeat of the second Irish Home Rule Bill in 1894 and revived with the third Bill in 1910, which was finally passed in September 1914 in spite of the increasingly militant resistance of the Ulster Unionists.[27] The Great War, however, put everything on hold. By the time the war was over, the Irish Easter Rising of 1916 and its aftermath had transformed the context in which Scottish Home Rulers had been operating. With the granting of independence to Ireland and the partition of the island in 1921, they would need to reconsider the place and character of Scottish Home Rule in a changed British polity.

For all the energy of some of the supporters of Scottish Home Rule, their fervour could hardly compare with the emotionally charged nationalism of turn-of-the-century Catalan campaigners for autonomy like Prat de la Riba. There were good reasons for this. After nearly two centuries of union, the lives of Scotland and England were closely intertwined at many levels. Intermarriage, especially at the elite level, had become commonplace, and numerous members of the Scottish aristocracy had been educated at English public schools; many Scots were chosen to represent English constituencies in the House of Commons, while English members represented Scottish constituencies; and the British Empire, for all the challenges posed by the Boer War, remained a successfully functioning all-British concern.

The economy, too, was strong. While Edinburgh was the cultural capital of Scotland, and prided itself on being the Athens of the North, with spec-tacular vistas of eighteenth- and early nineteenth-century classical build-ings to reinforce the claim,[28] Glasgow was its industrial capital. This contrasted sharply with the situation in Catalonia, where Barcelona played both parts. Glasgow was prospering, and the rise of the steel and iron indus-tries, the development of engineering, and the massive success of Clydeside shipbuilding more than made up for the decline of its older industries, like tobacco and textiles. The great international exhibitions staged in Kelvingrove Park in 1880 and 1901 can be seen as a proud assertion of confidence in the future of Scottish talent and industry, and as a triumphant affirmation of the global impact of the 'second city in the empire'.[29] Just as its international exhibition of 1888 proclaimed Barcelona's status as a great metropolis, the Kelvingrove Park exhibitions did the same for Glasgow.

Although the Barcelona exhibition was adjudged a great success, it left the city, as Almirall had warned, with a massive burden of debt.[30] This was partly the result of mismanagement, but the Catalan economy, after several years of impressive growth, was running into trouble. A long period of deflation had set in, cereal prices were collapsing, and the arrival of phylloxera from French vineyards in 1885 was to have a devastating impact on Catalan viticulture. Above all, Catalan industry was over-producing for a domestic market that was not growing fast enough to absorb its products, in part because of the high price of home-grown food. Patterns of landownership, especially in a southern Spain dominated by great landowners with a cheap labour force at their disposal, were not conducive to capital-intensive farming and limited the country's capacity to generate a sustained increase in agricultural production. Sheltering, like Catalan industrialists, behind high tariffs, the owners of Andalusian latifundias had no particular interest in improving the productivity of their estates and seeing wheat prices fall.

Although the late nineteenth and early twentieth centuries were to witness impressive agricultural improvements in the coastal zones of Catalonia and Mediterranean Spain as result of small-scale investments in market gardening, much Spanish farming remained traditional and backward, especially in the dryer regions. This backwardness, even if at times over-dramatized, was bound to have a negative impact on the sale of over-priced Catalan manufactures. The protectionist system that Catalan textile producers and industrialists had fought so hard to put in place was beginning to turn against them.[31]

Catalan industrialists were also facing increased competition, both from the industrializing Basque Country in northern Spain, and from foreign competitors; and although they responded to the challenge by investing in new plant and moving into new areas like chemicals, textiles remained the staple product, and saturation point had been reached. In 1891 the government came to the rescue of Catalan textile producers by introducing tariff legislation that extended their monopoly to Cuba and the Philippines, but the relief proved short-lived. Seven years later, in the brief and catastrophic war between Spain and the United States of 1898, Spain lost both colonies, along with Puerto Rico, and its once great American Empire was at an end.[32]

Since the colonies accounted for 34 per cent of all Spanish exports in 1897, with Cuba taking the preponderant share, the disaster of 1898[33] was bound to be widely felt in Catalonia, although not all its economic effects were negative. Repatriated capital from the lost overseas territories was invested in the domestic economy, and so helped recovery. But the impact of 1898 was more than economic, and extended far beyond Catalonia. Defeat by an upstart United States came as a traumatic shock to a Spain in which national self-confidence was already brittle, undermined not least by a recent string of terrorist attacks perpetrated by anarchists. These included the bombing of Barcelona's Corpus Christi religious procession on 7 June 1896, which prompted a savage bout of police repression by the captain-general, Valeriano Weyler, and the assassination of Conservative Prime Minister Antonio Cánovas del Castillo on 8 August 1897 while he was taking the waters in northern Spain. The publication in 1897 of Ángel Ganivet's inquiry into the origin of Spain's current troubles, *Idearium español*, is evidence that national soul-searching was already underway, but the loss of the colonies gave rise to an outpouring of publications by intellectuals, professional writers and journalists who came to be known collectively as 'the generation of '98'.[34]

Was Spain to be classed as a 'dying nation', as Lord Salisbury suggested in a speech after its first naval defeat in the war of 1898?[35] The disaster created a crisis of national identity, and generated a mood of brooding introspection, not untinged by that *fin de siècle* pessimism to which other European states also succumbed. Nevertheless, the introspection was not purely fatalistic. Defeat demanded renewal and national regeneration, and offered an opportunity to break free from the fatalism conjured up by the paralyzing image of 'two Spains', one decadent and traditional, the other modern and progressive. Those who thought they had an answer to the nation's troubles hastened to provide it. For the conservative regime that replaced the Liberal government in the wake of the disaster, as also for the Liberals themselves, it was vital to restore national self-confidence. Although in spite of the failure of the First Republic in 1873 republicanism remained strong, the monarchy was potentially a national rallying point. The effective inauguration of the reign of Alfonso XIII when, aged sixteen, he attained his majority in 1902 and took a solemn oath to observe the Constitution, provided an ideal opportunity to reinforce the prestige of the dynasty and the symbolic importance of the Crown.[36]

During the following years the king and the royal family paid numerous visits to all parts of the country, and engaged in an endless round of ceremonial activities designed to exploit the magic of royalty and bring the monarch closer to his people. At the turn of the nineteenth and twentieth centuries all the European monarchies were engaged in a similar enterprise, from Edwardian Britain to the Germany of Wilhelm II, a sovereign whom Alfonso particularly admired. Ceremonial and ritual, whether new or refashioned, made the monarch the living symbol of national unity and imperial strength.[37] With the help of royal ceremonial and through an increasingly assertive exercise of the substantial political power placed by the Constitution in the hands of Spanish monarchs, who could select and dismiss ministers as they saw fit, Alfonso began to acquire a popular reputation as the saviour of the nation. With his military upbringing he was well placed to rally the people behind him when military intervention in Morocco from 1904 onwards evolved during the second decade of the century into a full-blown colonial war – a war that, it was hoped, would restore Spain's standing as an imperial power and underline its new importance on the international stage.

The monarchy could also provide, as the Liberals hoped, a centre of stability at a time when a rising crescendo of regionalist and nationalist voices threatened the unity of the nation-state. But while some saw the revival of a strong monarchy as essential for political stability and national renewal, others had their own very different views about the most effective means for regenerating Spain. In the great debate launched in 1898 Prat de la Riba and his Catalan colleagues found a new opportunity to press for their long-standing objective of achieving not only self-government for Catalonia, but also a general reordering of Spanish political life.

In a *Compendium of Catalanist Doctrine*, written in 1894 jointly with a colleague, Pere Muntañola, and consisting of a set of questions and answers, Prat de la Riba indicated the main lines of thinking that he would later elaborate in his comprehensive *La nacionalitat catalana* of 1906. In one particular exchange between questioner and respondent he formulated in a few words a doctrine that was to have a profound long-term impact. Asked whether Spain was the *pàtria* of the Catalans, the respondent replied: 'It is no more than the state, or the political grouping that belongs to it.' He then went on to define the difference between state and *pàtria* in the following terms: 'The state is a political entity, artificial and voluntary; the *pàtria* is a historical, natural and necessary community.'[38] Such descriptions of the fatherland were common in nineteenth-century nationalist discourse, but in depicting Spain as no more than an artificial construct as contrasted with an organic national community like Catalonia, Prat de la Riba was drawing a distinction between state and nation that supporters of the movement for Catalan independence would exploit to the full a century later.[39]

Circumstances at the turn of the nineteenth and twentieth centuries were unusually propitious for what amounted to nothing less than the invention of Catalonia as a nation.[40] The *Renaixença*, in identifying the historic roots of Catalan distinctiveness, had laid firm foundations for the nationalist project of Prat de la Riba and his friends. Nations need proper capitals, and Catalonia could now boast with some justice that it had one. Barcelona by the 1890s possessed many of the characteristics of a national, as distinct from a provincial, capital. It was becoming a notably European city, absorbing the architectural and artistic influences of *fin de siècle* Paris and Vienna, and reshaping them in a *modernista* movement of its own that blended contemporary Art Nouveau with a revised and remodelled Catalan Gothic.

The *modernista* movement signalled the emergence of a truly Catalan intelligentsia as well as its success in winning over the middle and upper classes of Barcelona to its cause. The bourgeoisie's enthusiastic embrace of the new style in the 1880s and 1890s inaugurated a period of great creative vitality, in which artists, artisans and architects joined forces to create a distinctively Catalan language of the decorative arts, and produce extraordinary public and private buildings, like those designed by Antoni Gaudí and Lluís Domènech i Muntaner – buildings whose strange organic shapes and curious excrescences interrupted the respectable rhythm of the Eixample's all-too rational street-lines. A city as vital and creative as this stood in no doubt of its superiority to Madrid, which it was easy to dismiss as the second-class capital of a country now reduced to second-class status.[41]

The loss of empire in 1898 inevitably focused an unforgiving light on what was left – a shrunken Spain, whose failures were a source of deep frustration to many of the country's professional and entrepreneurial classes. The state had visibly failed, and the heightened rhetoric of later nineteenth-century Spanish nationalism, built around the Liberal concept of a unitary state, had shown itself inadequate to the task of merging state and nation to create an integrated polity. It was a rhetoric, too, that inevitably had the effect of heightening the opposing rhetoric of regionalist or nationalist movements that found it impossible to accept a centralizing Spanish nationalism imbued with strongly Castilian preconceptions.[42]

Alienated by the attitude and aspirations of a government unable to devise a form of Spanish nationhood that offered them an acceptable place within it, the Basques responded by emphasizing their racial uniqueness. The Catalans, for their part, singled out their history, language and culture as the source of their distinctive identity. Yet even as Prat de la Riba asserted that Catalonia's 'national personality' classified it not as a region but as an authentic nation, and hence entitled to statehood, he continued to set his projected nation-state within an Iberian context. 'Catalan nationalism,' he wrote, 'has never been separatist', and Catalonia's future, as he saw it, lay in a 'federative union of the states of Spain's other nationalities'. This federal union, joined by Portugal, would evolve into an 'imperial state', which might appropriate features from the Austro-Hungarian and German Empires, but would be modelled on the United States.[43] The way that Prat de la Riba's projected 'imperial state' would work in practice remains unclear, but at its heart was home rule for Catalonia and for those parts of Spain that had evolved from provinces into regions, and then from regions into nations. It was, however, home rule within a specifically federal structure. This would take the Catalan nationalist movement a step further than that taken by the advocates of home rule for Scotland. Nevertheless, Prat's project remained tied to an idealized concept of 'Spain'. This Spain would not be a Castilian Spain governed by a centralizing state which was no more than the artificial construct of an imperialistic Castile, but a plural Spain that found its unity in a voluntary association of all the Iberian peoples. The Catalan contribution to the construction of this decentralized Spain would be fundamental, and would restore it to the ranks of the great imperial powers.

The attempts of the government, headed by Francisco Silvela, to restore the nation's finances in the wake of the Spanish-American War widened still further the breach between Barcelona and Madrid. Industrialists, traders and shopkeepers, angered by new tax demands to meet the deficit and disgusted by the corruption generated by Cánovas's two-party system of government, were caught up in the nationalist movement and rallied to the cause of 'Catalonia for the Catalans'.[44] In 1901 Prat de la Riba and Francesc Cambó, at that time a young lawyer with high political ambitions, founded a new Catalan party, the Lliga Regionalista. With the creation of the Lliga, sectors of the big-business community formally identified themselves for the first time with the regionalist and nationalist cause. In the general election of May 1901 the new political grouping won four seats for the city of Barcelona, but it secured only two more in all the rest of Catalonia, where the clientage networks developed under the two-party system were strong.[45]

Often in the past Barcelona had claimed to speak for all Catalonia, when in fact it did not do so. Rural Catalonia always had its own priorities and was internally divided by sharp regional differences. For all the close personal and financial links between the Catalan capital and the countryside, the relations between the two were marked by a persistent tension. Small-town residents, villagers and peasantry were resentful of the way in which the capital siphoned off their wealth and tended to look down on them as provincials. The transformation of Barcelona into a strongly Europeanized industrial metropolis could only aggravate the tension.[46]

Not only did the nationalist Lliga not speak for the countryside, it did not even speak for much of Barcelona. It was primarily, although by no means exclusively, the party of industrialists and businessmen, who had no wish to break with Madrid, to which they were bound by too many ties of dependence. Under the pragmatic leadership of Cambó and Prat de la Riba, the party aspired to reform Spain, but shrank from any measures that could endanger Spanish unity. Other groups, however, were more radical, and republican politicians split off from the Lliga when Cambó, in defiance of his colleagues, went ahead and presented Alfonso XIII with a petition for Catalan autonomy during the king's visit to Barcelona in 1904. Consorting with the monarchy was not for them, and they followed their break-away movement by founding their own political party, the Republican Nationalist Centre.[47]

There were other weaknesses, too, in the nationalist cause as represented by the Lliga. Social tensions were rising in Barcelona, where a general strike was called in February 1902. Industrial workers, many of them immigrants into the city from rural Catalonia, were struggling to improve their terrible working conditions. This was fertile ground for socialists and anarchists, whose interests lay in social well-being and sheer survival, and not in the cause of Catalan autonomy. But anarchists and socialists were not the only political activists in this febrile city. Many members of the Barcelona working classes fell under the oratorical spell of Alejandro Lerroux, who was no *catalanista* but a radical republican with great organizational skills. In the 1904 elections his adherents defeated the Lliga, and four years later he founded a new political grouping, the Radical Republican Party, to promote the cause of social justice.[48]

With the Catalan nationalist cause divided between doctrinaire left and pragmatic right, with rising social tensions and with Lerroux throwing rhetorical hand-grenades from the sidelines, Cambó had a hard time navigating his way through the labyrinth of regional and national politics. He did, however, skilfully manage to paper over the internal differences between the different factions by promoting a Solidarity movement, Solidaritat Catalana. Successfully appealing to rural voters, he and his allies swept to power at the 1907 general election, which saw a substantial bloc of Catalan deputies, including Cambó himself, returned to the Cortes, and Prat de la Riba becoming president of the Diputació. Cambó's hope was to negotiate a settlement with Antonio Maura, a Mallorcan by origin and the Conservative prime minister, that would give Catalonia limited home rule.

Maura, no less eager than Cambó for the regeneration of Spain, saw decentralization as one way to reduce the level of corruption in Spanish life. This convergence of interests brought the two together, but Maura's proposed new law for local administration fell far short of what the Catalan left and the republicans demanded, not least in flouting the Universal Suffrage Law of 1890 by restricting suffrage in provincial and municipal elections.[49] With the government responding to a new upsurge of terrorism by suspending civil liberties, the opponents of the Lliga were well placed to recover the initiative from Solidarity. In the municipal elections of May 1909 the Catalan electorate made clear its hostility to the Maura-Cambó plan, and Lerroux's Radical Republicans took control of Barcelona.[50]

In July of that year Maura's government, already tainted by its plans for the reform of local administration and the heavy-handed responses of the authorities to unrest among the Barcelona workforce, made a disastrous miscalculation by calling up Catalan conscripts to fight in Spain's colonial war in Morocco. It compounded the error by making Barcelona their port of embarkation. Anti-militarist and anticlerical agitators – socialists, anarchists and republicans – seized the opportunity to organize movements of protest against the 'Bankers' War'. A call by a semi-anarchist 'workers solidarity' group for a twenty-four-hour strike for 26 July proved to be the prelude to Barcelona's 'tragic week', the *Setmana Tràgica* of 1909. Crowds rampaged through the streets, setting fire to eighty buildings, among them fourteen parish churches, sixteen convents and thirty schools, most of them run by the religious orders. Although the flames of anticlericalism were fanned by the close association of Maura's government with the Catholic Church, the alleged wealth of the religious orders traditionally singled them out as targets of popular hostility at times of high tension. In addition the schools were seen as obstacles to the development of a free public-school system and hence to democratic progress.[51] Against the advice of the city's civil governor martial law had been declared in response to the general strike, and the captain-general of Barcelona sent his forces into action. By 1 August they had restored order to the streets.[52]

Searching for a scapegoat the authorities picked on Francesc Ferrer i Guàrdia, a free-thinking educationalist with anarcho-syndicalist tendencies and a European reputation as a veteran revolutionary. In a show trial a military court sentenced him and four others to death, and the sentence was carried out in the face of international protests. Ferrer's trial and execution turned him into a hero and martyr, making anarcho-syndicalism the dominant force in the working-class movement during the succeeding decades. It also brought about the downfall of Maura, who had forfeited the confidence of the king. With Maura out of power Cambó had lost his best ally in Madrid.

Above all, the *Setmana Tràgica* laid bare the deep divisions and conflicts within Catalan society, profoundly affecting in the process the Barcelona bourgeoisie. Frightened by the display of anarchist terrorism, mob violence and trade union power, its overwhelming priority was the reestablishment of law and order on a lasting basis and the containment of the social forces that had been so alarmingly unleashed. The Lliga, reflecting these concerns, had supported Maura's hard line, but in so doing had exposed the vulnerability of a regionalist and nationalist movement that gave the appearance of being designed to further the interests of the rich and propertied, and seemed to offer no solution to the crying social problems of the age.

The *Setmana Tràgica* left a permanent imprint on the attitudes of a bourgeoisie which now, as in later moments of social and political crisis, would look for salvation to a strong-armed government. It also left the Lliga weakened. It would never again possess quite the dominance over Catalan political life that it enjoyed between 1907 and 1909, when it successfully combined its championship of Catalan regionalism with its bid to lead the movement for the national regeneration of Spain. It now found itself in the same situation as other moderate nationalist movements whose anxiety to avoid revolutionary upheaval leaves them exposed to the attacks of more radical nationalists to their left. Its enemies had little difficulty in depicting it as a party devoted to the defence of its members' class interests, although in reality it had many supporters much lower on the social scale. In this respect its situation was not unlike that of the Scottish Liberal Unionists, who equally saw themselves under attack from an increasingly well-organized labour movement. But where the Liberal Unionists found a degree of political salvation in fusing with a national Conservative Party, this was not a realistic option for Cambó once Maura fell from power and his Conservative Party ceased to speak with one voice.

Yet Cambó was nothing if not resilient. Divisions among the Lliga's opponents would allow it to recover the political initiative in 1911 and press ahead with the party's programme for Catalan autonomy as part of its plan for the decentralization of Spain through the devolution of power to its regions. Although Cambó had lost his most effective allies in Madrid, the pressing nature of the Catalan question and his own political skills allowed him to make *ad hoc* arrangements with whatever government happened to be in power. Whereas in Britain the advent of the Great War placed governmental initiatives for Irish and Scottish Home Rule on hold, Spain's neutrality in the conflict left Cambó with more room for manoeuvre than British Home Rulers enjoyed.[53] As an influential presence on the national political scene, he exploited his position to the full, and won his most important success when Madrid agreed to the amalgamation of the four Catalan deputations into a new regional entity, the *Mancomunitat*.

Set up in 1914, and presided over by Prat de la Riba until his death in August 1917, the Mancomunitat was intended as the first move in an ambitious experiment designed to restore life to the Spanish regions as a means of regenerating the country's politics and culture. As such, its creation would have major implications for the future both of Catalonia and of Spain. During its ten-year existence the Mancomunitat would devote much of its energy and resources to improving Catalonia's infrastructure and to consolidating and extending the hold of Catalan language and culture over the province's life, initially by conducting its own business in Catalan.[54]

The government's concession of a Mancomunitat for Catalonia was far from the decentralization envisaged in the nationalist programme of Prat de la Riba, but it offered at least a taste of home rule, and was the best that could be managed in the face of Madrid's opposition to anything that might jeopardize the unity of Spain. As it was, Catalonia was a constant source of exasperation to the government, which feared, with some reason, a process of creeping Catalanization. The Count of Romanones, with a long ministerial career behind him, would note in his memoirs that 'in my frequent passages through government I learnt that the attention of ministers was constantly absorbed by Catalonia; when it was not one thing it was another.'[55] Yet times were changing in Spain, as they were in Britain. In both countries new social forces were eroding old political affiliations, and in Spain the Catalan question was coming to be subsumed into the wider question of whether, and for how long, parliamentary monarchy itself could survive.

Post-War Transformations

Towards the end of the Great War in 1918 the shadow of Bolshevism hung over Europe, generating fear in the propertied classes while filling the landless and the urban proletariat with hopes of imminent revolution. By this time the rise of organized labour and of working-class movements was well on the way to transforming the political landscape in Spain and Great Britain alike. Catalan and Scottish labour were especially prominent in this more general transformation, and in both instances the Great War itself was a major precipitant of change.

Spain's neutrality in the conflict that convulsed other parts of the continent gave its manufacturers an unrivalled opportunity to break into markets where they had hitherto struggled to compete. The resulting economic boom gave rise to spectacular inflation, further encouraging already endemic labour unrest. As the prices of consumer goods rose and employers stood fast in their refusal to raise wages in line with inflation, Barcelona in particular became the scene of continual protests and strikes. Whereas in Britain the emerging Labour Party had no serious competitor in its bid to attract the support of a protesting workforce, in Spain its loyalties were divided between socialists and anarcho-syndicalists. Where the first saw themselves as participating in a national movement for the regeneration of Spain, the anarchists looked forward to mass revolution and the overthrow of the state. The foundation in 1910 of the CNT (Confederación Nacional del Trabajo, or National Confederation of Labour), as a national organization of anarchists who had been converted to syndicalism, held out momentary hopes that the rival movements of the UGT and the CNT might sink their differences, but two general strikes, called in 1917 and 1919, would only serve to underline the extent of their divisions.[56]

Social unrest, further aggravated by military repression, came at a time when Spain's parliamentary monarchy was in terminal decline. Maura's unwillingness as leader of the Conservative Party to do a deal with the Liberals split his party and precipitated the breakdown of the two-party system. Cambó worked hard to promote his programme for the democratization and modernization of Spain, but consistently overrated his chances of changing the system from within and found his efforts continuously frustrated. Early in 1917 he went to the Basque Country to win support for his grand design for the creation of an 'España Grande', in which an alliance of the Spanish regions would set out to break the political dominance of Castile. He followed this by initiating a parliamentary Assembly movement, designed to set up a constituent Cortes that would grant 'ample autonomy' to the regions. If these were once allowed to run their own affairs, the resulting liberation of Spain's creative energies would bring the long period of national decadence to an end.[57]

For a moment in the autumn of 1917 the regionalists seemed to be making headway, and for the first time since 1899 Catalonia was represented in the government when two Catalan politicians were given ministerial office in a coalition ministry. But, amidst great political instability, the government fell in March 1918, to be replaced by a 'national government' headed by Maura, in which Cambó himself held the post of Minister of Development. This government in turn survived for only eight months, and fell in November 1918.

The Lliga was now losing support in Catalonia, where Cambó was seen as selling out to the monarchists and the political establishment. Exasperation had been growing in Catalonia at what was felt to be the province's marginalization, and with the exasperation came an upsurge in sentiment that was becoming more nationalist than regionalist. Meanwhile, what was perceived as Catalan aggressiveness inevitably provoked rising anger in Madrid and in the more traditional Spain of the centre and south. Why should the Catalans, just because theirs was the most industrialized region of the country, claim that they alone had the answer to Spain's problems? Speeches in the Cortes and articles in the press denounced the Catalan 'separatists'. There was little disposition in Madrid to add to the concessions already made to Catalonia when it agreed to the establishment of the Mancomunitat.[58]

While the Lliga continued to play the political game in Madrid in a climate of growing suspicion about Cambó's intentions, weak governments proved incapable of tackling Spain's social problems, and were finding it increasingly hard to maintain law and order. Above all, the army was restless. There was an officers' strike in the summer of 1917 which, although called to secure better financial terms for the military, also exposed the degree of disgust among sections of the military at the rottenness that was corroding Spain's political life. Leading officers, their nationalist instincts sharpened by their experiences in Morocco, were beginning to see the armed forces as the last bulwark against national disaster in the form of social revolution and the political fragmentation of Spain.[59]

Their fears were deepened by European developments in the immediate post-war period. The collapse of the old continental empires, brought about or precipitated by the war, raised in an acute form the question of the rights of the minority peoples who lived within their borders. Over large parts of Central and Eastern Europe imperial states had enjoyed substantial success in checking and managing the aspirations of disaffected regions and ethnic minorities through a combination of accommodation, repression and the inculcation of loyalty to the ruling house. Now that monarchs had been toppled and empires had collapsed, the old restraints were gone. Minorities felt free to advance their claims for a place in the sun. As they did so, old passions and enmities rose to the surface, and the resulting nationalist upsurge was encouraged by President Woodrow Wilson's endorsement of national self-determination in January 1918.[60]

Wilson's Fourteen Points conferred international legitimacy on nationalist movements across the continent, and Catalan nationalists welcomed the opportunity this afforded them.[61] The petition drawn up in November 1918 after a meeting between the Council of the Mancomunitat and the Catalan deputies in the Congress (the lower chamber of the Cortes), spoke of 'this solemn moment of universal history, which throughout the world is witnessing the triumph of the principle of the collective right of peoples to dispose of themselves freely and to be ruled by the institutions to which they have given their assent'.[62] Encouraged by Alfonso XIII, who saw the crowned heads of Europe falling all around him and had come to see the elimination of the Catalan question as a way of strengthening the monarchy, the Lliga took the initiative in promoting a Statute of Autonomy.[63] But the leaders of the political parties in Madrid would have none of it, and Cambó responded by withdrawing his deputies from the Congress.

From this point on, Catalan nationalism acquired a new and more radical dimension. The monarchism of the Lliga proved too much for the maverick Colonel Francesc Macià, a former army officer and Lliga deputy, who broke with his party and lined up with the republican left. However, Macià was still a marginal figure, whose admiration for the armed struggle of the Irish Republican movement held little appeal for a Catalonia with no tradition of resorting to arms to further a nationalist agenda. Macià's time was yet to come.

More significant in weakening the party was the stance it took during the general strike of February 1919, known as the Canadenca, because it began with a pay dispute in the Canadian hydroelectric concern that supplied Barcelona with its light and power. The dispute paralysed the city and escalated into a bitter conflict between employers and the CNT. This culminated in the mass arrest of trade unionists, the weakening of the CNT, and the appointment of a general as the new civil governor. His attempts to root out the anarchists and the agitators inaugurated a still more violent period of conflict between workers and their employers, who were now increasingly dependent on the military to rescue them from trouble.[64] Between 1921 and 1923 the city was the scene of no fewer than 152 assassinations perpetrated by one side or the other. As the law of the gun took over, the chasm between Barcelona and Madrid widened still further.[65]

In placing itself firmly on the side of the employers, the Lliga had alienated many of its own members, and in 1922 disillusioned young party activists formed a new movement, Acció Catalana. The success of this movement in the provincial elections of June 1923 persuaded a defeated Cambó to abandon active political life. But the defeat was more than merely personal. Although he and the Lliga claimed to speak for all Catalonia, the trajectory of his career suggested that his brand of moderate and socially conservative Catalanism simply had no appeal to the masses, who had more urgent preoccupations than the invention of a Catalan nation with all the proper cultural trappings.

In 1921 the army's humiliating defeat in Morocco did much to exacerbate the already tense relationship between disaffected army officers and the political establishment. As law and order deteriorated, Alfonso XIII, disillusioned with parliamentary government, began looking for a way of escape from the impasse. The movement for national regeneration, launched with such high hopes at the beginning of the new century, had visibly failed, and the king's disillusionment with parliamentary democracy was widely shared. In turning against the Liberal constitutionalist regime under which it had lived for so long, the Spain of the early 1920s was by no means unique. Right across the continent parliamentary democracy, as practised at the time, had revealed its shortcomings. Political parties had shown themselves all too prone to succumb to pressures from interest groups; corruption was rife; and governments rose and fell with alarming rapidity. Between March 1918 and September 1923 Spain had eleven successive governments, but this was by no means unusual. In few continental countries did cabinets during this period last more than a year.[66] As weak governments failed to address the pressing economic and social problems of post-war Europe, mass electorates became restless and leaders in waiting seized their chance. In spite of the farcical character of the march of Mussolini's Fascists on Rome in October 1922, the King of Italy invited him to form a government that same month. The way was now open for the creation of a fascist state that in some respects continued the policies of its Liberal predecessors, but bore all the hallmarks of an authoritarian regime.[67]

The example was not lost on Spain's disaffected military, or on a country exasperated by the failure of governments to deliver on their promises. Everything pointed towards some sort of coup d'état. It came in September 1923 when General Primo de Rivera, the Captain-General of Catalonia, issued a manifesto, dissolved the Cortes, and established a military dictatorship.

In Catalonia the events of the past few years played into Primo de Rivera's hands by making him the beneficiary of the mutual exhaustion between 1917 and 1923 of the industrialists on one side and the competing workers' movements on the other. The employers and their political leadership had shown themselves unwilling to accept the idea of an effective unionization of the working classes. The syndicalists, for their part, had turned their backs on the Lliga's plans for the gradual creation in Catalonia of a regional civic culture. With the two sides cancelling each other out, a political vacuum had been created, and the military filled it.[68] The leadership of the Lliga reluctantly endorsed Primo de Rivera's coup. Colonel Macià fled to France, and the prospect of Catalan autonomy vanished with the installation of a dictatorial regime that had seized power in the name of national revival. Home rule was to have no place in the unitary Spain of Primo de Rivera's imagining. In 1924 his regime forbade the use of the Catalan flag and language in official ceremonies, and in the following year it abolished the Mancomunitat.[69]

By comparison, the Scots were fortunate. Their nation's symbols and identity faced no such challenge and, if anything, were reinforced by the experiences of 1914–18. In Spain, neutrality in the Great War did nothing to foster a sense of national cohesion or consolidate a national narrative designed to cut across regional and social boundaries. The wave of patriotism that swept across Great Britain and the warring nations of continental Europe simply passed it by. Great Britain's entry into a war that was seen as a fight for national survival did much to consolidate the image of the British nations as a single community battling for a common cause, while simultaneously increasing the pride of the Scots in their own nation's achievements.

These achievements were impressive. Scottish industry made a massive contribution to the war effort: in particular the Clydeside became a major manufacturing centre for war material and munitions, while its shipyards turned out warships of every kind, and kept the merchant fleet afloat by making good the heavy losses caused by German submarine warfare.[70] Above all, large numbers of young Scottish men went to France to fight, and die, in the trenches. Some 668,000 Scots enlisted in the Crown forces during the Great War, with a disproportionately higher number of volunteers than in England and Wales. The Scottish regiments, although no longer dominated by the Highlanders who had done so much to win Britain its empire, maintained the country's martial traditions, and were a source of immense patriotic pride.[71] Yet the patriotism was British as well as Scottish, for these regiments formed part of the British Army under the command of a Scottish general, Earl Haig. As so often in the Anglo-Scottish union, Scottishness went hand in hand with Britishness.

If the Great War tightened, at least for the moment, the bonds of the Anglo-Scottish union at a time when those of the Anglo-Irish union were unravelling,[72] it also had more long-lasting consequences, both positive and negative, for the future of the Anglo-Scottish relationship. The demands of a wartime economy imposed heavy new pressures on Scottish society. These found an explosive outlet in 1915, when the workforce in the engineering shops and shipyards of the Clyde went on strike. The strike involved confrontation not only with stony-faced employers but also with Herbert Asquith's Liberal government, whose overriding priority was to ensure that the war effort came to no harm. The government's response, which included the arrest of leaders of the protest movement on charges of sedition, was far from the kind of brutal repression with which the authorities sought to suppress labour unrest in Barcelona, but it had similar polarizing consequences. Many condemned the strikers as unpatriotic revolutionaries for going on strike in wartime, and agitators earned the enduring name of 'Red Clydeside' for the dockyards. The strikers, for their part, would neither forget nor forgive the alliance between the Liberal Party and the bosses. Meanwhile, another mass protest took the form of a Rent Strike in Glasgow over attempts to impose higher rents. This was a city where the influx of large numbers of munition workers aggravated the overcrowding in what were already horrific housing conditions. The protest, supported by the Labour movement, did much to strengthen the bonds of community in a depressed urban population, and showed what well-coordinated collective action could achieve.[73]

The advance of the Labour movement was itself a pan-British phenomenon that crossed regional and national borderlines, even if Scottish Labour had its own distinctive characteristics. Where Catalan regional politics failed to integrate successfully into Spanish national politics, Scottish politics, regardless of party affiliation, were firmly established in British political life, however much Scotland might at times feel itself to be marginalized or neglected.

So close were the connections between the different parts of the United Kingdom that developments in any one of the British nations were almost certain to influence the others. This was especially true of developments in Ireland. Nowhere did the Irish question have a deeper impact than in Scotland, with its large immigrant population of Irish origin. In the 1911 census 174,000 persons, or 3.7 per cent of Scotland's population, were recorded as Irish-born. As such, they belonged to an Irish immigrant community heavily concentrated in western-central Scotland. Many – perhaps a third of all Irish immigrants by 1914 – were Protestant Ulster men and women.[74] In a viscerally anti-popish Scottish society these were more easily assimilated than the Roman Catholic majority, which to some extent formed a community apart, with its own distinctive religious and social institutions. Inevitably the failure to deliver on the promise of home rule for Ireland weakened the adherence of the Catholic immigrant community to the Liberal Party, while the harsh repression of the Easter Rising increased its sympathy for the cause of Irish separatism and the militancy of Sinn Fein. With the creation in 1922 of the Irish Free State, however, tensions diminished, and the Irish Catholic vote moved over to the Labour Party.[75]

This was one more blow to a Liberal Party already in deep trouble on both sides of the border after David Lloyd George split the party by forcing Asquith's resignation from the premiership in 1916. In the 1922 general election Labour became the largest party in Scotland. It increased its share of the vote still more in the election of 1924, when the Liberals were reduced to a mere eight seats, five of them in the Highlands and Islands.[76] The age of Liberal ascendancy in Scotland was at an end.

The eclipse of the Liberals, however, did not mean the eclipse of the home rule movement. This had won the enthusiastic support of the Scottish Labour Party and the trade unions, which were inclined to see home rule as the best device for advancing social reform. A former Young Scot and Labour Party member, Roland Muirhead, refounded the Scottish Home Rule Association in 1918 but as a non-party organization, in a bid to avoid too close an identification with a damaged Liberal Party. In practice the Association, in line with the general political trend, came to be dominated by Labour, and the Association's hopes soared in 1924, when a minority Labour government led by a Scot, Ramsay MacDonald, was installed. At the very moment when Primo de Rivera was clamping down on the nationalist movement in Catalonia, there seemed a real possibility that Scotland would at last get its own parliament. But the Association had misjudged the political scene in Westminster. MacDonald's government was too weak, the Conservatives were opposed, and, as so often, the time did not seem right. With the Labour Party displaying more interest in socialist than nationalist causes, disillusionment grew, and the Association lost momentum. It was becoming clear to many of its members, including Muirhead, that British political parties were unlikely to place a Scottish parliament high on their agenda, especially at a time when the depressed state of the British economy was coming to overshadow all other considerations. The obvious answer seemed to be to organize a separate, exclusively Scottish, political party, and in 1928 the National Party of Scotland was formed.[77]

While Labour was the first beneficiary of the post-war political upheaval, the Conservatives, decked out for a Scottish electorate in the more attractive mantle of Unionism, showed themselves to be increasingly strong competitors. Although the Labour Party was far from revolutionary, fears of Bolshevism and socialism helped move the propertied and professional classes into the Unionist camp. But Unionism had other sources of strength. While its origins lay in a deep concern for the preservation of the Anglo-Irish union, it held an obvious appeal for the many Scots who were determined to preserve the Anglo-Scottish union, even though they may have felt that it was not working as well as it should. They could take comfort from the knowledge that the Unionists were firmly opposed to any concessions that might set Scotland on the slippery path that had led Ireland to disaster, while knowing that they remained firmly committed to the preservation of those distinctive cultural and social traditions that had made their country what it was.

The Unionist Party made skilful use of the new opportunities created by the decline and fall of Liberalism. It was well organized and proved adept in shaping its message to appeal to the newly enfranchised, and especially to women and younger voters. The press, abandoning the Liberals, came out strongly in its favour, and it won overwhelming support from the higher levels of the legal profession and from the leadership of the Church of Scotland.[78] Above all, the advent of the Great Depression in 1929 created a desire for firm and stable government at a time of high unemployment, hunger marches and the threat of social disorder. Scotland was particularly hard hit by the Depression, which threw thousands out of work and devastated the shipbuilding and engineering industries on which its economic strength was so heavily dependent.

The Westminster government, in response to the crisis, could only accept the unpalatable truth that Scotland was no longer, even theoretically, an equal partner in the union, and now needed life-support from England.[79] At the same time, there was a realization in Unionist and government circles that a formerly self-reliant people had suffered a profound psychological shock. In the words of a former Chancellor of the Exchequer, Sir Robert Horne, 'there is a sense of defeat among a considerable portion of the population, to which Scottish people are not accustomed'.[80] With extreme nationalist and right-wing movements sweeping the continent it was essential that the disease should not spread to a depressed Scotland, although the moderation of the new Scottish Nationalist Party (SNP), founded in 1934 and absorbing the more conservative elements of the National Party, hardly suggested that this was an imminent danger. The weakness of the nationalist cause was confirmed when the SNP failed to win a single seat in the 1935 election.

Nevertheless, as the government recognized, there were legitimate grounds for Scottish discontent. In times of economic crisis, a national and London-controlled policy for Great Britain and Northern Ireland seemed more than ever necessary, but to many Scots Whitehall was remote and had little or no understanding of their tribulations. One possible response to the complaints was to allow a measure of devolution, but not the legislative devolution demanded by the more radical nationalists. Administrative devolution was a different matter. A higher degree of management from Edinburgh could produce more efficient government. It would also make the administrative machine more responsive to local requirements, especially in matters of economic and social policy.

Administrative devolution was championed by the Unionist politician, Walter Elliot, who as Scottish Secretary engineered the transfer of the Scottish Office from London to Edinburgh in 1937.[81] Both in symbolic and practical terms this proved a highly effective measure. The presence in

Edinburgh of a better-organized Scottish Office, and one with a much higher degree of visibility, drew some of the sting from the cause of Home Rule. It also made it easier to manage the reforms in healthcare, housing and other areas of social concern being pushed by Sir John Gilmour and by Elliot himself, even though, behind the scenes, London still controlled the levers of power.

Yet it would take more than a handful of social reforms and administrative concessions to lift the mood of depression that settled over the Scotland of the 1930s – a mood that was caught in the writings of prominent figures of the 'Scottish Renaissance' like Edwin Muir and Hugh MacDiarmid.[82] Hardship and economic depression did not lead, however, as in so many parts of the continent, to political extremism of the right or the left. Scottish society remained remarkably stable, and the consensus in favour of moderation endured, in large part because Scottish politics were so deeply embedded in British politics, and these successfully avoided the extremes that in this same decade tore Catalonia and Spain apart.[83]

The Spanish Tragedy

The kind of consensus that was achieved in the Britain of the 1930s proved to be beyond the reach of Primo de Rivera's militaristic and authoritarian regime. If it won a temporary popularity by restoring order, its inability to reconcile the irreconcilable became increasingly clear with every year that passed. Caught between the demands of the new Spain and the resistance of the old, between pluralist aspirations and the intransigence of the defenders of a centralized unitary state, the dictator was out of his depth. As a former captain-general in Barcelona he had some knowledge of conditions in Catalonia, and possessed unbounded contempt for the Catalanism of the middle and upper classes. He did, though, attempt to buy off with job-creating projects the working classes, whose power he had seen for himself. Among them was his grandiose project for the 1929 World Fair in Barcelona. This involved the construction on the slopes of Montjuïc of a complex of buildings including a massive National Palace and the 'Pueblo Español', an artificial village composed of houses that would display the various architectural styles of the different Spanish regions.[84]

Regionalism at the level of folklore was as far as Primo de Rivera was willing to go in reply to regional demands for a degree of autonomy. His military background aligned him with the advocates of the ultranationalism that had been gathering force since the early years of the twentieth century in response to the crisis of Spain's parliamentary system and to the

danger of separatism created by the increasingly strident nationalist movements of the Basque provinces and Catalonia.[85] Spanish unity was believed
to be at stake, and the dictatorship instinctively adopted a form of reactionary nationalism that identified unity with the institutions of the centralizing state, and reflected – just as the regionalist movements reflected – the
nineteenth-century failure to articulate a Spanish nationalism capable of
integrating all the peoples of Spain.[86]

The contrast with contemporaneous developments in the British Isles is
striking. The generality of the Scots and the Welsh, although not of the Irish,
assimilated and interiorized the British national narrative of the nineteenth
and early twentieth centuries. This was true even at the level of higher
education, where the teaching of Scottish history was almost absent from
the university curriculum.[87] It is symptomatic of the contrast that shortly
after coming to power Primo de Rivera felt it necessary to outlaw Catalanist
schools and ban Catalanist textbooks, neither of which had a place within
his notion of a regenerated Spain.[88] Unlike the Spanish narrative that he was
attempting to write, the British national narrative was progressive rather
than regressive, and had liberty rather than unity as its central theme.

In pursuit of this elusive unity Primo de Rivera's regime trumpeted the
Spanishness of a Spanish *patria* that embraced religion, monarchy and
those traditional pursuits, like bull-fighting and *flamenco*, that made Spain
unique among the nations of the world. It was this authentic Spanish nation
that legitimized the Spanish state: 'the state exercises sovereignty as the
permanent organ of the nation'.[89] This grandiloquent assertion drew heavily
on the thinking of neo-romantic and conservative writers searching for
answers to the 'problem of Spain', but it was also indebted to the ideas of
those members of the 'generation of '98' and the successor generation who
were of a more liberal disposition, like the philosopher and essayist José
Ortega y Gasset. They, no less than conservatives, were anxious to bring
about the regeneration of Spain, and believed no less fervently than the
conservatives that the way to promote it was by reinforcing the sense of
national identity and civic consciousness. As Ortega proclaimed, it was the
duty of intellectuals to 'build Spain'.[90]

In the long run the Spanish nationalist message developed in the years
after 1900 by writers and intellectuals representing all shades of opinion
and coming from all parts of Spain would turn out to be counter-productive,
especially when presented in the reactionary version embraced by the
dictatorship. In self-defence, regionalists and nationalists from Catalonia
and the Basque Country would reiterate with growing assertiveness their
own alternative narratives, reinforcing, as they did so, not the positive image

of a single Spanish *patria* but the troubling and negative image of two Spains. In the early years of the dictatorship, however, the regime's message held an undoubted attraction for those broad sections of the population, in Catalonia and elsewhere, who applauded the dictator's success in restoring law and order.

The long-running conflict over collective identities was far from being the only source of division among Spaniards during the last stage of parliamentary government and the years of the dictatorship. Nor, for much of the time, was this conflict even the most urgent and demanding. Spain was undergoing change on a massive scale as people migrated in large numbers from the country into cities and towns, where they swelled the rapidly expanding industrial proletariat. It was a daunting challenge for any government, of whatever colour, to manage change in a country with a failed political system and in the throes of modernization. Somehow the masses had to be integrated into that society, whether they were workers living on the poverty line in the industrial cities of eastern and northern Spain or exploited rural labourers in the under-developed agricultural regions of the south. The challenge inevitably elicited a wide range of responses. This was a society racked by dissension between employers and workers, socialists and anarchists, clericals and anticlericals, monarchists and republicans. Nor was there anything clear-cut and predetermined about the stance that individuals would take when confrontation loomed. Anticlericalism was rampant, but the majority of nationalists, including those of a liberal stripe, were, to a greater or lesser degree, practising Catholics; nor did republicanism, now rapidly gathering strength, automatically preclude devotion to the faith. Above all, the Spain of the 1920s was caught up, like all Europe, in the great ideological conflict of the age, the conflict between left and right, socialists and fascists, even if that conflict was shaped in Spain by specifically Spanish circumstances and had its own distinctive Spanish colouring.

In grappling with the multitude of problems that faced him, Primo de Rivera sought to give coherence to society by reasserting the traditional alliance of throne and altar, and wrapping that alliance in the national flag. But his programme, while drawing on his reading of Spain's conflicted past, cannot simply be dismissed as purely regressive. It also contained elements of modernity like corporatism, which aligned it with contemporaneous authoritarian movements in the Europe of the 1920s and 1930s. It shared, too, their belief in the need for a strong national leader to turn programmes into action and make the trains run on time.

The Spanish nationalism of Primo de Rivera's Spain was not, then, that of the mid-nineteenth century. It was less focused on Castile and its historic construction of the Spanish state, and more on a united Spanish nation whose identity was enriched by its colourful regional diversity.[91] Contemporary Catalan nationalists may persist in regarding Catalonia as the permanent victim of an unchanging Spanish nationalism impelled by Castile's thirst for domination, but they have failed to recognize that this nationalism acquired new elements and adopted new forms as times and circumstances changed. In this, it resembled their own.

Even if Primo de Rivera's formula incorporated new ideas, both domestic and foreign, it was not one that appealed for any length of time to broad swathes of opinion in Spain. Towards the end of his dictatorship his policy failures were not only discrediting the whole system of monarchical centralism, but were also galvanizing the regionalist and nationalist movements of the Spanish periphery.[92] Facing growing opposition from both right and left to a mixture of policies that satisfied nobody, he lost the confidence of the king and his fellow generals, and resigned in January 1930. In August of that year republicans joined forces with Basque and Catalan nationalists in the 'Pact of San Sebastián' to form a united opposition. In the municipal elections of April 1931 the Republican-Socialist coalition captured almost all the provincial capitals, and Alfonso XIII followed the fallen dictator into exile. The king's sudden departure was followed by the proclamation of the Second Republic.

In Catalonia, the Lliga's association with Prima de Rivera's regime had left it discredited among broad sectors of the population, leaving the field open for republicans to unite among themselves and join forces with radical Catalan nationalists. This union had a strong appeal for the lower classes in Barcelona and the industrial towns, which had long resented the dominance of the Lliga as the party of the employers. But the appeal also reached into rural Catalonia, where there had long been a simmering conflict between landlords and the Union of *Rabassaires* – smaller tenants (vine growers) hit hard by the decision of the Institute of San Isidro (the landlords' organization) to rearrange and shorten tenancies following the introduction of shorter-lived American vines in the wake of the phylloxera epidemic.[93] It was the alliance of republicans, socialists and nationalists, and the link between workers' movements in urban Catalonia and the movement of social and economic protest in the countryside, that allowed a newly formed party of nationalist republicans, the Esquerra Republicana de Catalunya, to sweep to electoral victory.[94] Catalanism as a political cause had finally broken free from its conservative background and shifted decisively to the left.

On 14 April 1931 one of its leaders, Lluís Companys, went onto the balcony of the Barcelona city hall to proclaim a republic, and entrusted

Francesc Macià with the task of forming a provisional government. Colonel Macià, who had attempted a wild 'invasion' of Catalonia from France in 1926, then proceeded to proclaim, 'in the name of the people of Catalonia', the 'Catalan State, which we will cordially seek to integrate into the Federation of Iberian republics'.[95] Three days later, after consultation with the republican leaders in Madrid, the leadership agreed to draw back from their 'Catalan State'. Instead, Catalonia would be given its own governing institution, the Generalitat, a throwback to the institution abolished by Philip V, the full title of which was the Diputació de la Generalitat de Catalunya, the deputation of the 'generality' or community of Catalonia. The leaders were invited to draft a statute outlining the nature of the autonomy they wanted to see enacted.

The terms of the statute were worked out among left-wing republicans and socialists at a meeting held in a hotel in Núria. The so-called 'Núria Statute' opened with a preamble expressing the hope that Spain would be given a federal structure. It then went on to define Catalonia as 'an autonomous State within the Spanish Republic'. Its official language would be Catalan, and many competencies currently exercised by Madrid would be devolved to the Generalitat. Once the statute was drafted, Macià, without waiting for Madrid, pushed ahead in August with the holding of a referendum, in which 99 per cent of the voters approved the statute in a turnout of 75 per cent. It was not until December 1931 that the Constitution of the Second Spanish Republic, under the presidency of a recent recruit to the republican cause, Niceto Alcalá Zamora, was approved by the new Spanish Cortes. Only in May 1932 did Congress get round to discussing the Catalan statute.

The statute aroused strong emotions and provoked furious debate. Catalan deputies in the Congress complained, as usual, of the region's maltreatment by the Spanish state, arguing that, while Catalonia accounted for only 11 per cent of Spain's population, it furnished the state with over 19 per cent of its revenues.[96] The counter-arguments, again as usual, came from the forces of the right who believed in a strong state and feared that the granting of autonomy to Catalonia would lead to the disintegration of Spain. Eventually an attempted coup by General Sanjurjo helped concentrate minds and Congress approved a watered-down version of the statute in September. Manuel Azaña, the prime minister and future president of the Republic, was firmly set against a federal solution to the regional question and insisted that the statute had to be adjusted to make it conform to the new Constitution. This described Spain, in a careful attempt to combine unitary with pluralist requirements, as an integral state compatible with regional and municipal autonomy. Catalonia thus became 'an autonomous region within the Spanish State'. The transfer of competencies in the Núria statute was much reduced, with the control of education shared between the central and regional governments, and Castilian placed alongside Catalan as the region's official language.

The final version, skilfully negotiated by Azaña, was sufficient to satisfy moderate Catalan opinion, while successfully binding Catalonia into the democratic Republic. Azaña himself received a hero's welcome when he travelled to Barcelona in September 1932 to present the statute.[97] Elections held in November led to the victory of Esquerra Republicana. Companys was chosen as president of the new Catalan parliament, but then resigned the office when he became a short-lived minister in Azaña's government in 1933. Macià was elected president of the Generalitat, a post he held until his death in December 1933, when Companys succeeded him.

As Azaña's government wrestled with the enormous political and social problems that confronted it, it began to lose support. Meanwhile, the left-leaning Catalan government under Companys was also running into trouble. Delays in the transfer of powers to the Generalitat led to tensions with the government at a moment when the balance of forces in the country was tilting sharply to the right. Conservative and monarchist forces had rallied round the energetic figure of José María Gil Robles, an advocate of Social Catholicism who had founded the Confederación Española de Derechas Autónomas or CEDA (the Confederation of Autonomous Right-Wing Groups). Gil Robles himself, while anxious to restore the privileged position of the Church, was in many respects a pragmatic politician, who was prepared to accept the Republic, at least for the time being, and whose movement left a space for regional interests and concerns. CEDA was not therefore the rabidly anti-republican movement with centralizing ambitions depicted by its enemies, but its programme commanded the acquiescence, if not the wholesale support, of many of the most right-wing forces in Spanish society, who were determined to see the political and social reforms of the preceding two years overturned.

CEDA won the most votes in the general election of November 1933 – the first held in the Spanish Republic – although without securing an absolute majority, and a government of the centre-right was formed under the leadership of the veteran but now more moderate radical, Alejandro Lerroux. In the elections to the Catalan parliament the right also showed impressive signs of recovery, with Esquerra Republicana losing thirteen of its thirty-one deputies, and the tally of the Lliga, which changed its name in 1933 from 'Lliga Regionalista' to 'Lliga Catalana', rising from four to twenty-four.[98]

Spain's parties of the left, however, were unable to accept their defeat, and the appointment as ministers of three representatives of CEDA at the end of September 1934 confirmed the fears of the left that the forces of fascism were about to take over the country, and provided the occasion, or the pretext, for the socialist insurrection known as the 'October Revolution'.[99] The savage repression of the miners' strike in Asturias by troops of the Army of Africa was to be the prelude to the notorious 'black biennium' (*bienio negro*), during which conservative governments, while failing to restore political or social stability, managed to reverse much of the legislation of 1931–3.

In Catalonia, landowners were antagonized by the attempts of Companys to introduce agrarian reforms designed to help the vine-growing tenant farmers (the *rabassaires*) who had been hit by the phylloxera epidemic and the new tenancy contracts. Bringing their complaint to Spain's Tribunal of Constitutional Guarantees, they successfully challenged the legality of the new agrarian law approved by the Catalan parliament in the spring of 1934. Faced with this constitutional challenge, Companys refused to withdraw the legislation, and set up a new rural police force, the Mossos d'Esquadra, under the direction of the Generalitat, to contain the growing unrest in the countryside, where impatient *rabassaires* were threatening to take over the land.[100]

The confrontation between a Catalan government of the left and a central government of the right precipitated a nationalist upsurge in Catalonia, at a time when the Basque provinces, although divided among themselves, were now pressing their own demands for autonomy. As crisis conditions intensified, young Catalan extremists, organized into armed squads claiming allegiance to Josep Dencàs, the Generalitat's strongly nationalist minister of the interior and a would-be Mussolini, came out onto the streets. Companys, beleaguered from all sides and desperate to avoid the break-up of his disunited Esquerra party, was now under intense pressure from Dencàs to break with Madrid and declare Catalonia independent. At the last moment, on the evening of 6 October 1934, as Dencàs was about to proclaim his country's independence in front of a dense crowd, Companys seized the microphone and proclaimed, without great conviction, an independent Catalan state but one within the Spanish federal state. He then retreated to the Generalitat under the protection of the Mossos d'Esquadra to take refuge. Here he reached an agreement with General Domènec Batet i Mestres, a moderate Catalan in command of the Barcelona military district, who defied instructions from Madrid and succeeded in defusing the situation with minimum force. Dencàs, failing to secure the support he had expected, fled the city overnight. The whole farcical episode came to an end when Batet, as the servant of the Spanish Republic, took Companys and the Generalitat into custody to await trial on charges of rebellion.[101]

The events in Barcelona on 6 October 1934 revealed the weakness of the Catalan separatist movement, but also, more generally, that of Companys and the nationalist cause. Nationalism was only one of the many forces at work in a Catalan society torn in many directions, and at every point it interacted with, and was affected by, the larger movements in Spanish society as a whole, like the agrarian conflicts in Andalusia or the miners' strike in Asturias. Not only the anarcho-syndicalists but also the National Confederation of Labour, the CNT, displayed no interest in supporting an uprising of petit-bourgeois radical nationalists. Nor did it attract republicans or moderate nationalists. Following the collapse of the 'revolution' the central government closed down the Catalan parliament and suspended the agrarian law, but later lifted the state of siege. Government by the Generalitat could now be restored – a Generalitat composed this time of conservative nationalists and independents. All this, however, took place against a background of escalating violence between the forces of the right and left across Spain.

Along with his colleagues in government, Companys embraced the role of victim and martyr from behind his prison bars. The image was indelibly stamped on the popular imagination when he was sentenced in June 1935 to thirty years in prison, in spite of his known reluctance to take part in the uprising. When he and the others were amnestied after the victory of the Popular Front in the general election of February 1936, they returned from gaol as heroes. Companys himself resumed his former post as president of the Generalitat, and took his place alongside the late Colonel Macià as an iconic figure of the nationalist cause.[102]

As an ideologically divided country was gripped by violence, the government of the Republic, headed by Azaña, struggled unsuccessfully to maintain control. In July 1936 officers of the army of Africa rebelled, the commanders of the garrison towns of Spain followed suit, and Spain descended into civil war. It would end two and half years later when General Franco's troops entered Barcelona in triumph on 26 January 1939 and the last outposts of resistance collapsed.

The military uprising of July 1936 failed in Madrid, Valencia and Barcelona, where nationalist insurgents under the command of General Goded were defeated in street fighting by a combination of troops loyal to the Republic, the Civil Guard and anarcho-syndicalists and other members of the population who managed to get hold of arms. Their success quickly turned into a revolutionary and popular movement against real or alleged enemies. An orgy of church-burning was accompanied by the mass killing of priests and members of the religious orders. Many of those who saw themselves as potential targets of the left-wing forces fled the country, and some 400 adherents of the Lliga were murdered. President Companys and his Generalitat were powerless to put a stop to this reign of terror. The real power had passed into the hands of the Central Committee of Anti-Fascist Militias, its local committees across Catalonia and their militia units.[103]

In September 1936, in a bid to unite the resistance movement and organize more effective Catalan participation in the war against the insurgents, all the workers' unions, along with the anarchists, joined forces with the Generalitat to create a united anti-fascist government, headed by a salesman and politician, Josep Tarradellas. The power, however, lay with the workers. 'Practically every building of any size,' reported George Orwell, astonished by what he saw in Barcelona that autumn, 'had been seized by the workers and was draped with red flags or with the red and black flag of the Anarchists; every wall was scrawled with the hammer and sickle and with the initials of the revolutionary parties.'[104] Their unity did not last. The various political groupings and workers' unions were soon at loggerheads, while the communists manoeuvred to seize power and impose their own iron discipline on the motley array of anti-fascist forces – the socialists, the anarchists and the non-communist Partido Obrero de Unificación Marxista or POUM (Workers' Party of Marxist Unification). When the struggle came to a head on 3 May 1937, the Republican government in Madrid, itself convulsed by acute internal struggles, moved troops into Catalonia to restore order and assert its own authority. As the Moscow-controlled Communist Party tightened its grip on the region, a new Catalan government was formed at the end of June. It would last until the final defeat of the Republic.

The cause of Catalan autonomy was the principal casualty of the Catalan civil war within the Spanish Civil War. During the preceding months the Generalitat, in addition to salvaging as many artistic treasures as possible from the general conflagration, had seized the chance to press ahead with its plans for the consolidation and strengthening of Catalan culture and the severing of Catalan institutions from Madrid. The University of Barcelona now became the 'Autonomous University of Barcelona', and, in defiance of the terms of the 1932 statute of autonomy, the Generalitat assumed responsibility for education at all levels. It also took complete control of the administration of justice, reorganized local government into *comarques*, or regions, and even issued a new low-denomination coinage for circulation in Catalonia. Yet the effect of the events of May 1937 was to reduce it to political impotence. All that Companys and his colleagues could continue to do, although with considerable success, was to pursue the process of cultural Catalanization and promote the Republic's propaganda campaign at home and abroad. Artists, photographers and film directors received official encouragement, and the Catalan architect, Josep María Sert, was commissioned to design the Republic's official pavilion at the Paris International Exhibition of 1937, for which Pablo Picasso painted his *Guernica* and Joan Miró his great mural, the *Segador*, or *Reaper*, harking back to the insurrection of the Catalan peasantry in 1640.[105]

It was ironical that the programme promoted by Catalan nationalists ever since the advent of the *Renaixença* for generating a civic sense and making their country's cultural life and institutions more authentically Catalan should have reached its highpoint just as the cause of political autonomy sank into irrelevance. The various unions and working-class movements had never shown an interest in autonomy, or were openly hostile to it. This was a middle-class movement of little concern to them. Now, with the Nationalist forces of General Franco closing in on eastern Spain and the other areas of the peninsula still under republican control, the defeat of fascism and the salvation of the Republic was all that counted.

Barcelona became the capital of the Republic when Prime Minister Dr Juan Negrín moved his government out of Valencia in late October 1937. With the government physically present in the city the Generalitat's powers were still further reduced. Negrín made it clear that he had no use for Catalanist policies. 'I am not making war on Franco to allow a stupid and provincial separatism to sprout in Barcelona,' he declared. 'In no way. I am making war for Spain ... and for its greatness ... There is only one nation: Spain!' Negrín's concept of Spain, while coloured by recent events, harked back to the regenerationist movement of the early twentieth century and the centralizing liberalism of the nineteenth. Now, in the dying days of the Republic, the popular nationalism of the left that he embodied was proclaiming victory over the radical Catalan nationalism that had looked forward to building, in alliance with the various working-class movements, a distinctive Catalan state shaped by social revolution.[106]

It was obvious that Catalonia, and with it Catalan nationalist ideals, could expect no mercy from Franco and his troops. As they pushed into Catalonia in the spring of 1938, he issued a decree on 5 April proclaiming the abolition of the statute of autonomy granted by the Republic in 1932.[107] With the failure of the heroic Ebro counter-offensive launched by republican forces in the summer of 1938, their cause was doomed. The army of

Catalonia collapsed and the republican government abandoned Barcelona on 22 January 1939. The entry of Franco's forces into the city on 26 January without a shot being fired was preceded and accompanied by a mass exodus of over 400,000 soldiers and civilians across the frontier into France.

On 1 April Franco's Nationalist government announced that the war was officially at an end. Companys, who joined the flight to France, was arrested in August 1940, and was handed over by the Nazi authorities to the Spanish government. After being beaten, tortured and given a brief court martial on charges of military rebellion, he faced a firing squad in the castle of Montjuïc on 15 October 1940. His last words before he fell were *Per Catalunya* – 'For Catalonia'.[108] Josep Tarradellas, who also escaped to France, was more fortunate. President of the Generalitat in exile, a position he held from 1954, he was called back to Spain in 1977 following Franco's death two years earlier to negotiate with the government of Adolfo Suárez on Catalonia's future. As a result of the negotiations the Generalitat was officially re-established on 29 September. King Juan Carlos named him as its president on 19 October, and on 23 October he received a rapturous welcome on his return to Barcelona.[109] The symbolism of the event was powerful. Catalonia was on the way to recovering its liberties after the long, dark night of the Franco regime.

For Catalonia that night was exceptionally dark. The outbreak of the Second World War in September 1939 distracted the world's attention from Spain and shielded the new Franco regime from the hostile scrutiny of international public opinion. The first months of the occupation of Catalonia by Franco's Nationalist forces were a time of violent repression, motivated partly by revenge, but also by a determination to extinguish Catalan identity. As everywhere across Spain, supporters of the Republic were hunted down by the secret police, arraigned before military tribunals, imprisoned or summarily executed. A great purge was conducted, in which properties were confiscated, and many people – among them government officials, university professors and schoolteachers – were temporarily suspended. Others permanently lost their jobs, or, like the archaeologist Pere Bosch Gimpera, went into exile. Ramón Serrano Suñer, Franco's brother-in-law and minister of the interior, described the Catalans to a German newspaper as 'morally and politically sick', while the new civil governor of Barcelona stated that toleration of any kind of regionalism would lead once again to 'the putrefaction represented by Marxism and separatism that we have just surgically eradicated'.[110]

This vitriolic language faithfully reflected the views and the mental attitude of the man who was to govern Spain from the moment of victory in

1939 until his death in 1975. Francisco Franco was a military man through and through, whose life was dedicated to order, discipline and control. The regime that he established was no second instalment of the dictatorship of Primo de Rivera, and although it appropriated the totalitarian character of the two powers, Nazi Germany and Fascist Italy, that had helped him to victory, his system of government was and remained highly personal.[111] Cold, calculating and authoritarian, he knew what he wanted to do and how to get it done. His chosen method, well suited to his character, was to play off against each other his generals, his ministers and the Falangist movement that would be his chosen instrument for mobilizing the masses. As he saw it, nineteenth-century liberalism and parliamentary democracy were the root cause of the ills that had befallen his country. Thanks to them Spain had fallen victim to the principal scourges of the modern world – communism, atheism and Freemasonry. He, as the *Caudillo*, the divinely appointed leader, would rescue the *patria*, establish a well-ordered state under his firm personal control, and forge, with the help of the Church, a new sense of national unity founded on the ideals of Christian civilization.

Franco's was to be a confessional state that would dedicate itself to championing the transcendental values that, under the inspired leadership of those devout Christian monarchs, Isabella the Catholic, Charles V and Philip II, had transformed it into a bastion of the faith. As he saw it, it was they who had converted Spain into a unitary state, and in a unitary state anything that smacked of separatism was anathema. The defence of national unity therefore required the total extirpation of Basque and Catalan nationalism and any divisive form of regionalism. In pursuance of this aim the regime imposed a ban on the use of the Catalan language in public. Catalan street names were changed into Castilian and that of Pau Claris removed; publication of books and magazines in Catalan was immediately prohibited; and teaching in schools and universities was to be conducted in Castilian, 'the language of the empire' (*la lengua del imperio*) – a language that a Barcelona policeman admonished the author of this book to speak in 1955.

The linguistic prohibitions were initially extended to cover religious life, but the blanket banning of the Catalan language, or 'dialect' as it was called, soon proved to be unrealistic. From 1946, as Franco's regime sought respectability and international recognition after the defeat of the Axis powers, there was a slow relaxation of the prohibitions. Catalan classics began to be reprinted, permission was granted for the publication of poetry in Catalan, and by degrees scholarly works and other publications in Catalan were authorized.[112] Over the years the regime made efforts, within its self-imposed limits, to adapt itself to changing times, but throughout the dictatorship the media were tightly controlled, government propaganda was incessant, and censorship remained rigorous, if frequently erratic.

In spite of the repression, and in part because of it, the sense of Catalan identity emerged reinforced by the experiences of those years. With the pursuit of political autonomy out of the question, writers and academics, members of the professional classes, and sections of the clergy opposed to the pro-regime stance of the ecclesiastical hierarchy, devoted their efforts to affirming the distinctive character of a Catalan culture shaped by history, language and religion. Opponents of the regime united beneath the banners of Catalanism and the more liberal Catholicism inspired by the Second Vatican Council of 1962–5, and the abbey of Montserrat resumed its traditional place as a centre and symbol of national survival. In 1963 its abbot, Aureli M. Escarré, although initially a supporter of the regime who gave a warm welcome to Franco when he paid a visit to Montserrat, commented critically to a journalist from *Le Monde* on the situation in Catalonia and the lack of liberty. He was expelled from Spain two years later.[113]

With the passage of time the mass of the population came to take the dictatorship for granted as a fact of life, and many, especially in the middle classes, welcomed it as guaranteeing order, stability and returning prosperity. But the mid-1950s had already seen the beginnings of student protest in the University of Barcelona as a new generation with no memory of the Civil War came to maturity. At the popular level, football served as an outlet for suppressed anti-Franco and anti-Castilian sentiments, with every victory of the Barcelona team, El Barça, over Real Madrid hailed as a triumph of the enduring Catalan spirit. In the long run, repression, as so often, proved counter-productive.

While Catalonia under Franco successfully maintained the sense of identity forged for it by the nineteenth-century pioneers of cultural Catalanism, it was caught up from the 1960s, like the rest of Spain, in a process of economic and social upheaval that left it profoundly changed. The government's National Plan of 1959 for Economic Stabilization did much to rescue the country from the economic morass into which it had sunk, and helped release its long-stifled productive capacity. Catalonia was a prime beneficiary of the new wave of industrialization, which provoked a new migration from the countryside to the towns. The migratory movement also extended far beyond Catalonia itself as large numbers of immigrants – perhaps a million or more, and largely from south-eastern and southern Spain – headed to the region in search of employment. In the 1980s it was estimated that around 60 per cent of Catalonia's population came from outside Catalonia.[114] There were allegations at the time that the mass arrival of workers from other parts of the peninsula was the result of a policy adopted by the regime to suffocate Catalan identity. Yet while the assimilation into Catalan society of large numbers of Spaniards who spoke no Catalan presented a clear challenge to those anxious to preserve the nation's pristine purity, the principal explanation of the influx of immigrants lies in the drawing-power of an economy in a phase of rapid expansion.[115]

The economic and social changes, combined with the growing convergence of Spanish and international trends and the impact of mass tourism on a society isolated for many years from the outside world, inevitably led to some loosening of the iron grip of Franco's dictatorship. Political groups and workers' associations resurfaced or emerged; student unrest increased, and in November 1971 a 'Catalan Assembly' brought together the clandestine or semi-clandestine groups opposed to the regime. It demanded the restoration of political and social freedom; an amnesty for political prisoners; and the restoration of the 1932 statute of autonomy.[116] Strikes and demonstrations were organized, and active planning began for a post-Franco era.

During the 1950s, from his chair in the University of Barcelona, the leading Catalan historian of the second half of the twentieth century, Jaume Vicens Vives, set out to demythologize Catalan history, with a view to preparing a new generation of Catalans for the task of building a modern, democratic Catalonia and Spain. He died prematurely in 1960, long before there was any chance of seeing his ambition realized.[117] Nor was it clear whether his efforts, and those of his pupils, would succeed in stripping Catalan history of its myths and giving the new generation a more sophisticated picture of Catalonia's past than one that depicted it as a permanent victim. When Franco died at last, on 20 November 1975, this, like so much else, still remained uncertain. It was even far from clear whether his dictatorship would be replaced by democracy, and, if so, whether a Catalonia whose nationalism had been intensified by the long years of dictatorship would achieve, or be satisfied with, some form of home rule in a democratic Spain.

The British Consensus

If the years between the end of the Civil War in 1939 and the death of Franco in 1975 were years of imposed unity in Spain, they were years of unity through consensus in the British Isles. As the peoples of the United Kingdom stood shoulder to shoulder in a common cause, the Second World War gave a powerful impetus to the sense of British solidarity. Moreover, the war led to an unprecedented level of state intervention in the daily life of British citizens in response to the need for centralized planning and control, and with it an increased level of uniformity throughout the United Kingdom. This was carried over to post-war Britain, as the country, following the Labour Party's massive victory in the 1945 general election under Clement Attlee, embarked on the great experiment of creating a welfare state.

Scotland was fully engaged in these common enterprises of winning the war and building a better society in the post-war years. The war itself helped lift Scottish industry out of the depression of the interwar period, and industrial recovery continued in response to the requirements of post-war reconstruction. For a time it seemed as if the great days of Scottish heavy industry had returned as shipbuilding and engineering flourished in the late 1940s and the 1950s to meet the national and international demand.[118] The immediate post-war years might be years of shortage and austerity, but they were also years of confidence and hope as a generation that had grown accustomed to an enhanced level of direction from the central government automatically looked to the state to help industrial recovery and provide comprehensive welfare legislation.

For a Scotland that had always been wary of government from London, acceptance of large-scale state interventionism might in principle have seemed problematic. Inevitably conflicts of interest arose as wartime directives and regulations rained down from Westminster, but the conflicts were kept within bounds by the political skills and powers of persuasion of Tom Johnston, the Labour MP for West Stirlingshire, who was appointed Secretary of State for Scotland by Churchill in 1941 and remained in his post until the conclusion of the war. The most effective and influential Scottish Secretary of State of the twentieth century, Johnston, following in the footsteps of his great eighteenth-century predecessors, Archibald Campbell, Earl of Ilay, and Henry Dundas, acted as the mediator between London and Edinburgh, skilfully balancing the interests of the two. Himself a Home Ruler, he concentrated power in the hands of a Council of State for Scotland, thus effectively decentralizing government from London in order to recentralize it in his homeland. As a forceful member of the cabinet he was also not above exaggerating the dangers of Scottish separatism in order to win concessions from Westminster when it suited his purpose.[119]

Johnston's success in showing his fellow Scots the effectiveness of state intervention in the management of the war effort eased the way for the acceptance of Labour's programme of nationalization in Scotland, and for the foundation of the welfare state. Before the war the Labour Party had toyed with the idea of some form of devolution, and Johnston himself had said in 1936 that 'Scotland must have a legislative Assembly of its own, to

deal with its own special grievances and own special needs.'[120] With nationalization well under way, however, and the Scottish trade unions very much
a part of the wider British Trade Union movement, the Labour Party, both
north and south of the border, lost interest in plans for Scottish self-
government, and in its 1950 election manifesto Labour dropped its commitment to Home Rule.

Yet, as suggested by the spectacular theft of the Stone of Scone from
Westminster Abbey on Christmas Day 1950 and its subsequent deposit in
Arbroath Abbey, Scottish nationalism was far from dead. The Scottish National
Party, riven by feuds between Home Rulers and the advocates of outright independence, was so ineffective that a moderate nationalist, John MacCormick,
set up in exasperation a non-party Scottish Convention. In 1949 this collected
two million signatures, not all of them authentic, in support of a parliament for
Scotland with adequate legislative authority 'within the framework of the
United Kingdom'.[121] Nevertheless, nationalism had little impact on the broad
electoral picture. Disillusionment with Labour north and south of the border
brought Conservative governments to power between 1951 and 1964, respectively under Winston Churchill, Anthony Eden, Harold Macmillan and Alec
Douglas-Home. During this period devolution was effectively dropped from
the agenda of the major political parties, and the Anglo-Scottish union
appeared as strong as it had ever been. In part this was the result of intelligent
political management by the Unionists, and of effective administrative measures taken by the Scottish Office for the redress of some of Scotland's major
problems, like the acute shortage of housing.[122]

By the later 1950s, however, the Unionists, who would be rebranded
simply as Conservatives in 1965, were coming to look too anglicized and
were losing their touch. The Labour Party under Harold Wilson was
returned to power in 1964, but its victory led all too soon to disappointed
expectations. By the 1960s the post-war boom in Scotland's heavy industries was over. Demand had decreased as Europe recovered from the impact
of the Second World War and international competition grew more intense.
The economy was failing to diversify; west-central Scotland in particular
was suffering, the coal industry was dying, and the rise in Scottish GDP was
being easily outstripped by the British GDP, which itself was lagging inter-
nationally.[123] A faltering Scottish economy had left the country increasingly
dependent on government support and intervention, and inevitably, as the
British economy itself faltered, there was never enough money to meet the
growing demands. It was in this climate of disillusionment that the SNP
candidate, Winifred Ewing, won her spectacular victory over Labour at the
Hamilton by-election of November 1967. This was not a vote against the

Anglo-Scottish Union, the terms of which, according to the winner herself, had been violated. Still less was it a vote for independence. It was, rather, the expression of a widespread desire for a more effective working of the Union, based on a greater degree of autonomy for Scotland, and a higher recognition of its identity as an equal partner.[124]

Ironically, nobody was more of an enthusiast for this kind of 'constructive unionism', than Willie Ross, the formidable Scottish Secretary of State for Scotland in Harold Wilson's government. Himself a fervent nationalist, and an equally fervent opponent of the SNP, Ross worked hard, and with success, to divert public revenues to major development projects north of the border.[125] In the light of his efforts, the Hamilton by-election result came as all the more of a shock, forcing the political parties at Westminster to rethink their approach to their awkward northern neighbour.

The Conservatives, whose support in Scotland had been sliding, were the first to move, when their leader in opposition, Ted Heath, at his party conference in Perth in 1968, came out in favour of a Scottish assembly as the best means of halting the nationalist peril in its tracks. Harold Wilson, playing for time in the hope that the nationalist tide would recede, as indeed it did, set up a Royal Commission on the Constitution in 1969. In the long run, Labour's prevarication proved unsustainable, and in November 1975, the month of Franco's death, Wilson's government published its plans for a devolved Scottish Assembly. Both major parties, therefore, had now accepted, at least in principle, the need for more home rule.[126]

Yet times were changing, in Britain as in Spain. Britain was in the grip of a growing malaise over the state of the national economy and the country's place in Europe and the world. Meanwhile, the Scottish national cause had been given new grounds for hope by the discovery in 1970, some hundred miles off the coast of Aberdeen, of vast reserves of oil in the North Sea – a resource that was bound to change, perhaps decisively, the traditional equation between the two partners to the Union. For Scotland, as for Catalonia in the wake of Franco's death, there was now a chance of achieving the long-frustrated dream of home rule, or perhaps of something more.

CHAPTER 6

Breaking Away?
1975–2017

Constitutional Change

On 1 March 1979 Scotland voted in a referendum on whether it should have a form of home rule, now called 'devolution', that included the establishment of its own parliamentary assembly. Some eight months later, on 25 October, Catalans voted in a referendum on the statute of autonomy offered them under the new Spanish Constitution of 1978. How did the two referendums come about, and what does their outcome suggest about the national mood in the two countries at the end of the 1970s?

The Scottish referendum was the consequence of a feeling in both the Conservative and Labour parties, prompted by the growing electoral success of the Scottish National Party, that the constitutional status quo could no longer be sustained.[1] It had long been clear that Scots wanted more control over the way in which they were governed, and it was hoped in Westminster that the offer of an assembly sitting in Edinburgh would take the sting out of nationalism and satisfy what many saw as a legitimate aspiration that stopped well short of independence. In conjunction with a simultaneous referendum offering a devolved assembly to Wales, there were many who saw the projected constitutional reordering of 1979 as the best means of preserving the Anglo-Scottish union and holding the United Kingdom together at a time of generalized national malaise – a malaise generated by economic failure, widespread industrial unrest and disappointed popular expectations over the ability of successive governments to deliver on their promises. Yet from the beginning there were those, like the Scottish Labour MP Tam Dalyell and the historian Hugh

Trevor-Roper, who warned that devolution would set the United Kingdom on a slippery slope leading to the dissolution of the very union it was designed to uphold.[2]

In the aftermath of the referendums such fears appeared unfounded. Welsh voters heavily rejected the proposal for their own assembly. In Scotland, 1.23 million Scots, or 51.6 per cent of those voting, were in favour of devolution, and 48.4 per cent were against.[3] But by the terms of an amendment to the Scotland Act introduced by George Cunningham, a Scottish Labour MP sitting for a London constituency, the Act would be repealed if those voting in favour proved to comprise less than 40 per cent of the total electorate. In fact the figure reached was no more than 32.85 per cent. As a result, the devolution project advocated by Jim Callaghan's Labour government failed.[4]

The SNP, although disappointed by the obvious lack of popular enthusiasm for a change to the existing constitutional arrangements, was determined to press on, and tabled a parliamentary motion of no confidence that passed the Commons by one vote. The Callaghan government fell, and in the resulting general election of 1979 the Conservatives under the leadership of Margaret Thatcher swept into power. Not only Labour but also the SNP were routed, leaving the home rule campaign discredited and its leadership divided. Mrs Thatcher's government went on to repeal the Scotland Act and firmly set itself against any further talk of devolution. The United Kingdom was united, and so it must remain.[5]

Where the Scottish and Welsh referendums were the consequence of political manoeuvring and governmental concern, the Catalan referendum followed directly from the introduction of Spain's new written Constitution in 1978. With the death of General Franco in November 1975 and the restoration of monarchy in the person of Don Juan Carlos, Spain entered a period of deep political uncertainty. The country itself was changing and so was the world around it, with the overthrow in 1974 of dictatorships in Greece and Portugal and the active promotion of liberal democracy across the continent by the European Community. The restored monarchy needed the legitimacy that only democracy could bring, but there were deeply entrenched elements in the Spanish political establishment opposed to meaningful change. In addition, the terrorist activities of the Basque ETA movement strengthened the hands of those determined to ensure that there should be no relaxation of the iron grip that Franco had displayed in maintaining law and order. Yet at the same time there was a widespread feeling that a generous settlement for the Basques, and, by extension, for the Catalans, could bring an end to ETA.

The events of the following decades were to show that such confidence was misplaced.

It was the king's nomination as head of the government in July 1976 of Adolfo Suárez, a former Francoist of his own generation, that ended the impasse. With great adroitness Suárez dismantled the Francoist apparatus piece by piece, and successfully engineered the peaceful transition of the country from an authoritarian state into a parliamentary monarchy resting on democratic foundations. The enthusiastic celebration in June 1977 of the first free general elections in forty years marked the point at which there could no longer be any turning back other than by a military coup.

The transition could not have succeeded without a determination by all the leading politicians to avoid the horrors of another civil war. This entailed a willingness on all sides to make concessions for the sake of democracy, national unity, and a recognition of Basque and Catalan claims. Of the many problems that had to be addressed, one of the most pressing was that of the constitutional structure of the new democratic Spain. The centuries-old question of the relationship of the central government in Madrid to the different nations and regions of Spain was still unresolved, and was made all the more urgent when the lid imposed by the Franco regime on the festering nationalism of Catalonia and the Basque Country could no longer be held down.

Spain had lived under eight Constitutions between 1812 and 1931. In the last of these the Second Republic recognized Spain's inherent pluralism by describing it as an integral state but one compatible with regional and municipal autonomy. It was in accordance with this formulation that Catalonia was given the statute of 1932 that made it an 'autonomous region within the Spanish State'.[6] This was followed in 1936 by a statute of autonomy for the Basque provinces, and the preparation of a further statute for Galicia that never reached the stage of promulgation. The precedents set by the Second Republic and their fateful consequences, not least where the question of national unity was concerned, made the drafting of a new Constitution a delicate enterprise, whose success would again be dependent on the degree of compromise and consensus with which it was approached.[7]

Suárez prepared the ground skilfully by arranging for the return to Barcelona in October 1977 of the exiled Josep Tarradellas, as the president of a reinstituted Generalitat.[8] As a figure from the past, Tarradellas provided a perfect link between the old Republican Spain and its emerging democratic successor. The government followed its Catalan initiative by setting in train a far-reaching programme of decentralization that embraced not only the 'historic' communities of Catalonia, the Basque Country (Euskadi) and Galicia, but also raised the prospect of autonomy for several other regions and communities including Valencia, Aragon, Andalusia, Extremadura, Castile-León and the Balearic Islands. As other regions were later added to make an eventual total of seventeen, this distribution of what would come to be known as 'coffee for all' would create serious problems for the future, antagonizing the three 'historic' communities which believed that their historical distinctiveness created a 'differential fact' and entitled them to preferential treatment.

The decisions already taken by the government in pursuit of decentralization inevitably limited the room for manoeuvre of the distinguished seven-man commission set up to draft the new Constitution, although the political and social realities of the moment were bound to drive its members in the same direction. Representing all the major political parties, along with Catalan nationalists and Basques, they had somehow to strike a balance between national unity and national diversity. The difficulty in achieving this balance is suggested by the carefully ambiguous drafting of article 2 of the preliminary section of the Constitution, which describes it as being based on 'the indissoluble unity of the Spanish Nation, the common and indivisible *patria* of all Spaniards', and as recognizing and guaranteeing 'the right of autonomy for the nationalities and regions that integrate it and the solidarity between them all'. 'Nationalities' was seen as a more neutral term than 'nation', which was carefully avoided except when applied to Spain itself. A similar tension is apparent in article 3, which states that 'Castilian is the official language of the state. All Spaniards have the duty to know it and the right to use it. The other Spanish languages will also be official in the respective autonomous communities ...'[9] Title VIII of the Constitution was devoted to spelling out the practical implications of these defining principles, as it wrestled with the intractable question of the division of powers between the state and the 'autonomous communities', a term that sought to sidestep the awkward problem of drawing a clear dividing line between the Spanish regions and those parts of the country that laid claim to the title of 'nations'.

With the Basque terrorist organization ETA orchestrating 236 assassinations between 1975 and 1980 alone,[10] the issue of nationality was to be a continuing source of controversy, and it was ominous that the Partido Nacionalista Vasco or PNV (the Basque Nationalist Party) refused to vote in the Cortes for the new Constitution on the grounds that the Constitution did not recognize the sovereignty of the Basque Country. Franco's traditionalist and authoritarian concept of the 'Spanish Nation' was clearly unacceptable to the new political leaders, but was the opposing concept of Spain as a 'nation of nations' any more acceptable?[11] Might not the federalizing implications of such a concept open the way to the kind of political and constitutional engineering that would justify Prat de la Riba's dismissal of the state in 1894 as a purely artificial construct?[12]

Even though the new Constitution held back from conceding the word 'nation' to individual regions of Spain, it was approved by the electorate in a referendum held on 6 December 1978. The abstention rate in Catalonia was around 32 per cent, but 90 per cent of those who cast their votes showed themselves in favour, a figure above the national average. Following further constitutional discussions a statute of autonomy was agreed for Catalonia in August 1979 and was approved by over 88 per cent of those voting in the referendum held in October. The statute recognized Catalonia as a 'nationality', gave the Catalan language an official status equal to Castilian, and went much further than the statute of 1932 in the powers it conceded to the Generalitat in certain areas, notably those relating to education, culture and language. In the first elections for the new *parlament*, held in March 1980, the recently formed Convergència i Unió (CiU), drawing on non-nationalist centre and right-wing votes, emerged as the majority party. Its leader, Jordi Pujol, who had distinguished himself by his resistance to the Franco regime, became president of the Generalitat, a position he would hold for the next twenty-three years.[13] Catalans now had their own autonomous government, even if its competencies were not complete: its financial and judicial powers in particular were confined within the boundaries drawn by a Constitution that reserved a range of powers for Madrid. The limitations did not preclude the overall acceptance by Catalans of the new constitutional arrangements, which in fact gave Catalonia a greater degree of autonomy than the statute of 1932 had allowed it. As intended under the Constitution, Catalonia henceforth became an integral but largely self-governing part of what the bulk of its inhabitants had long wanted – a democratic, decentralized and modernizing Spain. Moreover, this was a Spain which, by joining the European Community in 1985 and NATO a year later, assumed its place as a fully fledged European state committed to upholding the democratic values that the Community espoused.

By contrast, the failure of devolution in 1979 left unchanged the constitutional ordering of Britain, which had finally secured membership of the European Community in 1973. Mrs Thatcher was an old-style Unionist with little or no understanding of Scottish sensitivities, and although Scottish Conservatives won 31.3 per cent of the votes in the 1979 general election, support in Scotland for her government began to wane as she privatized industry, closed down the mines and pushed through a series of policies that jarred with the sensibilities and aspirations of the Scottish electorate. These moves came at a time when the development of the North Sea oil deposits was beginning to yield rich rewards. The SNP was quick to see the political opportunities that this presented, and argued to great effect that, instead of being channelled southwards, the oil was a Scottish resource and that the large revenues it was generating should be placed under Scottish control and used for the benefit of a Scotland ravaged by high unemployment.[14]

Prime Minister Thatcher would have none of this. In her eyes and those of her Tory supporters Scotland had become a dependency culture that had grown lazy through excessive reliance on handouts from the government. In the eyes of many Scots, on the other hand, the state interventionism of the post-war era had successfully set Scottish industry on its feet again, and had brought the country the precious benefits of the welfare state. Now a Westminster party for which many of them had not voted seemed bent on systematically dismantling the legacy of the 1940s. As the Scotland of the 1980s slipped into a recession deeper than that in other parts of the United Kingdom, support for the Tories slumped. In the 1987 general election the Scottish Conservative Party, reduced to only ten MPs in Westminster, was almost wiped out. The electoral reverse may have encouraged, and certainly did not deter, the prime minister, when she made her fateful decision in 1989 to introduce her proposed new 'Poll Tax' in Scotland before implementing it south of the border.

The Community Charge, or 'Poll Tax', was the outcome of an attempt to fend off an impending crisis in the financing of Scottish local government, which was based, as in England, on a rating system. The revaluation of rates in 1984 infuriated Tory ratepayers, angered by what they saw as politically motivated spending by local authorities under Labour control and their disregard of rate-capping restrictions after the reduction of the block grant by the government. The revaluation hit homeowners hard, and led to the collapse of the Tory vote in the 1987 general election. Electoral disaster strengthened the feeling in Tory ranks and among Scottish ministers that an alternative system of financing had become essential. Ironically it was a group of free-market Scottish academics at St Andrews University and some of their former pupils who came up with the proposal for the replacement of rates by a Community Charge. Its introduction provoked a political storm as ratepayers discovered that their burdens were not substantially reduced, while most people found themselves having to pay much more than under the rate-paying system. This was bad enough, but Mrs Thatcher's 'catastrophic error', in the words of Tam Dalyell, was to impose a highly experimental poll tax in Scotland before introducing it in England. It could be argued that this contravened the stipulation in the Act of Union that the two kingdoms should have the same tax regimes, and it cast a glaring light on the prime minister's lack of understanding of Scottish affairs and the constitutional issues involved.[15]

By the time Mrs Thatcher's successor, John Major, had changed course and instituted a more emollient approach to Scotland, it was too late. His predecessor had turned her back on the flexible and pragmatic unionism long promoted by successive Tory governments in Westminster, and in so doing had left a legacy of bitterness that it would be hard to erase. The effect of the abandonment in the Thatcher years of old-style Tory unionism was to bring into the open, and accelerate the development of, a divergence between the political cultures of England and Scotland that would profoundly influence not only the politics but also the mutual perceptions of the two nations in the years that followed. Symptomatic of the divergence was an incipient tendency among Scots to speak of 'Westminster' in pejorative terms as a shorthand for all they disliked about being governed by the English.[16] For Scots of all persuasions, except for the outright advocates of independence, it was time to look again for ways to bridge the widening gap. The same held true for the Labour Party.[17]

In 1979 a civic Campaign for a Scottish Assembly had been launched to keep the cause of devolution alive at a time when Labour was divided over the best way forward and the SNP was in the doldrums. As the SNP recovered, it turned its eyes towards the continent, with which Scotland had traditionally enjoyed strong ties, and in 1988 adopted a policy of 'Independence in Europe'.[18] As some of its members had grasped, membership of the European Community had opened up a new range of possibilities for minority nationalist movements – something that the Catalans would also realize. What could not be achieved within the framework of the traditional nation-state might now be achieved by appealing over its head to a supra-national community with Brussels as its capital.

The Labour Party had toyed with home rule in the past and then drawn back. Now, under pressure from a reviving SNP, it once again came round to the idea of devolution. This was heavily promoted by Donald Dewar, MP for Glasgow Garscadden, who was to mastermind the moves that would lead to the Labour Party's eventual endorsement of plans for the creation of a Scottish parliament.[19] The first stage in this process was Labour's agreement to participate in a broad-based Convention called by the Campaign for a Scottish Assembly. In 1990 the Convention's report proposed that

Scotland should have its own legislative assembly elected by proportional representation, but evaded an answer to the tricky question of the assembly's relationship to the Westminster parliament. Given the general climate in the early 1990s and the fact that John Smith, MP for North Lanarkshire, a moderate supporter of devolution, became leader of the Labour Party in 1992, it seemed unlikely that the party would again reverse course, although Smith's death two years later raised new questions about its commitment. Labour retained this commitment under its new leader, Tony Blair, but added a proviso that Scots should be offered a referendum to decide whether in fact they wanted an assembly of their own in Edinburgh.[20] A referendum had the attraction of meeting the growing demand across the western world for greater popular participation in matters of outstanding import. Canada had resorted to the device in 1980 and again in 1995 as it grappled with Quebec's demands for independence. On both occasions the cause of independence went down to defeat.

Following Labour's massive victory in the general election of May 1997 the promised Scottish referendum was held in September, with an opposite outcome to that of the Quebec referendum. Under the skilful tactical management of Dewar, whom Blair appointed Secretary of State for Scotland, Labour joined forces with the Liberal Democrats and the SNP. This had been led since 1990 by the charismatic Alex Salmond. The united campaign of all three parties for a 'yes' vote won the support of 74.3 per cent of those voting, compared with 51.6 per cent in 1979. In response to a second question, as to whether the Edinburgh parliament should have tax-varying powers, 63.5 per cent were in favour. This time there could be no doubt about the electorate's wishes. The cause of home rule had finally triumphed, and Scotland would have its own legislative assembly for the first time since 1707.

The ending of direct rule in Northern Ireland with the Good Friday Agreement of April 1998 allowed the government to adopt a more relaxed attitude to devolution, which it hoped and expected would kill off the movement for independence. But it remained wary of the Scottish nationalists and crafted a system of proportional representation designed to prevent the dominance of the parliament by a single party, most obviously the SNP. It was under a form of proportional representation that the Scots went to the polls in May 1999 to choose their own government. The result of the election was that, with fifty-three seats for Labour, twelve for the Liberal Democrats, and seven for the SNP, Labour and Liberal Democrats would form a coalition government.[21] The parliament was formally opened by the Queen at Holyrood on 1 July, and Donald Dewar became the first minister of an executive which potentially possessed considerable room for manoeuvre.

In Spain the competencies transferred to the country's different autonomous communities varied widely and were subject to constant negotiation or renegotiation as they lobbied for more. In the event of disputes it was the task of the Constitutional Tribunal, sitting in Madrid, to pronounce on the legality of the actions of the Generalitat and the other autonomous governments.[22] Scottish legislators, on the other hand, were from the first given freedom of action, other than in those spheres, such as foreign policy and defence, where legislative powers were specifically reserved to the Westminster government. Where disagreements arose, the Judicial Committee of the Privy Council would fulfil the role played by Spain's Constitutional Tribunal.[23]

After such a hopeful beginning, the first years of Scotland's new devolved government were not happy ones. The strongest talents in the Scottish Labour Party – among them Gordon Brown, Robin Cook and Alistair Darling – were appointed to the cabinet of the half-Scottish prime minister, Tony Blair, leaving Dewar to carry the burden of Scottish politics. He was no administrator and his health was failing. He died in October 2000, at a moment when controversy was escalating over a number of issues, including the design and costs of the new parliament building opposite Holyroodhouse. Symbolically it was a Catalan, Enric Miralles, who won the international architectural competition, and his imaginative design suggested an instinctive identification with Scotland, its landscape and its people. His sudden death, a few months before that of Dewar, came when his plans were still incomplete. Although the project would continue, it would do so without his personal touch.

While Scotland was struggling with the challenge of getting its new government up and running, Catalonia under the presidency of Jordi Pujol was finding new ways to affirm its distinctive character. This was not the time to make a bid for independence, which anyhow would be a highly divisive issue in Catalonia itself. Instead, Pujol saw it as his task to consolidate and reinforce the concept of Catalan nationhood by deploying all the powers given to the Generalitat under the 1979 statute of autonomy, and adding to them incrementally whenever the balance of party politics in Madrid offered an opportunity to advance fresh demands. The 1979 statute transferred eighty-nine competencies to Catalonia – more than those allocated to any other of the autonomous communities, including the Basque Country. The success of the Generalitat in pushing its claims can be gauged by the fact that thirty years later the number of competencies had risen to 274.[24]

The aim of Pujol and his CiU party was to endow Catalonia with as many of the trappings of a sovereign state as they could. This, in their eyes, was an act of historical reparation. In a book published in 1987 a Catalan legal historian, Víctor Ferro, argued that Catalonia was once 'a "complete" state, with all the attributes of a sovereign entity and all the functions appropriate to a fully developed political community'.[25] The logical conclusion of this argument was that the Bourbons destroyed the Catalan 'state' when they used their victory in 1714 to abolish the principality's distinctive constitutional and institutional arrangements. This conclusion was readily embraced by Pujol in his bid to popularize the standard narrative of Catalonia as the victim of malign outside forces. It hardly seems a coincidence that Scottish historians at around the same time were initiating a debate as to whether or not Scotland could be classified as a 'state' in the years before the Union, although here the narrative of victimhood was more muted.[26]

Constructing, or reconstructing, a Catalan state, was not a straightforward task, not least because it had to be managed within the structure of a Spanish state regulated by organic laws passed by a Cortes that included Catalan representatives of different party affiliations – laws upheld in the final instance by Spain's Supreme Court. Pujol was faced, too, with grave suspicions, both in the PSOE (Partido Socialista Obrero Español), Spain's Socialist Party, and in its main rival, the PP (Partido Popular), about his ultimate intentions. His programme was also hampered by the fact that, while the Generalitat was in his hands and those of his party, the city government of Barcelona was the terrain of the Socialists. As so often in the past, the two institutions facing each other across the Plaça Sant Jaume were frequently at loggerheads, including over the candidature of Barcelona for the 1992 Olympic Games, for which the Generalitat showed no great enthusiasm.[27] Gradually, however, Pujol succeeded in building up a complex state apparatus, creating more layers of administration and, with them, more employees in the public service sector, and, as a consequence, more opportunities for clientage and corruption. A process that had begun in 1978 with the laudable intention of decentralizing an over-centralized Spanish state was now creating a series of over-centralized semi-states, with Catalonia among the leaders.[28]

Beyond the process of state-building Pujol was concerned to promote the larger, if vaguer, ambition of 'making a country' (fer país).[29] This meant turning it into a unified national polity, as Companys had sought to do in the 1930s. Nineteenth-century nationalists saw language as being at the very heart of national identity, and this Romantic notion was inherited by their twentieth-century Catalan successors. In practice, the country had grown accustomed to using Catalan in some situations and Castilian in others, although bilingualism only became fully established in the second half of the twentieth century, thanks in large part to the dominance of Castilian in the national media.[30]

The aim of the Generalitat was now to turn its aspiration into reality – a task that was complicated by the massive influx into Catalonia during the Franco years of Castilian-speaking immigrants from other parts of Spain. In 1983 the Catalan parliament passed a law for 'linguistic normalization', and everything possible was done in succeeding years to transform a bilingual Catalonia into a predominantly Catalan-speaking nation. Apart from the obvious measure of enhancing the teaching of Catalan in schools, this involved the promotion or creation of every kind of Catalan cultural institution, and the founding of a Catalan Corporation of Radio and Television, which began its operations in 1984. Castilian speakers inevitably felt discriminated against by the intensifying process of Catalanization, while the Generalitat claimed that it was simply reversing age-old policies designed to Castilianize Catalan society and suppress Catalonia's national identity.[31]

Following the near-extinction of Gaelic in the eighteenth and nineteenth centuries, Scotland, with fewer than 60,000 Gaelic speakers recorded in the 2011 census, differed from Catalonia in not having a seriously divisive linguistic question. But nationalism has many strings to its bow, and if one is missing there are always others, as long as the will exists and the time is right. The time would not be right until the advent of the twenty-first century. The Scottish economy, and with it Scottish society, was by now emerging from a painful period of transition in ways that seemed to offer real hope for the future. It was not only the development of the offshore oil industry that was opening up new vistas of prosperity after the long years of struggle. An economy dependent on dying or dead traditional manufacturing industries was being replaced by a more modern and varied economy, more attractive to foreign investors and better attuned to the requirements of international markets.

The new economy was led by a growing service sector, and was based on electronics and petrochemicals, banking and insurance, and the developing tourist industry. Where the share of this service sector stood at 24 per cent in 1951, it had risen to 33 per cent by 1971 and would be up to 70 per cent by the turn of the century – a growth that has been described as 'the greatest single identifiable motor of social change in Scotland since 1945'.[32] Such profound economic and social changes, while producing losers as well as winners, seemed likely to benefit a Scottish Labour Party which, while far from nationalist in outlook, was now firmly identified with devolution, rather than benefiting an SNP which had formally adopted the cause of Scottish independence.

The exact meaning of 'independence' was far from clear, even to SNP voters, of whom less than a quarter in 1997 were separatists.[33] The party was still insufficiently professional, and was struggling to convince an electorate wearying of constitutional issues.[34] A number of developments, however, were working in its favour. The Scottish Executive had a lacklustre appearance, and, as time went on, Tony Blair's New Labour, with its distinctively Westminster bias, no longer aroused among Scottish voters the enthusiasm it had generated in 1997, while the decline of the trade unions brought about by the collapse of the old manufacturing industries had weakened the Old Labour heartlands. Religion, too, was a declining force in the political arena. As old sectarian divisions diminished, the Kirk, traditionally supportive of the union, no longer exercised a commanding influence, while Roman Catholics of Irish descent were no longer automatically prepared to cast their votes for Labour. In addition, educational improvements had created an electorate that was becoming better informed, more critical in its assessments of politicians of all parties, and, above all, less deferential.[35]

At the start of 2007, the year that marked the third centenary of the Anglo-Scottish Union, it was by no means certain that the SNP could find a message that would allow it to capitalize on these various developments, although for some time it had been moving in the right direction. In particular, by adopting a gradualist approach to independence, it had positioned itself to broaden its appeal when the opportunity arose. This came with the extension by the Scottish Executive in 2007 of proportional representation to local government, a measure that had the effect of breaking the grip of the Labour Party at the local level.[36] The SNP came first in the 2007 election to the Scottish Parliament, although still winning less than a third of the vote,[37] and took power as a minority government with Alex Salmond as first minister. Twenty-seven years after Jordi Pujol came to power in Catalonia, Scottish nationalists, too, had the chance of turning their dream into reality.

Forging a State

Alex Salmond and his SNP colleagues were well aware of the parallels between Scotland's situation and that of Catalonia, and Salmond may well have had in mind the Catalan model when, on taking office, he changed the name of the Scottish Executive to that of Scottish Government (the Catalan

Govern). The change was a signal of the new administration's intention to follow Catalonia's example in leap-frogging the national capital and going directly to Brussels to win recognition of its statehood within the framework of a united Europe.

The example, although in many respects promising, was not devoid of dangers. Tom Nairn had presciently pointed this out as long ago as 1975 when, in commenting on the propensity of SNP ideologists to think of Scotland as already a fully fledged member of the European Union, he observed that its situation was far from unique. They would do well to recognize, he argued, that 'Catalonia has much more in common with us [Scotland] than Norway: we may end up as noisy outcasts and not as paid-up members of an elite club.'[38] Would the European Union really be willing to accept for membership the breakaway regions of existing member states?

Times had changed in Spain since 1975, but the movement in Catalonia towards nationhood and statehood had not run entirely smoothly since the advent of autonomy in 1980. During Pujol's twenty-three-year presidency the Generalitat's educational and cultural programmes did much to propagate among Catalans the idea that they were inhabitants of a distinctive nation. Yet in pressing for enhanced powers, the Generalitat came into conflict with successive governments in Madrid, although the deputies of Pujol's party, Convèrgencia i Unió, cleverly kept down the political temperature by supporting them in the Congress when they needed parliamentary help. Yet disputes continued. Between 1986 and 1988 alone the Catalan government complained to the Supreme Constitutional Tribunal of seventy-seven real or alleged breaches by the Spanish authorities of rights conferred on it by the statute of autonomy. For its part the Tribunal was called upon to pass judgement on numerous cases involving claims that the Generalitat had exceeded its constitutional powers.[39]

The year 2003 saw the retirement of Jordi Pujol, whose coalition government had been dependent on the support of the conservative Partido Popular, which assumed power in 1996 under the presidency of José María Aznar with the support of the Basque Nationalist Party, the Canarian coalition and Pujol's CiU. By the time of Pujol's retirement the relationship with Aznar's government had soured, and his party, tainted by corruption and by its association with the forces of the right, was losing popular support. In the 2003 elections to the Catalan parliament the Socialists won a majority of the votes. As a result, Pujol was unable to hand on the presidency of the Generalitat to his chosen heir, Artur Mas, and control of the autonomous government passed to a three-party coalition of parties of the left, with the former mayor of Barcelona, Pasqual Maragall, succeeding him as president.[40]

The return to power in the national elections of 2004 of the socialist PSOE, led by José Luis Rodríguez Zapatero, gave Maragall an opportunity to press ahead with the Catalan nationalist agenda at a time when the president of the Basque regional government was also making what proved to be an unsuccessful bid to redefine, in ways that clearly contravened the 1978 Constitution, the relationship between the Basque Country and the Spanish state. Maragall's aim was to settle the Catalan question by revising the 1979 statute of autonomy. His hope was that a revision would reinforce and extend Catalan autonomy, anchoring it within the constitutional framework of the genuinely federal Spain that he wanted to see created. A project for a new statute of autonomy, commonly but mistakenly known as the Estatut, was drafted with Zapatero's backing, and accepted by the Catalan parliament in September 2005. Its first article read 'Catalonia is a nation' – sensitive wording, since the 1978 Constitution had reserved the term 'nation' for Spain.

Sections of his own Socialist Party, worried by the threat to the Constitution and to Spanish unity, immediately brought pressure to bear on Zapatero to go back on his promise of support. After prolonged discussions the proposed statute was modified, leaving a deliberate ambiguity in the definition of Catalonia's 'national' status. Modifications were also made over the equally sensitive question of future financial arrangements. These eventually gave the autonomous government its own fiscal agency along with the control of 50 per cent of the taxes recovered in Catalonia. The modified version of the statute was then approved by the Congress and the Senate before being put to the Catalan population in a referendum held in June 2006. Here again it was approved, but with an abstention rate of 51 per cent, and officially became an Organic Law on 19 July.[41]

The modified statute did not satisfy those Catalan politicians who resented the way in which the original text had been watered down, and Maragall responded by announcing his withdrawal from political life. It was also totally unacceptable to the Partido Popular, the strongest and most inflexible of all the defenders of Spain's territorial integrity. The PP, after collecting more than four million signatures, proceeded to file a suit against the Estatut in the Constitutional Tribunal at the end of July 2006, claiming that the proposed changes amounted to a reform of the Constitution and should be treated as such. A suit was filed, too, by the Defensor del Pueblo, Spain's equivalent of the Ombudsman, over matters affecting civil rights, and objections were also raised by five of the autonomous communities, all of them except Aragon governed at the time by the PP. Their objections were mostly to do with such contentious points as the control of water supplies, where one or more of the autonomous communities argued that the Catalan statute impinged on their rights. These objections, like those of the Defensor del Pueblo, would be dealt with by brief separate judgements delivered after the handing down of the principal judgement and were made with reference to it. The prime issue was that of the constitutionality of the Estatut as a whole.[42]

The constitutional objections included references in the document to 'national symbols' and to Catalonia as a 'nation'; compulsory Catalan for all schoolchildren, at a time when Castilian was already being taught in the schools as a separate subject; a parallel system of judicial power to the Spanish system; and increased financial autonomy for the Catalan government.[43] All these alleged 'reforms' would, in the eyes of the PP and those who shared its objections, whittle down even further state powers already much reduced by the decentralizing measures introduced under the 1978 Constitution. If the Estatut were accepted, Catalonia would enjoy a status superior to that of all the other autonomous communities with the exception of the Basque provinces and Navarre, which still enjoyed their so-called 'historic rights' of fiscal and administrative autonomy, as guaranteed under the new arrangements negotiated with the government in 1878. This, of course, was exactly what Catalan nationalists believed was only right and proper, given the 'differential fact' of Catalonia's distinctive linguistic and 'historical' identity.

It would take four years for the Tribunal to reach its decision – four years of confusion in Catalonia's political life with its political parties, including the CiU, divided among themselves, and of growing resentment at continuous manifestations of anti-Catalan sentiment by the Partido Popular. The PP itself was again defeated in the national elections of 2008. These gave Zapatero a second term in office, but this coincided with the global financial crash that would doom his government three years later.

With the Scottish Nationalist Party having only just become the party of government, it was clearly not in the interest of Alex Salmond and his minority administration to plunge Scotland and the United Kingdom into the kind of polarization now afflicting Spain. Independence for Scotland was, and remained, the SNP's long-term goal, but the immediate need was to show, both to doubting Scots and to the British public in general, that the nationalists could run an efficient government. This they managed to do, and they reaped their reward in the 2011 election to the Scottish parliament, which followed the defeat of Gordon Brown's Labour government in the British general election of 2010 and the creation of a coalition government of Conservatives and Liberal Democrats headed by David Cameron. The decline in support for Labour had already been apparent in the Scottish local elections of 2007, but the extraordinary collapse of the Scottish Labour vote in the 2011 election took almost everyone by surprise. With the Conservatives still deeply discredited and Labour sinking drastically in popularity among its core voters, a now highly organized SNP was well placed to fill the vacuum, and it romped home with some 45 per cent of the votes and sixty-nine seats out of 129 in the new Scottish parliament. This was a remarkable result, and all the more so since the electoral system had been carefully designed to prevent a majority one-party government.

Having won power with a striking majority the SNP could now fulfil the promise in its election manifesto to seek a referendum on Scottish independence, although there was no guarantee that those who had voted for the party in such large numbers had actually voted for an independent Scotland. Indeed opinion polls at the time of the election indicated that only 29 per cent of the electorate wanted full independence, and that most would be satisfied with an increased devolution of power to the government in Edinburgh. While opening negotiations with the Westminster government, Salmond was therefore in no hurry for a referendum before assuring himself that there was a reasonable chance of winning it.[44] On the other hand, with independence as the proclaimed objective of the SNP, there was now no dodging the issue, especially as John Major had conceded as long ago as 1993 that if the Scots really wanted to secede they had the right to do so.[45]

Although the sovereignty of parliament, and not of the people, remains the bedrock of British political theory and practice, resort to referendums has in recent years become a convenient instrument of government when answers were sought to large and controversial questions, like devolution or membership of the European Union. In this, as in other respects, the absence of a written constitution affords the British government a degree of flexibility not shared by its Spanish counterpart. The 1978 Spanish Constitution gave the central government 'exclusive competence' to authorize a referendum. With seventeen autonomous communities anxious to assert themselves, however, it would be politically impossible for any Spanish administration of whatever political hue to allow one of them to call unilaterally a referendum that included the offer of independence. A change of such magnitude could only be brought about by a constitutional amendment, and this would first require the approval of a large majority in the Cortes, to be followed by the calling of a general election.[46]

It was the ruling on 28 June 2010 by the Supreme Constitutional Tribunal, on the allegations brought before it four years previously about the unconstitutionality of the Estatut, that dramatically raised the political temperature. Although the sentence was hailed by the Partido Popular as a major defeat for Catalan nationalism, the Tribunal did not strike down the statute, and instead made relatively mild modifications to fourteen of its articles, six of which were concerned with financing. But it did declare that the reference to Catalonia as a 'nation' in the preamble had no juridical status – a point conceded by Maragall when launching the project – and it pronounced as unconstitutional the addition of the words 'and preferred' in the reference to Catalan as 'the normal and preferred language of the public administration and the public media in Catalonia'.

The Tribunal's long-delayed ruling aroused fury in the Generalitat and in nationalist organizations, which saw it as the culmination of an unrelenting anti-Catalan campaign. With the majority of the judges on the Tribunal being political appointees, it was easy to condemn the judgement as politically biased, and to mobilize public opinion in defence of a Catalonia that was once again being victimized. On 10 July hundreds of thousands took to the streets of Barcelona in a mass demonstration under the slogan of 'We are a nation. We decide.' Once again the 'nation' was in open confrontation with the 'Spanish state'– the equivalent of Scotland's pejorative 'Westminster'. Growing disillusionment with both the main political parties, and with a Constitution that seemed incapable of meeting what were regarded as Catalonia's legitimate demands, gave a fresh impetus to the cause of independence.

The disillusionment was reflected in the results of the Catalan elections of November 2010, which came close to giving the Convergència i Unió an absolute majority in the parliament, and brought its leader, Artur Mas, to power as president of the Generalitat. With the new government came heightened rhetoric and growing talk of a unilateral referendum on the question of Catalan independence. In the spring of 2011 a pro-independence meeting was held, leading to the creation of a National Assembly of Catalonia (the ANC) which committed itself to working for full Catalan independence.[47] In the Spanish general election of November of that year the Partido Popular was returned to power in Madrid, and Mariano Rajoy succeeded Zapatero as president. With the return of the PP to government the prospect of some form of agreement between Madrid and the Generalitat was significantly diminished.

The attitude and behaviour of both were profoundly influenced by the global banking crisis of 2007–8 and its economic and social consequences. Rajoy's government was committed to new austerity measures to restore the public finances, and was in no mood to bail out a Catalan government whose debts had been rising steeply since Mas came to power. In the spring of 2012 the imposition of cuts by the central government on the Generalitat's spending on such public services as health and education began to turn public opinion against Mas and his party. Economic depression was affecting broad swathes of the population, and depression provides fertile ground for demagogues and opportunists. During the summer of 2012 mass demonstrations in many towns and cities under the banner of the 'march towards independence' made it clear to Mas that his only chance of survival was to swim with the tide. The 'march' reached its climactic point on Catalonia's national day, the *diada*, of 11 September, when a mass gathering in Barcelona of some one and a half million people demonstrated for 'Catalonia, a new State in Europe'. The regional administration not only associated itself with the 'march', but used the media under its control to launch a massive propaganda campaign. A critical choice now faced Mas. He could either distance himself and his Convergence party from the secessionists or make it the leading separatist party in Catalonia. He chose the second option. He now began to speak of Catalonia's right to decide, while the Catalan parliament adopted resolutions in the same vein. From this point on it would be hard to turn back.[48]

Although Artur Mas and the Generalitat were far from carrying with them the bulk of the population, the advocates of independence, both in the Generalitat and at the local level, had captured the initiative. They were helped by the fact that many Catalans held posts in the administration or were dependent on it in one way or another, while the Generalitat's influence over the media, and the possession of its own radio and television channels, gave it ample opportunities to propagate its message. Even the weather forecasts on Channel 3 were brought into play. These covered the western Mediterranean but did not include the Iberian Peninsula as a whole, and the weather in Madrid was simply listed alongside that of other major European cities.

Above all, the programme of Catalanization, or outright indoctrination, inaugurated by Pujol thirty years earlier was now yielding its fruits. A new generation had arisen, more fervently nationalist in its outlook than its predecessor – a generation that had learnt Catalan at the expense of Castilian in the schools, and had been taught a form of history in which the Catalan past was disconnected from that of Spain, now routinely described as the 'Spanish state'. Even the geography textbooks sponsored by the Generalitat tended, like the weather forecasts, to ignore the Iberian Peninsula, and concentrate instead on the western Mediterranean.[49] In Scotland, by contrast, the renaissance of Scottish history as an academic subject in the 1970s to 1990s had very limited political consequences, and it was not until the opening years of the twenty-first century that the history of Scotland achieved prominence as a compulsory element in school-leaving examinations.[50]

Hoping to capitalize on the euphoria created by the success of the *diada*, while simultaneously diverting attention from the inability of his government to come up with adequate responses to the economic and social challenges that faced it, Mas called new Catalan elections for November 2012, with the promise of a referendum on independence to be held in 2014. He also hoped to benefit from Rajoy's rejection of his proposal that Catalonia should be given the same fiscal privileges as those historically enjoyed by the Basque Country and Navarre, and from the government's unwillingness to permit any fiscal changes before the normal quinquennial financial adjustments, due in 2014. 'Spain is robbing us' (*Espanya ens roba*) was a useful slogan. Yet the results of the election proved disappointing for the CiU, which lost a dozen seats in the parliament. In spite of this setback Mas was re-elected as president of the Generalitat in December 2012 with the help of a pro-independence left-wing party, the Esquerra Republicana de Catalunya or ERC. He and his party were now clearly committed to the calling of a referendum as the starting point on the road to full independence. They faced strong resistance, however, from opponents of independence, notably the Partido Popular, along with the less militant Catalan Socialist Party, and a new constitutionalist 'citizens' party, Ciutadans (Ciudadanos). Both the PP and Ciutadans had gained ground in the elections, as had the pro-independence ERC at the opposite end of the political spectrum.

Although the Scotland Act of 1998 gave the British government the right to refuse a Scottish referendum, the triumph of the SNP in the 2011 elections persuaded David Cameron's government that the Scottish electorate should have its way, partly in the hope, or expectation, that this would put an end for the foreseeable future to the clamour for independence. As a result, and in contrast to contemporaneous developments in Spain, independence for Scotland became a matter to be resolved in negotiations between Edinburgh and London, with no explicit intervention by the non-English components of the United Kingdom, Wales and Northern Ireland. It was the 'Edinburgh Agreement' of 15 October 2012 signed in that city by David Cameron and an Alex Salmond triumphant in the wake of the SNP's election victory, that made possible the holding of a Scottish referendum on 18 September 2014. Concessions were made by both the negotiating parties. The prime minister was adamant in insisting on a two-question referendum – 'yes' or 'no' to Scotland becoming an independent country or remaining part of the United Kingdom – rather than permitting the inclusion of a third question offering a vote on maximum devolution ('Devo-max'), the option he feared and that Salmond wanted, suspecting that full independence was still a minority cause. On the other hand,

Cameron conceded that the Scottish government should decide on the wording of the questions to be put, the composition of the electorate, and the date on which the referendum should be held. In waiting until 2014 Salmond thus gave himself time to win over more of the sceptics to his cause. Once the agreement was reached, the Westminster parliament simply had to give its consent, and the referendum could go ahead.

In the event the referendum campaign was full of suspense, and the results and their aftermath produced moments of high drama.[51] With the eyes of the world upon them the Scots engaged in a passionate internal debate about their past, present and future. Nothing was excluded, from the events of 1707 to the brutal suppression of the 1745 rebellion, the persistent neglect, or worse, of Scotland's interests by an uncomprehending Westminster parliament, the decay of its traditional industries, and the prospects of a brighter future once the nation was allowed full control over the revenues from 'Scotland's' North Sea oil. But above all, this was a debate about the nation's sense of itself, in which everyone, whether young or old, had a view to express, and did not hesitate to do so.

With the leaders of the three main British parties, together with leading Scottish public figures, including the former prime minister, Gordon Brown, all actively campaigning for a 'No' vote, the rejection of an ill-defined 'independence' appeared at the start of the campaign to be a foregone conclusion. As with the campaign in the unofficial Catalan referendum that followed two months later, the debate exposed deep internal divisions in Scottish society, both generational and regional, and aroused much bitterness. Newspapers on both sides of the border were largely hostile to the nationalist cause, and the 'No' campaign drove home relentlessly the economic, social and financial risks to Scotland if it decided to cut loose from its British moorings and cast itself adrift on a sea of uncertainty. It would surely be folly to cast aside a union that over the course of three centuries had brought such benefits to both the contracting parties.

The argument was potent and undoubtedly swayed many votes, but it also showed itself to be dangerously double-edged. It smacked too much of English arrogance, as if Scotland, instead of being an equal partner, was no more than an appendage of England, and as such could not expect to continue receiving the financial and other benefits of a Union primarily funded by English taxpayers if it unwisely chose to dissolve it. The unionists were strikingly unsuccessful in articulating a strong positive case for the continuation of the Union, and a fundamentally negative campaign was not calculated to impress those swathes of Scottish society that had failed to experience any improvement in their living conditions over many decades and saw no cause for gratitude. Deeply antagonized by the policies of the Thatcher regime and disillusioned with a sclerotic Labour Party that had proved unable to deliver social justice, Scots were naturally ready to look elsewhere in their search for something better.

The negative message promoted by the 'Better Together' campaign gave Salmond and his supporters an opportunity they were quick to seize. Their obvious response was to project a sense of optimism about the capacity of the Scots to shape their own destiny. In delineating a brighter future for Scotland outside the United Kingdom but inside the European Union, the proponents of independence were in effect turning their back on the Britishness that had been a hallmark of Scottish identity since the eighteenth century. Instead, they purveyed a vision of an idealized Scotland released from the constraining shackles of the Union. This was a nation in which individual self-fulfilment went hand in hand with an ingrained sense of civic responsibility and a deep commitment to the cause of social justice. The notion that egalitarianism was an inherent and defining feature of Scottish society was one of those Scottish 'myths' – assumptions largely unquestioned and not amenable to proof – that had come to shape the image that Scots held of themselves.[52] It was not hard for campaigners for a 'Yes' vote to emphasize the contrast between an egalitarian Scotland rich in unrealized potential and an aloof and arrogant England that had been shaped over the centuries by its social distinctions and its deep-rooted inequalities.

The differences between the national cultures of Scotland and England had always been recognized and accepted as a fact of life, but the political divergence between the two parts of the United Kingdom in the 1970s and succeeding decades undoubtedly helped to sharpen and underline the contrast. This easily lent itself to depiction as a contrast between two national characters, both of them simplified and distorted for political purposes. Distorted images made for effective weapons when deployed in the referendum campaign, and did much to generate the enthusiasm for the cause of Scottish nationhood and statehood apparent across much of the country as voting day approached. The level of debate was intense in pubs, at street corners and at public gatherings. When the opinion polls showed a narrowing of the gap between the two sides, with one poll on 7 September 2014 even pointing to a possible victory for the 'Yes' campaign, Westminster panicked. At the risk of being accused of English intervention in Scotland's affairs the leaders of the three largest unionist parties – David Cameron of the Conservatives, Nick Clegg of the Liberal Democrats and Ed Miliband of Labour – flew north to make the case for the retention of the Union.

Then, two days before the vote, they signed a pledge, known as the 'Vow', promising Scotland 'extensive new powers'. An imprecisely defined 'Devo-max', so carefully kept off the balloting papers, was now again in play.

Referendum day, 18 September 2014, saw a record turnout of 85 per cent of registered voters. In spite of predictions based on the latest opinion polls, the outcome was decisive, with 55 per cent voting against independence and 45 per cent in favour. Stability had triumphed over risk, pragmatism over utopianism, fear over hope. The immediate consequence of the vote was the resignation of Alex Salmond as first minister and leader of the SNP, and his replacement by his deputy, Nicola Sturgeon, who would prove herself to be an equally artful but perhaps more strategic politician, and one capable of inspiring more confidence and a greater degree of trust than her predecessor.

More unexpectedly, defeat was followed over the next few months by a massive upsurge of support for all the pro-independence parties, as those disappointed by the result and by the subsequent failure of Westminster to honour immediately its promise of devolving 'extensive' new powers to Edinburgh rushed to join the ranks of the SNP. Within little over two months of the referendum the membership lists of the party had trebled in size to 84,000, and by early 2015 numbers had reached 100,000 and were continuing to rise.[53] New members included many who had formerly been disengaged from the world of politics but had now found a cause that brought new meaning to their lives. Their new-found enthusiasm carried over to the general election of May 2015, at which the SNP scored an over-whelming victory over its rivals. In Scotland itself the once dominant Labour Party was reduced to a single member of parliament. In the House of Commons the SNP now held fifty-four of the fifty-nine Scottish seats – a quite extraordinary result. This made it the third largest British party after the Conservatives, who were returned to power with a clear majority, and after a Labour Party that could no longer depend on Scotland to bring it electoral victories.

This was a political revolution with profound implications for the future of a still United Kingdom. Scottish MPs now had the possibility of exerting unprecedented political leverage, and with it came the chance of securing a second independence referendum much sooner than the outcome of the first might suggest. More immediately it raised to a new level of urgency the whole question of the future constitutional structure of Great Britain. The so-called 'West Lothian question' had long been lurking in the back-ground of parliamentary politics: why the Scots, once they had their own parliament and conducted their own business, should continue to have a vote on matters that were only of English concern.[54]

There were already indications of an English backlash against Scotland at the time of the referendum, as if nothing much had changed since that moment in the 1760s when the two Highland officers were greeted with cries of 'Out with them!' on entering a London theatre.[55] While the outcome of the referendum was met with a widespread sense of relief, there were some who now, as then, would have been happy to let the Scots leave the Union if this was what they wanted. The Scots caused nothing but trouble, and English taxpayers were always being called upon to foot their bills. As the emergence of the United Kingdom Independence Party (UKIP) showed, English nationalism had been on the rise long before the referendum, but the sudden and apparently spontaneous upsurge of Scottish nationalism found its mirror image in the dramatic upsurge of its English equivalent. Well aware of the dangers, not least to his own Conservative Party, David Cameron pandered to this English nationalism and attempted to control it when, in his first public statement after the Scottish referendum, he raised the potentially explosive issue of 'English votes for English laws'.

The slogan, tripping so easily off the tongue, implied a possible constitutional reconstruction of the United Kingdom, moving perhaps towards the creation of a federal system in which England, too, would have its own parliament. But with Scottish nationalism riding high in spite of the rejection of the independence option, there could be no long-term guarantee of the United Kingdom's survival as a single political unit, and the future of both Wales and Northern Ireland would then be at stake. Nicola Sturgeon made it clear that she was not about to abandon the cause of independence, although her conduct as first minister made it equally clear that she was not minded to launch a second bid for independence without being confident of a favourable outcome. Timing and context were everything, and the continued collapse in the world price of oil hardly suggested that the time was right for the transformation of Scotland into a viable sovereign state.

The very fact, however, that independence still remained on the cards gave heart to the defeated, while also keeping alive the hopes of other small nations with their own aspirations for statehood. The Scottish referendum campaign was nowhere followed with closer attention than in Catalonia, whose nationalists cherished their links with their Scottish counterparts. They were conscious of having much in common with them. The two nations shared a proud past, a strong sense of cultural distinctiveness, and an aggrieved feeling of alienation from an unsympathetic central government. Where population was concerned, Catalonia had the advantage: Scotland in

2010 had 5.22 million inhabitants; Catalonia at around the same time had some 7.5 million.[56] Catalonia was superior, too, in the relative contribution of the two peoples to the national gross domestic product. Scotland's contribution to British GDP was 9.2 per cent, whereas Catalonia's contribution to that of Spain was 20 per cent.[57] Did not the Catalans, then, have at least as much right as the Scots to decide their own fate?

The polarization of Catalan society between secessionists and anti-secessionists was painfully apparent, and was confirmed when the Generalitat, ignoring the Spanish Constitution, pressed ahead with an illegal 'referendum' on 9 November 2014. Families were deeply divided, the atmosphere was tense, and in the end less than 40 per cent of the electorate turned out to vote. Outright independence was looking increasingly like the preserve of a section of the political class and of the middle and professional classes, while the working class, many of them with a Castilian-speaking background, were either hostile to the idea, or were satisfied with the degree of autonomy that Catalonia already enjoyed. But the outcome was far from being determined simply by class division, itself by no means clear-cut. There was division, too, between speakers of Catalan and those who spoke Castilian, while ideological differences also came into play. Nationalism, in any event, has many faces, and as in Scotland, there was no necessary correlation between a profoundly felt nationalism and the wish for independence.

An electoral system that gives more weight to some provinces than others makes it difficult to calculate the true balance of forces in Catalan society, but the realization that the enthusiasm of the population for independence was substantially less than anticipated persuaded the Generalitat to pull back from its more exposed position, and rethink its strategy without abandoning its goal. This in turn led to internal divisions among the nationalists, and Mas gave up the presidency of the Generalitat and of the CiU in July 2016. His successor as president of the Generalitat, proposed by Mas, was a committed supporter of independence, Carles Puigdemont, a journalist and a political activist who served as mayor of Girona between 2011 and 2016.[58]

Just as in Scotland at the time of the 2011 election, it seems probable that a large majority of the Catalan population would have been satisfied with a recognition of their nation's distinctive status, expressed in a larger measure of home rule. Hard-core secessionists amounted to perhaps 25 per cent of the population as a whole.[59] Nevertheless, more home rule was not something that nationalists could expect to receive from Rajoy's PP government. In any event the government, like the separatists, was boxed in by a constitution that could only be changed after the process had surmounted the many obstacles to allowing an independence referendum to a single autonomous community without the participation of all the others.

The secessionists, however, were not to be thwarted, and the failure of two successive national elections in 2016 either to return Rajoy to power or to lead to the establishment of a new Spanish government created a vacuum at the centre of politics that they were happy to exploit. The party system that grew out of the transition to constitutional monarchy and parliamentary democracy in the 1970s was showing signs of breaking down. The two leading political parties, both mired in corruption scandals, were losing the confidence of the electorate, and new political parties were emerging to contest their dominance. The representatives in the Spanish Cortes of the autonomous communities, themselves politically divided, made coalition-building essential if neither the Socialists nor the Partido Popular could win an outright majority in the polls, and coalition-building looked likely to require concessions to nationalist demands that neither of the two parties felt they were willing or able to make.

The resulting political impasse left the electorate disenchanted, and created opportunities for populist politicians of whatever hue. In opinion polls taken in Catalonia after the failed national election of 26 June 2016, 47.7 per cent of those approached answered 'yes' to the question, 'Do you want Catalonia to become an independent state?', as against 42.4 per cent who answered 'no'.[60] Encouraged by such findings, a coalition of secessionist groups made use of their absolute majority in the Catalan parliament to win approval in July 2016 for the region to continue on the road to independence by way of a unilateral referendum as laid out by Artur Mas. Two months later Puigdemont gave the date of the referendum, to be held with or without the government's approval, as September 2017.

In Britain, too, the summer of 2016 saw a profound political change. In an event that turned British politics upside down, the national referendum held on 23 June saw a clear majority in England voting to leave the European Union. In Scotland, by contrast, every local authority area produced a majority in favour of remaining. Following the vote, Nicola Sturgeon was quick to argue the injustice of Scotland being forced to follow England's lead in turning its back on Europe, and raised the possibility of a new referendum on Scottish independence. Well aware, though, of the economic and financial uncertainties that were bound to follow the Brexit vote – uncertainties that might well persuade anxious Scottish voters that they would be better off remaining part of the United Kingdom – she delayed committing herself to a timetable. Conscious that another unsuccessful Scottish referendum could dash the dream of independence for many years to come, she preferred to bide her time.

When the new British prime minister, Theresa May, announced that Britain would begin the process of negotiating the country's withdrawal from the European Union by the end of March 2017, however, Nicola Sturgeon responded by demanding another referendum during 2018–19. The SNP had reserved the right at the time of the referendum on Europe to call a second Scottish referendum if Scotland's national interests appeared to be jeopardized by the outcome. She could now argue that the vote for Brexit represented so fundamental a change in the circumstances of the United Kingdom that any earlier promises to leave aside for a generation the issue of Scottish independence no longer held good. In her view the British government had failed to heed the wishes of the Scottish electorate and was doing nothing to negotiate a deal in Brussels that would take Scotland's European interests into account. But in pressing for a second referendum within a relatively short time frame Nicola Sturgeon still took care to give herself some latitude for manoeuvre in what was becoming an elaborate game of poker with her British counterpart.

Going for Broke[61]

Sturgeon's caution over calling for a second Scottish referendum stood in sharp contrast to the attitude of the dominant political parties in Catalonia, hell-bent on unilateral action to bring about an independence referendum within eighteen months, in open defiance of the government and the Constitutional Tribunal. On 1 August 2016, following the July vote in the Catalan parliament to press ahead along the road to a referendum, the Tribunal rejected parliament's road map as illegal. On 17 October 2016, after Puigdemont had announced that the referendum would be held the following September, the public prosecutor brought charges of disobedience against the president of the Catalan parliament, Carme Forcadell, for allowing parliament to vote on the road map in spite of the fact that the Tribunal on 2 December 2015 had rejected as illegal any unilateral declaration of Catalonia's sovereignty. The crisis intensified on 13 March 2017 when former Catalan president Artur Mas and three of his ministers were debarred from holding public office after allowing their 'consultative' vote of November 2014 on independence to go ahead.

For a moment, on 17 August 2017, the constitutional crisis, which occupied more and more media attention as the date for the referendum drew ever closer, was sidelined by the news of a terrorist attack in Barcelona. A twenty-two-year-old Moroccan, who later turned out to have been living in Ripoll since the age of five, drove his van into pedestrians thronging the

Ramblas, killing fourteen and injuring over a hundred more. In the next few hours a similar attack occurred in Cambrils, and members of a terrorist cell of radicalized Muslims, residents of the Ripoll area, were rapidly identified by the Mossos d'Esquadra, who shot some of the perpetrators as they tried to flee and arrested others on suspicion of participating in terrorist activities. A former imam from Ripoll who was believed to have radicalized the terrorists was killed in an explosion the night before the terrorist acts in a house in Alcanar where he had rented a room for the storage or fabrication of explosives.

Questions would later be asked about what, if anything, had been known about the suspects before the events of 17–18 August and whether the Mossos had been kept informed of any investigations by the national police. The immediate reaction to the news of the attacks, however, was a national outpouring of sympathy for the people of Catalonia. Philip VI, who had succeeded his father, Don Juan Carlos, as King of Spain three years earlier, travelled to Barcelona with President Rajoy, and led a minute's silence in the Plaça de Catalunya the day after the attacks. An unwonted harmony seemed to have materialized, but it proved short-lived. On 26 August, in a mass anti-terror demonstration, thousands marched down the Passeig de Gràcia waving independence flags, booing the king and members of Spain's political establishment whom they held responsible for the acts of home-grown terrorism by permitting the sale of arms to the Gulf states.

On 6 September the Catalan parliament approved a law, immediately accepted by the Govern, for the calling of a referendum on 1 October. The law made no provision for a minimum turnout and allowed a simple majority as sufficient for the proclamation of independence. Although the Catalan Statute of Autonomy of 1979, and its revised version of 2006, stipulated that any change to the statute required a two-thirds majority in parliament, this was not forthcoming. The law, therefore, was patently illegal both in terms of the Constitution and of the Catalan autonomy statutes, and was declared as such by the Constitutional Tribunal on the following day. Rajoy, whose preferred method of government always tended to follow Philip II's famous practice of 'giving time to time', was under mounting criticism for his apparent passivity in the face of what had now become the worst constitutional crisis in the history of post-Franco Spain. Yet in a democracy in which the executive and the judiciary are separate – a separation disputed by those who question the impartiality of politically appointed judges – the government could justifiably argue that this was a constitutional issue. As such, it should be handled by the judiciary and the Constitutional Tribunal, which was only doing its duty when it prohibited members of the Catalan administration, the municipal authorities and the media from participating in, or promoting, a referendum campaign.

On 20 September the officials of the Govern involved in organizing the referendum were placed under arrest. The police were instructed to seize ballot papers and campaign material, and the government announced that it would take partial control of the Govern's finances. Rajoy now felt able to take a more assertive stance, as it became clear that firm action against the secessionists enjoyed the support not only of Ciudadanos (Ciutadans), which had consistently shown itself to be a staunch upholder of the unity of Spain, but also, after some hesitation, of the Socialists. It was also becoming clear that Catalan society itself was deeply divided, although the opponents of secession had so far failed to speak out, perhaps from fear, or because no potential leader had emerged.

Hard economic realities were also intruding as referendum day approached. More and more major banks and companies, disconcerted by the febrile atmosphere and worried about their future in such a volatile environment, were beginning to vote with their feet and relocate their headquarters to Madrid and other Spanish cities. Their uncertainty about the future was increased by the probability that an independent Catalonia would find itself outside the European Union. By the end of November more than 3,000 companies had moved out of Catalonia, which no longer seemed to offer the political stability required for sound investment decisions. Nor were those companies likely to be reassured by the obvious failure of the Govern to do any forward planning regarding an independent Catalan state. Similar fears affected private individuals, many of whom opened new bank accounts across the border in Valencia and Aragon into which they transferred their savings and bank holdings.

None of this appeared to deter Puigdemont and his colleagues, who blithely assumed that, once independence was achieved, everything would fall neatly into place. For them, independence was everything, and they seem to have cherished a blind faith that the European Union would speak up on their behalf and that international public opinion could not fail to favour a people's right to choose its own destiny. After all, had not the Scots been allowed to vote on their future? The circumstances in Scotland, however, had been very different. Catalonia's was an illegal referendum, and, as such, Nicola Sturgeon resolutely refused to endorse it, although this did not inhibit members of the SNP from flocking to Barcelona to show their solidarity as plans for voting reached their final stages. Encouraging as these manifestations of popular support were, the Govern left nothing to chance. By this point it was spending €12 million a year on fifteen 'embassies' or 'cultural offices' located in major foreign capitals, and was running a sophisticated public relations campaign that deployed all the standard arguments for giving Catalans their 'freedom' – arguments that drew on the now familiar distorted history of Catalonia as a once independent state that had been deprived of its liberties and had been consistently victimized and oppressed by successive Spanish regimes.

This propaganda campaign proved highly effective in influencing opinion in the western democracies, and it was made all the more effective by the failure of the Spanish government and the pro-unity elements in Spanish society to offer a serious rebuttal. These missed a promising opportunity to produce a 'Spanish' national narrative that would avoid the crude centralism of earlier times and instead would point to the success of post-1978 Spain in reconciling unity and diversity to the benefit of all its peoples. Even if its proponents did not deploy it as effectively as they might have done, the Scottish referendum campaign had demonstrated that there was force in the slogan 'Better Together'. The Spanish failure to mount a comparable campaign can be ascribed in part to a lack of political imagination, but it also reflects the sensitivity surrounding the whole concept of regional autonomy, a sensitivity made all the more acute by the passions unleashed by the Catalan regional government's drive for independence, which it called the *procés*.

Yet, at stake in the *procés* was a fundamental issue that transcended, and transcends, purely Spanish considerations. Under the Spanish Constitution a unilateral secessionist move by any of the country's regions is illegal. A similar view of secession is taken by the European Commission and the Venice Commission of the Council of Europe, both of which insist that any regional referendum on independence can only be regarded as legal if it conforms to the constitution of the state to which the region belongs. This determination reflects the concerns of individual EU member states, several of which are faced by their own separatist movements and are naturally worried by the possibility that one or more of their partner states might succumb to political fragmentation. Yet to some extent they find themselves swimming against a populist tide. The increasing resort to referendums in western democracies has created a conflict over the most appropriate instrument for determining the national will. Does a referendum focused on a single issue provide a more authentic expression of the will of the people than the traditional system of parliamentary representation?

There are cogent arguments for both methods, and both have their weaknesses. A single-issue campaign concentrates minds, provides opportunities for the public to become better informed as the arguments are rehearsed, and is capable of generating a degree of popular enthusiasm that leads to a far higher turnout at the polls than is to be found in most general elections. In this sense it gives every appearance of producing a more authentic expression of the national will than a system that filters it through parliamentary institutions. These, at least in principle, subject the result to close debate and informed scrutiny that can improve the final outcome. Yet when this diverges from the expressed will of the people in its more pristine form, the divergence can be used to reinforce the now widely diffused conviction in western societies that the political class is, by its very nature, out of touch.

However, a referendum can hardly be regarded as a flawless device for gauging public opinion. Personal grievances and public discontents may weigh more heavily than the question on the ballot paper in deciding how a vote is cast, with consequent distortions when the result comes to be interpreted. But for those whose prime concern is the maintenance of political and social stability, the most serious argument against recourse to referendums relates less to their authenticity as the expression of the national will than to their potentially divisive effects. All too easily the posing of a question of fundamental importance in stark binary terms can split society into two warring tribes, reinforcing old divisions or creating new ones. These divisive effects were apparent in the referendum campaign on Scottish independence, and were to assume a still more alarming form in the run-up to and aftermath of the Catalan referendum of 1 October 2017.

The Catalan government and supporters of independence had no hesitation in behaving and speaking as if they were the repositories of the Catalan national will, and increasingly depicted those of a different opinion as traitors to the national cause. This became all the easier as the Spanish government took steps to prevent the referendum from going ahead. In practice these steps proved largely futile. The Mossos were torn by conflicting loyalties and showed themselves unwilling to enforce effectively the presiding judge's ruling. The 10,000 national police and members of the Civil Guard drafted into Catalonia for just such an eventuality had no hope of preventing the opening of 2,000 polling stations, many of them ringed by *independentistas*. Faced with the question 'Do you want Catalonia to become an independent state in the form of a republic?', a non-verified 92.01 per cent of those who managed to cast their vote – or 2,044,038 voters – were reported as voting 'Yes'. The remaining 177,547, or 7.99 per cent, voted 'No', but many Catalans refused to participate in an illegal referendum. Others, whatever their voting intentions, were prevented from doing so by the actions of the police.

Not surprisingly, heavy-handed action by members of the police was a gift to the Govern. Images of policemen firing rubber bullets and striking innocent voters with their batons spread like wildfire around the world and served to confirm the message that Puigdemont and his friends had all along sought to convey: that the government of Spain's vaunted parliamentary democracy was no less repressive than that of General Franco, and that Catalonia was once again the victim of a hostile Spanish state. In reality, while the impact of police brutality was enormous, its actual extent is mired in controversy. The Govern placed the number of civilian casualties at around 900, but only four people were actually hospitalized as a direct consequence of police action, and some of the widely disseminated images of blood-stained voters were carry-overs from earlier incidents quite unrelated to the 2017 referendum.

Yet, confronted by a barrage of manipulated images and false information, truth counted for little. Foreign opinion-makers, many of them knowing little about the Catalan domestic situation or the background to the secessionist movement, were all too happy to accept the images and stories that were being put about by the *independentistas*. Many were unaware of the campaign of harassment and intimidation to which prominent members of the Catalan cultural and academic worlds who spoke out against independence were being subjected. Nor were they aware that, for extreme nationalists, the referendum campaign was the logical culmination of the various educational, cultural and public relations programmes pursued by Jordi Pujol's government and its successors on the basis of a document entitled 'A Strategy for Catalanization', commissioned in 1990 from a group of Catalan intellectuals.[62] The fact that by 2017 over two million Catalans, or more than 40 per cent of the total electorate, were ready to vote for an independence denied them by their Spanish 'enemy' testifies to the achievement of successive Catalan regional governments in implementing those programmes.

In view of the gravity of the political situation in the aftermath of the referendum, King Philip, following the example set by his father at the moment of the attempted coup of 1981, went on national television on 3 October and made a powerful speech rebuking the Catalan government for seeking to destroy the unity of Spain. His address was not that of a head of government, but a head of state, whose duty was to uphold the Constitution and the law. His words had an immediate effect. There was an upsurge of Spanish national feeling across the country, and suddenly the national flag was everywhere to be seen. The speech also emboldened those Catalans opposed to the course chosen by the Govern to speak out publicly against it, although it may well have alienated others who were anxious to see the king offer some formal recognition of Catalonia's unique national character.

On 10 October, following through on the results of the referendum, Puigdemont declared Catalonia to be an independent republic. Then, perfectly conscious of the illegality of the pronouncement and of the perilous course on which he was embarked, he immediately suspended the declaration in a bid to resolve the dispute with Madrid through 'dialogue'. The government responded by demanding clarity as to whether or not the declaration remained in force, with a deadline of 10 a.m. on 16 October for an answer. This response was accompanied by the threat that, if no answer were forthcoming, the government would trigger Article 155 of the Constitution, an article, never previously implemented, authorizing the state to suspend a regional government if its actions breached the law. Since Puigdemont and his friends had no expectation that a dialogue would produce any tangible results, and Rajoy, with the support of the Socialists and Ciudadanos, refused to engage in a dialogue with a regional government that had so flagrantly contravened the Constitution, the impasse was total.

The same day, two political activists, Jordi Cuixart, the president of an independent cultural and social organization, Omnium Cultural, and Jordi Sànchez, president of a lobby movement, the self-styled Catalan National Assembly, were arrested on accusations of sedition and rebellion involving the inciting of mass protests and acts of violence that stopped the police from doing their duty. It was now clear that the judiciary and the authorities meant business, and that others within the regional administration might soon be following the 'two Jordis' into gaol. Puigdemont was well aware of the weakness of his position. His support depended, on the one hand, on a fragile coalition of radical Catalan nationalists like himself, and on the other, radical anti-capitalists. Some, including the vice-president of the Generalitat, Oriol Junqueras, the leader of the Esquerra Republicana de Catalunya, wanted to press ahead irrespective of the consequences. Puigdemont himself favoured playing for time in the hope of reaching a compromise with the government. That same day, 16 October, he reiterated his plea for dialogue, but he was never willing to come to the Senate to defend his position, and his pleas met with no success.

Puigdemont was not the only political leader to find himself caught between conflicting demands. Rajoy was also under pressure to find some form of compromise – pressure that came both from abroad and from inside Spain, where the Socialists were advocating a more accommodating approach than the Partido Popular, including suggestions for a revision of the Constitution along more federal lines. International public opinion exerted its own form of pressure, and was no doubt discreetly seconded by Spain's European allies, deeply troubled by the scenes of violence and brutality that accompanied the referendum.

The clock was now ticking. The government could not defer much longer the triggering of Article 155, and on 21 October Rajoy announced that it would be put into force once the Senate had given its approval. Between 23 and 25 October intense discussions were held in Barcelona in an atmosphere of high tension, as Puigdemont sought to build a consensus that would unite the different political groupings all struggling to win presidential support. It is not yet known exactly what happened during those three dramatic days, although there has been much informed speculation.[63] Puigdemont himself believed that he could avert the triggering of Article 155 if he called new regional elections, and was supported in this by his predecessor as president, Artur Mas, who argued that the time was not ripe for Catalonia to become an independent state.

Others, like Junqueras, felt that any reversal of direction would create bitter disappointment among the two million or more who had pinned their hopes on independence. Some of these saw the referendum as a chance at last to see the realization of the dream of a lifetime, while a younger generation, many of them students and seriously affected by the problem of securing adequate employment, had come to believe that a Catalan Republic would do for them what the Spanish state could not. Now that the Republic had been proclaimed into existence there must be no turning back. On the morning of Thursday, 26 October, Puigdemont's plans for calling elections instead of proceeding to make a reality of his new-born state made him the target of a protest by students gathered 'in defence of the Republic' in the Plaça Sant Jaume. The hero had now become a traitor, and social media took up the charge.

By this time, personal relations between the leaders of the independence movement were deeply fractured, and Puigdemont himself seems to have been near breaking-point. He had failed in his hope of extracting from Madrid a promise that, in return for the calling of new elections, the government would not invoke Article 155. At some point in the early afternoon of the 26th he backed down, and did not sign the electoral decree, as had been expected. Instead, uncomfortably aware of the near certainty that he and his fellow ministers would be following the 'two Jordis' into prison, Puigdemont chose the independence option, making his announcement at 5 o'clock that evening. The following day, with constitutionalists boycotting the vote, Catalonia's parliament decided by secret ballot for the unilateral declaration of an independent Catalan Republic.

The secessionists had apparently made no plans for putting such a declaration into effect, and in the event it could be no more than an empty gesture, although one heavily freighted with symbolism. On learning of the declaration the government immediately reacted, as expected, by invoking Article 155. This meant the dissolution of the Govern and the application of direct rule over Catalonia, but not the suppression of Catalan autonomy. Regional government officials went back to work the next day as if nothing had happened, but they, like the Mossos, now found themselves operating under the control of the Spanish government. Arrest warrants on charges of sedition, rebellion and the embezzling of public funds for referendum purposes were issued against Puigdemont and those of his ministerial colleagues committed to secession. Six were taken into custody and removed to prison in Madrid, while Puigdemont and four of his cabinet colleagues fled the country and arrived in Brussels on 30 October to seek asylum – a move likely to cause the maximum trouble for the host country, by complicating Belgium's relationship with Spain, and potentially upsetting the delicate balance of internal power between Walloons and Flemish separatists.

Rajoy, in addition to imposing direct rule on Catalonia, had another card up his sleeve and played it to general surprise. He announced the calling of new Catalan elections to be held on 21 December, the first date they could be legally held under the Statute of Autonomy. This had been Puigdemont's original plan before he talked himself out of it. Rajoy was no doubt calculating that the combination of a deteriorating Catalan economy, the humiliation of Puigdemont's flight and the failure of his government to make good on its independence promises would swing public opinion in favour of a return to normality. Nevertheless, it was a risky move. Opinion polls indicated that the Catalan electorate, although showing a strong majority in favour of the right to self-determination, was almost equally divided between separatists and anti-separatists.

The campaign, which opened on 5 December, was likely to be hard-fought, and showed early signs of turning ugly. Threats and abuse seem to have come mostly from the separatists, who denounced constitutionalists as 'Francoists' and 'Fascists'. Overshadowing the campaign, even before it started, was the question of whether the ministers under arrest should be allowed to take part. What right, it could legitimately be asked, had politicians facing charges of rebellion against the Spanish state to move freely around the country voicing their obnoxious opinions in a campaign being held under the auspices of the state they had so persistently denounced? Yet if they were not allowed to do so, it might equally be asked whether the outcome of the election could properly be called free and fair.

Both sides were faced with a dilemma. If the ministers imprisoned in Madrid were refused the right to campaign, they would be given the perfect opportunity to present themselves to the electorate and the world as political prisoners and martyrs for the cause – something they themselves wanted and which the government was anxious to prevent at all costs. On the other hand, Junqueras, as president of the ERC, which was expected to emerge as easily the largest party in the next parliament, was naturally keen to participate.

It fell to the judiciary to make the decision. On 4 December the new public prosecutor, only recently appointed following the sudden death of his predecessor, decided to release on bail six of the arrested former ministers who now said they were ready to recant the declaration of independence, insisting that it had been a purely symbolic gesture. Their release, after five weeks in prison, would allow them to take part in the campaign. The former vice-president of the Govern, Junqueras, and its former interior minister, Joaquim Forn, were not willing to be so explicit, and remained in prison along with the 'two Jordis'. On the same day the judicial authorities withdrew on technical grounds the European arrest warrant against Puigdemont in Brussels, allowing him to remain there indefinitely without fear of extradition, although liable for immediate arrest if he should choose to return to Spain.

Now that Puigdemont was free to come and go as he wished, it was hard for him to continue convincingly presenting himself to the world as a political prisoner, though this did not deter him or his followers. Seizing the opportunity provided by Spanish national holidays on 6 and 8 December, thousands of his supporters travelled from Catalonia to Belgium to show their devotion to the man who was still for them 'the president' and who had brought them within sight of the Promised Land. On the night of Thursday, 7 December, some 45,000 Catalan and Flemish separatists marched through the quarter of Brussels that houses the buildings of the European Union. The marchers not only presented Puigdemont as the victim of Franco-style repression, but joined him in denouncing the European Union, so recently the great hope of the secessionists, for its refusal to uphold a nation's right to self-determination.

Once more, Puigdemont faced a dilemma. If he returned home he would wear a martyr's crown, but its price was likely to be thirty years in prison. On the other hand, if he remained in Belgium he ran the risk of discrediting both himself and his cause, having apparently failed to win his chosen game of identity politics. For the time being at least, he chose to keep his options open. Meanwhile in Catalonia an unprecedented election campaign was getting under way. It was unprecedented in the sense that it was the first election held in Spain under the shadow of Article 155 of the Constitution and the imposition of direct rule over one of its regions. It was also unprecedented because Puigdemont, the region's former president and also the leader of one of its political parties, Junts per Catalunya (JpC), was living abroad in self-imposed exile, while the head of the more dominant ERC, Oriol Junqeras, was behind bars.

One of the tragedies of the election was that it inescapably revolved around the *procés* at a time when much of the population was anxious to get back to more traditional issues like the economy, health, transport and education – issues that since 2010 had been relegated to the sidelines by the stand-off between Barcelona and Madrid and the all-consuming drive for independence. Yet Catalonia's was such a polarized society that the issue of independence inevitably dominated the campaign. The election exposed to the full light of day the uncomfortable reality that there was not one Catalonia but two: one, with its heartland in the provinces of Girona and Lleida, that would be satisfied with nothing less than an independent state, and another, centred on the populous Barcelona region, that saw Catalonia as a natural, although distinctive, part of Spain.

If the great divide was that between secessionists and constitutionalists, it quickly became apparent that both groups were also divided among themselves. Rajoy's Partido Popular stood low in the polls and was haemorrhaging support to Ciutadans, a party that was sweeping up potential constitutionalist votes attracted by the determination and vigour of its regional leader, Inés Arrimadas. The separatists were even more divided, with Junqueras's ERC refusing to stand on a joint ticket with Puigdemont's Junts per Catalunya and the smaller political groupings. Relations between the two men were now so bad that they were trading barbed comments on the eve of the election.

All the final polls suggested that the secessionists and the constitutionalists were running neck and neck, and that, given the electoral system in Catalonia, which does not automatically guarantee that a majority of votes translates into a majority of seats in parliament, the next government would almost certainly consist of some sort of coalition. The number of seats won by smaller parties was therefore likely to determine whether it would be the *independentistas* or the constitutionalists who won the upper hand.

In spite of the heightened rhetoric generated by the campaign, it was not accompanied by violence, and election day itself, 21 December, passed off peacefully. Voters turned out in their masses, and voting lines were long and orderly. By the time the polls were closed it was clear that, with over four million votes cast, participation, at around 82 per cent, had beaten all records for Spanish regional elections, although it was 3 per cent below the turnout in the Scottish referendum campaign of 2014. Given the importance of the issues at stake and the intensity of the campaign, a high participation rate was only to be expected. Less expected were some, though not all, of the results, which themselves were complicated by the lack of correlation between the number of votes cast and the allocation of parliamentary seats – the consequence of a voting system weighted in favour of rural areas and against the province of Barcelona.

Even though the secessionists won 47 per cent of the vote, their dominance in the provinces of Girona, Lleida and Tarragona gave them 70 of the 135 seats in parliament, sufficient to ensure them a parliamentary majority if the various political factions of which they were composed could reach agreement among themselves. This was an outcome that sent shock waves through Spain and Europe. It was immediately obvious that Rajoy's gamble in calling an early regional election had failed to do what he had expected of it by returning Catalonia to 'normality'. The discomfiture of Rajoy, who had personally campaigned in Catalonia, was compounded by the Partido Popular's loss of seven seats, leaving it with a mere four, and effectively wiping it out at the regional level. This humiliating defeat was bound to have national implications, both for the party and for Rajoy himself, and did not bode well for any general election, although Rajoy, in commenting on the results the day after the Catalan vote, was quick to say that he would not call one before the expiry of the current legislature in 2020. But the date might not be his for the choosing.

Even more striking was the upsurge of Ciutadans under the leadership of Inés Arrimadas, which, with thirty-six seats, emerged as the largest political party in the new parliament. This electoral success marked the first time that a national, non-Catalan, political party, Ciudadanos, headed by its national leader Albert Rivera, won the most seats in a regional election, and suggested that the Partido Popular was now faced with a powerful competitor for the right-wing vote in any future national election. Ciutadans did not, however, win enough seats to form the new Catalan regional government, even with the help of minor parties. Although 1.9 million Catalans, or 43.5 per cent of the voters, had come out in support of the unionist cause, secessionism had shown itself to possess a stronger appeal.

The Socialists, and their Catalan branch, had no more reason than the Partido Popular to feel satisfied with the results, which added only one seat to their previous sixteen. They were paying the price for their ambiguity throughout the campaign, at moments flirting with separatists and then drawing back. The election in fact confirmed what had for long been apparent – that the two great national parties, the PP and the PSOE, both tarnished by corruption, had become stale and sclerotic, and lacked any vision for the future of Spain. In this they resembled the Conservative and Labour parties in twenty-first-century Britain, whose degeneration into little more than increasingly unsuccessful vote-getting machines had left the field wide open for the SNP, a party that combined passion with a strong and clear message.

Yet there was an important difference between the Scottish Nationalists and the Catalan separatists. Whereas the movement for Scottish independence was broadly united in the run-up to the 2014 referendum, the advocates of an independent Catalan Republic were a heterogeneous bunch, from the ERC with its leftist preoccupations to Puigdemont's Junts per Catalunya, all of whose energies were directed to the realization of the long-held radical programme for the creation of a 'free' Catalonia. Oriol Junqueras's refusal to join forces with Puigdemont in the campaign suggested that, even if his imprisonment debarred him from campaigning in person, he had every confidence that his ERC would emerge triumphant. The results showed him to have been badly mistaken. His party secured thirty-two seats in parliament to JpC's thirty-four.

The electoral success of the party headed by the self-exiled former president came as a startling surprise to the many who had assumed that his flight to Brussels had left him discredited. On the contrary, the narrow legalistic response of Rajoy's government to the developing crisis seems to have had the effect of transforming Puigdemont into the most visible symbol of the secessionist cause. Puigdemont himself was quick to make the most of his unexpected success, claiming that the illegal referendum and the subsequent 'legal referendum' called by Madrid showed that a majority of Catalans favoured independence, a claim that was patently untrue. He then went on to ask for a personal dialogue with Rajoy anywhere outside Spain, since he could not safely return home until he had been formally recognized for what he had always been, Catalonia's legitimate president.

By late December 2017 it was all too clear that there would be no quick or easy resolution to what had become a full-scale national crisis. Prolonged negotiations between the various political groupings would be needed for the formation of a new Catalan regional government of whatever hue; and constitutionally, a new president, who might or might not be Puigdemont, had to be chosen by 6 February 2018. Failing this, new elections would have to be called, and there was every reason to believe that their outcome would simply repeat the stalemate of the 2017 vote.

Whatever was to happen, it was obvious that the Rajoy government had seriously underestimated the strength of Catalan separatism – a strength that its own mistakes had done much to increase. For the foreseeable future the independence movement was here to stay, and no amount of legalistic and constitutional correctness could wish it away. Only a political solution could offer a way forward, and as long as the government and the *independentistas* remained locked into their chosen positions, no political solution was likely to emerge.

The impasse was a tragedy for Spain, and for Catalonia itself, and one capable of producing Europe-wide repercussions. By the time the voters went to the polls the damage caused to the Catalan economy by the region's political instability was obvious, and by the end of 2017 it was also affecting the Spanish economy as a whole. Yet economic problems do not seem to have carried much weight with confirmed secessionists, many of them members of a relatively affluent middle class. Their priorities lay elsewhere, in the realization of a dream that had little connection to the world around them.

Their decision to press ahead with a unilateral declaration of independence was an act of folly, unleashing consequences that never seemed to have crossed the proponents' minds as they took the plunge. They had plainly put themselves outside the law and the Constitution, a Constitution that Catalonia itself had accepted and endorsed when Spain made its transition to a parliamentary democracy. In doing so they created fissures not only in the Spanish body politic, but also inside their own country. In arrogantly claiming to speak for all Catalonia, and systematically branding Spain as the 'enemy', they drove a wedge down the middle of Catalan society. This had been a prosperous, friendly and outward-looking society, fully engaged with the rest of Spain and the world. Now it turned inwards and began to tear itself apart. Families and communities were divided, long-standing friendships cooled or were ruptured, and unionists and secessionists faced each other across a widening gulf of misunderstanding and mutual recrimination.

In a story to which there will be no clear-cut conclusion for many years to come, one at least stands out. In spite of the numerous failings of the Spanish government and the Spanish political class over many years – a class that proved unable or unwilling to transform the combination of unity and diversity written into the Constitution into a coherent political project – the prime responsibility for this tragic situation rests with part of the Catalan establishment. This sector of the elite decided to take the law into its own hands and forge ahead with its plans, regardless of the price to be paid. In many respects, indeed, it was oblivious to the price because it lived in a fantasy world of its own. This world was partly of its own making but it also had long antecedents, drawing on a mixture of true and false history, and of memories filtered through the collective imagination. Whatever the *independentistas* might claim, twenty-first-century Spain was not the Spain of General Franco, nor had Spain been for centuries little more than a repressive state apparatus. To exclude alternative readings is to shut down alternative options. By embarking on this unhappy process, which all too easily metamorphosed into the *procés*, Catalan nationalism, for all its smiling face, was unable to hide the ugliness that lay behind the smile.

Epilogue

The histories of Scottish and Catalan nationalism have many differences, but they also have much in common. Both are histories of hopes kept alive only to be dashed, of aspirations after home rule and of moves towards secession. Yet for all the differences between the national histories of the two countries, they converge markedly from the 1970s onwards. Both saw a powerful resurgence of nationalism in the 1970s and 1980s. Such resurgences were in themselves nothing new, and, on this occasion as in the past, they occurred in very different contexts. But this time the reassertion of a sense of national identity gave rise to more durable and more persistent separatist movements than any that preceded them, to the point that a breakaway from the political entities in which they had been embedded for many centuries became, if not a certainty, at least a strong possibility.

Where Scotland was concerned, the background to the nationalist resurgence was the slow post-war decline of the heavy industries which had made the country for many generations an international powerhouse. This accompanied the parallel decline of Britain's global standing and the dismantling of the British Empire after 1945. Almost three centuries of close Scottish engagement with the British imperial project, which saw kilted Scottish regiments fighting alongside English, Irish and Welsh regiments in numerous colonial and continental wars, had given generations of Scots a sense of belonging to a community larger than their own. This made them Britons as well as Scots, reinforcing their commitment to a Union that had offered them innumerable opportunities to make their mark in the world. It would therefore be natural to expect that the post-war loss of empire should have strengthened the Scottish component of the British-Scottish equation at the expense of the British, but the ending of empire seems to have been accepted in Scotland with relative equanimity, and had no immediate impact on the working of the Anglo-Scottish relationship. This may reflect the growth of a disillusionment with empire and its value to Scotland in the decades that followed the end of the First World War, but the relatively peaceful and long-drawn-out nature of the decolonizing process is also likely to be part of the explanation. There was certainly none of the trauma that accompanied the final loss of empire in the Spain of 1898. The creation of the welfare state in post-war Britain also helped to fill the vacuum by offering an alternative British project that many Scots could enthusiastically embrace.[1]

Yet, as in Spain, the end of empire, in largely reducing a formerly expansive territorial space to the narrower geographical confines of the mother country, inevitably had profound, if slow-burning, consequences for the ways in which the component nations of the United Kingdom thought about themselves and about their relationship to each other and to the larger polity to which they belonged. There had always been marked differences between the political cultures of Scotland and England, but by the dawn of the twenty-first century the two countries gave an increasing impression of travelling in different directions. The creation of a Scottish parliament and a Scottish Executive inevitably widened the gap that had always existed between Westminster and Edinburgh, and in this respect seemed to justify the fears of those who argued that the implementation of home rule for Scotland was bound to set the Anglo-Scottish Union on a slippery slope. But as long as the major British political parties could command strong support among Scottish voters, the resulting participation in the political life of the United Kingdom as a whole served to counterbalance the tendencies towards the distancing of interests and concerns that was always likely to follow from the establishment of a Scottish parliament. It was the collapse of the Tory vote in Scotland during the 1990s, followed two decades later by that of the Labour and Liberal Democrat vote, that left the field open for Scottish Nationalists to impose their own agenda.

In doing so, they claimed to be speaking for the entire Scottish electorate, instead of only a part of it – a part that was less than half when their agenda included a drive for independence. The same was true of the Catalan nationalists. Here the 1978 Constitution had given the Catalans a degree of autonomous government not equalled in Scotland until after 1997, but the two countries would move along similar lines although on different time scales. Participation by the autonomous communities in Spanish national politics remained high in the years after 1978, and the two major Spanish parties commanded extensive support from the Catalan electorate in Spain's national elections. From the beginnings of the Pujol government in 1980, however, the degree of autonomy conceded by Madrid to the Generalitat enabled it to pursue the kind of nationalist agenda that the SNP could only start to implement after its electoral success in 2007. But the trajectory was similar. In Catalonia, as in Scotland, the major Spanish political parties, the PSOE and PP, progressively lost support, thus leaving the field open for radical nationalists to pursue, as in Scotland, an agenda whose goal was independence.

In Scotland and Catalonia alike, therefore, radical nationalism began to spread its wings in a changing environment. The traditional two-party political system was now showing signs of collapse, while old institutions were everywhere being questioned by electorates alienated from rulers who seemed incapable of finding answers to the challenges posed by globalization, economic crisis, the dominance of supra-national corporations and organizations, and widespread social inequality. This was an environment ready-made for nationalist populism and for politicians who knew how to exploit it. Separatism appeared to offer an easy answer to those who felt that they had lost control over their own lives. Independence would allow them once again to be the masters in their own house.

Much of this was nostalgia for a world that never was. Scotland had lost the last vestiges of its sovereign statehood in 1707; Catalonia had never been an independent sovereign state in any modern definition of the term; and in both nations government had largely been exercised by elites in conjunction with the Crown. Yet both had developed over the course of the centuries national narratives that prioritized certain sections of their past at the expense of others, as they struggled to assert their own distinctiveness in the face of the real or perceived threat of assimilation by a more powerful neighbour. The Scots, as was natural, looked back to the wars their medieval ancestors had fought to save their independence from an expansionist England, and found their heroes in Wallace and Bruce, who had led them to victory. They exulted in the unbroken continuity of a monarchy stretching far back into the mists of antiquity, but also in the community of a realm in which monarch and social elites, acting in the name of the people, enjoyed a reciprocal relationship to the benefit of both. The Catalans, equally, looked back to a glorious medieval past, to the legendary Otger Cataló and the counts of Barcelona who had freed the principality from Moorish domination. They looked back, too, to the great age of Mediterranean empire and to the creation of a community in which, as in Scotland, their medieval ancestors had institutionalized contractual arrangements that protected the liberties of the people from the arbitrary exercise of power.

Inevitably these were selective, and in many respects mythologized, histories, but they proved sufficiently powerful to retain their hold over the collective imagination, providing each generation in turn with an enduring concept of nationhood. It was a concept that grew by accretion as memories accumulated. The Catalan revolt of 1640 and the surrender of Barcelona in 1714 followed by the annulment of the principality's Constitutions, left a lasting legacy of bitterness, together with an enduring image of Catalonia as the victim of malign external forces. Scotland, too, had a tendency to cast itself in the role of victim, and the story gained credibility from the horrors of the aftermath of 1745 and the Highland clearances. Yet although Scotland's sense of itself as a victim was never entirely dispelled, it was tempered by an accompanying narrative of the country's upwards trajectory during the first two centuries of Anglo-Scottish union – a trajectory that was acknowledged, if somewhat grudgingly, to have started with the Union itself. The Catalans, for their part, could take pride, like the Scots, in creating a vibrant industrial society, a success that gave them a sense of superiority and a degree of confidence in their own unaided capacity that was not calculated to endear them to their fellow Spaniards, although it might win their admiration. At the same time, continuous confrontation with the state and its often incompetent or repressive apparatus during the nineteenth and much of the twentieth century created a conviction that success had been achieved in spite of their inclusion within a larger polity which they came to regard as an artificial construct. Victims they were, and victims they remained.

The persistence of these national narratives – glossed, enhanced and reinterpreted in response to new events – furnished ammunition for twentieth-century nationalists as they sought to weaken, and perhaps demolish, the structural ties that attached them to London and Madrid. Unwelcome government intervention, and equally unwelcome government neglect, both provided an opportunity to turn this ammunition to account. The past, however remote, created the context in which to fight the battles of the present. In shaping the national self-image, it opened vistas onto a future in which both countries would be unfettered to realize their potential to the full.

If group identity has its roots in 'primordial attachments' like ethnicity, custom and language,[2] changing historical circumstances do much to determine the intensity of its expression at any given time. Nationalism waxes and wanes as circumstances dictate, but there always remains an element of unpredictability about its upsurge and relapse. Trivial events can trigger responses out of all proportion to the size of a perceived outrage, and reason falls silent as emotion takes over. Sir Walter Scott noted the power of mass emotion in commenting on the Darien disaster of the late 1690s. In remarking on what he called 'the strangest inconsistencies' in 'human character', whether national or individual, Scott found:

> few more striking than that which the Scots exhibit in their private conduct, contrasted with their views when united together for any general or national purpose. In his own personal affairs the Scotsman is remarked as cautious, frugal and prudent, in an extreme degree ... But when a number of the natives of Scotland associate for any speculative project, it would seem that their natural caution becomes thawed and dissolved by the union of their joint hopes, and that their imaginations are liable to be heated and influenced by any splendid prospect held out to them. They appear, in particular, to lose the power of calculating and adapting their means to the end which they desire to accomplish, and are readily induced to aim at objects magnificent in themselves but which they have not, unhappily, the wealth or strength necessary to attain.[3]

A comparable observation was made by the mid-twentieth-century Catalan historian Jaume Vicens Vives about the character of the Catalans. It is ironical that a historian who had devoted much of his career to combating an essentialist approach to the past should have adopted just such an approach in his extremely influential *Noticia de Cataluña*, first published in Castilian in 1954, and then in a revised Catalan edition published shortly before his death in 1960. Here he discussed two contrasting psychological characteristics, *seny* and *rauxa*, which he saw as shaping the history of Catalonia since the seventeenth century. *Seny* is the practical sense that comes from a realistic appraisal of possibilities, whereas *rauxa* entails the sudden abandonment of all measure and reason as passion grips the masses. According to Vicens, while *rauxa* is by its nature transitory, *seny* is the norm. Similarly, caution and prudence are the natural characteristics of his compatriots in the eyes of Sir Walter Scott until there comes a moment when they are suddenly gripped by some mass illusion.[4]

Such 'inconsistencies' can hardly be regarded as the exclusive preserve of Scots and Catalans. Yet historical circumstances, and most notably the frequent marginalization of the two countries by their politically more powerful neighbours, may have given the inconsistencies a special intensity in both Scotland and Catalonia. The Darien mania and the sudden upsurges of violence in nineteenth- and twentieth-century Catalonia can well be described as manifestations of *rauxa* in societies that prided themselves on their *seny*. In assessing the causes of unexpected contemporary or historical events there is always a temptation to give greater weight to 'rational' considerations than to the force of sentiment and emotion, and then be surprised when the dictates of reason fail to prevail. The current independence movements in Catalonia and Scotland suggest that societies or nations do not necessarily respond in the way that detached analysis of the arguments for and against independence suggest that they should.

On the face of it there seems no good reason why the more forceful and aggressive forms of Catalan and Scottish nationalism should have enjoyed such a resurgence at the turn of the twentieth and twenty-first centuries, and still less why in both countries the more extreme nationalists should have succeeded in wresting the initiative from the moderates and launched their often reluctant compatriots on a road towards independence. Spain after 1978 was an infinitely more benign country than the Spain of General Franco, and its new Constitution gave the Catalans an unprecedented measure of self-government. After 1997 the Scots, like the Catalans, were managing more of their business than at any time since the early eighteenth century. In addition, the North Sea oil bonanza had done much to revive the ravaged economy of the Thatcher years, although many would argue that the government could have done far more to prevent the ravages from occurring. But in neither instance can oppression be held responsible for the upsurge of nationalism, even if radical Catalan nationalists, as if by some instinctive reflex, still used, and continue to use, oppression as an argument for independence.

Oppression, though, is far from being the sole explanation for nationalist revivals, and success can be as powerful a stimulus as failure or defeat. The opponents of devolution had always insisted that the granting of a degree of autonomy created an appetite for more, and the course of events appeared to bear them out. Successful management of large areas of public life by the Catalan government generated self-belief. Similarly, if a SNP government demonstrated the ability of the Scots, when left to themselves, to rule their country efficiently, then surely there was no good reason why they should not go on to enjoy full sovereignty.

There was, however, one serious objection that had first to be overcome. Did either of the two countries have the economic and financial resources to launch out on its own? In 1888, in an attempt to 'kill Home Rule by kindness', the British government under Lord Salisbury and his Chancellor of the Exchequer, George Goschen, introduced the 'Goschen formula' for Ireland and Scotland, under which the two countries would benefit from a share of public money based on the ratio of their populations to those of

England and Wales. As the proportion was fixed and the size of England's population grew relative to that of Scotland, the Scots increasingly benefited from the operation of the funding formula. Successive Secretaries of State for Scotland in the years after the end of the Second World War managed to keep Viscount Goschen's funding arrangements in place by deploying arguments like the remote and sparsely settled character of some parts of the country and chronic poverty in others. In 1978 a new formula, the 'Barnett formula', was introduced by Joel Barnett, the Chief Secretary of the Treasury.[5] While this was rather less generous than its predecessor, it still meant that the Scots received a disproportionate share of the United Kingdom's tax revenues. This in turn helped to keep the unionist cause strong and worked to the benefit of Scottish Labour, as the Callaghan government intended.

The discovery of North Sea oil transformed Scotland's economic prospects and its expectations for the future, although all too often these failed to take into account the possibility that accessible reserves were not limitless and that oil prices could go down as well as up. As early as 1973 the leader of the SNP was asserting that 'the wealth of the oil destroys the myth that Scotland is too poor for self-government'. Then, as oil wealth poured into the British treasury, the cry went up that 'it's oor oil and we'll keep it'.[6] So it was that a new grudge was born.

Catalonia, too, harboured its grudges, and not least those related to its money. 'Spain is robbing us' (*Espanya ens roba*) was the nationalist cry. There has been endless academic and public debate about the validity of this cry, which became more strident as the community's fiscal deficit escalated under the combined pressure of the global financial crisis of 2008 and chronic over-spending by the Generalitat. Even as late as 2015 separatists continued to claim that the Spanish state was seizing €16 million a year of Catalan money that would otherwise be available to finance an independent Catalonia.

This 'independence dividend' fails to take into account the cost of services financed by the central state which an independent Catalonia would be forced to assume. More generally, many of the figures commonly adduced by the advocates of independence as proof of the injustice of Catalonia's treatment by the central government have not stood up to serious analysis. As the economic powerhouse of modern Spain, Catalonia has not unreasonably been called upon to help out the poorer regions of the country, and the level of its contributions has been roughly in line with that expected of similarly prosperous regions in other contemporary European states. On the other hand, the fiscal advantages enjoyed by the Basque provinces have reinforced the impression among Catalans that they are hard done by, and it has become clear, whatever the rights and wrongs of Catalonia, that the current system under which the autonomous regions are financed has created serious disparities and is in urgent need of revision.[7]

In turn-of-the-century Scotland and Catalonia alike, separatists expressed the confidence that native resources and skills were sufficient to make independence viable, while arguing that in times of trouble it would always be possible to take shelter under the European umbrella. The message of self-sufficiency fell on fertile ground in a Catalonia where the Generalitat had exploited all the resources at its disposal to inculcate a sense of the nation's historic and linguistic distinctiveness. The same message would be relayed in Scotland once the SNP was in the saddle. It was a message well attuned to an age in which people everywhere were looking for greater individual and collective empowerment, and in which the new social media offered unprecedented opportunities for the rapid mobilization of large sections of the population in support of a cause with a strong emotional charge.

If the climate of the age has proved particularly conducive to propagating the idea of independence, its acceptance by broad swathes of society cannot be attributed solely to the organizational skills and missionary fervour of its advocates. Its opponents also helped, if unwittingly, to advance the secessionist cause. All too often governments in Britain and Spain dismissed or failed to take seriously issues that were sometimes felt deeply by many Scots and Catalans but which looked relatively insignificant when viewed from London and Madrid.

Some of these issues were symbolic, like the proper styling of the monarch (Elizabeth II or I?) in post-Union Scotland, or the flying of Spanish and Catalan flags. But symbolism often masks, or stands proxy for, a preoccupation with more fundamental concerns. In London, both government and parliament had a long record of neglecting or downplaying Scotland's genuine economic or administrative grievances until the point came when they could no longer be ignored. In Madrid, nineteenth-century governments proved responsive to pressures emanating from Barcelona for the protection of Catalan industry, but less responsive to the social problems that industrial development brought in its train. In the twentieth century the authoritarian regimes of Primo de Rivera and Franco rode roughshod over so many sensibilities that in both instances the demise of those regimes brought a backlash that made Catalans especially sensitive to real or perceived affronts. Language, in particular, was to prove a powerful lightning conductor.

The inability or unwillingness of central governments to reach out across cultural and emotional barriers to communities that feel themselves to be marginalized is a natural source of discontent. Dialogue is a central function of democratic government, and on both sides of the barrier are to be found those who, for one reason or another, have no interest in pursuing it. Often, however, the failure of dialogue is the result of a failure of imagination – of the inability to put oneself into another's shoes and grasp the power of emotion and sentiment. This failure of imagination has all too often bedevilled relations between London and Edinburgh on the one hand and Madrid and Barcelona on the other, creating an impasse where bridges might otherwise have been built.

Dialogue alone is not enough to solve long-standing and complex problems of mutual accommodation, but, whenever dialogue ceases, one more obstacle on the road to independence is removed, and secession comes closer to being the final response.[8] Secession was the response chosen by the Netherlands in the 1560s and by Britain's North American colonies in 1776, each time with success. Yet it was Thomas Jefferson, the future president of a newly independent United States of America, who wrote that 'governments long established should not be changed for light and transient causes'.[9] Proponents of independence in the twenty-first century would do well to bear his maxim in mind as they contemplate the road that lies ahead.

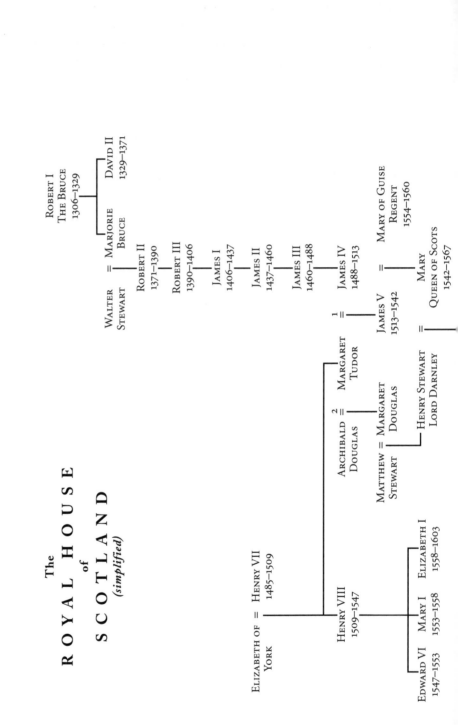

The
ROYAL HOUSE
of
SCOTLAND
(simplified)

ROBERT I
THE BRUCE
1306–1329

DAVID II
1329–1371

WALTER
STEWART = MARJORIE
BRUCE

ROBERT II
1371–1390

ROBERT III
1390–1406

JAMES I
1406–1437

JAMES II
1437–1460

JAMES III
1460–1488

JAMES IV
1488–1513 = MARY OF GUISE
REGENT
1554–1560

JAMES V
1513–1542

MARY
QUEEN OF SCOTS
1542–1567

ELIZABETH OF = HENRY VII
YORK   1485–1509

ARCHIBALD =² MARGARET
DOUGLAS   TUDOR

MATTHEW = MARGARET
STEWART   DOUGLAS

HENRY STEWART
LORD DARNLEY

HENRY VIII
1509–1547

EDWARD VI
1547–1553

MARY I
1553–1558

ELIZABETH I
1558–1603

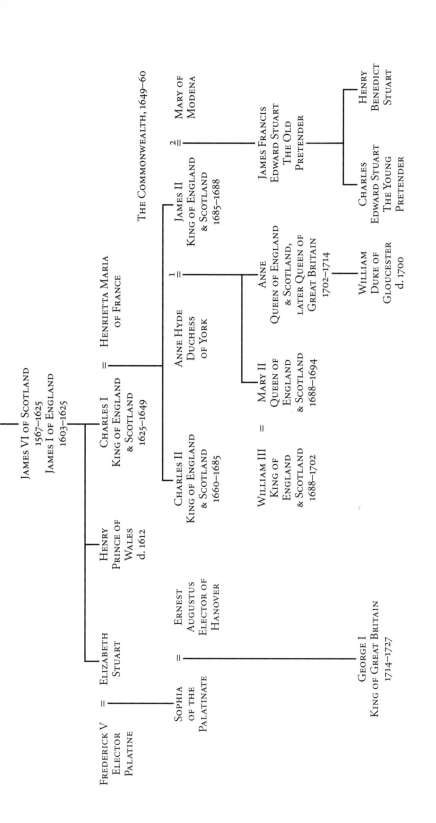

FREDERICK V
ELECTOR
PALATINE

= ELIZABETH
STUART

JAMES VI OF SCOTLAND
1567–1625
JAMES I OF ENGLAND
1603–1625

= HENRIETTA MARIA
OF FRANCE

SOPHIA
OF THE
PALATINATE

= ERNEST
AUGUSTUS
ELECTOR OF
HANOVER

HENRY
PRINCE OF
WALES
d. 1612

CHARLES I
KING OF ENGLAND
& SCOTLAND
1625–1649

ANNE HYDE
DUCHESS
OF YORK

THE COMMONWEALTH, 1649–60

MARY OF
MODENA

GEORGE I
KING OF GREAT BRITAIN
1714–1727

WILLIAM III
KING OF
ENGLAND
& SCOTLAND
1688–1702

=

MARY II
QUEEN OF
ENGLAND
& SCOTLAND
1688–1694

CHARLES II
KING OF ENGLAND
& SCOTLAND
1660–1685

1
=

ANNE
QUEEN OF ENGLAND
& SCOTLAND,
LATER QUEEN OF
GREAT BRITAIN
1702–1714

WILLIAM
DUKE OF
GLOUCESTER
d. 1700

JAMES II
KING OF ENGLAND
& SCOTLAND
1685–1688

2
=

JAMES FRANCIS
EDWARD STUART
THE OLD
PRETENDER

CHARLES
EDWARD STUART
THE YOUNG
PRETENDER

HENRY
BENEDICT
STUART

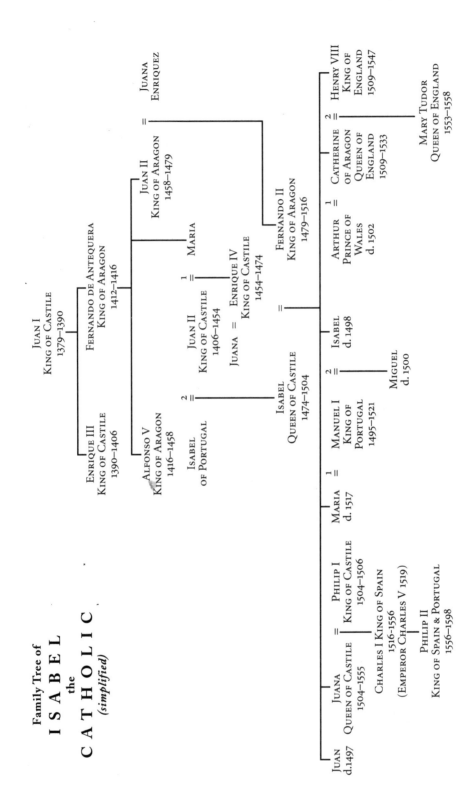

Family Tree of
I S A B E L
the
C A T H O L I C
(simplified)

JUAN I
KING OF CASTILE
1379–1390

FERNANDO DE ANTEQUERA
KING OF ARAGON
1412–1416

JUANA
ENRIQUEZ

ENRIQUE III
KING OF CASTILE
1390–1406

ALFONSO V
KING OF ARAGON
1416–1458

JUAN II
KING OF ARAGON
1458–1479

MARIA

JUAN II
KING OF CASTILE
1406–1454

1
=
ENRIQUE IV
KING OF CASTILE
1454–1474

JUANA =

FERNANDO II
KING OF ARAGON
1479–1516

ISABEL
of PORTUGAL

2
=

ISABEL
QUEEN OF CASTILE
1474–1504

=

ARTHUR
PRINCE OF
WALES
d. 1502

1
=
CATHERINE
OF ARAGON
QUEEN OF
ENGLAND
1509–1533

2
=
HENRY VIII
KING OF
ENGLAND
1509–1547

ISABEL
d. 1498

2
=
MANUEL I
KING OF
PORTUGAL
1495–1521

MIGUEL
d. 1500

MARY TUDOR
QUEEN OF ENGLAND
1553–1558

MARIA
d. 1517

1
=

JUANA
QUEEN OF CASTILE
1504–1555

=
PHILIP I
KING OF CASTILE
1504–1506

JUAN
d.1497

CHARLES I KING OF SPAIN
1516-1556
(EMPEROR CHARLES V 1519)

PHILIP II
KING OF SPAIN & PORTUGAL
1556–1598

NOTES

Introduction

1. The concept of nations as 'imagined communities' belongs to Benedict Anderson, and is explained and developed in his acclaimed *Imagined Communities: Reflections on the Origin and Spread of Nationalism* (London, 1983). The concept as he defines it (pp. 14–16) involves historical continuity – the ways in which communities see or imagine themselves over time. The modern literature on nationalism is enormous. Eric Hobsbawm, *Nations and Nationalism since 1780* (Cambridge, 1990), and Anthony D. Smith, *The Nation in History: Historiographical Debates about Ethnicity and Nationalism* (Hanover, NH, 2000), have been particularly influential in shaping recent discussions.
2. Joaquín Tornos Mas, *De Escocia a Cataluña. Referendum y reforma constitucional* (Madrid, 2015), p. 12.
3. David McCrone, *Understanding Scotland: The Sociology of a Nation* (1992; 2nd edn London and New York, 2001), p. 1.

1 Dynastic Union, 1469–1625

1. For a survey of the reign of James IV, see Jane E. A. Dawson, *Scotland Re-formed, 1488–1587* (Edinburgh, 2007), chs. 1–3.
2. The political and institutional history of the Iberian kingdoms in the later Middle Ages is usefully covered by J. N. Hillgarth, *The Spanish Kingdoms, 1250–1516* (2 vols., Oxford, 1978). See also A. MacKay, *Spain in the Middle Ages: From Frontier to Empire, 1000–1500* (London, 1977).
3. T. N. Bisson, *The Medieval Crown of Aragon: A Short History* (Oxford, 1986). For a brief survey of the history of the Crown of Aragon from beginning to end, see Norman Davies, *Vanished Kingdoms: The History of Half-Forgotten Europe* (London, 2011), ch. 4.
4. Jaime Vicens Vives, *Noticia de Cataluña* (Barcelona, 1954), pp. 22–5. For the role of geography in the creation of Catalonia see Pierre Vilar, *La Catalogne dans l'Espagne moderne* (3 vols., Paris, 1962), vol. 1, pp. 199–280 ('Le Milieu Naturel').
5. Paul Freedman, *The Origins of Peasant Servitude in Medieval Catalonia* (Cambridge, 1991), pp. 18–19; Bisson, *Medieval Crown of Aragon*, p. 25.
6. Roger B. Merriman, *The Rise of the Spanish Empire in the Old World and the New* (4 vols., New York, 1918–34, repr. 1962), vol. 1, p. 120.

7. For the Visigoths and the influence of the 'Gothic model' on later generations, see J. N. Hillgarth, *The Visigoths in History and Legend* (Toronto, 2009). For Margarit, see Robert B. Tate, *Joan Margarit i Pau, Cardinal-Bishop of Gerona* (Manchester, 1955).

8. Xavier Gil Pujol, 'La fábrica de la monarquía. Traza y conservación de la monarquía de España', *Discurso leído en la Real Academia de La Historia* (Madrid, 2016), p. 73, citing the chronicle of Hernando del Pulgar. I am grateful to Professor Gil Pujol for his advice on this point.

9. For composite monarchies, see J. H. Elliott, 'A Europe of Composite Monarchies', *Past and Present*, 137 (1992), pp. 48–71, reprinted in J. H. Elliott, *Spain, Europe and the Wider World, 1500–1800* (New Haven, CT, and London, 2009), ch. 1. See also Robert Frost, *The Oxford History of Poland-Lithuania* (Oxford, 2015), vol. 1, ch. 4, for a perceptive discussion of the historiography of composite states and ideas of union.

10. Cited by R. R. Davies, *The First English Empire: Power and Identities in the British Isles 1093–1343* (Oxford, 2000), p. 83; and see his ch. 1 for 'The High Kingship of the British Isles' in this period.

11. Reginald Coupland, *Welsh and Scottish Nationalism: A Study* (London, 1954), pp. 47–8.

12. M. Perceval-Maxwell, 'Ireland and the Monarchy in the Early Stuart Multiple Kingdom', *Historical Journal*, 34 (1991), pp. 279–95.

13. Gordon Donaldson, *Scotland: The Shaping of a Nation* (Newton Abbot, 1974), pp. 9ff for this and what follows.

14. Dauvit Broun, *Scottish Independence and the Idea of Britain from the Picts to Alexander III* (Edinburgh, 2007), pp. 7–8. The implications of this geographical divide for the medieval Scottish imagination constitute a major theme of Broun's book.

15. Ibid., pp. 3 and 11, and ch. 6.

16. See, for this and further observations on the Anglo-Scottish relationship to the end of the Middle Ages, the valuable short survey by Stringer and Grant in Alexander Grant and Keith J. Stringer (eds.), *Uniting the Kingdom? The Making of British History* (New York and London, 1995), ch. 6.

17. For the development of this territorialized aristocracy in the twelfth and early thirteenth centuries, and for the simultaneous development of bureaucratic institutions and practices in the government of the kingdom, see Alice Taylor, *The Shape of the State in Medieval Scotland, 1124–1290* (Oxford, 2016). 'Alba' (Britain) and 'Scotia', pp. 6–7.

18. Davies, *First English Empire*, p. 62.

19. I owe this point to Professor Hamish Scott.

20. Taylor, *Shape of the State*, p. 20 and *passim*.

21. Davies, *First English Empire*, p. 87.

22. G. W. S. Barrow, *Robert Bruce and the Community of the Realm of Scotland* (1965; 2nd edn., Edinburgh, 1976), pp. 288, 362.

23. Ibid., pp. xiv–xv.

24. Ibid., p. 428. See also Edward J. Cowan, 'Identity, Freedom and the Declaration of Arbroath', in Dauvit Broun, R. J. Finlay and Michael Lynch (eds.), *Image and Identity: The Making and Re-making of Scotland Through the Ages* (Edinburgh, 1998), pp. 38–68.

25. Davies, *First English Empire*, pp. 177–8.

26. Roger A. Mason (ed.), *Scots and Britons: Scottish Political Thought and the Union of 1603* (Cambridge, 1994), p. 169.

27. Cited by Coupland, *Welsh and Scottish Nationalism*, p. 78. For a recent useful survey of the history of sixteenth-century Scotland, see Dawson, *Scotland Re-formed*.

28. Conyers Read, *Mr. Secretary Cecil and Queen Elizabeth* (London, 1955; repr. 1962), chs. 7 and 8.

29. See Davies, *First English Empire*, pp. 39–41.

30. Colin Kidd, *Subverting Scotland's Past: Scottish Whig Historians and the Creation of an Anglo-British Identity, 1689–c.1830* (Cambridge, 1993), pp. 16–17.

31. Mason (ed.), *Scots and Britons*, pp. 164–5. For later influence of the concept of imperial crowns, see William Ferguson, 'Imperial Crowns: A Neglected Facet of the Background to the Treaty of Union of 1707', *Scottish Historical Review*, 53 (1974), pp. 22–44.

32. Davies, *First English Empire*, p. 49.
33. Ibid., p. 47.
34. See Colin Kidd, *British Identities Before Nationalism: Ethnicity and Nationhood in the Atlantic World, 1600–1800* (Cambridge, 1999), ch. 2.
35. For a helpful summary of these developments, to which I am indebted, see Richard L. Kagan, *Clio and the Crown: The Politics of History in Medieval and Early Modern Spain* (Baltimore, MD, 2009), ch. 1.
36. Cited by Alan Deyermond, 'La ideología del estado moderno en la literatura española del siglo XV', in Adeline Rucquoi (ed.), *Realidad e imágenes del poder: España a fines de la Edad Media* (Valladolid, 1988), p. 177.
37. J. H. Elliott, *Empires of the Atlantic World: Britain and Spain in America 1492–1830* (New Haven, CT, and London, 2006), pp. 120–1.
38. Alfredo Floristán Imízcoz, *El reino de Navarra y la conformación política de España, 1512–1841* (Madrid, 2014), pp. 67–70.
39. For a recent account, including a summary of differing views about the causes of what he calls 'the fifteenth-century catastrophe', see Alan Ryder, *The Wreck of Catalonia: Civil War in the Fifteenth Century* (Oxford, 2007). Vilar, *La Catalogne*, vol. 1, pp. 461–586, although in part superseded by subsequent research, remains an essential point of reference both for the economic and social problems of the principality, and also for the shift in the balance of power in the peninsula over the fifteenth and sixteenth centuries. See also Josep Fontana, *La formació d'una identitat. Una història de Catalunya* (Barcelona, 2014), pp. 78–81.
40. Spanish population figures as given in Vicente Pérez Moreda and David-Sven Reher (eds.), *Demografía histórica en España* (Madrid, 1988), Table 1, p. 40. The figure for Scotland is no more than a guess. See T. M. Devine and Jenny Wormald (eds.), *The Oxford Handbook of Modern Scottish History* (Oxford, 2012), p. 40.
41. Cited in J. H. Elliott, *The Revolt of the Catalans: A Study in the Decline of Spain, 1598–1640* (Cambridge, 1963), p. 13.
42. Cited in Ricardo García Cárcel, *La herencia del pasado. Las memorias históricas de España* (Barcelona, 2011), p. 197.
43. Cited in Jaime Vicens Vives, *Política del rey católico en Cataluña* (Barcelona, 1940), pp. 26–7.
44. For Catalan interpretations of the principality's past, see García Cárcel, *La herencia del pasado*, especially pp. 207–9 and 284–356; Fernando García de Cortázar, *Los mitos de la historia de España* (Barcelona, 2003), ch. 4; Albert Balcells (ed.), *Història de la historiografia catalana* (Barcelona, 2004); Eulàlia Duran i Grau, *Sobre la mitificació dels orígens històrics nacionals catalans* (Institut d'Estudis Catalans, Barcelona, 1991); Jesús Villanueva López, *Política y discurso histórico en la España del siglo XVII. Las polémicas sobre los orígines medievales de Cataluña* (Alicante, 2004). See also Paul Freedman's survey of Catalan foundation myths, 'Cowardice, Heroism, and the Legendary Origins of Catalonia', *Past and Present*, 121 (1988), pp. 3–28, which is particularly concerned with the deployment of these myths by the Catalan nobility to justify the serfdom of the peasantry.
45. While this is the central theme of Villanueva López, *Política y discurso*, he also provides an excellent account of earlier Catalan historiography leading up to 1640.
46. Eulàlia Duran i Grau, 'Historiografia del temps de l'Humanisme', in Balcells (ed.), *Història de la historiografia catalana*, pp. 82–3.
47. Freedman, 'Cowardice, Heroism', pp. 20–1. The story was picked up, or concocted, in the middle of the sixteenth century by a Valencian, Pedro Antonio Beuter.
48. The genealogical obsessions of early modern Europeans are described and acutely examined by Roberto Bizzocchi, *Généalogies fabuleuses. Inventer et faire croire dans l'Europe moderne* (Paris, 2010), the French version of the original Italian edition (Bologna, 1995). I am grateful to Professor Hamish Scott for bringing this book to my attention.
49. The attribution is the result of the detective work of Dauvit Broun, whose *Scottish Independence* lays out the evidence in detail in chapters 8 and 9.

50. Ibid., p. 279. For an entertaining account of these mythical histories, see Hugh Trevor-Roper, *The Invention of Scotland: Myth and History* (New Haven, CT, and London, 2008), ch. 1.
51. See Kidd, *British Identities Before Nationalism*, ch. 6 ('The Gaelic Dilemma in Early Modern Scottish Political Culture'); and for the complex question of the Pictish antecedents of the kingdom of Scotland, see Broun, *Scottish Independence*, ch. 3.
52. For the covenanting tradition see below, pp. 48–9.
53. For a lively, if unsympathetic, account of the queen and her reign, see Jenny Wormald, *Mary Queen of Scots: A Study in Failure* (London, 1988). For a more sympathetic study see the perceptive biography by Antonia Fraser, *Mary Queen of Scots* (London, 1969).
54. John Barbour, *The Bruce*, ed. and trans. A. A. M. Duncan (Edinburgh, 1997).
55. Mason (ed.), *Scots and Britons*, ch. 5 ('George Buchanan, James VI and the Presbyterians'); Quentin Skinner, *The Foundations of Modern Political Thought*, 2 vols. (Cambridge, 1978), vol. 2, pp. 339–45. For the invisibility of the Declaration of Arbroath before 1680 and its later deployment, including in the United States, see Roger Mason's essay, 'Beyond the Declaration of Arbroath', in Steve Boardman and Julian Goodare (eds.), *Kings, Lords and Men in Scotland and Britain, 1300–1625: Essays in Honour of Jenny Wormald* (Edinburgh, 2014), ch. 12.
56. See Ralph A. Giesey, *If Not, Not* (Princeton, NJ, 1968).
57. Villanueva López, *Política y discurso*, pp. 59–71.
58. Josep Iglésies i Fort, *Pere Gil, S.I. (1551–1622) i la seva Geografia de Catalunya* (Barcelona, 1949), p. 275. For Counter-Reformation Catalonia, see Henry Kamen, *The Phoenix and the Flame: Catalonia and the Counter Reformation* (New Haven, CT, and London, 1993).
59. Antoni Simon i Tarrés, *Els orígens ideològics de la revolució catalana de 1640* (Barcelona, 1999), pp. 43–4.
60. For an account of the image of the *pàtria* in the Catalonia of this period and its identification with the liberty derived from, and preserved by, its Constitutions, see Xavier Torres i Sans, 'Making and Remaking Patriotism: The Catalan Revolt against the Spanish Monarchy (1640–1659)', in Robert von Friedeburg (ed.), *'Patria' und 'Patrioten' vor dem Patriotismus* (Wiesbaden, 2005), pp. 139–68. A more extended version is in Xavier Torresi Sans, *Naciones sin nacionalismo. Cataluña en la monarquía hispánica, siglos XVI–XVII* (Valencia, 2008), especially pp. 104–13 and 123–70.
61. Cited in Elliott, *Revolt of the Catalans*, p. 45.
62. For the dispute of 1622–3 over the appointment of the viceroy, see ibid., ch. 6.
63. For questions of sovereignty and allegiance in Spain's composite monarchy, see Xavier Gil Pujol, 'Un rey, una fe, muchas naciones. Patria y nación en la España de los siglos XVI–XVII', in Antonio Álvarez-Ossorio Alvariño and Bernardo J. García García (eds.), *La monarquía de las naciones* (Madrid, 2004), pp. 39–76 (English version, Xavier Gil Pujol, 'One King, One Faith, Many Nations: *Patria* and Nation in Spain, 16th–17th Centuries', in Friedeburg (ed.), *'Patria' und 'Patrioten'*, pp. 105–37).
64. Mason (ed.), *Scots and Britons*, p. 63.
65. Denys Hay, 'The Use of the Term "Great Britain" in the Middle Ages', *Proceedings of the Society of Antiquaries of Scotland*, 89 (1955–6), pp. 55–66; Andrew D. Nicholls, *The Jacobean Union: A Consideration of British Civil Policies Under the Early Stuarts* (Westport, CT, 1999), pp. 4–5.
66. Colin Kidd, *Union and Unionisms: Political Thought in Scotland, 1500–2000* (Cambridge, 2008), pp. 44–8; for Whitelaw's speech, see Grant and Stringer (eds.), *Uniting the Kingdom?*, p. 108.
67. Mason (ed.), *Scots and Britons*, p. 176; Brian P. Levack, *The Formation of the British State: England, Scotland and the Union 1603–1707* (Oxford, 1987), pp. 32–4.
68. Mason (ed.), *Scots and Britons*, p. 184.
69. Conrad Russell, 'Composite Monarchies in Early Modern Europe: The British Example', in Grant and Stringer (eds.), *Uniting the Kingdom?*, pp. 143–4.
70. See Bruce R. Galloway and Brian P. Levack (eds.), *The Jacobean Union: Six Tracts of 1604* (Edinburgh, 1985).

71. For unions, or attempted unions, in eastern and northern Europe in this period, placed in a comparative context, see Robert Frost, 'The Limits of Dynastic Power: Poland-Lithuania, Sweden and the Problem of Composite Monarchy in the Age of the Vasas', in Tonio Andrade and William Reger (eds.), *The Limits of Empire: European Imperial Formations in Early Modern World History. Essays in Honor of Geoffrey Parker* (Farnham, Surrey, 2012), ch. 7.

72. See Jon Arrieta Alberdi, 'Forms of Union: Britain and Spain, a Comparative Analysis', in Jon Arrieta Alberdi and John H. Elliott (eds.), *Forms of Union: The British and Spanish Monarchies in the Seventeenth and Eighteenth Centuries* (*Riev. Revista Internacional de Estudios Vascos*, Cuadernos 5, 2009), pp. 23–52.

73. James Spedding (ed.), *The Works of Francis Bacon*, vol. 10 (London, 1868), pp. 96–7.

74. Ibid., p. 98.

75. For a suggestive but controversial assessment of James's policy and the motivations behind it, see Jenny Wormald, 'James VI, James I and the Identity of Britain', in Brendan Bradshaw and John Morrill (eds.), *The British Problem, c.1534–1707* (Basingstoke, 1996), ch. 6.

76. Nicholls, *The Jacobean Union*, p. 151; Wormald, 'James VI, James I and the Identity of Britain', pp. 154–5.

77. Johann P. Somerville (ed.), *King James VI and I: Political Writings* (Cambridge, 1994), pp. 159–78.

78. Ibid., p. 162.

79. Brian P. Levack, 'Law, Sovereignty and the Union', in Mason (ed.), *Scots and Britons*, pp. 216–19.

80. Somerville (ed.), *King James*, p. 163.

81. Levack, *Formation of the British State*, p. 72.

82. David Stevenson, *The Scottish Revolution 1637–1644: The Triumph of the Covenanters* (Newton Abbot, 1973), pp. 22–4.

83. For the short- and long-term impact of the Articles of Perth, see Laura M. Stewart, 'The Political Repercussions of the Five Articles of Perth: A Reassessment of James VI and I's Religious Policies in Scotland', *Sixteenth Century Journal*, 38 (2007), pp. 1,013–36. This article takes issue with David Stevenson and other historians who see the king making a prudent tactical retreat in the face of mass opposition.

84. For recent work on viceroys and the viceregal system, see Pedro Cardim and Joan-Lluis Palos (eds.), *El mundo de los virreyes en las monarquías de España y Portugal* (Madrid, 2012).

85. Wormald, 'James VI, James I and the Identity of Britain', p. 151.

86. Levack, *Formation of the British State*, pp. 60–2; Russell, 'Composite Monarchies', in Grant and Stringer (eds.), *Uniting the Kingdom?*, pp. 138–41; Julian Goodare, *The Government of Scotland, 1560–1625* (Oxford, 2004), ch. 6, including a reference (p. 142) to similar travelling distances of four days in Britain and Spain; Maurice Lee Jr., *The 'Inevitable' Union and Other Essays on Early Modern Scotland* (East Linton, 2003), ch. 9 ('James VI's Government of Scotland after 1603').

87. Galloway and Levack (eds.), *The Jacobean Union*, pp. xiv–xvi.

88. Cited by Romà Pinya i Homs, *La debatuda exclusió catalano-aragonesa de la conquesta d'Amèrica* (Barcelona, 1992), p. 123.

89. For the vexed and still debated question of nationality and naturalization in the Hispanic world, and particularly in the Indies, see, in addition to Pinya i Homs, *La debatuda exclusió*, Richard Konetzke, 'La legislación sobre inmigración de extranjeros en América durante el reinado de Carlos V', in *Charles-Quint et son temps* (Paris, 1959), pp. 93–111. More generally for citizenship in the Hispanic world, see Tamar Herzog, *Defining Nations: Immigrants and Citizens in Early Modern Spain and Spanish America* (New Haven, CT, and London, 2003), and 'Una monarquía, dos territorios. La frontera entre españoles y portugueses: España y Portugal durante (y después) de la unión', in Carlos Martínez Shaw and José Antonio Martínez Torres (eds.), *España y Portugal en el mundo, 1581–1668* (Madrid, 2014), pp. 139–55, at pp. 143–5.

90. Somerville (ed.), *King James*, p. 167.
91. D. H. Willson, *King James VI and I* (London, 1956), pp. 254–7.
92. For the figures for Anglo-Scottish marriages and a valuable discussion of the failure of James's dream of social integration, see Keith M. Brown, 'The Origins of a British Aristocracy: Integration and its Limitations before the Treaty of Union', in Steven G. Ellis and Sarah Barber (eds.), *Conquest and Union: Fashioning a British State, 1485–1725* (New York and London, 1995), ch. 9.
93. Modesto Ulloa, *La hacienda real de Castilla en el reinado de Felipe II* (Madrid, 1977), pp. 233–4, 259; Levack, *Formation of the British State*, p. 148.
94. Sir William Alexander, *An Encouragement to Colonies* (London, 1624), p. 32.
95. For the Ulster plantation, see M. Perceval-Maxwell, *The Scottish Migration to Ulster in the Reign of James I* (London, 1973). The figure of 'perhaps 30,000' Scottish emigrants to Ireland by the time of the uprising of 1641 is suggested, on the basis of the figures for muster roles recorded by Perceval-Maxwell, in Nicholas Canny (ed.), *Europeans on the Move: Studies on European Migration 1500–1800* (Oxford, 1994), p. 78.
96. Somerville (ed.), *King James*, p. 161.
97. See Jenny Wormald, ' "A Union of Hearts and Minds?": The Making of the Union Between Scotland and England, 1603', in Arrieta Alberdi and Elliott (eds.), *Forms of Union*, pp. 110–11.
98. Galloway and Levack (eds.), *The Jacobean Union*, p. xvi.

2 Rebellion and Its Aftermath, 1625–1707/1716

1. Anna Groundwater, 'The Middle Shires Divided: Tensions at the Heart of the Anglo-Scottish Union', in Sharon Adams and Julian Goodare (eds.), *Scotland in the Age of Two Revolutions* (Woodbridge, 2014), ch. 2; Cicely. V. Wedgwood, 'Anglo-Scottish Relations, 1603–1640', *Transactions of the Royal Historical Society*, 4, ser. 32 (1950), pp. 31–48, at pp. 33 and 36–9.
2. Elliott, *Revolt of the Catalans*, p. 52; and for Catalan banditry in general see Xavier Torres i Sans, *Els bandolers (s. XVI–XVII)* (Vic, 1991).
3. Elliott, *Revolt of the Catalans*, ch. 6; and see subsequent chapters for the events of the following years recounted below.
4. Cited in ibid., p. 102.
5. For the text of the 'Gran Memorial' see John H. Elliott, José F. de la Peña and Fernando Negredo del Cerro (eds.), *Memoriales y cartas del Conde Duque de Olivares* (2nd edn. Madrid, 2013), vol. 1, doc. iv.
6. For Olivares's phrase see J. H. Elliott, *The Count-Duke of Olivares: The Statesman in an Age of Decline* (New Haven, CT, and London, 1986), p. 197; that of James is quoted by Jenny Wormald, 'James VI, James I and the Identity of Britain', p. 149, from C. H. McIlwain (ed.), *The Political Works of James I* (New York, 1965), p. 292. Also in Somerville (ed.), *King James*, p. 162.
7. Mason (ed.), *Scots and Britons*, p. 63.
8. Above, p. 32.
9. Stevenson, *The Scottish Revolution*, p. 169; Goodare, *The Government of Scotland*, ch. 3 ('Law and Legislation').
10. This point is well made by Pablo Fernández Albaladejo, *La crisis de la monarquía* (*Historia de España*, ed. Josep Fontana and Ramón Villares, vol. 4, Madrid, 2009), pp. 88–9.
11. Elliott, La Peña and Negredo (eds.), *Memoriales y cartas*, p. 167.
12. For the Union of Arms see Elliott, *Count-Duke*, ch. 7.
13. Cited in Elliott, *Revolt of the Catalans*, p. 204, n. 2.
14. See the essays by Pablo Fernández Albaladejo and Jenny Wormald in Arrieta Alberdi and Elliott (eds.), *Forms of Union*.
15. Pere Molas i Ribalta, *Catalunya i la Casa d'Àustria* (Barcelona, 1996), pp. 145–64.
16. Alistair Malcolm, *Royal Favouritism and the Governing Elite of the Spanish Monarchy, 1640–1665* (Oxford, 2017), pp. 111–15.
17. Elliott, La Peña and Negredo (eds.), *Memoriales y cartas*, Document ix, p. 177.

18. For a collection of excellent essays on the concept of the *patria* in the British Isles and continental Europe (including Spain and Catalonia) in the early modern period, see Friedeburg (ed.), *'Patria' und 'Patrioten'*. Also for Spain, I. A. A. Thompson, 'Castile, Spain and the Monarchy: The Political Community from *patria natural* to *patria nacional*', in Richard L. Kagan and Geoffrey Parker (eds.), *Spain, Europe and the Atlantic World: Essays in Honour of John H. Elliott* (Cambridge, 1995), ch. 5.

19. Charles W. J. Withers, *Gaelic Scotland: The Transformation of a Culture Region* (London, 1988), pp. 4–5.

20. Cited in Elliott, *Count-Duke*, p. 564.

21. Stevenson, *The Scottish Revolution*, pp. 33–41.

22. *Calendar of State Papers Domestic, 1625–1649. Addenda*, pp. 241–2.

23. For the resumption of alienated Crown lands in Catalonia and its possible connection with the Union of Arms, see Elliott, *Revolt of the Catalans*, p. 210.

24. For the direct link between the Act of Revocation and the proposal for a British Union of Arms, see Geoffrey Parker, *Global Crisis: War, Climate Change and Catastrophe in the Seventeenth Century* (New Haven, CT, and London, 2013), p. 750, n. 18.

25. Edward Hyde, Earl of Clarendon, *The History of the Rebellion and Civil Wars in England* (ed. W. D. Macray, 6 vols., Oxford, 1888), vol. 1, p. 113. Also cited by Keith Brown, 'The Vanishing Emperor: British Kingship and its Decline, 1603–1707', in Mason (ed.), *Scots and Britons*, p. 58.

26. For the ways in which the word *provincia* was used and understood in Catalonia see Torres i Sans, *Naciones sin nacionalismo*, pp. 114–21. In Portugal fears were expressed as early as 1600 that the appointment of a non-royal viceroy would lead to the kingdom's reduction to the status of a province. See Fernando Jesús Bouza Álvarez, 'La "soledad" de los reinos y la "semejanza del rey". Los virreinatos de príncipes en el Portugal de los Felipes', in Massimo Ganci and Ruggiero Romano (eds.), *Governare il Mondo. L'impero spagnolo dal XV al XIX secolo* (Palermo, 1991), p. 137.

27. Stevenson, *The Scottish Revolution*, p. 42.

28. Elliott, *Revolt of the Catalans*, p. 251.

29. For Charles's religious policies, see especially Stevenson, *The Scottish Revolution*, pp. 42–55, and chs. 2 and 3 for an account of their impact.

30. For the covenant and bonding see Jane E. A. Dawson, *John Knox* (New Haven, CT, and London, 2015), pp. 115–16 and 240, and Laura M. Stewart, *Rethinking the Scottish Revolution* (Oxford, 2016), pp. 88 and 90–3.

31. John Morrill (ed.), *The Scottish National Covenant in its British Context, 1638–51* (Edinburgh, 1990), p. 11. See also for the covenanting tradition and its theology, ch. 2 of this collection of essays, Margaret Steele, 'The "Politick Christian": The Theological Background to the National Covenant'.

32. Stevenson, *The Scottish Revolution*, pp. 193–5.

33. For these events and their aftermath see Elliott, *Revolt of the Catalans*, chs. 14–16.

34. Ibid., pp. 522–3; José Sanabre, *La acción de Francia en la pugna por la hegemonía de Europa, 1640–1659* (Barcelona, 1956), ch. 2; Ricardo García Càrcel, *Pau Claris. La revolta catalana* (Barcelona, 1980); Antoni Simon i Tarrés, *Pau Claris, líder d'una classe revolucionària* (Barcelona, 2008), ch. 6; Xavier Gil Pujol, 'Republican Politics in Early Modern Spain: The Castilian and Catalano-Aragonese Traditions', in Martin Van Gelderen and Quentin Skinner (eds.), *Republicanism: A Shared European Heritage* (2 vols., Cambridge, 2002), vol. 1, ch. 13, at pp. 283–4.

35. For Anglo-Scottish relations during the Commonwealth and Protectorate see below, pp. 57–9.

36. Lee, *The 'Inevitable' Union*, ch. 8 ('Scotland and the General Crisis of the Seventeenth Century'), argues that the Scottish example was unique, and that it cannot be fitted into any theory of the existence of a general crisis of the seventeenth century, which he rejects as 'a figment of the scholarly imagination'. While religion was not central to the Catalan rebellion, the desecration of churches by elements of the royal army in the spring and summer of 1640 was one among the many motives for the original uprising and helped to cement the sense of solidarity between parish priests and their parishioners.

37. Elliott, *Revolt of the Catalans*, pp. 550–1; Simon i Tarrés, *Orígens ideològics*, pp. 192–3; Villanueva López, *Política y discurso*, pp. 112 and 118.

38. See García Càrcel, *Pau Claris*, pp. 105–8.

39. See Elliott, *Spain, Europe and the Wider World*, ch. 4 ('A Non-Revolutionary Society: Castile in the 1640s').

40. It has been estimated that as many as 30,000 Scottish soldiers served in the army of Gustavus Adolphus alone. See Canny (ed.), *Europeans on the Move*, p. 83. n. 24.

41. Julian Goodare, 'The Scottish Revolution', in Adams and Goodare (eds.), *Scotland in the Age of Two Revolutions*, ch. 6, pp. 88–9.

42. For a suggestive discussion of Scottish attitudes to the idea of Britain between 1603 and 1707 and of Scotland's place in the British composite monarchy, see Roger A. Mason, 'Debating Britain in Seventeenth-Century Scotland: Multiple Monarchy and Scottish Sovereignty', *Journal of Scottish Historical Studies*, 35 (2015), pp. 1–24.

43. For the covenanters' programme see David Stevenson, *Union, Revolution and Religion in 17th-Century Scotland* (Aldershot, 1997), ch. 3 ('The Early Covenanters and the Federal Union of Britain'). Also Stewart, *Rethinking the Scottish Revolution*, esp. pp. 128–68.

44. Quoted by John Morrill, *The Nature of the English Revolution* (London, 1993), pp. 116–17.

45. For Cromwell and Scotland see Derek Hirst, 'The English Republic and the Meaning of Britain', in Bradshaw and Morrill (eds.), *The British Problem*, ch. 8; Sharon Adams, 'In Search of the Scottish Republic', in Adams and Goodare (eds.), *Scotland in the Age of Two Revolutions*, ch. 6; Hugh R. Trevor-Roper, *Religion, the Reformation and Social Change* (London, 1967), chs. 8 and 9.

46. Cited from Clarendon, *History of the Rebellion*, vol. 4, p. 307, by Keith M. Brown, 'The Origins of a British Aristocracy', in Ellis and Barber (eds.), *Conquest and Union*, p. 225.

47. Stevenson, *Union, Revolution and Religion*, ch. 4 ('Cromwell, Scotland and Ireland'), p. 164.

48. Cited by Hirst, 'The English Republic', p. 203.

49. For this distinction, as drawn by Olivares, see above, p. 43.

50. For the successes and failures of Cromwellian government in Scotland, see Stevenson, *Union, Revolution and Religion*, ch. 4, pp. 170–80.

51. Paul Slack, *The Invention of Improvement* (Oxford, 2014), p. 97.

52. Danielle McCormack, 'Highland Lawlessness and the Cromwellian Regime', in Adams and Goodare (eds.), *Scotland in the Age of Two Revolutions*, ch. 7. See also for English hegemony in the Cromwellian period Keith M. Brown, *Kingdom or Province? Scotland and the Regal Union, 1603–1715* (Basingstoke, 1992), pp. 135–40.

53. Michael Lynch, 'A Nation Born Again? Scottish Identity in the Sixteenth and Seventeenth Centuries', in Broun, Finlay and Lynch (eds.), *Image and Identity*, ch. 5.

54. Adams, 'In Search of the Scottish Republic', pp. 101–2; John R. Young, 'The Scottish Parliament and National Identity from the Union of the Crowns to the Union of Parliaments, 1603–1707', in Broun, Finlay and Lynch (eds.), *Image and Identity*, pp. 108–9.

55. Mason, 'Debating Britain in Seventeenth-Century Scotland', p. 15.

56. Cited in Clare Jackson, *Restoration Scotland: Royalist Politics, Religion and Ideas* (Woodbridge, 2003), p. 47.

57. William Ferguson, *Scotland's Relations with England: A Survey to 1707* (Edinburgh, 1977), p. 150. In his chapter 8, devoted to the years 1660–88, Ferguson emphasizes the 'unique importance' of the late Stuart period for the understanding of Anglo-Scottish relations (p. 143). For succinct but helpful accounts of Restoration Scotland, in addition to that by Ferguson, see in particular Mark Goldie, 'Divergence and Union: Scotland and England, 1660–1707', in Bradshaw and Morrill (eds.), *The British Problem*, ch. 9; Alasdair Raffe, 'Scotland Restored and Reshaped: Politics and Religion, c. 1660–1712', in Devine and Wormald (eds.), *Oxford Handbook of Modern Scottish History*, ch. 12; Allan I.

MacInnes, *Union and Empire: The Making of the United Kingdom in 1707* (Cambridge, 2007), ch. 4. A fuller treatment is in Jackson, *Restoration Scotland*, which is primarily concerned with the political and religious culture of Scotland in the Restoration period.

58. Maurice Lee Jr., 'The Worcester Veterans and the Restoration Regime in Scotland', in Adams and Goodare (eds.), *Scotland in the Age of Two Revolutions*, ch. 8.

59. Cited by Jackson, *Restoration Scotland*, p. 79.

60. Ibid., p. 132.

61. For the surrender of Barcelona and its aftermath, see Fernando Sánchez Marcos, *Cataluña y el gobierno central tras la Guerra de los Segadores (1652–1679)* (Barcelona, 1983), ch. 1.

62. For the history of the two counties, now known as Roussillon and Cerdagne, both before and after the Peace of the Pyrenees, Peter Sahlins, *Boundaries: The Making of France and Spain in the Pyrenees* (Berkeley and Los Angeles, CA, and Oxford, 1989), is fundamental. Further observations in Àngel Casals (ed.), *Les fronteres catalanes i el Tractat dels Pirineus* (Cabrera de Mar, 2009), which cites Bishop Margarit telling the Corts of 1473 that 'Rosselló and Cerdanya are inseparable members of the body of this principality' (p. 109).

63. Elliott, *Revolt of the Catalans*, pp. 263–6.

64. For French immigrants, who are estimated to have oscillated between 10 and 20 per cent of Catalonia's male population between 1570 and 1620, see Jordi Nadal and Emili Giralt i Raventós, *La population catalane de 1553 à 1717. L'immigration française* (Paris, 1960). Estimates of the French presence, p. 62.

65. Vilar, *La Catalogne*, vol. 1, p. 368, and for the complicated process involved in drawing the border line, and the effects of the separation, see Sahlins, *Boundaries*.

66. The Council's recommendations are analysed by Sánchez Marcos, *Cataluña y el gobierno central*, pp. 55–65. See also Josep M. Torras i Ribé, 'El projecte de repressió dels catalans de 1652', in Eva Serra et al., *La revolució catalana de 1640* (Barcelona, 1991), pp. 241–90.

67. Torras i Ribé, 'El projecte', pp. 268–71.

68. The court's preoccupation with the possibility of further Catalan unrest emerges clearly from the contemporary diary of the marqués de Osera, *Escribir la corte de Felipe IV. El diario del marqués de Osera 1657–1659*, ed. Santiago Martínez Hernández (Madrid, 2013). See, for instance, p. 43.

69. Sánchez Marcos, *Cataluña y el gobierno central*, p. 246.

70. For the 1688 rebellion and its repression see Henry Kamen, 'A Forgotten Insurrection of the Seventeenth Century: The Catalan Peasant Rising of 1688', *Journal of Modern History*, 49 (1977), pp. 210–30; Christopher Storrs, *The Resilience of the Spanish Monarchy 1665–1700* (Oxford, 2006), pp. 196–201; Antonio Espino López, *Catalunya durante el reinado de Carlos II. Política y guerra en la frontera catalana, 1679–1697* (Bellaterra, 1999), pp. 63–98; Joaquim Albareda i Salvadó, 'Catalunya a finals del segle XVII', in Eva Serra et al., *La revolució catalana*, pp. 291–317.

71. *Memorial* of the Duke of Villahermosa, 15 December 1690, printed as Appendix 2 in Jaume Dantí, *Aixecaments populars als Països catalans, 1687–1693* (Barcelona, 1990). Citations, pp. 214 and 219.

72. Storrs, *Resilience of the Spanish Monarchy*, pp. 200–1.

73. For a brief but acute discussion of this theme, which has dominated much of the historiography of this period, see Xavier Gil Pujol, 'La Corona de Aragón con el neoforalismo', in Pablo Fernández Albaladejo (ed.), *Los Borbones. Dinastía y memoria de nación en la España del siglo XVIII* (Madrid, 2001). Also Storrs, *Resilience of the Spanish Monarchy*, ch. 5.

74. The urbanization of the Barcelona region and its growing commercial and economic prosperity between 1550 and 1640 is documented in detail in the pioneering work of Albert García Espuche, *Un siglo decisivo. Barcelona y Cataluña, 1550–1640* (Madrid, 1998). For Catalans and the Indies trade see his ch. 7, which makes later seventeenth-century developments less novel than they appear in the previously standard account by Carlos Martínez Shaw, *Cataluña en la carrera de Indias* (Barcelona, 1981).

75. Cited in Vilar, *La Catalogne*, vol. 1, pp. 671–2.

76. Vilar, *La Catalogne*, vol. 1, pp. 655–67; Fernández Albaladejo, *La crisis de la monarquía*, pp. 477–8; Henry Kamen, 'El Fénix catalán: la obra renovadora de Narciso Feliu de la Penya', *Estudis*, 1 (1973), pp. 185–203. Feliu's implausible but significant description of Carlos II comes from his *Anales de Cataluña* (3 vols., Barcelona, 1709), vol. 3, p. 458, and has been repeatedly cited by historians of the reign.

77. Albrecht Graf von Kalnein, *Juan José de Austria en la España de Carlos II* (Lleida, 2001), ch. 4 and pp. 499–500; Gil Pujol, 'La Corona de Aragón', p. 101.

78. See Henry Kamen, *Spain in the Later Seventeenth Century 1665–1700* (London and New York, 1980), pp. 75–81.

79. Núria Sales, 'Institucions polítiques catalanes en vigílies de la seva abolició', *Pedralbes*, 13:1 (1993), pp. 275–9, at pp. 278–9; Joaquim Albareda i Salvadó, *Felipe V y el triunfo del absolutismo. Cataluña en un conflicto europeo, 1700–1714* (Barcelona, 2002), pp. 69–70.

80. Jackson, *Restoration Scotland*, p. 21.

81. Ibid., pp. 96–9.

82. Goldie, 'Divergence and Union', pp. 227–8; Jackson, *Restoration Scotland*, pp. 26–7.

83. Jackson, *Restoration Scotland*, pp. 81–2, 143.

84. Trevor-Roper, *The Invention of Scotland*, pp. 30–1

85. Goldie, 'Divergence and Union', pp. 229–30.

86. See Ferguson, *Scotland's Relations with England*, pp. 157–61.

87. Tim Harris, *Revolution: The Great Crisis of the British Monarchy, 1685–1720* (London, 2006), p. 145, and succeeding pages for what follows.

88. For the revolutionary events of 1688–9, see Harris, *Revolution*, ch. 9; Jackson, *Restoration Scotland*, ch. 8; Alasdair Raffe, 'Scottish State Oaths and the Revolution of 1688–1690', in Adams and Goodare (eds.), *Scotland in the Age of Two Revolutions*, ch. 10.

89. Harris, *Revolution*, p. 179.

90. Ibid., p. 369.

91. Ibid., p. 366.

92. Ibid., p. 408; Jackson, *Restoration Scotland*, pp. 193–203, for the arguments adopted. Quotation on p. 197; Goldie, 'Divergence and Union', p. 232.

93. Ferguson, *Scotland's Relations with England*, p. 172; Harris, *Revolution*, pp. 401–3.

94. For a succinct account of competing conceptions of Scottish nationhood in the years leading up to 1707, see Clare Jackson, 'Conceptions of Nationhood in the Anglo-Scottish Union Debates of 1707', in Stewart J. Brown and Christopher A. Whatley (eds.), *Union of 1707: New Dimensions* (Edinburgh, 2008), ch. 4.

95. Ferguson, *Scotland's Relations with England*, pp. 152–6; Christopher A. Whatley, *The Scots and the Union* (Edinburgh, 2006), pp. 91–2, 95–6.

96. MacInnes, *Union and Empire*, pp. 157–64.

97. Ibid., p. 87.

98. Canny (ed.), *Europeans on the Move*, pp. 88–90.

99. Whatley, *Scots and the Union*, p. 143.

100. Slack, *Invention of Improvement*, pp. 161 and 189; T. Christopher Smout, *A History of the Scottish People 1560–1830* (London, 1969), pp. 242–3.

101. John Robertson, 'An Elusive Sovereignty: The Course of the Union Debate in Scotland 1698–1707', in John Robertson (ed.), *A Union for Empire: Political Thought and the British Union of 1707* (Cambridge, 1995), pp. 198–227, at pp. 199–200.

102. For the Darien scheme see Douglas Watt, *The Price of Scotland: Darien, Union and the Wealth of Nations* (Edinburgh, 2007); David Armitage, 'The Scottish Vision of Empire: Intellectual Origins of the Darien Venture', in Robertson (ed.), *Union for Empire*, ch. 4; Whatley, *Scots and the Union*, pp. 166–73; Ferguson, *Scotland's Relations with England*, pp. 176–9.

103. Whatley, *Scots and the Union*, p. 173; Watt, *The Price of Scotland*, p. 63; Sir Walter Scott, *The Tales of a Grandfather* (3 vols., 1827–30, repr. London, 1933), p. 728.

104. See Andrew Fletcher, *Political Works*, ed. John Robertson (Cambridge, 1997).

105. For an account of Fletcher's life and thought, see Robertson's Introduction to Fletcher, *Political Works*.

106. Robertson, 'An Elusive Sovereignty', pp. 201–2; and for the different status of Scotland and Ireland see Ferguson, 'Imperial Crowns'.

107. Cited from Burnet's *History* by William Ferguson, 'The Making of the Treaty of Union 1707', *Scottish Historical Review*, 43 (1964), pp. 89–110, at p. 96.

108. For the complicated story of the political developments of these years, see Ferguson, *Scotland's Relations with England*, ch. 11; Whatley, *Scots and the Union*, ch. 5; MacInnes, *Union and Empire*, ch. 9; Robertson, 'An Elusive Sovereignty', ch. 8.

109. For Philip in Barcelona and the Corts of 1701–2, see Albareda i Salvadó, *Felipe V y el triunfo del absolutismo*, pp. 45–51.

110. Henry Kamen, *Philip V of Spain: The King Who Reigned Twice* (New Haven, CT, and London, 2001), pp. 24–7.

111. Albareda i Salvadó, 'Catalunya a finals del segle XVII', pp. 316–17.

112. The most recent full account of these events is to be found in Joaquim Albareda i Salvadó, *La guerra de sucesión en España, 1700–1714* (Barcelona, 2010), chs. 5 and 6.

113. See Albareda i Salvadó, *Felipe V y el triunfo del absolutismo*, pp. 55–73.

114. Kamen, *Philip V*, pp. 25–6.

115. See Antonio Domínguez Ortiz, *Sociedad y estado en el siglo XVIII español* (Barcelona, 1976), p. 47.

116. See Francisco Javier Palao Gil, 'The Crown of Aragon in the War of the Spanish Succession', in Trevor J. Dadson and J. H. Elliott (eds.), *Britain, Spain and the Treaty of Utrecht, 1713–2013* (Leeds, 2014), ch. 3.

117. Albareda i Salvadó, *La guerra de sucesión*, p. 171.

118. Rosa María Alabrús Iglesias, *Felip V i l'opinió dels catalans* (Lleida, 2001), pp. 431–2.

119. For the continuing uncertainty about the motivations of the Catalan merchant class and the circle of Feliu de la Peña in coming out in support of the archduke, see Ricardo García Cárcel, *Felipe V y los españoles* (Barcelona, 2002), pp. 79–83.

120. Ricardo García Cárcel and Rosa María Alabrús Iglesias, *España en 1700. Austrias o Borbones?* (Madrid, 2001), p. 113.

121. For a discussion of the extent to which the word 'rebellion' was justified, see Palao Gil, 'The Crown of Aragon'.

122. The course of the negotiations and of the events leading up to the Union of 1707 have been extensively treated by numerous historians. For a summary of the recent literature see Clare Jackson, 'Union Historiographies', in Devine and Wormald (eds.), *Oxford Handbook of Modern Scottish History*, ch. 17.

123. MacInnes, *Union and Empire*, ch. 8 ('Going Dutch?'), esp. pp. 202 and 235.

124. Kidd, *Union and Unionisms*, pp. 66–8; Robertson, 'An Elusive Sovereignty', pp. 207–8; Jackson, 'Conceptions of Nationhood'.

125. Whatley, *Scots and the Union*, p. 243.

126. William Ferguson, *Scotland: 1689 to the Present* (Edinburgh, 1968), pp. 49–50.

127. For the bail-out and its impact, see Watt, *The Price of Scotland*, ch. 17.

128. George Macaulay Trevelyan, *England Under Queen Anne* (3 vols., London, 1930–4, repr. 1948), vol. 2, p. 283.

129. Cited in ibid., pp. 284–5.

130. Cited in Albareda i Salvadó, *La guerra de sucesión*, p. 229.

131. Cited in ibid., pp. 230–1.

132. See Jon Arrieta Alberdi, 'L'antítesi pactisme-absolutisme durant la guerra de Successió a Catalunya', in Joaquim Albareda i Salvadó (ed.), *Del patriotisme al catalanisme: societat i política (segles XVI–XIX)* (Vic, 2001), pp. 105–28.

133. García Cárcel, *Felipe V y los españoles*, pp. 86–8.

134. MacInnes, *Union and Empire*, p. 272. Although Roger L. Emerson, *An Enlightened Duke: The Life of Archibald Campbell (1682–1751), Earl of Ilay and Third Duke of Argyll* (Kilkerran, 2013), is devoted to the life and political career of Argyll's younger brother, whose life was overshadowed by the second duke until he succeeded to the dukedom

on the latter's death in 1743, the close if often conflictive relationship of the two brothers, who between them dominated so much of Scotland's political life in the post-Union decades, means that the elder brother is never far from the scene.

135. Albareda i Salvadó, *La guerra de sucesión*, pp. 265 and 327–8.
136. For a succinct account of the internal disputes and the last days of Barcelona, see Albareda Salvadó, *Felipe V y el triunfo del absolutismo*, ch. 5.
137. *The Case of the Catalans Consider'd* (London, 1714), facsimile reprint, p. 17, in Michael B. Strubell (ed.), *Consideració del cas dels catalans, seguit de La deplorable història dels catalans* (Barcelona, 1992).
138. Jon Arrieta Alberdi, 'Una recapitulación de la Nueva Planta, a través del austracista Juan Amor de Soria', in Marina Torres Arce and Susana Truchuelo García (eds.), *Europa en torno a Utrecht* (Santander, 2014), pp. 353–87, at pp. 376–80.
139. Albareda i Salvadó, *La guerra de sucesión*, pp. 168–72.
140. Above, p. 41.

3 Incorporating Unions, 1707–1789

1. See above, p. 82.
2. The arguments in court circles following Philip V's victory at Almansa on 25 April 1707, in which 'prudence' was pitted against 'innovation', are closely examined in José María Iñurritegui, *Gobernar la ocasión. Preludio político de la Nueva Planta de 1707* (Madrid, 2008).
3. For the origins of the decree, see Albareda i Salvadó, *La guerra de sucesión*, pp. 226–30 (quotation from Louis XIV, p. 228).
4. See Jon Arrieta Alberdi, 'The Anglo-Scottish Union and the Nueva Planta', in Dadson and Elliott (eds.), *Britain, Spain and the Treaty of Utrecht*, at pp. 40 and 45.
5. Cited by Albareda i Salvadó, *La guerra de sucesión*, p. 432.
6. See Palao Gil, 'The Crown of Aragon', pp. 32–7.
7. Levack, *Formation of the British State*, ch. 3 ('The Union of Laws'); Carlos A. Garriga Acosta, 'Sobre el gobierno de Cataluña bajo el régimen de la Nueva Planta. Ensayo historiográfico', *Anuario de Historia del Derecho Español* LXXX (2010), pp. 716–65.
8. Domínguez Ortiz, *Sociedad y estado*, p. 88.
9. Ferguson, *Scotland: 1689 to the Present*, pp. 110–14.
10. For a summary of legal developments after the Union see John W. Cairns, 'Scottish Law, Scottish Lawyers and the Status of the Union', in Robertson (ed.), *A Union for Empire*, ch. 10. Also Colin Kidd, 'Eighteenth-Century Scotland and the Three Unions', in T. C. Smout (ed.), *Anglo-Scottish Relations from 1603 to 1900* (Oxford, 2005), ch. 9, at pp. 177–80. Anglicization and modernization, p. 183.
11. Ferguson, *Scotland: 1689 to the Present*, pp. 134–8.
12. Lluís Roura i Aulinas, 'Subjecció i militarització a la Catalunya del segle XVIII', in Albareda i Salvadó (ed.), *Del patriotisme al catalanisme*, pp. 289–315.
13. Josep M. Fradera, *Passat i identitat: la Guerra de Successió en la política i la literatura del segle XIX català* (Acte commemoratiu de'l 11 de septembre de 1714, Ajuntament de Barcelona, 1993). It was finally demolished during the liberal 'biennium' of 1854–6.
14. Martín M.ª Gay Escoda, *El corregidor a Catalunya* (Madrid, 1997).
15. Josep M. Torras i Ribé, *Els municipis catalans de l'antic règim, 1453–1808* (Barcelona, 1983), p. 159.
16. Fontana, *La formació d'una identitat*, p. 227.
17. Alabrús Iglesias, *Felip V i l'opinió dels catalans*, p. 436.
18. Vilar, *La Catalogne*, vol. 1, pp. 702–4; Joan Mercader i Riba, *Felip V i Catalunya* (Barcelona, 1968), pp. 171–3; Albareda i Salvado, *Felipe V y el triunfo del absolutismo*, pp. 207–11.
19. Whatley, *The Scots and the Union*, p. 314.

20. Mercader i Riba, *Felip V*, pp. 175–6; Jesús Astigarraga, 'Economic Integration Models and Processes of Political Union: The Contrasting Fates of Scotland and the Basque Country after 1707', in Arrieta Alberdi and Elliott (eds.), *Forms of Union*, p. 146.

21. Joseph Townsend, *Journey Through Spain in the Years 1786 and 1787* (3 vols., London, 1791), vol. 1, p. 154.

22. Mercader i Riba, *Felip V*, ch. 9.

23. Albareda i Salvadó, *Felipe V y el triunfo del absolutismo*, pp. 214–16.

24. Ernest Lluch, *La Catalunya vençuda del segle XVIII* (Barcelona, 1996), pp. 122–6.

25. See James S. Amelang, *Honored Citizens of Barcelona: Patrician Culture and Class Relations, 1490–1714* (Princeton, NJ, 1986), pp. 190–5, and Bruce P. Lenman, *Jacobite Risings in Britain 1689–1746* (London, 1980), p. 79.

26. For a suggestive discussion of questions of linguistic diversity and uniformity, primarily but not exclusively in the context of revolutionary France, see David A. Bell, 'Lingua Populi, Lingua Dei: Language, Religion and the Origins of French Revolutionary Nationalism', *American Historical Review*, 100 (1995), pp. 1,403–37.

27. For the complexities of the linguistic question in Catalonia before the twentieth century, see Joan-Lluís Marfany, *La llengua maltractada. El castellà i el català a Catalunya del segle XVI al segle XIX* (Barcelona, 2001).

28. Cited in Alabrús Iglesias, *Felip V l'opinió dels catalans*, p. 423.

29. Cited ibid., from Ignasi Farreras, *Apologia de l'idioma català* (1780).

30. Albareda i Salvadó, *Felipe V y el triunfo del absolutismo*, pp. 212–13.

31. The text of the decree is reproduced in Francesc Ferrer i Gironès, *La persecució política de la llengua catalana* (Barcelona, 1985), pp. 35–8. The relevant article is Article VII. For comments on its interpretation and effectiveness, see Marfany, *La llengua maltractada*, pp. 408–13.

32. Salvador Sanpere i Miquel, *Fin de la nación catalana* (Barcelona, 1905). For Sanpere as a historian see Roberto Fernández Dìaz, *Cataluña y el absolutismo borbónico. Historia y política* (Lleida, 2014), pp. 291–302.

33. Cited by Fernández Dìaz, *Cataluña y el absolutismo borbónico*, p. 295.

34. Sanpere i Miquel, *Fin de la nación catalana*, p. 690.

35. The concept of the 'horizontal' Spain of the Habsburgs and the 'vertical' Spain of the Bourbons was formulated by Ricardo García Cárcel in his *Felipe V y los españoles*. See pp. 112 and 114.

36. See ibid., pp. 120–4; Floristán Imízcoz, *El reino de Navarra*, pp. 239–46; Astigarraga, 'Economic Integration Models', pp. 141–63.

37. Víctor Ferro Pomà, *El dret públic català. Les institucions a Catalunya fins al Decret de Nova Planta* (Vic, 1987), p. 442.

38. P. W. J. Riley, *The English Ministers and Scotland, 1707–1727* (London, 1964), pp. 90–7. Riley's book remains a valuable account of the complex politics of the period.

39. Ibid., pp. 166–7, 246–7, 254–5.

40. Andrew Mackillop, 'A Union for Empire? Scotland, the English East India Company and the British Union', in Brown and Whatley (eds.), *Union of 1707*, ch. 7.

41. See above, p. 84.

42. Lenman, *Jacobite Risings*, p. 86; Whatley, *The Scots and the Union*, p. 330.

43. Lenman, *Jacobite Risings*, pp. 95–6.

44. Riley, *English Ministers*, pp. 230–1.

45. For an analysis of the background to the '15, see Daniel Szechi, *1715: The Great Jacobite Rebellion* (New Haven, CT, and London, 2006), and Lenman, *Jacobite Risings*, ch. 6. Rosalind Mitchison, 'The Government and the Highlands, 1707–1745', in Nicholas Phillipson and Rosalind Mitchison (eds.), *Scotland in the Age of Improvement* (Edinburgh, 1996), ch. 2, for the Highland regional setting.

46. Szechi, *1715*, chs. 8 and 9; Lenman, *Jacobite Risings*, pp. 107–8, 158–70.

47. Lenman, *Jacobite Risings*, pp. 190–5. For clear-eyed accounts of the Stuarts in exile, their attempts to recover the Crown, and the uprisings of their Jacobite supporters, see the contributions to David Forsyth (ed.), *Bonnie Prince Charlie and the Jacobites* (Edinburgh, 2017). This is the catalogue of the remarkable exhibition held in Edinburgh's National

Museum of Scotland in 2017, which displayed numerous objects and relics that cast fresh light on important aspects of Jacobite history and culture.

48. See Riley, *English Ministers*, ch. 16 ('Walpole and the Scots') for Walpole's approach to the government of Scotland. For Argyll's following in the House of Commons, p. 273.
49. See Emerson, *An Enlightened Duke*, for Ilay's varied life and political career.
50. García Cárcel, *Felipe V y los españoles*, pp. 124–6; Fontana, *La formació d'una identitat*, pp. 229–30.
51. García Cárcel, *Felipe V y los españoles*, pp. 161–4.
52. Ferguson, *Scotland: 1689 to the Present*, p. 90; Thomas M. Devine, *The Scottish Nation, 1700–2000* (London, 1999), p. 95.
53. Eric Cregeen, 'The Changing Role of the House of Argyll in the Scottish Highlands', in Phillipson and Mitchison (eds.), *Scotland in the Age of Improvement*, p. 5. I have relied on this chapter, and the succeeding chapter by Rosalind Mitchison on 'The Government and the Highlands, 1707–1745', as also on Lenman, *Jacobite Risings*, and Emerson, *An Enlightened Duke*, ch. 15, for my discussion of the Highlands and the Jacobite movement.
54. Mitchison, 'The Government and the Highlands', p. 35.
55. Lenman, *Jacobite Risings*, pp. 146–9.
56. Cregeen, 'Changing Role of the House of Argyll', pp. 10–2.
57. Cited by Mitchison, 'The Government and the Highlands', p. 38.
58. Smout, *History of the Scottish People*, p. 343.
59. Lenman, *Jacobite Risings*, pp. 278–80.
60. Smout, *History of the Scottish People*, p. 229.
61. See Amelang, *Honored Citizens*, ch. 2.
62. Joan Mercader i Riba, *Els capitans generals. El segle xviii* (Barcelona, 1957), pp. 112–14; Fernández Díaz, *Cataluña y el absolutismo borbónico*, p. 475; and for municipal government in general see Torras i Ribé, *Els municipis catalans*.
63. Fernández Díaz, *Cataluña y el absolutismo borbónico*, p. 474; Szechi, *1715*, pp. 236–50.
64. Stephen Jacobson, *Catalonia's Advocates: Lawyers, Society, and Politics in Barcelona, 1759–1900* (Chapel Hill, NC, 2009), pp. 47–8.
65. Vilar, *La Catalogne*, vol. 2, pp. 420–5; Domínguez Ortiz, *Sociedad y estado*, pp. 250–3. For a succinct explanation of emphyteusis and the Catalan system of property rights, based on a study of the Igualada region in central Catalonia, see Julie Marfany, *Land, Proto-Industry and Population in Catalonia, c. 1680–1829: An Alternative Transition to Capitalism?* (Farnham, Surrey, 2012), pp. 25–53.
66. Figures as given in García Espuche, *Un siglo decisivo*, pp. 415–16; and see above, p. 67.
67. Smout, *History of the Scottish People*, pp. 258–9. For Catalonia, Antoni Simon i Tarrés, *La població catalana a l'edat moderna. Deu estudis* (Barcelona, 1996), pp. 84–5; Joaquim Albareda i Salvadó and Pere Gifre i Ribas, *Història de la Catalunya moderna* (Barcelona, 1999), p. 131. Both these authors regard the total population figures at the beginning and end of the eighteenth century, as given by Pierre Vilar in his extensive account of Catalan demography in *La Catalogne*, vol. 2, ch. 1, as underestimates.
68. Devine, *The Scottish Nation*, pp. 152–4.
69. Regina Grafe, *Distant Tyranny: Markets, Power, and Backwardness in Spain, 1650–1800* (Princeton, NJ, 2012), pp. 215–16. For Madrid's population, see David Ringrose, *Spain, Europe and the 'Spanish Miracle', 1700–1900* (Cambridge, 1996), p. 258, and Domínguez Ortiz, *Sociedad y estado*, p. 200.
70. Arrieta Alberdi, 'L'antítesi pactisme-absolutisme', p. 133.
71. Elliott, *Revolt of the Catalans*, p. 538.
72. For Feliu de la Peña see above, pp. 67 and 82. The essential starting point for the history of Catalan economic growth in the second half of the seventeenth century is Vilar, *La Catalogne*, vol. 1, pp. 638–70. Brief overviews, incorporating more recent work, in Albareda i Salvadó and Gifre i Ribas, *Història de la Catalunya moderna*, pp. 88–98; Fontana, *La formació d'una identitat*, pp. 192–8. For the Atlantic trade, Martínez Shaw, *Cataluña en la carrera de Indias*, pp. 72–82.
73. Michael Fry, *A Higher World: Scotland 1707–1815* (Edinburgh, 2014), p. 4.

74. Devine, *The Scottish Nation*, p. 51. For surveys of agrarian development in Scotland between the Restoration and the Union, see Ferguson, *Scotland: 1689 to the Present*, ch. 3, and Smout, *History of the Scottish People*, chs. 5 and 6. For competing versions, optimistic and pessimistic, of the state of the Scottish economy in this period, see Karin Bowie, 'New Perspectives on Pre-Union Scotland', in Devine and Wormald (eds.), *Oxford Handbook of Modern Scottish History*, pp. 313–18.

75. Vilar, *La Catalogne*, vol. 2, p. 481.

76. See J. K. J. Thomson, *A Distinctive Industrialization: Cotton in Barcelona 1728–1832* (Cambridge, 1992), especially ch. 4. Also, for proto-industrialization, see Marfany, *Land, Proto-Industry and Population*.

77. For a synthesis of recent work on this entrepreneurial class and its activities and attitudes, see Joan-Lluís Marfany, *Nacionalisme espanyol i catalanitat. Cap a una revisió de la Renaixença* (Barcelona, 2017), pp. 81–111.

78. Cited from Estrada, *Población general de España*, vol. III, p. 125, by Miguel Herrero García, *Ideas de los españoles del siglo XVII* (Madrid, 1966), pp. 303–4. For other contemporary observations on Catalan industriousness see Jaime Carrera Pujal, *Historia política y económica de Cataluña* (4 vols., Barcelona, 1946–7), vol. 3, pp. 76–105.

79. Vicens Vives, *Noticia de Cataluña*, pp. 41–3.

80. Thomson, *A Distinctive Industrialization*, pp. 132–8.

81. Fernández Díaz, *Cataluña y el absolutismo borbónico*, p. 458.

82. Albareda i Salvadó and Gifre i Ribas, *Història de la Catalunya moderna*, p. 154.

83. Pierre Vilar, *Estat, nació, socialisme. Estudis sobre el cas espanyol* (Barcelona, 1982), p. 76; Fernández Díaz, *Cataluña y el absolutismo borbónico*, p. 466; and see below, pp. 137–8.

84. Richard Herr, *The Eighteenth-Century Revolution in Spain* (Princeton, NJ, 1958), pp. 154–63. The first societies of Amigos del País were set up in the Basque provinces, beginning on an unofficial basis at Azcoitia in 1748 on the initiative of a group of nobles. Government approval came in 1765. By the end of the reign of Charles III fifty-six of these societies had come into existence across Spain, but Catalonia was a notable absentee. Barcelona's Junta de Comercio, established in 1758, was felt to be sufficient as an institution for promoting economic growth.

85. Above, pp. 98–9, and Grafe, *Distant Tyranny*, p. 145. Grafe's book is an important, if controversial, reassessment of the eighteenth-century Spanish economy and of obstacles to its growth.

86. Ferguson, *Scotland: 1689 to the Present*, pp. 169–70; Fry, *A Higher World*, pp. 14 and 25.

87. Ferguson, *Scotland: 1689 to the Present*, pp. 180–6; Devine, *The Scottish Nation*, pp. 55 and 58.

88. Thomson, *A Distinctive Industrialization*, pp. 248–60, 305–7.

89. Devine, *The Scottish Nation*, p. 62; Fry, *A Higher World*, p. 42.

90. Devine, *The Scottish Nation*, p. 58.

91. Fry, *A Higher World*, p. 60.

92. Thomas M. Devine and Gordon Jackson (eds.), *Glasgow* (2 vols., Manchester, 1995), vol. 1, ch. 4 ('The Golden Age of Tobacco'); Ferguson, *Scotland: 1689 to the Present*, pp. 183–4.

93. Martínez Shaw, *Cataluña en la carrera de Indias*, p. 274.

94. Stanley J. Stein and Barbara H. Stein, *Apogee of Empire: Spain and New Spain in the Age of Charles III, 1759–1789* (Princeton, NJ, 2003), pp. 204–9. For the *comercio libre* legislation and its impact see, in addition to Stein and Stein, John R. Fisher, *The Economic Aspects of Spanish Imperialism in America, 1492–1810* (Liverpool, 1997), chs. 9 and 10, and the essays by various hands in Antonio-Miguel Bernal Rodríguez (ed.), *El comercio libre entre España y América Latina, 1765–1824* (Madrid, 1987). I am indebted to Professor Josep M.ª Fradera for his advice on aspects of legislation on the Atlantic trade during the reigns of Ferdinand VI and Charles III.

95. See Josep M.ª Delgado Ribas, 'El modelo catalán dentro del sistema de libre comercio (1765–1820)', in Bernal Rodríguez (ed.), *El comercio libre,* pp. 64–6.

96. Stein and Stein, *Apogee*, pp. 206–7.

97. Thomas M. Devine, *Scotland's Empire 1600–1815* (London, 2003), and see his ch. 13 ('Warriors of Empire') for Scotland's overall contribution, Highland and Lowland, to the acquisition and defence of empire.

98. The concept of the 'fiscal-military state' was first developed by John Brewer in his *The Sinews of Power: War, Money and the English State, 1688–1783* (London, 1988), a book that has generated much discussion and inspired much new research. For the most recent assessment of Brewer's contribution see Aaron Graham and Patrick Walsh (eds.), *The British Fiscal-Military States, 1660–c.1783* (Abingdon, 2016). I am indebted to Hamish Scott for bringing this book to my notice. Previous important discussions include Patrick K. O'Brien and Philip A. Hunt, 'The Rise of a Fiscal State in England', *Bulletin of the Institute of Historical Research*, 66 (1993), pp. 129–76, and Patrick O'Brien and Leandro Prados de la Escosura (eds.), 'The Costs and Benefits of European Imperialism from the Conquest of Ceuta, 1415, to the Treaty of Lusaka, 1974,' (papers of the Twelfth International Economic History Congress), *Revista de Historia Económica*, 16 (Madrid, 1998). For the development of the Spanish fiscal-military state in the first half of the eighteenth century see also Christopher Storrs, *The Spanish Resurgence, 1713–1748* (New Haven, CT, and London, 2016).

99. See the ground-breaking essay by Andrew Mackillop, 'Subsidy State or Drawback Province? Eighteenth-Century Scotland and the British Fiscal-Military Complex', in Graham and Walsh (eds.), *British Fiscal-Military States*, ch. 9, which I follow here.

100. See above, p. 37.

101. Canny (ed.), *Europeans on the Move*, p. 35.

102. 'The Journal of a Tour to the Hebrides with Samuel Johnson L.L.D' (first published 1786) in James Boswell and Samuel Johnson, *A Journey to the Western Islands of Scotland and the Journal of a Tour to the Hebrides*, ed. Peter Levi (London, 1984), p. 253 (8 September 1773).

103. For a synthesis by T. C. Smout, N. C. Landsman and T. M. Devine of recent research on Scottish emigration, see Canny (ed.), *Europeans on the Move*, ch. 5. This includes a consideration of the findings of Bernard Bailyn in his fundamental work, *Voyagers to the West: A Passage in the Peopling of America on the Eve of the Revolution* (New York, 1986). Eric Richards provides a valuable short survey of Scottish activities on both sides of the Atlantic in the post-Union period in 'Scotland and the Uses of the Atlantic Empire', in Bernard Bailyn and Philip D. Morgan (eds.), *Strangers Within the Realm* (Chapel Hill, NC, and London, 1991), pp. 67–114. For Highland emigration, pp. 92–5.

104. Thomas M. Devine, 'Scottish Elites and the Indian Empire, 1700–1815', in Smout (ed.), *Anglo-Scottish Relations*, ch. 9. This chapter examines service for the East India Company in the context of social and economic pressures in Scotland and the workings of the patronage system. Much the same ground is covered in ch. 11 of Devine's *Scotland's Empire* ('Colonizing the Indian Empire').

105. Devine, 'Scottish Elites', pp. 227–9.

106. Devine, *Scotland's Empire*, pp. 237–8; Christopher A. Bayly, *Imperial Meridian: The British Empire and the World, 1780–1830* (London, 1989), pp. 83–4.

107. The Johnstones and their global activities have been traced by Emma Rothschild, *The Inner Life of Empires: An Eighteenth-Century History* (Princeton, NJ, 2011). For the Scots and empire, see Devine, *Scotland's Empire*, and the brief survey by Douglas Hamilton, 'Scotland and the Eighteenth-Century Empire', in Devine and Wormald (eds.), *Oxford Handbook of Modern Scottish History*, ch. 22.

108. See David Hancock, *Citizens of the World: London Merchants and the Integration of the British Atlantic Community, 1735–1765* (Cambridge, 1995), and Devine, *Scotland's Empire*, pp. 245–6 and p. 110.

109. John Lynch, *Bourbon Spain 1700–1800* (Oxford, 1989), pp. 298–9.

110. Ibid., p. 340; John R. Fisher, *Bourbon Peru 1750–1824* (Liverpool, 2003), p. 148.

111. Frederick A. Pottle (ed.), *Boswell's London Journal, 1762–1763* (New York, 1950), pp. 71–2; and for the Scots and anti-Scottish sentiment at this time, see Janet Adam Smith, 'Some Eighteenth-Century Ideas of Scotland', in Phillipson and Mitchison (eds.), *Scotland in the Age of Improvement*, Linda Colley, *Britons: Forging the Nation 1707–1837* (New Haven, CT, and London, 1982), pp. 117–32, and Bruce P. Lenman, *Integration, Enlightenment, and Industrialization. Scotland 1746–1832* (London, 1981), pp. 39–40.

112. See Kidd, 'Eighteenth-Century Scotland and the Three Unions'.

113. See above, p. 24.

114. See the suggestive article by Allan I. MacInnes on a Scottish *patria* transcending Jacobite and Whig divisions, 'Jacobitism in Scotland: Episodic Cause or National Movement?', *Scottish Historical Review*, 86 (2007), pp. 225–52.

115. Smith, 'Some Eighteenth-Century Ideas of Scotland'; Withers, *Gaelic Scotland*, pp. 59–60; Devine, *Scotland's Empire*, p. 351.

116. Devine, *Scotland's Empire*, p. 353; Colley, *Britons*, p. 130.

117. Below, p. 138.

118. This is the argument advanced by Marfany in his *Nacionalisme espanyol i catalanitat*, as on pp. 174–6, although most of his examples are taken from the period after 1800.

119. Pere Anguera, 'Entre dues posibilitats: espanyols o catalans?', in Albareda i Salvadó (ed.), *Del patriotisme al catalanisme*, at pp. 317–19.

120. Alexander Broadie, 'The Rise (and Fall?) of the Scottish Enlightenment', in Devine and Wormald (eds.), *Oxford Handbook of Modern Scottish History*, p. 380. The term 'Scottish Enlightenment' seems not to have come into existence until around 1900. See Emerson, *An Enlightened Duke*, p. 359.

121. John Robertson, *The Case for the Enlightenment. Scotland and Naples 1680–1760* (Cambridge, 2005), pp. 109–11 and 136–7. For the background and character of the Scottish Enlightenment, in addition to Robertson's book, see also his essay, 'The Scottish Contribution to the Enlightenment', in Paul Wood (ed.), *The Scottish Enlightenment. Essays in Reinterpretation* (Rochester, NY, 2000), ch. 2, and Alexander Broadie in Devine and Wormald (eds.), *Oxford Handbook of Modern Scottish History*, ch. 19.

122. Richards, 'Scotland and the Atlantic Empire', pp. 84–7.

123. Robertson, 'The Scottish Contribution', p. 52.

124. For a comparison of Edinburgh and Barcelona, see James Amelang, 'Comparing Cities: A Barcelona Model?', *Urban History*, 34 (2007), pp. 173–80. On the relative size of Edinburgh and London, see R. A. Houston, *Social Change in the Age of Enlightenment: Edinburgh, 1660–1760* (Oxford, 1994), p. 148.

125. Bob Harris, *The Scottish People and the French Revolution* (London, 2008), pp. 20–2.

126. Bernard Bailyn and John Clive, 'England's Cultural Provinces: Scotland and America', first published in the *William and Mary Quarterly* (1954) and reprinted as ch. 7 of Bernard Bailyn, *Sometimes an Art: Nine Essays on History* (New York, 2015). For the travelling time see p. 185. The essay remains a suggestive treatment of the implications of provincial status. The stagecoach service between Madrid and Barcelona by way of Zaragoza or Valencia was also weekly, and in this same year, 1763, was reported as taking six days, travelling at six hours a day (Gonzalo Menéndez Pidal, *Los caminos en la historia de España*, Madrid, 1951, p. 125). I am grateful to Dr Bob Harris for informing me that by the mid-1780s improvements had reduced the travelling time between London and Edinburgh to sixty hours, or ten days if travelling, like the Spanish coach, at six hours a day.

127. Robertson, *The Case for Enlightenment*, p. 373.

128. Houston, *Social Change*, pp. 143–4; Smout, *History of the Scottish People*, pp. 370–2; Felipe Fernández-Armesto, *Barcelona: A Thousand Years of the City's Past* (London, 1991), pp. 174–5 and 130–1; Robert Hughes, *Barcelona* (London, 1992), pp. 193–4, 198–204, 276–8.

129. Ferran Soldevila i Zubiburu, *Història de Catalunya* (3 vols., 2nd edn., Barcelona, 1962–3), vol. 3, pp. 1,220–1.

130. See especially Antonio de Capmany, *Memorias históricas sobre la marina, comercio y artes de la antigua ciudad de Barcelona* (Barcelona, 1779–92).

131. Jorge Cañizares-Esguerra, *How to Write the History of the New World* (Stanford, CA, 2001), pp. 174–8.

132. José M. López Piñero, *La introducción de la ciencia moderna en España* (Barcelona, 1969); Iris M. Zavala, *Clandestinidad y libertinaje erudito en los albores del siglo XVIII* (Barcelona, 1978), pp. 17–18.

133. For a recent assessment of impediments to the reception of the ideas of the Enlightenment in Spain, see Javier Fernández Sebastián, 'Toleration and Freedom of Expression in the Hispanic World between Enlightenment and Liberalism', *Past and Present*, 211 (2011), pp. 159–97.

134. Townsend, *Journey Through Spain*, vol. 2, p. 420.

135. Herr, *Eighteenth-Century Revolution in Spain*, pp. 357–8.

136. Soldevila i Zubiburu, *Història de Catalunya*, vol. 3, pp. 1,221–3, 1,227.

137. Cited in Carrera Pujal, *Historia política y económica*, vol. 3, p. 78; and see Fernández Díaz, *Cataluña y el absolutismo borbónico*, pp. 461–4.

138. Townsend, *Journey Through Spain*, vol. 2, p. 321.

139. Quoted in Albareda i Salvadó, *La guerra de sucesión*, p. 432.

140. See above, p. 125.

4 Nations and States, 1789–1860

1. See especially, for the summary account that follows, Lynch, *Bourbon Spain*, ch. 10. For events in Catalonia, see Soldevila i Zubiburu, *Història de Catalunya*, vol. 3, chs. 36 and 37.

2. Soldevila i Zubiburu, *Història de Catalunya*, vol. 3, p. 1,265.

3. Manuel Moreno Alonso, *El nacimiento de una nación. Sevilla, 1808–1810. La capital de una nación en guerra* (Madrid, 2010), pp. 264–8.

4. Antoni Moliner i Prada, *La Catalunya resistent a la dominació francesa (1808–1812). La Junta Superior de Catalunya* (Barcelona, 1989); Angel Smith, *The Origins of Catalan Nationalism, 1770–1898* (Basingstoke, 2014), p. 26.

5. Moliner i Prada, *La Catalunya resistent*, pp. 9–10; citation, p. 41.

6. Francisco Martínez Marina, *Teoría de las Cortes*, ed. J. A. Escudero (Oviedo, 2002); Ricardo García Cárcel, *El sueño de la nación indomable. Los mitos de la guerra de la independencia* (Madrid, 2007), pp. 236–41, for Martínez Marina and the constitutionalist thinking of the period.

7. Enric Jardí i Casany, *Els catalans de les corts de Cadis* (Barcelona, 1963), pp. 21–3.

8. Ibid., pp. 15 and 59.

9. José Álvarez Junco, *Dioses útiles. Naciones y nacionalismos* (Barcelona, 2016), pp. 158–9.

10. Josep M. Fradera, *Cultura nacional en una societat dividida* (Barcelona, 1992), ch. 1 ('El llenguatge del doble patriotisme').

11. Moliner i Prada, *La Catalunya resistent*, ch. 12, examines and quantifies the use of 'nation', *patria* and other key words in the Acts of the Junta Superior. For a more general discussion of the uses of *patria* and *nación* in this period, see Javier Varela Tortajada, 'Nación, patria y patriotismo en los orígenes del nacionalismo español', *Studia Historica-Historia Contemporánea*, 12 (1994), pp. 31–43, and, above all, Marfany, *Nacionalisme espanyol i catalanitat*.

12. Above, p. 131.

13. Antonio de Capmany, *Centinela contra franceses*, ed. Françoise Étienvre (London, 1988), pp. 133 and 125.

14. Cited in Juan J. Trías Vejarano, *Almirall y los orígenes del catalanismo* (Madrid, 1975), p. 31.

15. See Marfany, *Nacionalisme espanyol i catalanitat*, pp. 174, 427 and *passim*.

16. Cited in Jardí i Casany, *Els catalans de les corts*, p. 49.

17. Manuel Moreno Alonso, *La forja del liberalismo en España. Los amigos españoles de Lord Holland 1793–1840* (Madrid, 1997), pp. 18–19, 295–301.

18. Antonio Moliner i Prada (ed.), *La guerra de la independencia en España (1808–1815)* (Barcelona, 2007), p. 565.

19. Vilar, *La Catalogne*, vol. 1, p. 194; Raymond Carr, *Spain, 1808–1939* (Oxford, 1966), pp. 98–9.

20. Goldie, 'Divergence and Union', p. 222.

21. Sir Walter Scott, *Waverley* (rev. edn., Oxford 2015), p. 375 (ch. lxxii).

22. Cited from *The Scotsman*, 1 May 1907, by Michael Keating, *The Independence of Scotland: Self-Government and the Shifting Politics of Union. Understanding the Union* (Oxford Scholarship Online, 2009), p. 1.

23. Kidd, *Union and Unionisms*, p. 136.

24. Kidd, *Subverting Scotland's Past*, p. 271.
25. Murray G. H. Pittock, *The Invention of Scotland: The Stuart Myth and the Scottish Identity, 1638 to the Present* (London, 1991), p. 72. For Macpherson's place in attempts to reconstruct a Scottish Whig historiography, see Kidd, *Subverting Scotland's Past*, ch. 10.
26. Carr, *Spain*, pp. 111–15.
27. Michael Broers, *The Napoleonic Mediterranean* (London and New York, 2017), pp. 132–4. Chapter 4, which is devoted to Catalonia, is primarily concerned with French attempts to impose Napoleonic legal reforms on the province.
28. Soldevila i Zubiburu, *Història de Catalunya*, vol. 3, pp. 1,273–4; Broers, *Napoleonic Mediterranean*, pp. 178–82.
29. Smith, *Origins of Catalan Nationalism*, pp. 26–38; García Cárcel, *El sueño de la nación*, pp. 213–14; Lluís Puig i Oliver, *Tomàs Puig: catalanisme i afrancescament* (Barcelona, 1985). For a less favourable view of Puig and his importance see Marfany, *Nacionalisme espanyol i catalanitat*, pp. 148–9 and 381–2.
30. Ferguson, *Scotland: 1689 to the Present*, p. 252; Harris, *The Scottish People*, p. 51.
31. For the militia issue and its ramifications, see John Robertson, *The Scottish Enlightenment and the Militia Issue* (Edinburgh, 1985).
32. Harris, *The Scottish People*, pp. 166–7. I have drawn extensively on Harris's work, and also his chapter on 'Scottish-English Connections in British Radicalism in the 1790s', in Smout (ed.), *Anglo-Scottish Relations*, ch. 10, for my account of Scottish reactions to the events of this period.
33. For a sustained comparison of the Scottish and Irish Unions see Alvin Jackson, *The Two Unions: Ireland, Scotland and the Survival of the United Kingdom, 1707–2007* (Oxford, 2012). Also, for the Anglo-Irish union of 1801, S. J. Connolly, 'Varieties of Britishness: Ireland, Scotland and Wales in the Hanoverian State', in Grant and Stringer (eds.), *Uniting the Kingdom?*, ch. 11.
34. David Cannadine, *Aspects of Aristocracy: Grandeur and Decline in Modern Britain* (New Haven, CT, and London, 1994), pp. 30–1. For the 1711 Hamilton decision, see above, p. 102.
35. Joanna Innes, 'Legislating for Three Kingdoms: How the Westminster Parliament Legislated for England, Scotland and Ireland, 1707–1830', in Julian Hoppit (ed.), *Parliaments and Identities in Britain and Ireland, 1660–1850* (Manchester, 2003), ch. 2, for these figures and the account that follows. I am indebted to Professor Innes for drawing my attention to this volume and to her suggestive comparative survey.
36. Bob Harris, 'The Scots, the Westminster Parliament, and the British State in the Eighteenth Century', in Hoppit (ed.), *Parliaments and Identities*, ch. 7. Quotation, p. 30.
37. Harris, *The Scottish People*, p. 197, and 'Scottish-English Connections', pp. 191–2.
38. *La constitución de Cádiz (1812)*, ed. Antonio Fernández García (Madrid, 2002), título II, capítulo II.
39. Vicente Palacio Atard, *Los españoles de la ilustración* (Madrid, 1964), p. 94, cited by Pere Molas i Ribalta, *La burguesia mercantil en la España del antiguo régimen* (Madrid, 1985), p. 160.
40. See Arno Mayer, *The Persistence of the Old Regime: Europe to the Great War* (New York, 1981).
41. See Robert J. W. Evans, *Austria, Hungary, and the Habsburgs: Central Europe c. 1683–1867* (Oxford, 2006), esp. pp. 126–31.
42. Rafael Sánchez Mantero, *Los cien mil hijos de San Luis y las relaciones franco-españolas* (Seville, 1981).
43. Cited by Rafael Sánchez Mantero, *Fernando VII* (Madrid, 2001), p. 142.
44. Gordon Pentland, *The Spirit of the Union: Popular Politics in Scotland, 1815–1820* (London, 2011), p. 9.
45. Ibid., pp. 25–6.
46. Cited in ibid., p. 127. For the impact among reformers of Riego's mutiny, ibid., pp. 94–5.
47. Scott, *Waverley*, p. 272 (ch. lii).
48. Smith, *Origins of Catalan Nationalism*, pp. 99–100, 107.
49. Marfany, *Nacionalisme espanyol i catalanitat*, p. 492.

50. Josep M. Fradera, *Colonias para después de un imperio* (Barcelona, 2005), pp. 18–19.
51. Thomson, *A Distinctive Industrialization*, pp. 270–1; Carr, *Spain*, pp. 200–1.
52. Smith, *Origins of Catalan Nationalism*, pp. 102–4. For the 'agro-commercial oligarchy' and its emergence, see David Ringrose, *Madrid and the Spanish Economy, 1560–1850* (Berkeley and Los Angeles, CA, and London, 1983).
53. Benoît Pellistrandi, *Histoire de l'Espagne. Des guerres napoléoniennes à nos jours* (Paris, 2013), pp. 102–3.
54. Ringrose, *Spain, Europe*, pp. 211–16.
55. Jaime Vicens Vives and Jordi Nadal Oller, *Historia económica de España* (3rd edn., Barcelona, 1964), p. 565.
56. See Ringrose, *Spain, Europe*, pp. 249–55, and, for some suggestive points of comparison between the two cities, see Amelang, 'Comparing Cities'.
57. Fernández-Armesto, *Barcelona*, p. 197.
58. See above, p. 130; Hughes, *Barcelona*, pp. 257–60.
59. Thomson, *A Distinctive Industrialization*, pp. 307–9; Fernández-Armesto, *Barcelona*, p. 175; Pellistrandi, *Histoire de l'Espagne*, p. 230.
60. T. M. Devine, C. H. Lee and G. C. Peden (eds.), *The Transformation of Scotland: The Economy Since 1700* (Edinburgh, 2005), p. 40.
61. '. . . a comparison . . . that would merit further scrutiny', in Devine and Wormald (eds.), *Oxford Handbook of Modern Scottish History*, p. 405.
62. William W. Knox, *Industrial Nation: Work, Culture and Society in Scotland, 1800–Present* (Edinburgh, 1999), p. 34.
63. Devine, Lee and Peden (eds.), *Transformation of Scotland*, ch. 3.
64. Knox, *Industrial Nation*, p. 36.
65. Devine and Jackson (eds.), *Glasgow*, vol. 1, p. 172.
66. Jaime Vicens Vives and Montserrat Llorens, *Industrials i polítics del segle XIX* (Barcelona, 2010, 1st edn., 1958), pp. 21–9; Devine, Lee and Peden (eds.), *Transformation of Scotland*, p. 51.
67. Devine and Jackson (eds.), *Glasgow*, vol. 1, p. 161, and see above, pp. 128–9.
68. Smith, *Origins of Catalan Nationalism*, pp. 51–2; Vicens Vives and Llorens, *Industrials*, pp. 137–8.
69. Smith, *Origins of Catalan Nationalism*, p. 67; Hughes, *Barcelona*, pp. 295–8.
70. Smith, *Origins of Catalan Nationalism*, p. 207.
71. Jaime Torras Elías, *Liberalismo y rebeldía campesina, 1820–1823* (Barcelona, 1976), p. 43. This study, while not confined to Catalonia, is particularly strong on the insurrection in the Catalan countryside.
72. Torras Elías, *Liberalismo y rebeldía*, p. 83.
73. Sánchez Mantero, *Fernando VII*, pp. 197–8.
74. Jordi Canal, *Historia mínima de Cataluña* (Madrid, 2015), pp. 130–1.
75. Vicens Vives and Llorens, *Industrials*, pp. 219–25, and Carr, *Spain*, p. 150, for España's repressive regime.
76. Smith, *Origins of Catalan Nationalism*, pp. 39–40.
77. Trías Vejarano, *Almirall*, pp. 66–8.
78. Canal, *Historia mínima de Cataluña*, pp. 131–3; Hughes, *Barcelona*, pp. 216–18.
79. Vicens Vives and Llorens, *Industrials*, pp. 231–3, 243–4.
80. Juan Pablo Fusi, *Historia mínima de España* (Madrid, 2012), pp. 191–2.
81. Canal, *Historia mínima de Cataluña*, pp. 132–3; Fontana, *La formació d'una identitat*, pp. 272–4. For the attack on the Ciutadella see above, pp. 94–5.
82. Pellistrandi, *Histoire de l'Espagne*, p. 110; Fusi, *Historia mínima de España*, p. 194.
83. Fusi, *Historia mínima de España*, pp. 195–9.
84. Percentages as given in Pellistrandi, *Histoire de l'Espagne*, p. 123.
85. Ferguson, *Scotland: 1689 to the Present*, p. 290.
86. Devine, Lee and Peden (eds.), *Transformation of Scotland*, pp. 143–4.
87. See Knox, *Industrial Nation*, pp. 63–78; Devine, *The Scottish Nation*, pp. 276–80.
88. Knox, *Industrial Nation*, pp. 73–4.
89. Vicens Vives and Llorens, *Industrials*, pp. 156–9, for workers' associations.

90. Ibid., pp. 159–60; Hughes, *Barcelona*, pp. 277–8. For the War of the *Matiners* see Fontana, Laformació d'una identitat, pp. 277–8.

91. For Scotland's virtual self-government see Graeme Morton, *Unionist Nationalism: Governing Urban Scotland 1830–1860* (East Linton, 1999), especially pp. 11–13 and 35–7.

92. For attacks on 'centralization' and the rather imprecise demands for 'decentralization' that accompanied them, see Marfany, *Nacionalisme espanyol i catalanitat*, pp. 643–50.

93. 'Unionist nationalism' is the term used by Graeme Morton in *Unionist Nationalism*. Colin Kidd has adopted the term 'banal unionism' to describe a unionism 'so dominant that it does not need to be assertive'. Kidd, *Union and Unionisms*, pp. 25ff.

94. Colley, *Britons*, p. 209.

95. José Álvarez Junco, *Mater Dolorosa. La idea de España en el siglo XIX* (Madrid, 2001), pp. 552–5; Smith, *Origins of Catalan Nationalism*, p. 49.

96. Carr, *Spain*, pp. 235–6.

97. Fusi, *Historia mínima de España*, pp. 196–7; Smith, *Origins of Catalan Nationalism*, pp. 41–2, 46–8.

98. For the current debate among historians over the relative strength or weakness of the nineteenth-century Spanish state, see especially Álvarez Junco, *Mater Dolorosa*, pp. 533–45; Smith, *Origins of Catalan Nationalism*, pp. 46–50.

99. Jackson, *The Two Unions*, pp. 172–4.

100. Pellistrandi, *Histoire de l'Espagne*, p. 118.

101. Trías Vejarano, *Almirall*, pp. 59–63, for the political weakness of the Catalan bourgeoisie.

102. Borja de Riquer i Permanyer, 'Sobre el lugar de los nacionalismos-regionalismos en la historia contemporánea española', *História Social*, 7 (1990), pp. 104–26, at p. 119.

103. García Cárcel, *La herencia del pasado*, p. 195. See also Álvarez Junco, *Mater Dolorosa*, ch. 4, for the construction of the Spanish national narrative.

104. Álvarez Junco, *Mater Dolorosa*, pp. 144–9; García Cárcel, *La herencia del pasado*, pp. 542–62.

105. Álvarez Junco, *Mater Dolorosa*, p. 219.

106. Ferran Toledano González, 'La guerra de la Independencia como mito fundamental de la memoria y de la historia nacional española', in Moliner i Prada (ed.), *La guerra de la independencia*, ch. 15. For Barcelona as the publishing centre for translations of Scott's works, and their Spanish and Catalan impact, see Edgar Allison Peers, 'Studies in the Influence of Sir Walter Scott in Spain', *Revue Hispanique*, 68 (1926), pp. 1–160. For Bofarull, see Smith, *Origins of Catalan Nationalism*, pp. 53–4.

107. Above, pp. 24 and 25. For Thomas Innes, see Trevor-Roper, *The Invention of Scotland*, pp. 64–71.

108. Kidd, *Union and Unionisms*, pp. 152–3.

109. Sir Walter Scott in his *Tales of a Grandfather* (1827–30) talks of thirteenth-century Scots rising up to 'recover the liberty and independence of their country' (p. 48), presumably reflecting the new and widespread currency that the American Declaration of Independence gave to the word 'independence' as meaning a national struggle for liberty. William Burns, in *The Scottish War of Independence* (2 vols., Glasgow, 1874), may have been the first author to choose it for a book title, and Evan M. Barron, in *The Scottish War of Independence: A Critical Study* (London, 1914), follows suit. It seems that 'Wars of Independence' became the commonly used term only in the course of the twentieth century, but the question of nomenclature deserves closer consideration. I am grateful to Professor Dauvit Broun for his advice and for the references above.

110. For Scottish historical writing in this period in relation to national identity, see especially, in addition to his *Union and Unionisms*, ch. 4, Colin Kidd's *Subverting Scotland's Past*, where he writes (p. 267) of a 'historical failure of nerve' in Scottish culture in the age of Walter Scott. For the question of the preservation of national identity from a different angle, see Graeme Morton, 'What If? The Significance of Scotland's Messy Nationalism', in Broun, Finlay and Lynch (eds.), *Image and Identity*, ch. 8.

111. See Marinell Ash, *The Strange Death of Scottish History* (Edinburgh, 1980), ch. 1 ('The Historical World of Walter Scott').
112. Kidd, *Union and Unionisms*, pp. 153–4, 198–210; I. G. C. Hutchison, 'Anglo-Scottish Political Relations in the Nineteenth Century, c.1815–1914', in Smout (ed.), *Anglo-Scottish Relations*, ch. 13 at pp. 252–3.
113. Ferguson, *Scotland: 1689 to the Present*, pp. 306–15.
114. I am grateful to Josep M.ª Fradera for his observations to this effect.
115. Jacobson, *Catalonia's Advocates*, pp. 135–45.
116. See ibid., ch. 6 ('The Nationalist Profession'), and Smith, *Origins of Catalan Nationalism*, pp. 189–93.
117. Pittock, *Invention of Scotland*, ch. 4.
118. Smith, *Origins of Catalan Nationalism*, pp. 79–80; Ewen A. Cameron, 'Embracing the Past: The Highlands in Nineteenth-Century Scotland', in Broun, Finlay and Lynch (eds.), *Image and Identity*, ch. 10.
119. Above, p. 106.
120. Withers, *Gaelic Scotland*, p. 59; Kidd, *Union and Unionisms*, pp. 154–7.
121. An account, now dated, of the origins of the *Renaixença* in Soldevila i Zubiburu, *Història de Catalunya*, vol. 3, Epilogue. For more recent discussions of the revival of Catalan as a literary language see Joan-Lluís Marfany, '"Minority" Languages and Literary Revivals', *Past and Present*, 184 (2004), pp. 137–67, and his *La llengua maltractada*, especially pp. 479–87; Fradera, *Cultura nacional*, pp. 212–33; Fontana, *La formació d'una identitat*, pp. 305–9; Smith, *Origins of Catalan Nationalism*, pp. 72–3.
122. For disglossia in Catalonia see Marfany's *La llengua maltractada*. Also Smith, *Origins of Catalan Nationalism*, pp. 88–90.
123. Fradera, *Passat i identitat*, pp. 20–1.
124. Smith, *Origins of Catalan Nationalism*, pp. 78 and 238, n. 34.
125. Ringrose, *Madrid*, p. 324.
126. Carr, *Spain*, pp. 162–4, for the political views of the two factions.
127. Cited by Josep M. Fradera, *Jaume Balmes. Els fonaments d'una política catòlica* (Vic, 1996), p. 181. Fradera's book provides a subtle assessment of Balmes's thought, which is notorious for its apparent internal contradictions. See also Daniel Fernández Cañueto, *La iglesia católica y la nacionalización de Cataluña* (Lleida, 2016), pp. 79–82.
128. For the conservative version of the history of Spain, see Álvarez Junco, *Mater Dolorosa*, pp. 405–31.
129. See above, pp. 162–3.
130. Ash, *Strange Death of Scottish History*, p. 149. Chairs of universal history were established in Edinburgh and St Andrews in the first half of the eighteenth century, and lectures might include an occasional illustration from the history of Scotland. Chairs of specifically Scottish history were founded in Edinburgh in 1901 and Glasgow in 1913. See Bruce P. Lenman, 'The Teaching of Scottish History in the Scottish Universities', *Scottish Historical Review*, 52 (1973), pp. 165–90.
131. *Hazañas y recuerdos de los catalanes*. See Fradera, *Cultura nacional*, pp. 83–4.
132. *Historia de Cataluña y de la Corona de Aragón*. For a helpful summary of the movement for the writing of Catalan patriotic history in this period, see Smith, *Origins of Catalan Nationalism*, pp. 73–9.
133. Cited in Trías Vejarano, *Almirall*, p. 115.
134. Smith, *Origins of Catalan Nationalism*, pp. 77–8.
135. Ibid., p. 82; Hughes, *Barcelona*, pp. 287–8; Álvarez Junco, *Mater Dolorosa*, pp. 652–3.
136. Morton, 'What If?', ch. 8, and ch. 4 of his *Unionist Nationalism* ('Governing Civil Society').
137. Marfany, *Nacionalisme espanyol i catalanitat*, pp. 646–9. The author of the articles was Estanislau Reynals i Rabassa.
138. *Selected Letters of Robert Louis Stevenson*, ed. Ernest Mehew (New Haven, CT, and London, 1997), pp. 37–8, letter of 28/29 July 1873.

5 The Call for Home Rule, 1860–1975

1. Cited in H. J. Hanham, *Scottish Nationalism* (London, 1969), p. 79.
2. See Angel Smith, 'Nationalisms Against the Spanish State, 1808–1923: Cuba, Catalonia and the Basque Country', in Paul Garner and Angel Smith (eds.), *Nationalism and Transnationalism in Spain and Latin America, 1808–1923* (Cardiff, 2017), pp. 117–53.
3. Josep M. Fradera, *La pàtria dels catalans. Historia, política, cultura* (Barcelona, 2009), p. 230.
4. Borja de Riquer i Permanyer, *Identitats contemporànies: Catalunya i Espanya* (Vic, 2000), pp. 108–9; Josep R. Llobera, *Foundations of National Identity: From Catalonia to Europe* (New York and Oxford, 2004), p. 151; Jackson, *The Two Unions*, pp. 140–1 (prime ministers of Scottish origin: William Gladstone, Lord Rosebery, Arthur Balfour, Henry Campbell-Bannerman, Andrew Bonar Law, Ramsay MacDonald).
5. Marfany, *Nacionalisme espanyol i catalanitat*, p. 492.
6. For Pi's career and ideas see especially A. M. Hennessy, *The Federal Republic in Spain: Pi y Margall and the Federal Republican Movement 1868–74* (Oxford, 1962). For a brief survey of republicanism and federalism in Catalonia, see pp. 63–72.
7. See Josep M. Fradera, *La nación imperial, 1750–1918* (2 vols., Barcelona, 2013), vol. 1, pp. 555–74.
8. Smith, 'Nationalisms Against the Spanish State', p. 142; and see Raphael Minder, *The Struggle for Catalonia: Rebel Politics in Spain* (London, 2017), pp. 44 and 262–5 for current disputes over the flying of the *estelada*.
9. Josep M. Batista i Roca, 'Martí d'Eixalà i la introducció de la filosofia escocesa a Catalunya', *Hispanic Studies in Honour of I. González Llubera*, ed. Frank Pierce (Oxford, 1959), pp. 41–60.
10. Francisco Pi y Margall, *Las nacionalidades*, ed. Jordi Solé Tura (Madrid, 1986). Citations from pp. 9, 18, 257–8, 276–7. Also Hennessy, *Federal Republic*, appendix ('The Political Ideas of Pi y Margall').
11. 'Pacificus' [Frederick Scott Oliver], *Federalism and Home Rule* (London, 1910), p. liii. See also Jackson, *The Two Unions*, p. 232; Kidd, *Union and Unionisms*, pp. 111–12.
12. Pi y Margall, *Las nacionalidades*, p. 88.
13. For Almirall and his ideas see, in addition to Trías Vejarano, *Almirall*, Carr, *Spain*, pp. 543–5; Smith, *Origins of Catalan Nationalism*, pp. 153–60; Vicens Vives and Llorens, *Industrials*, pp. 292–3; Fontana, *La formació d'una identitat*, pp. 311–13.
14. Cited in Fradera, *La pàtria dels catalans*, pp. 230–1.
15. See above, p. 171.
16. Smith, *Origins of Catalan Nationalism*, p. 165. For what follows I have made extensive use of Smith's book, which seeks to untangle the complex strands of the Catalanist movement between 1885 and the end of the century.
17. Accounts of the exhibition in Ramón Grau, Mariana López and Pere Anguera (eds.), *Exposició universal de Barcelona. Llibre del centenari* (Barcelona, 1988); Smith, *Origins of Catalan Nationalism*, pp. 140–5; Hughes, *Barcelona*, pp. 362–73.
18. As suggested by Smith, *Origins of Catalan Nationalism*, pp. 169–70.
19. Carr, *Spain*, pp. 546–7.
20. For summary surveys of Scottish grievances and the Home Rule question, see Jackson, *The Two Unions*, ch. 7; Ferguson, *Scotland: 1689 to the Present*, pp. 323–9; Devine, *The Scottish Nation*, ch. 13.
21. Cited by Morton, *Unionist Nationalism*, p. 139.
22. Cited by Ferguson, *Scotland: 1689 to the present*, p. 321.
23. Hutchison, 'Anglo-Scottish Political Relations', pp. 253–4.
24. Devine and Wormald (eds.), *Oxford Handbook of Modern Scottish History*, pp. 486–7.
25. For relations between the Liberal Unionists and the Conservative Party, see Catriona Burness, '*Strange Associations': The Irish Question and the Making of Scottish Unionism, 1886–1918* (East Linton, 2003).
26. Burness, '*Strange Associations*', pp. 206–7; Devine, *The Scottish Nation*, p. 308; Kidd, *Union and Unionisms*, pp. 283–4, for the programme of the Young Scots.

27. Hutchison, 'Anglo-Scottish Political Relations', pp. 264–5.
28. The title of 'Athens of the North' was first given to Edinburgh by the poet Hugh William Williams in the 1820s. See Devine, *The Scottish Nation*, p. 329.
29. Burness, 'Strange Associations', pp. 4–5.
30. Hughes, *Barcelona*, p. 364.
31. Enric Ucelay Da Cal, *La Catalunya populista. Imatge, cultura i política en l'etapa republicana, 1931–1939* (Barcelona, 1982), p. 22. David Ringrose, *Spain, Europe*, pp. 283–5, notes the successes as well as the failures of Spanish agriculture in the nineteenth and early twentieth centuries. See also Carr, *Spain*, pp. 400–5.
32. Vicens Vives and Llorens, *Industrials*, pp. 180–1; Carr, *Spain*, pp. 390–4.
33. Export statistics in Borja de Riquer i Permanyer, *Lliga regionalista: la burgesia catalana i el nacionalisme, 1898–1904* (Barcelona, 1977), p. 60.
34. See H. Ramsden, *The 1898 Movement in Spain* (Manchester, 1974); and for summary accounts of a much studied movement, Álvarez Junco, *Mater Dolorosa*, pp. 586–7, and Pellistrandi, *Histoire de l'Espagne*, pp. 188–206.
35. Álvarez Junco, *Mater Dolorosa*, p. 586.
36. For what follows see Javier Moreno-Luzón, 'Performing Monarchy and Spanish Nationalism, 1902–1913', in Milinda Banerjee, Charlotte Backerra and Cathleen Sarti (eds.), *Transnational Histories of the 'Royal Nation'* (Cham, Switzerland, 2017), ch. 10.
37. For the British example see David Cannadine, 'The Context, Performance and Meaning of Ritual: The British Monarchy and the "Invention of Tradition", c. 1820–1977', in Eric Hobsbawm and Terence Ranger (eds.), *The Invention of Tradition* (Cambridge, 1983) ch. 4.
38. The *Compendi* is included in Enric Prat de la Riba, *La nacionalitat catalana*, ed. Jordi Casassas i Ymbert (Barcelona, 1993). Citation from p. 83.
39. Enric Ucelay Da Cal, *El imperialismo catalán. Prat de la Riba, D'Ors y la conquista moral de España* (Barcelona, 2003), p. 73; Llobera, *Foundations of National Identity*, p. 79.
40. See especially Canal, *Historia mínima de Cataluña*, pp. 151–3.
41. For *modernisme* and its impact, see Ucelay Da Cal, *La Catalunya populista*, pp. 33–6 and *El imperialismo catalán*, pp. 155 and 160; Hughes, *Barcelona*, pp. 391–411, and Mireia Freixa, 'El protomodernisme en la arquitectura y las artes plásticas', in Grau, López and Anguera (eds.), *Exposició universal*, pp. 490–7.
42. For the complex relationship of state and nation in later nineteenth- and twentieth-century Spain, see Borja de Riquer i Permanyer, 'Aproximación al nacionalismo español contemporáneo', *Studia Histórica*, 12 (1994), pp. 11–29.
43. Prat de la Riba, *La nacionalitat catalana*, pp. 68 and 71. For the idea of empire as central to Prat's thinking, see Ucelay Da Cal, *El imperialismo catalán*.
44. Prat de la Riba, *La nacionalitat catalana*, p. 33.
45. Riquer i Permanyer, *Lliga regionalista*, is fundamental for the political and economic context from which the Lliga emerged.
46. Ucelay Da Cal, *La Catalunya populista*, p. 47.
47. Fontana, *La formació d'una identitat*, p. 322.
48. For anarchism, unrest and strikes in turn-of-the-century Barcelona, see Angel Smith, *Anarchism, Revolution and Reaction: Catalan Labour and the Crisis of the Spanish State, 1898–1923* (New York and Oxford, 2007), ch. 4. For the rise of Lerroux see Joaquín Romero Maura, *La rosa de fuego: la política de los obreros barceloneses entre el desastre colonial y la semana trágica, 1899–1903* (Barcelona, 1975), ch. 2.
49. Joan Connelly Ullman, *The Tragic Week: A Study of Anticlericalism in Spain, 1875–1912* (Cambridge, MA, 1968), pp. 51–2.
50. Carr, *Spain*, p. 550; Riquer i Permanyer, *Identitats contemporànies*, pp. 181–212; María Jesús González Hernández, *El universo conservador de Antonio Maura. Biografía y proyecto de Estado* (Madrid, 1997), pp. 150–9, and pp. 288–300 for the law on local administration and the convergence of interests between Maura and Cambó.
51. Ullman, *The Tragic Week*, pp. 326–7.
52. Ullman, *The Tragic Week*, provides a day-by-day narrative of events. For brief accounts see Hughes, *Barcelona*, pp. 522–3; Carr, *Spain*, pp. 483–5.

53. For the Great War and its impact on Catalan politics and life, see Angel Smith, 'Cataluña y la gran guerra: de la reforma democrática al conflicto social', *Hispania Nova. Revista de Historia Contemporánea*, 15 (2017), pp. 472–99.

54. Enric Ucelay Da Cal, 'La Diputació y la Mancomunitat: 1914–1923', in Borja de Riquer i Permanyer (ed.), *Historia de la Diputació de Barcelona*, vol. 2 (Barcelona, 1987), pp. 36–177, at pp. 38–9; Canal, *Historia mínima de Cataluña*, pp. 164–6.

55. Cited by Romero Maura, *La rosa de fuego*, p. 41.

56. Carr, *Spain*, pp. 445–55; Canal, *Historia mínima de Cataluña*, p. 164 and pp. 169–71.

57. Carr, *Spain*, pp. 502–3; Smith, 'Cataluña y la gran guerra', pp. 482–4.

58. Smith, 'Cataluña y la gran guerra', p. 496.

59. Fusi, *Historia mínima de España*, pp. 214–15; Carr, *Spain*, pp. 497–508.

60. For the demands of minorities and the upsurge of nationalism as a European phenomenon in the post-war era, see Mark Mazower, *Dark Continent: Europe's Twentieth Century* (London, 1998), ch. 2.

61. For the Fourteen Points and their interaction with nationalist movements in the Austro-Hungarian Empire, see Robert Gerwarth, *The Vanquished: Why the First World War Failed to End, 1917–1923* (London, 2016), pp. 179–81. There are some obvious parallels between the Spanish and Austro-Hungarian situations, with similar tensions between demands for autonomy within a more federal structure and movements for independence.

62. Cited by Edgar Allison Peers, *Catalonia Infelix* (London, 1937), p. 168.

63. Riquer i Permanyer, *Identitats contemporànies*, p. 197.

64. For the Canadenca and its aftermath, see Smith, *Anarchism, Revolution*, pp. 290ff; Ucelay Da Cal, *La Catalunya populista*, pp. 70–2.

65. Carr, *Spain*, pp. 511–12; Fontana, *La formació d'una identitat*, pp. 327–8.

66. Pellistrandi, *Histoire de l'Espagne*, pp. 274–5; Mazower, *Dark Continent*, p. 18.

67. Mazower, *Dark Continent*, pp. 13–14.

68. The mutual exhaustion of the two sides is a central theme of Ucelay Da Cal, *La Catalunya populista*. See especially p. 341 for a succinct summary.

69. Riquer i Permanyer, *Identitats contemporànies*, pp. 198–9; Fusi, *Historia mínima de España*, pp. 214–15; Pellistrandi, *Histoire de l'Espagne*, pp. 286–7.

70. Ferguson, *Scotland: 1689 to the Present*, pp. 352–3.

71. Jackson, *The Two Unions*, pp. 167–8; T. M. Devine, *Independence or Union: Scotland's Past and Scotland's Present* (London, 2016), pp. 100–1, 102–3; and, for Scotland and the Great War, see Devine and Wormald (eds.), *Oxford Handbook of Modern Scottish History*, ch. 29.

72. For valuable suggestions of possible reasons for the contrast between the two relationships, see Jackson, *The Two Unions*.

73. Ferguson, *Scotland: 1689 to the Present*, pp. 355–6; Devine, *The Scottish Nation*, pp. 309–12.

74. For statistics on the immigrant population and observations on its characteristics, see Devine and Wormald (eds.), *Oxford Handbook of Modern Scottish History*, pp. 491–50.

75. Devine, *The Scottish Nation*, pp. 491–507, for the immigrants and politics.

76. Ibid., pp. 313–14.

77. Richard J. Finlay, *A Partnership for Good? Scottish Politics and the Union Since 1880* (Edinburgh, 1997), pp. 70–6; Kidd, *Union and Unionisms*, pp. 284–6.

78. Jackson, *The Two Unions*, pp. 246–53; Devine, *The Scottish Nation*, pp. 315–16; Thomas M. Devine (ed.), *Scotland and the Union, 1707–2007* (Edinburgh, 2008), pp. 123–9.

79. See Finlay, *A Partnership for Good?*, pp. 102–13, for Unionist attitudes and government responses in the 1930s. Also Finlay, 'The Interwar Crisis', in Devine and Wormald (eds.), *Oxford Handbook of Modern Scottish History*, ch. 30.

80. Cited in Finlay, *A Partnership for Good?*, p. 104.

81. Devine, *Independence or Union*, p. 106.

82. Devine, *The Scottish Nation*, pp. 320–1; Devine and Wormald (eds.), *Oxford Handbook of Modern Scottish History*, p. 578.

83. Devine and Wormald (eds.), *Oxford Handbook of Modern Scottish History*, pp. 580–2.

84. Pellistrandi, *Histoire de l'Espagne*, pp. 299–301; Fernández-Armesto, *Barcelona*, pp. 219–20.
85. See Riquer i Permanyer, 'Aproximación', pp. 21–2, for Spanish 'ultranationalism' and the ideological currents that went into its making.
86. Álvarez Junco, *Mater Dolorosa*, pp. 601–3; Riquer i Permanyer, *Identitats contempòranies*, p. 14.
87. See above, p. 175.
88. Carolyn P. Boyd, *Historia Patria: Politics, History and National Identity in Spain, 1875–1975* (Princeton, NJ, 1997), p. 171.
89. Cited by Álvarez Junco, *Dioses útiles*, p. 178, on whose succinct account, pp. 174–82, of Primo de Rivera's and other 'regenerationist' narratives I have drawn here.
90. 'Construir España', cited by Álvarez Junco, *Dioses útiles*, pp. 174–5.
91. Pellistrandi, *Histoire de l'Espagne*, pp. 300–1.
92. Riquer i Permanyer, 'Aproximación', p. 20.
93. Ucelay Da Cal, *La Catalunya populista*, ch. 3, and summary, p. 342; Carr, *Spain*, p. 420.
94. For the account that follows I have drawn in particular on Canal, *Historia mínima de Cataluña*, pp. 178–81, and Fontana, *La formació d'una identitat*, pp. 334–9.
95. Citation in Canal, *Historia mínima de Cataluña*, p. 179.
96. Pellistrandi, *Histoire de l'Espagne*, p. 329.
97. Gabriel Jackson, *The Spanish Republic and the Civil War 1931–1939* (Princeton, NJ, 1965), pp. 73–7.
98. Pellistrandi, *Histoire de l'Espagne*, pp. 332–4.
99. Fusi, *Historia mínima de España*, pp. 219–20.
100. Jackson, *The Spanish Republic*, p. 150.
101. Ibid., pp. 151–2; Carr, *Spain*, pp. 633–4; Canal, *Historia mínima de Cataluña*, pp. 186–9; Gerald Brenan, *The Spanish Labyrinth* (2nd edn., Cambridge, 1950), pp. 282–4.
102. Canal, *Historia mínima de Cataluña*, pp. 190–1.
103. Ibid., pp. 200, 204.
104. George Orwell, *Homage to Catalonia* (1938; new edn., London, 1951), p. 2.
105. Peers, *Catalonia Infelix*, pp. 268–9; Canal, *Historia mínima de Catalunya*, p. 209.
106. Ucelay Da Cal, *La Catalunya populista*, pp. 332–40; Negrín quotation, p. 333.
107. Canal, *Historia mínima de Cataluña*, p. 211.
108. Paul Preston, *The Spanish Holocaust: Inquisition and Extermination in Twentieth-Century Spain* (New York and London, 2012), p. 493.
109. Fontana, *La formació d'una identitat*, pp. 416–17.
110. Cited by Preston, *Spanish Holocaust*, pp. 466–7.
111. For an excellent brief account of Franco's personalized style of government and the essential characteristics of his dictatorship, see Borja de Riquer i Permanyer, 'La dictadura de Franco' (vol. 9 of Josep Fontana and Ramón Villares, eds., *Historia de España*, Barcelona and Madrid, 2010), ch. 1. See also Paul Preston, *Franco: A Biography* (London, 1993).
112. Canal, *Historia mínima de Cataluña*, pp. 219–20, 232–3.
113. Fusi, *Historia mínima de España*, p. 235; Canal, *Historia mínima de Cataluña*, p. 244. Whether or not Escarré underwent a genuine change of heart or was simply an opportunist remains a subject of dispute. See Minder, *Struggle for Catalonia*, pp. 62–3.
114. Henry Kamen, *España y Cataluña. Historia de una pasión* (Madrid, 2014), p. 279.
115. For economic and social change in Catalonia under Franco, see Fontana, *La formació d'una identitat*, pp. 381–6; Canal, *Historia mínima de Cataluña*, pp. 224–7; Gabriel Tortella Casares, *Cataluña en España. Historia y mito* (Madrid, 2016), p. 249.
116. Tortella Casares, *Cataluña en España*, pp. 252–3.
117. Josep M. Muñoz i Lloret, *Jaume Vicens i Vives. Una biografia intel·lectual* (Barcelona, 1997), p. 389.
118. Devine, *The Scottish Nation*, p. 556.
119. Ferguson, *Scotland: 1689 to the Present*, pp. 383–4; Jackson, *The Two Unions*, pp. 270–4; Devine, *The Scottish Nation*, pp. 551–4.
120. Cited by Finlay, *A Partnership for Good?*, p. 119.

121. Ferguson, *Scotland: 1689 to the Present*, pp. 388–90; Devine, *The Scottish Nation*, pp. 565–7.
122. Ewen A. Cameron, 'The Politics of Union in an Age of Unionism', in Devine (ed.), *Scotland and the Union*, pp. 135–6.
123. Devine, *The Scottish Nation*, pp. 570–1.
124. Kidd, *Union and Unionisms*, pp. 260–1.
125. Devine, *The Scottish Nation*, pp. 579–80.
126. Finlay, *A Partnership for Good?*, pp. 148–54.

6 Breaking Away? 1975–2017

1. See above, p. 224.
2. See the editor's foreword to Trevor-Roper, *The Invention of Scotland*, p. xi, and Tam Dalyell, *The Question of Scotland: Devolution and After* (Edinburgh, 2016).
3. Jackson, *The Two Unions*, pp. 277–8; Devine, *Independence or Union*, p. 132.
4. For the Cunningham amendment and the background to it, see Dalyell, *The Question of Scotland*, ch. 8.
5. Devine, *Independence or Union*, pp. 131–4, for these events.
6. See above, pp. 212–13.
7. For a good summary of the background to the 1978 Constitution and the outcome of the deliberations, see Pellistrandi, *Histoire de l'Espagne*, pp. 494–504.
8. See above, pp. 216 and 218. For an account of the delicate negotiations between Suárez and Tarradellas, see Juan Francisco Fuentes Aragonés, *Adolfo Suárez. Biografía política* (Barcelona, 2011), pp. 216–19.
9. *Constitución española, aprobada por las Cortes el 31 de octubre de 1978*, título preliminar.
10. Fusi, *Historia mínima de España*, p. 239.
11. 'Nation of nations' was a term that was in the air when the constitution was under discussion and may first have been coined by the Valencian historian José María Jover in an article published in 1950 on seventeenth-century Spanish concepts of monarchy and nation (José María Jover Zamora, 'Sobre los conceptos de monarquía y nación en el pensamiento político español del XVII', *Cuadernos de Historia de España*, 13, Buenos Aires, 1950, pp. 101–50). See Antonio Papell, 'Nación de naciones', *e-SLegal History Review*, 24 (January, 2017). The term has gained a wider currency in recent years. I am grateful to Xavier Gil Pujol for looking into its origins for me, and bringing Papell's article to my attention.
12. See above, p. 193. Previously, in a speech given in 1890, he had said: 'Today there are many who see clearly that Spain is not a nation but a State', *La nacionalitat catalana*, p. 31. See also Tortella Casares, *Cataluña en España*, pp. 298–9.
13. Canal, *Historia mínima de Cataluña*, pp. 262–5, for voting figures and the outcome.
14. Devine, *The Scottish Nation*, pp. 585–6.
15. Mrs Thatcher's 'catastrophic error', Dalyell, *The Question of Scotland*, p. 110. For the poll tax see Jackson, *The Two Unions*, pp. 265–8; Richard J. Finlay, *Modern Scotland 1914–2000* (London, 2004), pp. 165–6; Devine, *Independence or Union*, pp. 179–81.
16. Dalyell, *The Question of Scotland*, p. 118.
17. For the divergence of the 1980s and its consequences, see Finlay, *Modern Scotland*, ch. 10, and Ewen A. Cameron, *Impaled upon a Thistle: Scotland since 1880* (Edinburgh, 2010), p. 354.
18. Devine, *Independence or Union*, pp. 191–2.
19. For an unsympathetic assessment of Dewar and his activities in support of devolution, see Dalyell, *The Question of Scotland*, pp. 101–4.
20. For the course of events and their analysis see Devine, *Independence or Union*, pp. 193–200.
21. For constituency voting figures, see Devine, *Independence or Union*, p. 208.
22. Tortella Casares, *Cataluña en España*, pp. 305–6.
23. See Devine, *Independence or Union*, pp. 200–12, for the results of the referendum and the 1999 election. For the Judicial Committee of the Privy Council, see Cameron, *Impaled upon a Thistle*, p. 354.

24. Tortella Casares, *Cataluña en España*, p. 305.
25. Ferro, *El dret públic català*, p. 442.
26. The argument for seventeenth-century Scotland's statehood was put forward in particular by Julian Goodare in *State and Society in Early Modern Scotland* (Oxford, 1999) and *The Government of Scotland, 1560–1625* (Oxford, 2004). For a summary of the points at issue see Laura M. Stewart, 'The Rise of the State?', in Devine and Wormald (eds.), *Oxford Handbook of Modern Scottish History*, ch. 10.
27. Canal, *Historia mínima de Cataluña*, pp. 268 and 275.
28. For critical assessments see Tortella Casares, *Cataluña en España*, pp. 306–8, and Canal, *Historia mínima de Cataluña*, p. 281.
29. Fontana, *La formació d'una identitat*, p. 420.
30. See Marfany, *La llengua maltractada*, p. 476.
31. Canal, *Historia mínima de Cataluña*, p. 265; Tortella Casares, *Cataluña en España*, p. 315.
32. Finlay, *Modern Scotland*, p. 381; for statistics and quotation, McCrone, *Understanding Scotland*, p. 74.
33. Devine (ed.), *Scotland and the Union*, pp. 185–6.
34. Devine, *Independence or Union*, pp. 210–12.
35. Ibid., pp. 224–6.
36. Ibid., p. 217.
37. See the analysis of the election results by John Curtice in Devine (ed.), *Scotland and the Union*, pp. 224–5.
38. Tom Nairn, *The Break-Up of Britain: Crisis and Neo-Nationalism* (3rd edn., Altona, Victoria, Australia, 2003), p. 180.
39. Tortella Casares, *Cataluña en España*, p. 306.
40. Canal, *Historia mínima de Cataluña*, pp. 281–2; Fontana, *La formació d'una identitat*, p. 421.
41. For an account of the history of the statute and its modifications, see Carsten Humlebæck, *Spain: Inventing the Nation* (London, 2015), pp. 187–8. See also Canal, *Historia mínima de Cataluña*, pp. 283–4; Fusi, *Historia mínima de España*, p. 264; Fontana, *La formació d'una identitat*, pp. 421–2. Under the 1978 Constitution an Organic law requires an absolute majority in the Congress of Deputies, and not simply a majority of those voting. Statutes of autonomy fall under this rubric.
42. I am indebted to Professor Josep M.ª Castellà Andreu for the clarification of some of these points.
43. Humlebæck, *Spain: Inventing the Nation*, pp. 189–91.
44. Devine, *Independence or Union*, pp. 219–21.
45. Michael Keating (ed.), *Debating Scotland: Issues of Independence and Union in the 2014 Referendum* (Oxford, 2017), p. 9.
46. William Chislett, *A New Course for Spain: Beyond the Crisis* (Madrid, 2016), p. 82.
47. Humlebæck, *Spain: Inventing the Nation*, p. 195, for this and what follows.
48. Minder, *Struggle for Catalonia*, p. 12. I am grateful to Professor Castellà Andreu for information and advice on the course of events in 2012 and their long-term implications.
49. For an extensive examination of the manipulation of geography, and especially of history, in Catalan manuals for use in the schools, see Tortella Casares, *Cataluña en España*, pp. 379–427.
50. I am grateful to Hamish Scott for his advice on this point.
51. For a succinct coverage which captures something of the atmosphere before and after the referendum campaign, see Devine, *Independence or Union*, chs. 16 and 17; and, for an immediate post-campaign assessment, Ian Jack, 'How the Scots Are Still Scaring Britain', *New York Review of Books*, 6 November 2014. For a personal view on the background to the referendum by the most high-profile Scottish figure to campaign for the retention of the Union, see Gordon Brown, *My Scotland, Our Britain* (London, 2014).
52. For the 'myth' of Scottish egalitarianism, McCrone, *Understanding Scotland*, pp. 90–3.
53. Devine, *Independence or Union*, p. 257.

54. Named after Tam Dalyell, the former MP for that constituency, who pointed out that, while Scottish MPs could continue to vote on English matters after the creation of a Scottish parliament, English MPs would no longer be able to have a say on Scottish laws.
55. See above, p. 125.
56. Brown, *My Scotland, Our Britain*, p. 314; Canal, *Historia mínima de Cataluña*, p. 279.
57. Figures as given in Tornos Mas, *De Escocia a Cataluña*, p. 13.
58. Canal, *Historia mínima de Cataluña*, pp. 287–9; Humlebæk, *Spain: Inventing the Nation*, pp. 195–8.
59. Chislett, *A New Course for Spain*, p. 82.
60. Polls taken by the Centro de Estudios de Opinión, as reported by Angels Piñol, *El País*, 22 July 2016 ('El 26-J da aire al independentismo').
61. This section, summarizing the events of 2017, is based on the extensive coverage of the Catalan crisis in the Spanish and international press, and on the author's impressions derived from visits to Spain and from communications with Spanish friends and colleagues. William Chislett's 'Inside Spain', 143, 19 September–19 October, published by the Elcano Institute in Madrid, has proved very helpful in following the course of events, and I am grateful to Raphael Minder, the *New York Times* correspondent in Madrid, for information on specific points. Neither can be held responsible for the views expressed here, which are purely personal.
62. See Javier Ayuso, 'Estrategia de construcción del enemigo español', *El País*, 1 December 2017.
63. One such account by Xavier Vidal-Folch and Miquel Noguer, 'Los tres días que conmocionaron Cataluña', was published in *El País*, 26 November 2017.

Epilogue

1. For the 'conundrum' of the relatively limited impact of the end of empire on Scottish politics, see Devine, *The Scottish Nation*, ch. 26 ('conundrum', p. 622).
2. Clifford Geertz, *The Interpretation of Cultures* (New York, 1973), p. 259.
3. Scott, *Tales of a Grandfather*, pp. 725–6.
4. The word *rauxa* is used in the Catalan version of the book, replacing *arrauxament* in the original Castilian version (*Noticia de Cataluña*, p. 152). See Jaime Vicens Vives, *Notícia de Catalunya* (Barcelona, 2010), pp. 211–16. For *seny* see also above, p. 183.
5. Jackson, *The Two Unions*, pp. 352–3; Dalyell, *The Question of Scotland*, pp. 91–5, for Barnett and the 'formula', which he would later have liked to see scrapped.
6. Devine, *Independence or Union*, p. 151; Dalyell, *The Question of Scotland*, p. 93.
7. See Joseph Borrell and Joan Llorach, *Las cuentas y los cuentos de la independencia* (Madrid, 2015), especially ch. 6, and Tortella Casares, *Cataluña en España*, pp. 438–44, for critical assessments of Catalan claims ('Espanya ens roba', p. 441). The complexities of the funding system of the autonomous communities are such that it has proved impossible to produce exact and generally accepted figures. The article by Antonio Maqueda, 'No, Catalonia is not Being Robbed', in *El País*, 26 September 2017, offers a useful breakdown of disbursements to the different autonomous communities. This suggests that Catalonia is slightly underfunded compared to the national average. Under Spain's tax system the richer regions, of which Catalonia is one, 'pay more taxes in a bid to redistribute wealth', while state investment in Catalonia between 1995 and 2013 was an average of 14.6 per cent, which is under its GDP and population, although correlating to its size. Two other wealthy regions, the Basque Country and Navarre, live under a separate fiscal arrangement that allows them to keep most of their tax receipts rather than turn them over to the state. They subsequently pay in a certain amount of money for the state's services, an amount generally thought to be too low.
8. See Don H. Doyle (ed.), *Secessionism as an International Phenomenon: From America's Civil War to Contemporary Separatist Movements* (Athens, GA, and London, 2010).
9. 'Thomas Jefferson's "Original Rough Draft" of the Declaration of Independence', in David Armitage, *The Declaration of Independence* (Cambridge, MA, and London, 2007), p. 158.

BIBLIOGRAPHY

Adams, Sharon, and Goodare, Julian (eds.). *Scotland in the Age of Two Revolutions*. Woodbridge, 2014.

Alabrús Iglesias, Rosa María. *Felip V i l'opinió dels catalans*. Lleida, 2001.

Albareda i Salvadó, Joaquim. 'Catalunya a finals del segle XVII', in Eva Serra i Puig et al., *La revolució catalana de 1640*. Barcelona, 1991.

Albareda i Salvadó, Joaquim. *Felipe V y el triunfo del absolutismo. Cataluña en un conflicto europeo, 1700–1714*. Barcelona, 2002.

Albareda i Salvadó, Joaquim. *La guerra de sucesión en España, 1700–1714*. Barcelona, 2010.

Albareda i Salvadó, Joaquim (ed.). *Del patriotisme al catalanisme: societat i política (segles XVI–XIX)*. Vic, 2001.

Albareda i Salvadó, Joaquim, and Gifre i Ribas, Pere. *Història de la Catalunya moderna*. Barcelona, 1999.

Alexander, Sir William. *An Encouragement to Colonies*. London, 1624.

Álvarez-Ossorio Alvariño, Antonio, and García García, Bernardo J. (eds.). *La monarquía de las naciones*. Madrid, 2004.

Álvarez Junco, José. *Mater Dolorosa. La idea de España en el siglo XIX*. Madrid, 2001.

Álvarez Junco, José. *Dioses útiles. Naciones y nacionalismos*. Barcelona, 2016.

Amelang, James S. *Honored Citizens of Barcelona: Patrician Culture and Class Relations, 1490–1714*. Princeton, NJ, 1986.

Amelang, James S. 'Comparing Cities: A Barcelona Model?', *Urban History*, 34 (2007), pp. 173–80.

Anderson, Benedict. *Imagined Communities: Reflections on the Origin and Spread of Nationalism*. London, 1983.

Andrade, Tonio, and Reger, William (eds.). *The Limits of Empire: European Imperial Formations in Early Modern World History. Essays in Honor of Geoffrey Parker*. Farnham, Surrey, 2012.

Anguera, Pere. 'Entre dues posibilitats: espanyols o catalans?', in Joaquim Albareda i Salvadó (ed.), *Del patriotisme al catalanisme: societat i política (segles XVI–XIX)*. Vic, 2001.

Armitage, David. 'The Scottish Vision of Empire: Intellectual Origins of the Darien Venture', in John Robertson (ed.), *A Union for Empire: Political Thought and the British Union of 1707*. Cambridge, 1995.

Armitage, David. *The Declaration of Independence*. Cambridge, MA, and London, 2007.

Arrieta Alberdi, Jon. 'L'antítesi pactisme-absolutisme durant la guerra de Successió a Catalunya', in Joaquim Albareda i Salvadó (ed.), *Del patriotisme al catalanisme: societat i política (segles XVI–XIX)*. Vic, 2001.

Arrieta Alberdi, Jon. 'Forms of Union: Britain and Spain, a Comparative Analysis', in Jon Arrieta Alberti and John H. Elliott (eds.), *Forms of Union: The British and Spanish Monarchies in the Seventeenth and Eighteenth Centuries.* Riev. *Revista Internacional de Estudios Vascos*, Cuadernos 5, 2009, pp. 23–52.

Arrieta Alberdi, Jon. 'The Anglo-Scottish Union and the Nueva Planta', in Trevor J. Dadson and John H. Elliott (eds.), *Britain, Spain and the Treaty of Utrecht, 1713–2013*. Leeds, 2014.

Arrieta Alberdi, Jon. 'Una recapitulación de la Nueva Planta, a través del austracista Juan Amor de Soria', in Marina Torres Arce and Susana Truchuelo García (eds.), *Europa en torno a Utrecht*. Santander, 2014.

Arrieta Alberdi, Jon, and Elliott, John H. (eds.). *Forms of Union: The British and Spanish Monarchies in the Seventeenth and Eighteenth Centuries.* Riev. *Revista Internacional de Estudios Vascos*, Cuadernos 5, 2009.

Ash, Marinell. *The Strange Death of Scottish History.* Edinburgh, 1980.

Astigarraga, Jesús. 'Economic Integration Models and Processes of Political Union: The Contrasting Fates of Scotland and the Basque Country after 1707', in Jon Arrieta Alberdi and John H. Elliott (eds.), *Forms of Union: The British and Spanish Monarchies in the Seventeenth and Eighteenth Centuries.* Riev. *Revista Internacional de Estudios Vascos*, Cuadernos 5, 2009, pp. 141–63.

Bailyn, Bernard. *Voyagers to the West: A Passage in the Peopling of America on the Eve of the Revolution.* New York, 1986.

Bailyn, Bernard. *Sometimes an Art: Nine Essays on History.* New York, 2015.

Bailyn, Bernard, and Clive, John. 'England's Cultural Provinces: Scotland and America', in Bernard Bailyn, *Sometimes an Art: Nine Essays on History.* New York, 2015 (first published in the *William and Mary Quarterly*, 1954).

Bailyn, Bernard, and Morgan, Philip D. (eds.). *Strangers Within the Realm.* Chapel Hill, NC, and London, 1991.

Balcells, Albert (ed.). *Història de la historiografia catalana.* Barcelona, 2004.

Balcells, Albert (ed.). *Historiografia del temps de l'Humanisme.* Barcelona, 2004.

Banerjee, Milinda, Backerra, Charlotte, and Sarti, Cathleen (eds.). *Transnational Histories of the 'Royal Nation'.* Cham, Switzerland, 2017.

Barbour, John. *The Bruce*, ed. and trans. A. A. M. Duncan. Edinburgh, 1997.

Barron, Evan M. *The Scottish War of Independence: A Critical Study.* London, 1914.

Barrow, G. W. S. *Robert Bruce and the Community of the Realm of Scotland.* Edinburgh, 1965 (2nd edn., 1976).

Batista i Roca, Josep M. 'Martí d'Eixalà i la introducció de la filosofia escocesa a Catalunya', in *Hispanic Studies in Honour of I. González Llubera*, ed. Frank Pierce. Oxford, 1959.

Bayly, Christopher A. *Imperial Meridian: The British Empire and the World, 1780–1830.* London, 1989.

Bell, David A. 'Lingua Populi, Lingua Dei: Language, Religion and the Origins of French Revolutionary Nationalism', *American Historical Review*, 100 (1995), pp. 1,403–37.

Bernal Rodríguez, Antonio-Miguel (ed.). *El comercio libre entre España y América Latina, 1765–1824.* Madrid, 1987.

Bisson, T. N. *The Medieval Crown of Aragon: A Short History.* Oxford, 1986.

Bizzocchi, Roberto. *Genéalogies fabuleuses. Inventer et faire croire dans l'Europe moderne.* Paris, 2010.

Boardman, Steve, and Goodare, Julian (eds.). *Kings, Lords and Men in Scotland and Britain, 1300–1625: Essays in Honour of Jenny Wormald.* Edinburgh, 2014.

Borrell, Joseph, and Llorach, Joan. *Las cuentas y los cuentos de la independencia.* Madrid, 2015.

Boswell, James, and Johnson, Samuel. *A Journey to the Western Islands of Scotland and the Journal of a Tour to the Hebrides*, ed. Peter Levi. London, 1984.

Bouza Álvarez, Fernando Jesús. 'La "soledad" de los reinos y la "semejanza del rey". Los virreinatos de príncipes en el Portugal de los Felipes', in Massimo Ganci and Ruggiero Romano (eds.), *Governare il Mondo. L'impero spagnolo dal XV al XIX secolo.* Palermo, 1991.

Bowie, Karin. 'New Perspectives on Pre-Union Scotland', in Thomas M. Devine and Jenny Wormald (eds.), *The Oxford Handbook of Modern Scottish History.* Oxford, 2012.

Boyd, Carolyn P. *Historia Patria: Politics, History and National Identity in Spain, 1875–1975*. Princeton, NJ, 1997.

Bradshaw, Brendan, and Morrill, John (eds.). *The British Problem, c.1534–1707*. Basingstoke, 1996.

Brenan, Gerald. *The Spanish Labyrinth* (2nd edn.). Cambridge, 1950.

Brewer, John. *The Sinews of Power: War, Money and the English State, 1688–1783*. London, 1988.

Broadie, Alexander. 'The Rise (and Fall?) of the Scottish Enlightenment', in Thomas M. Devine and Jenny Wormald (eds.), *The Oxford Handbook of Modern Scottish History*. Oxford, 2012.

Broers, Michael. *The Napoleonic Mediterranean*. London and New York, 2017.

Broun, Dauvit. *Scottish Independence and the Idea of Britain from the Picts to Alexander III*. Edinburgh, 2007.

Broun, Dauvit, Finlay, R. J., and Lynch, Michael (eds.). *Image and Identity: The Making and Re-making of Scotland Through the Ages*. Edinburgh, 1998.

Brown, Gordon. *My Scotland, Our Britain*. London, 2014.

Brown, Keith M. *Kingdom or Province? Scotland and the Regal Union, 1603–1715*. Basingstoke, 1992.

Brown, Keith M. 'The Vanishing Emperor: British Kingship and its Decline, 1603–1707', in Roger A. Mason (ed.), *Scots and Britons: Scottish Political Thought and the Union of 1603*. Cambridge, 1994.

Brown, Keith M. 'The Origins of a British Aristocracy: Integration and its Limitations before the Treaty of Union', in Steven G. Ellis and Sarah Barber (eds.), *Conquest and Union: Fashioning a British State, 1485–1725*. New York and London, 1995.

Brown, Stewart J., and Whatley, Christopher A. (eds.). *Union of 1707: New Dimensions*. Edinburgh, 2008.

Burness, Catriona. *'Strange Associations': The Irish Question and the Making of Scottish Unionism, 1886–1918*. East Linton, 2003.

Cairns, John W. 'Scottish Law, Scottish Lawyers and the Status of the Union', in John Robertson (ed.), *A Union for Empire: Political Thought and the British Union of 1707*. Cambridge, 1995.

Calendar of State Papers Domestic, 1625–1649. Addenda.

Cameron, Ewen A. 'Embracing the Past: The Highlands in Nineteenth-Century Scotland', in Dauvit Broun, R. J. Finlay and Michael Lynch (eds.), *Image and Identity: The Making and Re-making of Scotland Through the Ages*. Edinburgh, 1998.

Cameron, Ewen A. 'The Politics of Union in an Age of Unionism', in Thomas M. Devine (ed.), *Scotland and the Union, 1707–2007*. Edinburgh, 2008.

Cameron, Ewen A. *Impaled upon a Thistle: Scotland since 1880*. Edinburgh, 2010.

Canal, Jordi. *Historia mínima de Cataluña*. Madrid, 2015.

Cañizares-Esguerra, Jorge. *How to Write the History of the New World*. Stanford, CA, 2001.

Cannadine, David. 'The Context, Performance and Meaning of Ritual: The British Monarchy and the "Invention of Tradition", c. 1820–1977', in Eric Hobsbawm and Terence Ranger (eds.), *The Invention of Tradition*. Cambridge, 1983.

Cannadine, David. *Aspects of Aristocracy: Grandeur and Decline in Modern Britain*. New Haven, CT, and London, 1994.

Canny, Nicholas (ed.). *Europeans on the Move: Studies on European Migration 1500–1800*. Oxford, 1994.

Capmany y de Montpalau, Antonio de. *Memorias históricas sobre la marina, comercio y artes de la antigua ciudad de Barcelona*. Barcelona, 1779–92.

Capmany y de Montpalau, Antonio de. *Centinela contra franceses*, ed. Françoise Étienvre. London, 1988.

Cardim, Pedro, and Palos, Joan-Lluís (eds.). *El mundo de los virreyes en las monarquías de España y Portugal*. Madrid, 2012.

Carr, Raymond. *Spain, 1808–1939*. Oxford, 1966.

Carrera Pujal, Jaime. *Historia política y económica de Cataluña* (4 vols.). Barcelona, 1946–7.

Casals, Àngel (ed.). *Les fronteres catalanes i el Tractat dels Pirineus*. Cabrera de Mar, 2009.

The Case of the Catalans Consider'd. London, 1714 (facsimile). See under Strubell, Michael B. (ed.).

Chislett, William. *A New Course for Spain: Beyond the Crisis.* Madrid, 2016.

Colley, Linda. *Britons: Forging the Nation 1707-1837.* New Haven, CT, and London, 1982.

Connolly, S. J. 'Varieties of Britishness: Ireland, Scotland and Wales in the Hanoverian State', in Alexander Grant and Keith J. Stringer (eds.), *Uniting the Kingdom? The Making of British History.* New York and London, 1995.

La constitución de Cádiz de 1812, ed. Antonio Fernández García. Madrid, 2002.

Constitución española, aprobada por las Cortes el 31 de octubre de 1978.

Coupland, Reginald. *Welsh and Scottish Nationalism: A Study.* London, 1954.

Cowan, Edward J. 'Identity, Freedom and the Declaration of Arbroath', in Dauvit Broun, R. J. Finlay and Michael Lynch (eds.), *Image and Identity: The Making and Re-making of Scotland Through the Ages.* Edinburgh, 1998.

Cregeen, Eric. 'The Changing Role of the House of Argyll in the Scottish Highlands', in Nicholas Phillipson and Rosalind Mitchison (eds.). *Scotland in the Age of Improvement.* Edinburgh, 1996.

Dadson, Trevor J., and Elliott, John H. (eds.). *Britain, Spain and the Treaty of Utrecht, 1713-2013.* Leeds, 2014.

Dalyell, Tam. *The Question of Scotland: Devolution and After.* Edinburgh, 2016.

Dantí, Jaume. *Aixecaments populars als països catalans, 1687-1693.* Barcelona, 1990.

Davies, Norman. *Vanished Kingdoms: The History of Half-Forgotten Europe.* London, 2011.

Davies, R. R. *The First English Empire: Power and Identities in the British Isles 1093-1343.* Oxford, 2000.

Dawson, Jane E. A. *Scotland Re-formed, 1488-1587.* Edinburgh, 2007.

Dawson, Jane E. A. *John Knox.* New Haven, CT, and London, 2015.

Delgado Ribas, Josep M.ª 'El modelo catalán dentro del sistema de libre comercio (1765-1820)', in Antonio-Miguel Bernal Rodríguez (ed.), *El comercio libre entre España y América Latina, 1765-1824.* Madrid, 1987.

Devine, Thomas M. *The Scottish Nation, 1700-2000.* London, 1999.

Devine, Thomas M. *Scotland's Empire 1600-1815.* London, 2003.

Devine, Thomas M. 'Scottish Elites and the Indian Empire, 1700-1815', in T. C. Smout (ed.), *Anglo-Scottish Relations from 1603 to 1900.* Oxford, 2005.

Devine, Thomas M. (ed.). *Scotland and the Union, 1707-2007.* Edinburgh, 2008.

Devine, Thomas M. *Independence or Union: Scotland's Past and Scotland's Present.* London, 2016.

Devine, Thomas M., and Jackson, Gordon (eds.). *Glasgow* (2 vols.). Manchester, 1995.

Devine, Thomas M., Lee, Clive H., and Peden, George C. (eds.). *The Transformation of Scotland: The Economy Since 1700.* Edinburgh, 2005.

Devine, Thomas M., and Wormald, Jenny (eds.). *The Oxford Handbook of Modern Scottish History.* Oxford, 2012.

Deyermond, Alan. 'La ideología del estado moderno en la literatura española del siglo XV', in Adeline Rucquoi (ed.). *Realidad e imágenes del poder: España a fines de la Edad Media.* Valladolid, 1988.

Domínguez Ortiz, Antonio. *Sociedad y estado en el siglo XVIII español.* Barcelona, 1976.

Donaldson, Gordon. *Scotland: The Shaping of a Nation.* Newton Abbot, 1974.

Doyle, Don H. (ed.). *Secessionism as an International Phenomenon: From America's Civil War to Contemporary Separatist Movements.* Athens, GA, and London, 2010.

Duran i Grau, Eulàlia. *Sobre la mitificació dels orígens històrics nacionals catalans.* Barcelona (Institut d'Estudis Catalans), 1991.

Duran i Grau, Eulàlia. 'Historiografia del temps de l'Humanisme', in Albert Balcells (ed.). *Història de la Historiografia.* Barcelona, 2004.

Elliott, John H. *The Revolt of the Catalans: A Study in the Decline of Spain, 1598-1640.* Cambridge, 1963.

Elliott, John H. *The Count-Duke of Olivares: The Statesman in an Age of Decline.* New Haven, CT, and London, 1986.

Elliott, John H. *Empires of the Atlantic World: Britain and Spain in America 1492–1830*. New Haven, CT, and London, 2006.

Elliott, John H. 'A Europe of Composite Monarchies', *Past and Present*, 137 (1992), pp. 48–71. Reprinted in John H. Elliott, *Spain, Europe and the Wider World, 1500–1800*. New Haven, CT, and London, 2009.

Elliott, John H. *Spain, Europe and the Wider World, 1500–1800*. New Haven, CT, and London, 2009.

Elliott, John H., de la Peña, José F., and Negredo del Cerro, Fernando (eds.). *Memoriales y cartas del Conde Duque de Olivares* (2nd edn.). Madrid, 2013.

Ellis, Steven G., and Barber, Sarah (eds.). *Conquest and Union: Fashioning a British State, 1485–1725*. New York and London, 1995.

Emerson, Roger L. *An Enlightened Duke: The Life of Archibald Campbell (1682–1751), Earl of Ilay and Third Duke of Argyl*. Kilkerran, 2013.

Espino López, Antonio. *Catalunya durante el reinado de Carlos II. Política y guerra en la frontera catalana, 1679–1697*. Bellaterra, 1999.

Evans, Robert J. W. *Austria, Hungary, and the Habsburgs: Central Europe c.1683–1867*. Oxford, 2006.

Feliu de la Peña y Farell, Narcisco. *Anales de Cataluña* (3 vols.). Barcelona, 1709.

Ferguson, William. *Scotland: 1689 to the Present*. Edinburgh, 1968.

Ferguson, William. *Scotland's Relations with England: A Survey to 1707*. Edinburgh, 1977.

Ferguson, William. 'The Making of the Treaty of Union 1707', *Scottish Historical Review*, 43 (1964), pp. 89–110.

Ferguson, William. 'Imperial Crowns: A Neglected Facet of the Background to the Treaty of Union of 1707', *Scottish Historical Review*, 53 (1974), pp. 22–44.

Fernández Albaladejo, Pablo. *La crisis de la monarquía*, in Josep Fontana and Ramón Villares (eds.), *Historia de España*. Madrid, 2009, vol. 4.

Fernández Albaladejo, Pablo (ed.). *Los Borbones. Dinastía y memoria de nación en la España del siglo XVIII*. Madrid, 2001.

Fernández Cañueto, Daniel, *La iglesia católica y la nacionalización de Cataluña*. Lleida, 2016.

Fernández Díaz, Roberto. *Cataluña y el absolutismo borbónico. Historia y política*. Lleida, 2014.

Fernández Sebastián, Javier. 'Toleration and Freedom of Expression in the Hispanic World between Enlightenment and Liberalism', *Past and Present*, 211 (2011), pp. 159–97.

Fernández-Armesto, Felipe. *Barcelona: A Thousand Years of the City's Past*. London, 1991.

Ferrer i Gironès, Francesc. *La persecució política de la llengua catalana*. Barcelona, 1985.

Ferro Pomà, Víctor. *El dret públic català. Les institucions a Catalunya fins al Decret de Nova Planta*. Vic, 1987.

Finlay, Richard J. *A Partnership for Good? Scottish Politics and the Union Since 1880*. Edinburgh, 1997.

Finlay, Richard J. *Modern Scotland 1914–2000*. London, 2004.

Finlay, Richard J. 'The Interwar Crisis', in Thomas M. Devine and Jenny Wormald (eds.). *The Oxford Handbook of Modern Scottish History*. Oxford, 2012.

Fisher, John R. *The Economic Aspects of Spanish Imperialism in America, 1492–1810*. Liverpool, 1997.

Fisher, John R. *Bourbon Peru 1750–1824*. Liverpool, 2003.

Fletcher, Andrew. *Political Works*, ed. John Robertson. Cambridge, 1997.

Floristán Imízcoz, Alfredo. *El reino de Navarra y la conformación política de España, 1512–1841*. Madrid, 2014.

Fontana, Josep. *La formació d'una identitat. Una història de Catalunya*. Barcelona, 2014.

Fontana, Josep, and Villares, Ramón (eds.). *Historia de España* (12 vols.). Barcelona and Madrid, 2007–.

Forsyth, David (ed.). *Bonnie Prince Charlie and the Jacobites*. Edinburgh, 2017.

Fradera, Josep M. *Cultura nacional en una societat dividida*. Barcelona, 1992.

Fradera, Josep M. *Passat i identitat: la Guerra de Successió en la política i la literatura del segle XIX català (Acte commemoratiu de'l 11 de septembre de 1714)*. Barcelona (Ajuntament de Barcelona), 1993.

Fradera, Josep M. *Jaume Balmes. Els fonaments d'una política catòlica.* Vic, 1996.

Fradera, Josep M. *Colonias para después de un imperio.* Barcelona, 2005.

Fradera, Josep M. *La pàtria dels catalans. Historia, política, cultura.* Barcelona, 2009.

Fradera, Josep M. *La nación imperial, 1750–1918* (2 vols.). Barcelona, 2013.

Fraser, Antonia. *Mary Queen of Scots.* London, 1969.

Freedman, Paul. *The Origins of Peasant Servitude in Medieval Catalonia.* Cambridge, 1991.

Freedman, Paul. 'Cowardice, Heroism, and the Legendary Origins of Catalonia', *Past and Present*, 121 (1988), pp. 3–28.

Freixa, Mireia. 'El protomodernismo en la arquitectura y las artes plásticas', in Ramón Grau, Mariana López and Pere Anguera (eds.), *Exposició universal de Barcelona. Llibre del centenari.* Barcelona, 1988.

Friedeburg, Robert von (ed.). *'Patria' und 'Patrioten' vor dem Patriotismus.* Wiesbaden, 2005.

Frost, Robert I. 'The Limits of Dynastic Power: Poland-Lithuania, Sweden and the Problem of Composite Monarchy in the Age of the Vasas', in Tonio Andrade and William Reger (eds.), *The Limits of Empire: European Imperial Formations in Early Modern World History. Essays in Honor of Geoffrey Parker.* Farnham, Surrey, 2012.

Frost, Robert I. *The Oxford History of Poland-Lithuania: The Making of the Polish-Lithuanian Union, 1385–1569,* vol. 1. Oxford, 2015.

Fry, Michael. *A Higher World: Scotland 1707–1815.* Edinburgh, 2014.

Fuentes Aragonés, Juan Francisco. *Adolfo Suárez. Biografía política.* Barcelona, 2011.

Fusi, Juan Pablo. *Historia mínima de España.* Madrid, 2012.

Galloway, Bruce R., and Levack, Brian P. (eds.). *The Jacobean Union: Six Tracts of 1604.* Edinburgh, 1985.

Ganci, Massimo, and Romano, Ruggiero (eds.). *Governare il Mondo. L'impero spagnolo dal XV al XIX secolo.* Palermo, 1991.

García Cárcel, Ricardo. *Pau Claris. La revolta catalana.* Barcelona, 1980.

García Cárcel, Ricardo. *Felipe V y los españoles.* Barcelona, 2002.

García Cárcel, Ricardo. *El sueño de la nación indomable. Los mitos de la guerra de la independencia.* Madrid, 2007.

García Cárcel, Ricardo. *La herencia del pasado. Las memorias históricas de España.* Barcelona, 2011.

García Cárcel, Ricardo, and Alabrús Iglesias, Rosa María. *España en 1700. Austrias o Borbones?* Madrid, 2001.

García de Cortázar, Fernando. *Los mitos de la historia de España.* Barcelona, 2003.

García Espuche, Albert. *Un siglo decisivo. Barcelona y Cataluña, 1550–1640.* Madrid, 1998.

Garner, Paul, and Smith, Angel (eds.). *Nationalism and Transnationalism in Spain and Latin America, 1808–1923.* Cardiff, 2017.

Garriga Acosta, Carlos A. 'Sobre el gobierno de Cataluña bajo el régimen de la Nueva Planta. Ensayo historiográfico', *Anuario de Historia del Derecho Español* LXXX (2010), pp. 716–65.

Gay Escoda, Martín M.ª. *El corregidor a Catalunya.* Madrid, 1997.

Geertz, Clifford. *The Interpretation of Cultures.* New York, 1973.

Gelderen, Martin Van, and Skinner, Quentin (eds.). *Republicanism: A Shared European Heritage* (2 vols.). Cambridge, 2002.

Gerwarth, Robert. *The Vanquished: Why the First World War Failed to End, 1917–1923.* London, 2016.

Giesey, Ralph A. *If Not, Not.* Princeton, NJ, 1968.

Gil Pujol, Xavier. 'La Corona de Aragón con el neoforalismo', in Pablo Fernández Albaladejo (ed.). *Los Borbones. Dinastía y memoria de nación en la España del siglo XVIII.* Madrid, 2001.

Gil Pujol, Xavier. 'Republican Politics in Early Modern Spain: The Castilian and Catalano-Aragonese Traditions', in Martin Van Gelderen and Quentin Skinner (eds.), *Republicanism: A Shared European Heritage* (2 vols.). Cambridge, 2002.

Gil Pujol, Xavier. 'Un rey, una fe, muchas naciones. Patria y nación en la España de los siglos XVI–XVII', in Antonio Álvarez-Ossorio Alvariño and Bernardo J. García García (eds.), *La monarquía de las naciones.* Madrid, 2004.

Gil Pujol, Xavier. 'La fábrica de la monarquía. Traza y conservación de la monarquía de España', *Discurso leído en la Real Academia de la Historia*. Madrid, 2016.

Goldie, Mark. 'Divergence and Union: Scotland and England, 1660–1707', in Brendan Bradshaw and John Morrill (eds.), *The British Problem, c.1534–1707*. Basingstoke, 1996.

González Hernández, María Jesús. *El universo conservador de Antonio Maura. Biografía y proyecto de Estado*. Madrid, 1997.

Goodare, Julian. *State and Society in Early Modern Scotland*. Oxford, 1999.

Goodare, Julian. *The Government of Scotland, 1560–1625*. Oxford, 2004.

Graf von Kalnein, Albrecht. *Juan José de Austria en la España de Carlos II*. Lleida, 2001.

Grafe, Regina. *Distant Tyranny: Markets, Power, and Backwardness in Spain, 1650–1800*. Princeton, NJ, 2012.

Graham, Aaron, and Walsh, Patrick (eds.). *The British Fiscal-Military States, 1660–c.1783*. Abingdon, 2016.

Grant, Alexander, and Stringer, Keith J. (eds). *Uniting the Kingdom? The Making of British History*. New York and London, 1995.

Grau, Ramón, López, Mariana, and Anguera, Pere (eds.). *Exposició universal de Barcelona. Llibre del centenari*. Barcelona, 1988.

Groundwater, Anna. 'The Middle Shires Divided: Tensions at the Heart of the Anglo-Scottish Union', in Sharon Adams and Julian Goodare (eds.). *Scotland in the Age of Two Revolutions*. Woodbridge, 2014.

Hamilton, Douglas. 'Scotland and the Eighteenth-Century Empire', in Thomas M. Devine and Jenny Wormald (eds.), *The Oxford Handbook of Modern Scottish History*. Oxford, 2012.

Hancock, David. *Citizens of the World: London Merchants and the Integration of the British Atlantic Community, 1735–1765*. Cambridge, 1995.

Hanham, H. J. *Scottish Nationalism*. London, 1969.

Harris, Bob. 'The Scots, the Westminster Parliament, and the British State in the Eighteenth Century', in Julian Hoppit (ed.). *Parliaments and Identities in Britain and Ireland, 1660–1850*. Manchester, 2003.

Harris, Bob. 'Scottish-English Connections in British Radicalism in the 1790s', in T. C. Smout (ed.), *Anglo-Scottish Relations from 1603 to 1900*. Oxford, 2005.

Harris, Bob. *The Scottish People and the French Revolution*. London, 2008.

Harris, Tim. *Revolution: The Great Crisis of the British Monarchy, 1685–1720*. London, 2006.

Hay, Denys. 'The Use of the Term "Great Britain" in the Middle Ages', *Proceedings of the Society of Antiquaries of Scotland*, 89 (1955–6), pp. 55–66.

Hennessy, A. M. *The Federal Republic in Spain: Pi y Margall and the Federal Republican Movement 1868–74*. Oxford, 1962.

Herr, Richard. *The Eighteenth-Century Revolution in Spain*. Princeton, NJ, 1958.

Herrero García, Miguel. *Ideas de los españoles del siglo XVII*. Madrid, 1966.

Herzog, Tamar D. *Defining Nations: Immigrants and Citizens in Early Modern Spain and Spanish America*. New Haven, CT, and London, 2003.

Herzog, Tamar D. 'Una monarquía, dos territorios. La frontera entre españoles y portugueses: España y Portugal durante (y después) de la unión', in Carlos Martínez Shaw and José Antonio Martínez Torres (eds.), *España y Portugal en el mundo, 1581–1668*. Madrid, 2014.

Hillgarth, J. N. *The Spanish Kingdoms, 1250–1516*. Oxford, 1978.

Hillgarth, J. N. *The Visigoths in History and Legend*. Toronto, 2009.

Hirst, Derek. 'The English Republic and the Meaning of Britain', in Brendan Bradshaw and John Morrill (eds.), *The British Problem, c.1534–1707*. Basingstoke, 1996.

Hobsbawm, Eric. *Nations and Nationalism since 1780*. Cambridge, 1990.

Hobsbawm, Eric, and Ranger, Terence (eds.). *The Invention of Tradition*. Cambridge, 1983.

Hoppit, Julian (ed.). *Parliaments and Identities in Britain and Ireland, 1660–1850*. Manchester, 2003.

Houston, R. A. *Social Change in the Age of Enlightenment: Edinburgh, 1660–1760*. Oxford, 1994.

Hughes, Robert. *Barcelona*. London, 1992.

Humlebæk, Carsten. *Spain: Inventing the Nation*. London, 2015.

Hutchison, I. G. C. 'Anglo-Scottish Political Relations in the Nineteenth Century, c.1815–1914', in T. C. Smout (ed.), *Anglo-Scottish Relations from 1603 to 1900*. Oxford, 2005.

Hyde, Edward (Earl of Clarendon). *The History of the Rebellion and Civil Wars in England*, ed. W. D. Macray (6 vols.). Oxford, 1888.

Iglésies i Fort, Josep. *Pere Gil, S.I. (1551–1622) i la seva Geografia de Catalunya*. Barcelona, 1949.

Innes, Joanna. 'Legislating for Three Kingdoms: How the Westminster Parliament Legislated for England, Scotland and Ireland, 1707–1830', in Julian Hoppit (ed.), *Parliaments and Identities in Britain and Ireland, 1660–1850*. Manchester, 2003.

Iñurritegui, José María. *Gobernar la ocasión. Preludio político de la Nueva Planta de 1707*. Madrid, 2008.

Jack, Ian. 'How the Scots Are Still Scaring Britain', *New York Review of Books*, 6 November 2014.

Jackson, Alvin. *The Two Unions: Ireland, Scotland and the Survival of the United Kingdom, 1707–2007*. Oxford, 2012.

Jackson, Clare. *Restoration Scotland: Royalist Politics, Religion and Ideas*. Woodbridge, 2003.

Jackson, Clare. 'Conceptions of Nationhood in the Anglo-Scottish Union Debates of 1707', in Stewart J. Brown and Christopher A. Whatley (eds.), *Union of 1707: New Dimensions*. Edinburgh, 2008.

Jackson, Clare. 'Union Historiographies', in Thomas M. Devine and Jenny Wormald (eds.), *The Oxford Handbook of Modern Scottish History*. Oxford, 2012.

Jackson, Gabriel. *The Spanish Republic and the Civil War 1931–1939*. Princeton, NJ, 1965.

Jacobson, Stephen. *Catalonia's Advocates: Lawyers, Society, and Politics in Barcelona, 1759–1900*. Chapel Hill, NC, 2009.

Jardí i Casany, Enric. *Els catalans de les corts de Cadis*. Barcelona, 1963.

Jover Zamora, José María. 'Sobre los conceptos de monarquía y nación en el pensamiento político español del XVII', *Cuadernos de Historia de España*, 13 (Buenos Aires, 1950), pp. 101–50.

Kagan, Richard L. *Clio and the Crown: The Politics of History in Medieval and Early Modern Spain*. Baltimore, MD, 2009.

Kagan, Richard L., and Parker, Geoffrey (eds.). *Spain, Europe and the Atlantic World: Essays in Honour of John H. Elliott*. Cambridge, 1995.

Kamen, Henry. *Spain in the Later Seventeenth Century 1665–1700*. London and New York, 1980.

Kamen, Henry. *The Phoenix and the Flame: Catalonia and the Counter Reformation*. New Haven, CT, and London, 1993.

Kamen, Henry. *Philip V of Spain: The King Who Reigned Twice*. New Haven, CT, and London, 2001.

Kamen, Henry. *España y Cataluña. Historia de una pasión*. Madrid, 2014.

Kamen, Henry. 'El Fénix catalán: la obra renovadora de Narciso Feliu de la Penya', *Estudis*, 1 (1973), pp. 185–203.

Kamen, Henry. 'A Forgotten Insurrection of the Seventeenth Century: The Catalan Peasant Rising of 1688', *Journal of Modern History*, 49 (1977), pp. 210–30.

Keating, Michael. *The Independence of Scotland: Self-Government and the Shifting Politics of Union. Understanding the Union*. Oxford Scholarship Online, 2009.

Keating, Michael (ed.). *Debating Scotland: Issues of Independence and Union in the 2014 Referendum*. Oxford, 2017.

Kidd, Colin. *Subverting Scotland's Past: Scottish Whig Historians and the Creation of an Anglo-British Identity, 1689–c.1830*. Cambridge, 1993.

Kidd, Colin. *British Identities Before Nationalism: Ethnicity and Nationhood in the Atlantic World, 1600–1800*. Cambridge, 1999.

Kidd, Colin. *Union and Unionisms: Political Thought in Scotland, 1500–2000*. Cambridge, 2008.

Kidd, Colin. 'Eighteenth-Century Scotland and the Three Unions', in T. C. Smout (ed.), *Anglo-Scottish Relations from 1603 to 1900*. Oxford, 2005.

Knox, William W. *Industrial Nation: Work, Culture and Society in Scotland, 1800–Present.* Edinburgh, 1999.

Konetzke, Richard. 'La legislación sobre inmigración de extranjeros en América durante el reinado de Carlos V', in *Charles-Quint et son temps.* Paris, 1959.

Lee, Maurice Jr. *The 'Inevitable' Union and Other Essays on Early Modern Scotland.* East Linton, 2003.

Lee, Maurice Jr. 'The Worcester Veterans and the Restoration Regime in Scotland', in Sharon Adams and Julian Goodare (eds.), *Scotland in the Age of Two Revolutions.* Woodbridge, 2014.

Lenman, Bruce P. *Jacobite Risings in Britain 1689–1746.* London, 1980.

Lenman, Bruce P. *Integration, Enlightenment, and Industrialization. Scotland 1746–1832.* London, 1981.

Lenman, Bruce P. 'The Teaching of Scottish History in the Scottish Universities', *Scottish Historical Review*, 52 (1973), pp. 165–90.

Levack, Brian P. *The Formation of the British State: England, Scotland and the Union 1603–1707.* Oxford, 1987.

Levack, Brian P. 'Law, Sovereignty and the Union', in Roger A. Mason (ed.), *Scots and Britons: Scottish Political Thought and the Union of 1603.* Cambridge, 1994.

Llobera, Josep R. *Foundations of National Identity: From Catalonia to Europe.* New York and Oxford, 2004.

Lluch, Ernest. *La Catalunya vençuda del segle XVIII.* Barcelona, 1996.

López Piñero, José M. *La introducción de la ciencia moderna en España.* Barcelona, 1969.

Lynch, John. *Bourbon Spain 1700–1800.* Oxford, 1989.

Lynch, Michael. 'A Nation Born Again? Scottish Identity in the Sixteenth and Seventeenth Centuries', in Dauvit Broun, R. J. Finlay and Michael Lynch (eds.), *Image and Identity: The Making and Re-making of Scotland Through the Ages.* Edinburgh, 1998.

MacInnes, Allan I. *Union and Empire: The Making of the United Kingdom in 1707.* Cambridge, 2007.

MacInnes, Allan I. 'Jacobitism in Scotland: Episodic Cause or National Movement?', *Scottish Historical Review*, 86 (2007), pp. 225–52.

MacKay, A. *Spain in the Middle Ages: From Frontier to Empire, 1000–1550.* London, 1977.

Mackillop, Andrew. 'A Union for Empire? Scotland, the English East India Company and the British Union', in Stewart J. Brown and Christopher A. Whatley (eds.), *Union of 1707: New Dimensions.* Edinburgh, 2008.

Mackillop, Andrew. 'Subsidy State or Drawback Province? Eighteenth-Century Scotland and the British Fiscal-Military Complex', in Aaron Graham and Patrick Walsh (eds.), *The British Fiscal-Military States, 1660–c.1783.* Abingdon, 2016.

Malcolm, Alistair. *Royal Favouritism and the Governing Elite of the Spanish Monarchy, 1640–1665.* Oxford, 2017.

Marfany, Joan-Lluís. *La llengua maltractada. El castellà i el català a Catalunya del segle XVI al segle XIX.* Barcelona, 2001.

Marfany, Joan-Lluís. *Nacionalisme espanyol i catalanitat. Cap a una revisió de la Renaixença.* Barcelona, 2017.

Marfany, Joan-Lluís. '"Minority" Languages and Literary Revivals', *Past and Present,* 184 (2004), pp. 137–67.

Marfany, Julie. *Land, Proto-Industry and Population in Catalonia, c. 1680–1829: An Alternative Transition to Capitalism?* Farnham, Surrey, 2012.

Martínez Hernández, Santiago (ed.). *Escribir la corte de Felipe IV. El diario del marqués de Osera, 1657–1659.* Madrid, 2013.

Martínez Marina, Francisco. *Teoría de las Cortes*, ed. J. A. Escudero. Oviedo, 2002.

Martínez Shaw, Carlos. *Cataluña en la carrera de Indias.* Barcelona, 1981.

Martínez Shaw, Carlos, and Martínez Torres, José Antonio (eds.). *España y Portugal en el mundo, 1581–1668.* Madrid, 2014.

Mason, Roger A. 'Beyond the Declaration of Arbroath', in Steve Boardman and Julian Goodare (eds.), *Kings, Lords and Men in Scotland and Britain, 1300–1625: Essays in Honour of Jenny Wormald.* Edinburgh, 2014.

Mason, Roger A. 'Debating Britain in Seventeenth-Century Scotland: Multiple Monarchy and Scottish Sovereignty', *Journal of Scottish Historical Studies*, 35 (2015), pp. 1–24.

Mason, Roger A. (ed.). *Scots and Britons: Scottish Political Thought and the Union of 1603.* Cambridge, 1994.

Mayer, Arno. *The Persistence of the Old Regime: Europe to the Great War.* New York, 1981.

Mazower, Mark. *Dark Continent: Europe's Twentieth Century.* London, 1998.

McCormack, Danielle. 'Highland Lawlessness and the Cromwellian Regime', in Sharon Adams and Julian Goodare (eds.), *Scotland in the Age of Two Revolutions.* Woodbridge, 2014.

McCrone, David. *Understanding Scotland: The Sociology of a Nation.* New York and London, 2001.

McIlwain, C. H. (ed.). *The Political Works of James I.* New York, 1965.

Menéndez Pidal, Gonzalo. *Los caminos en la historia de España.* Madrid, 1951.

Mercader i Riba, Joan. *Els capitans generals. El segle XVIII.* Barcelona, 1957.

Mercader i Riba, Joan. *Felip V i Catalunya.* Barcelona, 1968.

Merriman, Roger B. *The Rise of the Spanish Empire in the Old World and the New* (4 vols.). New York, 1918–34 (repr. 1962).

Minder, Raphael. *The Struggle for Catalonia: Rebel Politics in Spain.* London, 2017.

Mitchison, Rosalind. 'The Government and the Highlands, 1707–1745', in Nicholas Phillipson and Rosalind Mitchison (eds.), *Scotland in the Age of Improvement.* Edinburgh, 1996.

Molas i Ribalta, Pere. *La burguesia mercantil en la España del antiguo régimen.* Madrid, 1985.

Molas i Ribalta, Pere. *Catalunya i la Casa d'Àustria.* Barcelona, 1996.

Moliner i Prada, Antoni. *La Catalunya resistent a la dominació francesa (1808–1812). La Junta Superior de Catalunya.* Barcelona, 1989.

Moliner i Prada, Antoni (ed.). *La guerra de la independencia en España (1808–1815).* Barcelona, 2007.

Moreno Alonso, Manuel. *La forja del liberalismo en España. Los amigos españoles de Lord Holland 1793–1840.* Madrid, 1997.

Moreno Alonso, Manuel. *El nacimiento de una nación. Sevilla, 1808–1810. La capital de una nación en guerra.* Madrid, 2010.

Moreno-Luzón, Javier. 'Performing Monarchy and Spanish Nationalism, 1902–1913', in Milinda Banerjee, Charlotte Backerra and Cathleen Sarti (eds.), *Transnational Histories of the 'Royal Nation'.* Cham, Switzerland, 2017.

Morrill, John. *The Nature of the English Revolution.* London, 1993.

Morrill, John (ed.). *The Scottish National Covenant in its British Context, 1638–51.* Edinburgh, 1990.

Morton, Graeme. 'What If? The Significance of Scotland's Messy Nationalism', in Dauvit Broun, R. J. Finlay and Michael Lynch (eds.), *Image and Identity: The Making and Re-making of Scotland Through the Ages.* Edinburgh, 1998.

Morton, Graeme. *Unionist Nationalism: Governing Urban Scotland 1830–1860.* East Linton, 1999.

Muñoz i Lloret, Josep M. *Jaume Vicens i Vives. Una biografia intel·lectual.* Barcelona, 1997.

Nadal, Jordi, and Giralt i Raventós, Emili. *La population catalane de 1553 à 1717. L'immigration française.* Paris, 1960.

Nairn, Tom. *The Break-Up of Britain: Crisis and Neo-Nationalism* (3rd edn.). Altona, Victoria, Australia, 2003.

Nicholls, Andrew D. *The Jacobean Union: A Consideration of British Civil Policies Under the Early Stuarts.* Westport, CT, 1999.

O'Brien, Patrick K., and Hunt, Philip A. 'The Rise of a Fiscal State in England', *Bulletin of the Institute of Historical Research*, 66 (1993), pp. 129–76.

O'Brien, Patrick K., and Prados de la Escosura, Leandro (eds.). 'The Costs and Benefits of European Imperialism from the Conquest of Ceuta, 1415, to the Treaty of Lusaka, 1974' (papers of the Twelfth International Economic History Congress), *Revista de Historia Económica*, 16, Madrid, 1998.

Oliver, Frederick Scott ('Pacificus'). *Federalism and Home Rule.* London, 1910.

Orwell, George. *Homage to Catalonia.* London, 1938 (new edn., 1951).

The Oxford Handbook of Modern Scottish History, eds. Thomas M. Devine and Jenny Wormald. Oxford, 2012.

Palacio Atard, Vicente. *Los españoles de la ilustración*. Madrid, 1964.

Palao Gil, Francisco Javier. 'The Crown of Aragon in the War of the Spanish Succession', in Trevor J. Dadson and John H. Elliott (eds.), *Britain, Spain and the Treaty of Utrecht, 1713–2013*. Leeds, 2014.

Papell, Antonio. 'Nación de naciones', *e-SLegal History Review*, 24 (January 2017).

Parker, Geoffrey. *Global Crisis: War, Climate Change and Catastrophe in the Seventeenth Century*. New Haven, CT, and London, 2013.

Peers, Edgar Allison. *Catalonia Infelix*. London, 1937.

Peers, Edgar Allison. 'Studies in the Influence of Sir Walter Scott in Spain', *Revue Hispanique*, 68 (1926), pp. 1–160.

Pellistrandi, Benoît. *Histoire de l'Espagne. Des guerres napoléoniennes à nos jours*. Paris, 2013.

Pentland, Gordon. *The Spirit of the Union: Popular Politics in Scotland, 1815–1820*. London, 2011.

Perceval-Maxwell, M. *The Scottish Migration to Ulster in the Reign of James I*. London, 1973.

Perceval-Maxwell, M. 'Ireland and the Monarchy in the Early Stuart Multiple Kingdom', *Historical Journal*, 34 (1991), pp. 279–95.

Pérez Moreda, Vicente, and Reher, David-Sven (eds.). *Demografía histórica en España*. Madrid, 1988.

Phillipson, Nicholas, and Mitchison, Rosalind (eds.). *Scotland in the Age of Improvement*. Edinburgh, 1996.

Pí y Margall, Francisco. *Las nacionalidades*, ed. Jordi Solé Tura. Madrid, 1986.

Pinya i Homs, Romà. *La debatuda exclusió catalano-aragonesa de la conquesta d'Amèrica*. Barcelona, 1992.

Pittock, Murray G. H. *The Invention of Scotland: The Stuart Myth and the Scottish Identity, 1638 to the Present*. London, 1991.

Pottle, Frederick A. (ed.). *Boswell's London Journal, 1762–1763*. New York, 1950.

Prat de la Riba, Enric. *La nacionalitat catalana*, ed. Jordi Casassas i Ymbert. Barcelona, 1993.

Preston, Paul. *Franco: A Biography*. London, 1993.

Preston, Paul. *The Spanish Holocaust: Inquisition and Extermination in Twentieth-Century Spain*. New York and London, 2012.

Puig i Oliver, Lluís. *Tomàs Puig: catalanisme i afrancescament*. Barcelona, 1985.

Raffe, Alasdair. 'Scotland Restored and Reshaped: Politics and Religion, c.1660–1712', in Thomas. M. Devine and Jenny Wormald (eds.), *The Oxford Handbook of Modern Scottish History*. Oxford, 2012.

Raffe, Alasdair. 'Scottish State Oaths and the Revolution of 1688–1690', in Sharon Adams and Julian Goodare (eds.), *Scotland in the Age of Two Revolutions*. Woodbridge, 2014.

Ramsden, H. *The 1898 Movement in Spain*. Manchester, 1974.

Read, Conyers. *Mr. Secretary Cecil and Queen Elizabeth*. London, 1955 (repr. 1962).

Richards, Eric. 'Scotland and the Uses of the Atlantic Empire', in Bernard Bailyn and Philip D. Morgan (eds.), *Strangers Within the Realm*. Chapel Hill, NC, and London, 1991.

Riley, P. W. J. *The English Ministers and Scotland, 1707–1727*. London, 1964.

Ringrose, David. *Madrid and the Spanish Economy, 1560–1850*. Berkeley and Los Angeles, CA, and London, 1983.

Ringrose, David. *Spain, Europe and the 'Spanish Miracle', 1700–1900*. Cambridge, 1996.

Riquer i Permanyer, Borja de. *Lliga regionalista: la burgesia catalana i el nacionalisme, 1898–1904*. Barcelona, 1977.

Riquer i Permanyer, Borja de. 'Sobre el lugar de los nacionalismos-regionalismos en la historia contemporánea española', *História Social*, 7 (1990), pp. 104–26.

Riquer i Permanyer, Borja de. 'Aproximación al nacionalismo español contemporáneo', *Studia Histórica*, 12 (1994), pp. 11–29.

Riquer i Permanyer, Borja de. *Identitats contemporànies: Catalunya i Espanya*. Vic, 2000.

Riquer i Permanyer, Borja de. 'La dictadura de Franco', in Josep Fontana and Ramón Villares (eds.), *Historia de España*, vol. 9. Barcelona and Madrid, 2010.

Riquer i Permanyer, Borja de (ed.). *Historia de la Diputació de Barcelona* (3 vols.). Barcelona, 1987.

Robertson, John. *The Scottish Enlightenment and the Militia Issue*. Edinburgh, 1985.

Robertson, John (ed.). *A Union for Empire: Political Thought and the British Union of 1707*. Cambridge, 1995.

Robertson, John. 'An Elusive Sovereignty: The Course of the Union Debate in Scotland 1698–1707', in John Robertson (ed.), *A Union for Empire: Political Thought and the British Union of 1707*. Cambridge, 1995, pp. 198–227.

Robertson, John. 'The Scottish Contribution to the Enlightenment', in Paul Wood (ed.), *The Scottish Enlightenment. Essays in Reinterpretation*. Rochester, NY, 2000.

Robertson, John. *The Case for the Enlightenment. Scotland and Naples 1680–1760*. Cambridge, 2005.

Romero Maura, Joaquín. *La rosa de fuego: la política de los obreros barceloneses entre el desastre colonial y la semana trágica, 1899–1903*. Barcelona, 1975.

Rothschild, Emma. *The Inner Life of Empires: An Eighteenth-Century History*. Princeton, NJ, 2011.

Roura i Aulinas, Lluís. 'Subjecció i militarizació a la Catalunya del segle XVIII', in Joaquim Albareda i Salvadó (ed.), *Del patriotisme al catalanisme: societat i política (segles XVI–XIX)*. Vic, 2001.

Rucquoi, Adeline (ed.). *Realidad e imágenes del poder: España a fines de la Edad Media*. Valladolid, 1988.

Russell, Conrad. 'Composite Monarchies in Early Modern Europe: The British Example', in Alexander Grant and Keith J. Stringer (eds.), *Uniting the Kingdom? The Making of British History*. New York and London, 1995.

Ryder, Alan. *The Wreck of Catalonia: Civil War in the Fifteenth Century*, Oxford, 2007.

Sahlins, Peter. *Boundaries: The Making of France and Spain in the Pyrenees*. Berkeley and Los Angeles, CA, and Oxford, 1989.

Sales, Núria. 'Institucions polítiques catalanes en vigílies de la seva abolició', *Pedralbes*, 13:1 (1993), pp. 275–9.

Sanabre, José. *La acción de Francia en la pugna por la hegemonía de Europa, 1640–1659*. Barcelona, 1956.

Sánchez Mantero, Rafael. *Los cien mil hijos de San Luis y las relaciones franco-españolas*. Seville, 1981.

Sánchez Mantero, Rafael. *Fernando VII*. Madrid, 2001.

Sánchez Marcos, Fernando. *Cataluña y el gobierno central tras la Guerra de los Segadores (1652–1679)*. Barcelona, 1983.

Sanpere i Miquel, Salvador. *Fin de la nación catalana*. Barcelona, 1905.

Scott, Sir Walter. *The Tales of a Grandfather* (3 vols.). London, 1827–30 (repr. 1933).

Scott, Sir Walter. *Waverley* (rev. edn.). Oxford, 2015.

Serra i Puig, Eva et al. *La revolució catalana de 1640*. Barcelona, 1991.

Simon i Tarrés, Antoni. *La població catalana a l'edat moderna. Deu estudis*. Barcelona, 1996.

Simon i Tarrés, Antoni. *Els orígens ideològics de la revolució catalana de 1640*. Barcelona, 1999.

Simon i Tarrés, Antoni. *Pau Claris, líder d'una classe revolucionària*. Barcelona, 2008.

Skinner, Quentin. *The Foundations of Modern Political Thought* (2 vols.). Cambridge, 1978.

Slack, Paul. *The Invention of Improvement*. Oxford, 2014.

Smith, Angel. *Anarchism, Revolution and Reaction: Catalan Labour and the Crisis of the Spanish State, 1898–1923*. New York and Oxford, 2007.

Smith, Angel. *The Origins of Catalan Nationalism, 1770–1898*. Basingstoke, 2014.

Smith, Angel. 'Nationalisms Against the Spanish State, 1808–1923: Cuba, Catalonia and the Basque Country', in Paul Garner and Angel Smith (eds.), *Nationalism and Transnationalism in Spain and Latin America, 1808–1923*. Cardiff, 2017.

Smith, Angel. 'Cataluña y la gran guerra: de la reforma democrática al conflicto social', *Hispania Nova. Revista de Historia Contemporánea*, 15 (2017), pp. 472–99.

Smith, Anthony D. *The Nation in History: Historiographical Debates about Ethnicity and Nationalism*. Hanover, NH, 2000.

Smith, Janet Adam. 'Some Eighteenth-Century Ideas of Scotland', in Nicholas Phillipson and Rosalind Mitchison (eds.), *Scotland in the Age of Improvement*. Edinburgh, 1996.

Smout, T. Christopher. *A History of the Scottish People 1560–1830*. London, 1969.

Smout, T. Christopher (ed.). *Anglo-Scottish Relations from 1603 to 1900*. Oxford, 2005.

Soldevila i Zubiburu, Ferran. *Història de Catalunya* (3 vols.). Barcelona, 1962–3.

Somerville, Johann P. (ed.). *King James VI and I: Political Writings*. Cambridge, 1994.

Spedding, James (ed). *The Works of Francis Bacon* (14 vols.). London, 1868, vol. 10.

Steele, Margaret. 'The "Politick Christian": The Theological Background to the National Covenant', in John Morrill (ed.), *The Scottish National Covenant in its British Context, 1638–51*. Edinburgh, 1990.

Stein, Stanley J., and Stein, Barbara H. *Apogee of Empire: Spain and New Spain in the Age of Charles III, 1759–1789*. Princeton, NJ, 2003.

Stevenson, David. *The Scottish Revolution 1637–1644: The Triumph of the Covenanters*. Newton Abbot, 1973.

Stevenson, David. *Union, Revolution and Religion in 17th-Century Scotland*. Aldershot, 1997.

Stevenson, Robert Louis. *Selected Letters of Robert Louis Stevenson*, ed. Ernest Mehew. New Haven, CT, and London, 1997.

Stewart, Laura M. 'The Rise of the State?', in Thomas M. Devine and Jenny Wormald (eds.), *The Oxford Handbook of Modern Scottish History*. Oxford, 2012.

Stewart, Laura M. *Rethinking the Scottish Revolution*. Oxford, 2016.

Stewart, Laura M. 'The Political Repercussions of the Five Articles of Perth: A Reassessment of James VI and I's Religious Policies in Scotland', *Sixteenth Century Journal*, 38 (2007), pp. 1,013–36.

Storrs, Christopher. *The Resilience of the Spanish Monarchy 1665–1700*. Oxford, 2006.

Storrs, Christopher. *The Spanish Resurgence, 1713–1748*. New Haven, CT, and London, 2016.

Strubell, Michael B. (ed.). *Consideració del cas dels catalans, seguit de La deplorable història dels catalans*. Barcelona, 1992.

Szechi, Daniel. *1715: The Great Jacobite Rebellion*. New Haven, CT, and London, 2006.

Tate, Robert B. *Joan Margarit i Pau, Cardinal-Bishop of Gerona*. Manchester, 1955.

Taylor, Alice. *The Shape of the State in Medieval Scotland, 1124–1290*. Oxford, 2016.

Thompson, I. A. A. 'Castile, Spain and the Monarchy: The Political Community from *patria natural* to *patria nacional*', in Richard L. Kagan and Geoffrey Parker (eds.), *Spain, Europe and the Atlantic World: Essays in Honour of John H. Elliott*. Cambridge, 1995.

Thomson, J. K. J. *A Distinctive Industrialization: Cotton in Barcelona 1728–1832*. Cambridge, 1992.

Toledano González, Lluís Ferran. 'La guerra de la Independencia como mito fundamental de la memoria y de la historia nacional española', in Antoni Moliner i Prada (ed.), *La guerra de la independencia en España (1808–1815)*. Barcelona, 2007.

Tornos Mas, Joaquín. *De Escocia a Cataluña. Referendum y reforma constitucional*. Madrid, 2015.

Torras Elías, Jaime. *Liberalismo y rebeldía campesina, 1820–1823*. Barcelona, 1976.

Torras i Ribé, Josep M. *Els municipis catalans de l'antic règim, 1453–1808*. Barcelona, 1983.

Torras i Ribé, Josep M. 'El projecte de repressió dels catalans de 1652', in Eva Serra i Puig et al., *La revolució catalana de 1640*. Barcelona, 1991.

Torres Arce, Marina, and Truchuelo García, Susana (eds.). *Europa en torno a Utrecht*. Santander, 2014.

Torres i Sans, Xavier. *Els bandolers (s. XVI–XVII)*. Vic, 1991.

Torres i Sans, Xavier. 'Making and Remaking Patriotism: The Catalan Revolt against the Spanish Monarchy (1640–1659)', in Robert von Friedeburg (ed.), *'Patria' und 'Patrioten' vor dem Patriotismus*. Wiesbaden, 2005.

Torres i Sans, Xavier. *Naciones sin nacionalismo. Cataluña en la monarquía hispánica, siglos XVI–XVII*. Valencia, 2008.

Tortella Casares, Gabriel. *Cataluña en España. Historia y mito*. Madrid, 2016.

Townsend, Joseph. *Journey Through Spain in the Years 1786 and 1787* (3 vols.). London, 1791.

Trevelyan, George Macaulay. *England Under Queen Anne* (3 vols.). London, 1930–4 (repr. 1948).

Trevor-Roper, Hugh R. *Religion, the Reformation and Social Change*. London, 1967.

Trevor-Roper, Hugh R. *The Invention of Scotland: Myth and History*. New Haven, CT, and London, 2008.

Trías Vejarano, Juan J. *Almirall y los orígenes del catalanismo*. Madrid, 1975.

Ucelay Da Cal, Enric. *La Catalunya populista. Imatge, cultura i política en l'etapa republicana, 1931-1939*. Barcelona, 1982.

Ucelay Da Cal, Enric. 'La Diputació y la Mancomunitat: 1914-1923', in Borja de Riquer i Permanyer (ed.), *Historia de la Diputació de Barcelona* (3 vols.). Barcelona, 1987, vol. 2.

Ucelay Da Cal, Enric. *El imperialismo catalán. Prat de la Riba, D'Ors y la conquista moral de España*. Barcelona, 2003.

Ullman, Joan Connelly. *The Tragic Week: A Study of Anticlericalism in Spain, 1875-1912*. Cambridge, MA, 1968.

Ulloa, Modesto. *La hacienda real de Castilla en el reinado de Felipe II*. Madrid, 1977.

Varela Tortajada, Javier. 'Nación, patria y patriotismo en los orígenes del nacionalismo español', *Studia Historica-Historia Contemporánea*, 12 (1994), pp. 31-43.

Vicens Vives, Jaime. *Política del rey católico en Cataluña*. Barcelona, 1940.

Vicens Vives, Jaime. *Noticia de Cataluña*. Barcelona, 1954.

Vicens Vives, Jaime. *Notícia de Catalunya*. Barcelona, 2010.

Vicens Vives, Jaime, and Llorens, Montserrat. *Industrials i polítics del segle XIX*. Barcelona, 2010 (1st edn., 1958).

Vicens Vives, Jaime, and Nadal Oller, Jordi. *Historia económica de España* (3rd edn.). Barcelona, 1964.

Vilar, Pierre. *La Catalogne dans l'Espagne moderne* (3 vols.). Paris, 1962.

Vilar, Pierre. *Estat, nació, socialisme. Estudis sobre el cas espanyol*. Barcelona, 1982.

Villanueva López, Jesús. *Política y discurso histórico en la España del siglo XVII. Las polémicas sobre los orígenes medievales de Cataluña*. Alicante, 2004.

Watt, Douglas. *The Price of Scotland: Darien, Union and the Wealth of Nations*. Edinburgh, 2007.

Wedgwood, Cicely V. 'Anglo-Scottish Relations, 1603-1640', *Transactions of the Royal Historical Society*, 4, ser. 32 (1950), pp. 31-48.

Whatley, Christopher A. *The Scots and the Union*. Edinburgh, 2006.

Willson, D. H. *King James VI and I*. London, 1956.

Withers, Charles W. J. *Gaelic Scotland: The Transformation of a Culture Region*. London, 1988.

Wood, Paul (ed.). *The Scottish Enlightenment. Essays in Reinterpretation*. Rochester, NY, 2000.

Wormald, Jenny. *Mary Queen of Scots: A Study in Failure*. London, 1988.

Wormald, Jenny. 'James VI, James I and the Identity of Britain', in Brendan Bradshaw and John Morrill (eds.), *The British Problem, c.1534-1707*. Basingstoke, 1996.

Wormald, Jenny. '"A Union of Hearts and Minds?": The Making of the Union Between Scotland and England, 1603', in Jon Arrieta Alberdi and John H. Elliott (eds.), *Forms of Union: The British and Spanish Monarchies in the Seventeenth and Eighteenth Centuries*. Riev. *Revista Internacional de Estudios Vascos*, Cuadernos 5, 2009, pp. 109-24.

Young, John R. 'The Scottish Parliament and National Identity from the Union of the Crowns to the Union of Parliaments, 1603-1707', in Dauvit Broun, R. J. Finlay and Michael Lynch (eds.), *Image and Identity: The Making and Re-making of Scotland Through the Ages*. Edinburgh, 1998.

Zavala, Iris M. *Clandestinidad y libertinaje erudito en los albores del siglo XVIII*. Barcelona, 1978.

INDEX